A BED OF]

TÜRKİYE

A Simplified Map of Turkey

Ankara: the capital city, located in central Anatolia

Batman: a small town on the train line to Kurtalan and Lake Van

Diyarbakır: an ancient walled city, the largest in the southeast region, with an air strip, several hotels, many small shops and open markets

Istanbul: the largest and most cosmopolitan city, located partially in Europe, but mostly in Asia [the Anatolian side], separated by the Bosphorus strait connecting the Sea of Marmara to the Black Sea

Kurtalan: a small southeastern town, located near Lake Van and the end of the railroad line *[not shown]*

Raman Dagi: an early oil exploration camp, located on Raman Mountain 20 km north of Batman *[not shown]*

Sürmene: a small seacoast town on the eastern end of the Black Sea

Trabzon: an ancient seaport on the Black Sea

A BED OF ROSES

An American Woman's Memoirs from Turkey

by

ANNA MARIA MALKOÇ

To Orhan Ertugaay,
with very best wishes,
Anna Maria Malkoç
Seattle TURKFEST 2007

eBookstand Books
http//www.ebookstand.com
http//www.cyberread.com

Published by
eBookstand Books
Division of CyberRead, Inc.
Houston, TX 77079
1927_6

ISBN 1-58909-286-4

Cover artwork by Birsen Malkoç
Cover design by Ron Carraher
Back cover photograph by Melike Eden Malkoç

*The names of long-ago neighbors and friends (with two exceptions, so indicated
in the text) are those recorded in the letters written at the time, or supplied later
in the journal notes as accurately as memory allows. This holds for the dates
herein as well. The author trusts any unintentional discrepancies will be met with
a forgiving heart.*

Printed in the United States of America

ACKNOWLEDGEMENTS

First of all, I thank my mother, Marie Harms Jones, who saved every letter I ever wrote to her, and who was one of my guiding inspirations in this work. I thank also my father, Ethelbert Jones, who, as a young lad in England, was sent out perforce, to make his own way in the world, and who inspired in me a life-long love of adventurous travel.

My sister, Camilla Jones Phillipson in Lake Coeur d'Alene ID, who saved all my letters from Turkey and, years later, sent them back for me to share with my children.

All my other family members and many friends, whose messages from home kept my spirits up during bleak times. Each letter was a bright spot in the day.

Charismatic college friend Bill Brownfield in Tulsa OK, who cajoled mutual friends to type up these rambling handwritten accounts to share, and sent many copies on to my mother and family in Spokane.

Pamela Glasco and the Beta Sigma Phi women's club members in Mukilteo WA, who volunteered to type out the first fifty of these fading letters: Ann Biderbost, Mary Kaye Bredeson, Cindy Cornell, Dianne Cowman, Chris Hotton, Rhonda Kaleiwahea, Joni Marsicano, Linda Ray, Trish Russell, Peggy Simpson, Debbie Stratton and Alison Taylor. They inspired me to tackle this compilation.

Lynn Stafford-Yilmaz, free-lance editor/book reviewer in Bellevue WA, who read the first rough draft for style, balance, flow, and readers' expectations. With great respect for her critical powers, and gratitude for her helpful words of encouragement.

Jane Fields, Mary Hovander, Nancy Lambert, Camilla Phillipson, and Connie Copeland Malone for their insightful comments as "general readers."

Ron Carraher, Seattle artist/photographer, for his invaluable work on the cover design, and for his technical advice to daughter Hikmet on reviving the worn-out snapshots which add such an essential dimension to the book.

Sirin Özger, my brother-in-law Muammer's daughter in Ankara, who researched the Turkish Petroleum Company archives for old photos of Raman Camp;
Serdar Malkoç, Muammer's son in Izmir, who checked data and e-mailed precious artwork; and Birsen Malkoç, his daughter-in-law, who, inspired by antique Turkish illuminations, created the artwork for the book cover. Illuminator Birsen hanım, a modern-day Malkoç bride, lends a poetic nuance to the life-story of this earlier "Black Sea bride."

The Author

DEDICATION

To my husband, Selahattin Eyubi Malkoç

and our children,

Hikmet, Cemile*, Timur, Kâmuran, and Melike Malkoç

TABLE OF CONTENTS

APPENDIX

PREFACE

The author/compiler was born in Spokane, Washington in 1925. Following World War II, while studying literature and language classes at the University of Washington, she met a student of mining engineering, born in Turkey in 1921. His name was Selahattin Malkoç; his American friends called him Sam, or Sela.

For several years, they dated off and on. She was working part time at various odd jobs. He was immersed in his classes and struggling to improve his English. During vacations, he went with school friends to look for mining jobs in Montana and Washington.

In time, he wrote to his father that he had met an American girl and had serious intentions of marrying her when he finished his courses. His father made several serious attempts to dissuade him, not because of religious reasons (his father was not an ultra-strict Moslem), but because as a government scholarship student he had an obligation to return and work in his field of study. Finally, his father relented and sent his blessings.

The third year, he went to Spokane to meet her parents. He was quietly self-confident, well-mannered, likable. Her whole family liked him — her parents, her sister, and five brothers. He was the first Turk, in fact, the first person from that part of the world they had ever met, and the first Moslem. The subject of religion never arose, although her mother had been reared a German Lutheran and her father in the Church of England.

Sela had "a good work ethic," everyone agreed. He could discuss chemical formulas, her father's amateur hobby. He could talk to her brothers about farming and mechanical equipment. He could play any kind of ball with the kids, and was willing to lend a hand whenever necessary.

Most memorably during his visit, he helped her mother weed tomatoes in the garden, holding long discussions in German (which was, coincidentally, her mother's first language). He talked about his experiences as a student in Freiberg. He told her about his life there as a student of mining engineering in the midst of World War Two. Then when Turkey (who had fought with Germany during WWI but had remained neutral in WWII) entered on the side of the Allies in late 1944, he and the other Turkish students were interned as aliens in a mountain-top resort. He learned how to ski there while waiting for a Swedish Red Cross ship to escort them back to Turkey. This was shortly before the end of the war; he returned home safely. While waiting for his academic records and new travel papers to arrive, he worked in his father's dry goods/hardware store in the small town of Sürmene on the Black Sea. Sometime in 1946, his government sent him to Queens College in Flushing, New York for six weeks of English study. Then he was sent on to study at the University of Washington's School of Mining Engineering. At this time, the Turkish government was planning to establish a state enterprise for petroleum exploration and development. In 1950, he and a number of other Turkish students were transferred from UW to Tulsa University in Oklahoma to study petroleum engineering.

When the author finished her undergraduate courses, she took a Greyhound bus to Tulsa to marry him. At this point in her life, her romantic dream was to marry someone with whom she was in love and whom she respected. And who could offer her "an adventurous future." Whatever that meant.

They were married by a Justice of the Peace. She worked as a file clerk for "The Oil and Gas Journal" and took a basic course in education at TU. The summer before their daughter, Hikmet, was born, he went off to work in a Green Giant corn cannery, then completed his Master's degree in petroleum engineering. She took the train to Spokane with baby Hikmet (her mother's first grandchild) to say goodbye to her family, while he spent several months working in the Wyoming oilfields to help defray travel expenses to Turkey.

At the beginning of this story-in-letters documenting their dramatic life together in Turkey, they are about to set off for Istanbul. He will be returning, after nearly seven years of study abroad, to work as a petroleum engineer in his government's newly developing oil fields. It will be her first travel outside her own country. At one point in preparing for departure, she asks him seriously: "What is life really like in Turkey?"

After a long, thoughtful pause, he answers her: "Where we're going, I think life is not a bed of roses." 🐝

Sela & Anna Maria, Tulsa 1950

INTRODUCTION TO THE READER

This autobiography is based on a large collection of old letters and living memories of the most exciting and productive years of my life in Turkey, one of the most exotic and dearest places in my world. Before embarking on this romantic roller-coaster of a reading adventure, it will be helpful, I think, to have an idea about these letters and the circumstances under which they were written.

The Letter Collection In 1989, Bill Brownfield, a dear school friend from Tulsa University days and one of the main recipients of these letters, was diagnosed with cancer and advised by his doctor to "put his house in order." One of the first things Bill did was to make copies of the "Turkey letters" he'd stored away in his attic, and mail them back to me in a large manila envelope. Unfortunately, when I retired from the Foreign Service and moved back to my hometown, the envelope got lost. I was heartbroken.

One day the following year, Bill called to say he'd just seen his doctor and was telling everyone goodbye. He was so pleased he'd sent me the Turkey letters. I had to confess then about the lost envelope. "Well, I think I have one more trip to the attic left in me," he said, and we had a last, bittersweet chuckle together.... Sometime after his funeral, I received a second manila envelope, stuffed with the originals: dog-eared pages, torn and tattered envelopes. That packet sat carefully stored in my attic in Spokane for some ten years, until I retired again and moved to my son's home in Mukilteo, Washington. Then it sat in Timur's garage for two years while I finished an ongoing book project.

My new formatter friend in Mukilteo, Pamela Glasgo, half-jokingly asked whether I'd be working on another book project (at my age!). I told her about the precious manila envelope I'd just unpacked. I should compile the Turkey letters into a book for my children, I told her, but typing all those dim pages would be so eye-straining, the project would be such an emotionally daunting task, I wasn't sure if I was up to it....

The next time Pamela and I met, she announced she'd found ten volunteers in her Beta Sigma Phi women's group ready to type up the 50 or so letters in the manila envelope. I was flabbergasted. It seemed like a sign.

About this same time, my sister Camilla was also retiring and clearing out files. Quite unaware of my new project, she sent me a packet of letters and clippings she'd saved for me and my children. Another sign. It inspired me to go through the rest of the old storage boxes, where I unearthed dozens of letters my mother had saved for decades, and most amazingly of all, a neat bundle tied up with a pink ribbon, marked "Ankara 1965," the date I left Turkey. The several dozen fresh and unweathered letters inside were in my husband's handwriting and had passed from his hands to mine alone.

How many more signs did I need? That day, I began to sort and organize the letters, which eventually numbered over 130. They are the nucleus of this book.

The Letter Writers/Addressees: The principal writers were myself; my husband Selahattin Malkoç (Sela for short); my mother Marie Harms Jones (Ma, Mom, or

Grandmother) in Spokane, Washington; my sister Camilla Phillipson, of Coeur d'Alene, Idaho; and William G. Brownfield (Bill) of Tulsa, Oklahoma. He was Sela's classmate in petroleum geology at Tulsa U, and a dear friend of the Malkoç family.

Some of the letters are addressed to specific persons, but the longer ones are usually addressed to Family and Friends, or Tulsa and Spokane, as they were intended to be copied and/or passed around because of the shortage of writing supplies, stamps, and mailing facilities when we were living in the oilfield.

The Compiling/Writing Process: The letters are in chronological order, for the most part, with some minor changes and the gentlest of editing and/or splicing. I've added journal notes (vignettes, anecdotes, newspaper articles) here and there for several reasons: to provide backgrounding or details omitted from the letters; to give a richer feel and flavor of the times; or simply to aid in transition from one setting to another. The compilation has been like creating a patchwork quilt, arranging the pieces into interlocking patterns, connecting them to form a multifaceted, multicolored, phantasmagoric map of memories from long ago and far away.

For me, this kind of writing process requires entering a kind of time warp, to recapture emotions and scenes in my mind's eye. It requires solitude; I find it necessary, as Wordsworth would say, "to recollect in tranquility." Although sometimes I draw a complete blank, at other times, memories not only pop into my mind with astounding clarity, they set into motion whole trains of other recollections. Fifty years have passed since the first of these epistles from Turkey, yet the people and events I wrote about then still seem vividly alive. Their memories continue to enrich my life and my view of the world.

The Author

PROLOGUE

WESTERN UNION TELEGRAM
New York City
December 16, 1952
Addressee: William G. Brownfield, Tulsa, Oklahoma

ENJOYING NEW YORK STOP SAILING DELAYED TO DECEMBER
TWENTY THIRD STOP WISH YOU WERE HERE STOP WITH FIFTY
DOLLARS STOP IF YOU CAN'T COME PLEASE SEND MONEY CARE OF
GLORIA GASTON TWO NINETY WEST TWELFTH STREET STOP HOPE
YOU ARE ALL HEALTHY AND WEALTHY STOP WITH GREAT
ANTICIPATION STOP SELA

Predeparture Letter to Tulsa Friends

New York City
December 19, 1952

Dear Brownfields and Rakestraw,

I am writing this on my trusty traveling typewriter in our temporary
lodgings. Hope our wire didn't startle you too much. Rather desperate situation at
the moment, and while the situation has not become less provoking, it is not
without humor.

Third cancellation — sailing date is now set at December 26. The third
time is usually final, right?

The hotel — $6.00 per day — was not bad. But, egad! the valet service!
Never, never send laundry out in a hotel. It's a painful experience paying the bill.
Prefer not to recall. So, we finagled my old UW school friend Gloria Gaston, bless
her heart, to find us lodgings. And her friend Charlotte, a total stranger, bless her
soul, moved out of her bohemian apartment in Greenwich Village, where we are
now holing up, practically in the East River.

Our temporary port in the storm turned into a bad situation when the
suspicious super threatened to throw us out. (People have a habit of moving in on
other people's leases.) He apologized when he found out we were just visiting.
The woman below threatened to call the police because the bath tub overflowed
and leaked down on her refrigerator. A nasty moment. Sela apologized
charmingly and saved the day.

Anyway, we have free lodging until the original leasee comes back from
U. of Chicago. (From whom Charlotte sublet.) The original leasee may return
anytime now, but I have faith in Gloria. It's all very involved. The Villagers
where Gloria lives have a way of loaning beds, rooms, apartments and so forth, to
friends of friends with utmost trust and also abandon. She tells us not to worry,
something will turn up.

I hope you can meet each other. Her interests are more socio-political, Bill, but her friends and their friends are varied [in religion and race] and of truly stimulating character. The few we've met seem genuine and interesting. I've told her you would appear sometime this spring, so don't fail to call her. She works at the Educational Travel Association, 1790 Broadway. Her home address is 290 West 12th, telephone Chelsea 2-4062.

Haven't seen much here except the inside of the United Nations building. Just the cathedral-ceilinged lobby, though. We were standing there, drinking in the historic atmosphere, when baby Hikmet emitted a huge chortle of pleasure, followed by a series of gigantic echoes. We departed hastily.

Babies are seldom seen uptown. I feel like an oddity lugging her about; Sela and I take turns. She falls asleep anywhere, if you can imagine, even on the subways and while dodging traffic under the Third Avenue El.

Met the Turkish Educational Attaché in his office. Not an ogre at all. (I'd had several long-distance telephone calls with him, Worland to New York, while making arrangements for the trip.)

All our papers seem to be in order now. The Office of Internal Revenue finally cleared both Sela and me; all aliens and spouses leaving the country have to be cleared. It was like a miniature Ellis Island station, only everyone seemed more or less prosperous and not like the weary travelers in the old silent movies.

Many, many thanks for the loan. Hope it didn't cut you short. Sela should receive the tax refund early in the year and will reimburse you then. And don't be worried about us. If you are, and the thought crossed my mind you just may be, don't! This little adventure is of the sort you afterwards relish in retrospect. I must admit I *am* looking forward to looking back on it, but we're getting our kicks!

Much fondness to all. And since we might not write again too soon, pass this on to the Tulsa contingent, please. The Days called us from there while we were in Kansas City, enroute. Heartwarming. A big kiss back to Moe from Hikmet. Freulicher Weinachten! Anna-Maria, Sela, and Baby Hikmet

---

Journal: Predeparture from New York
December 27, 1952 We have been here in New York City for three hectic and indecisive weeks, traipsing to the travel office for news every day, waiting for our freighter to arrive in New York harbor. One disappointing departure cancellation after another. Apparently, freighters can't guarantee departure dates, which accounts in part for our unbelievably cheap fare of $300: a second-class cabin for two adults and one infant, New York-Istanbul, estimated travel time 30 days, with three stops en route.

During the discouraging series of delays and setbacks, we eventually went totally broke and had to wire school friends in Tulsa for money. The wired money arrived forthwith, and we enjoyed a hot meal for Christmas. Two days later, we were informed that we could board the ship this evening.

Our first bit of good luck occurred on the long walk down the pier, past other ships in various stages of loading. Eagle-eyed Sela spied our trunk on a cart waiting to be loaded onto a ship bound for Iceland! He yelled out to stop the longshoreman and sprinted down to the loading slip, waving a pink bill of lading under the worker's nose, just in time to retrieve the trunk and reroute it. "That was a close call!" he muttered afterward.

Actually, we won't sail until sometime tomorrow, but because the authorities had previously assured us we were going to sail today, we are being allowed to spend the night aboard. Our trunk and last bits of baggage are now safely on board. Hikmet is in her sleeping gear in the lower bunk. My trusty portable typewriter is unpacked on the folding table under the porthole, whence I am writing this. Since my mother has never really had an opportunity to travel, I hope to keep notes for her vicarious reading pleasure. All is well, I am happy to report. ❦

Journal: Thirty Days aboard a Greek Freighter

December 28, 1952 Today is the Day! Somehow, when the tugboat towing us to open sea cast clear, I had no great feeling of exhilaration or adventure. Anticipation has been stretched to the limit by three penniless weeks spent in Lower Manhattan, waiting for the freighter's arrival.

We may as well be occupying a small but compact hotel room, except for the motion, sudden and rather violent. Sela assures me this is nothing and scoffs at my Dramamine tablets. With appetites undulled, we enjoyed our first Greek dinner aboard ship: White cheese, olives, sausage for appetizers; spaghetti with grated cheese and tomato sauce for the first course; sliced veal with diced carrots, potatoes and celery for the entrée; tangerines for dessert; and Turkish coffee after dinner.

The food, although not in great abundance, is well prepared and deftly served. I have a suspicion I may gain weight! We eat in the only room free to us outside our cabins, which is a combination dining room, salon, and officer's council room. I haven't seen a uniform and I don't understand Greek, so I can't tell the passengers from the officers.

December 29, 1952 Everything on this ship is Greek to me. (Couldn't resist this pun.) For breakfast, I declined oatmeal, asked for one egg, with what I thought were appropriate gestures. I was served two eggs and oatmeal — which is the one food I actually dislike. The steward was trying very hard to please, so I downed the oatmeal. Also the six pieces of toast on the tray.

Our one fellow passenger introduced himself this morning, an elderly and distinguished-looking Turkish gentleman, making his twenty-ninth round trip, he informs us. He speaks excellent English and is very informative.

We learned that we three are the only Turks/Americans on board this cargo freighter, and that there is another woman aboard — a pale, mysterious Greek lady traveling with her sick husband. They take their meals in their first-class suite on the Captain's deck. There are also several dozen Greek passengers below deck in steerage class, traveling to Piraeus/Athens. They sit with the deck hands and we see them occasionally on our way to and from the mess hall.

December 30, 1952 Our fellow travelers — the Greek crew members — are unbending. We now manage to converse during mealtimes with the help of the Turkish gentleman, who also speaks Greek. Even the two engineers who speak only Greek keep up with the general run of the multilingual conversations.

Whenever the talk idles or gets fouled up, Baby Hikmet always starts it up again. She holds no favorites and welcomes attention from all. At coffee time, the chief cook appeared and silently offered her a tiny birdcage filled with candies. For once, Hikmet was awestruck, so I said "thank you" in Greek, my first accomplishment.

December 31, 1952 We landed in Halifax, Nova Scotia late last night. This was a surprise to us as we expected to sail directly to Genoa, Italy. We'll be here about three days to take on special cargo. The Canadian immigration officer came aboard this morning to grant landing permits to the passengers. No one expected to stop here and so no one had a visa. With my American birth certificate, I was allowed to go ashore, since no visa is required of Americans. The immigration officer escorted me to the end of the pier and directed me to town. In the biting wind, I managed to find the post office to mail some postcards.

Coming back to the ship, I lost my way and wandered through several loading sheds. It was worth the time; I got to see the stevedores loading our cargo, supplies for the Greek army. Gesticulations, shouting, hustle-bustle, winches lifting, lowering, thumping, bumping. Thrilling!

Much later in the evening, the New Year was ushered in with every foghorn, pipe and ship whistle in the Halifax harbor. Here, on board our ship, nothing stirred.

January 1, 1953 On New Year's morning, I am learning, the Greek custom is to shake hands with the others present, and then sit down to a New Year's breakfast of brandy, nuts, buttery-rich pastry dipped in sugar, and little cups of strong, sweet coffee. Or so it was celebrated aboard ship.

Lunch and dinner were even more sumptuous. The cook outdid himself with chicken and fish, and ended with puffy egg pastry covered with cinnamon and syrup. Oh, the gluttony of it all! Usually each meal ends with fresh fruit — apples, oranges, tangerines, pears. I guess this compensates in part for the exceedingly heavy dishes, either cooked in olive oil or served with oil and lemon.

We take turns playing Canasta between meals, since no one knows bridge or pinochle. Canasta is a new game to everyone here, and onlookers stop to look curiously at the maneuvers. It helps to pass the time, which hangs heavy.

January 2, 1953 Another trip ashore to buy baby food for Hikmet. Halifax is built on a hillside and reminds me of Ketchikan, Alaska, where my Aunt Birdie lives, although the streets seem even steeper and more treacherous to descend on foot in the ice and snow.

Life seems leisurely and complacent, with quaint streets and shops. I was told by a meandering dockworker that the largest pier in the world is here in Halifax.

It is now eleven o'clock and we have just slipped away. One hoarse toot from the horn and we're off for Genoa.

January 3, 1953 My first real look at the main deck today. We are heavily loaded; almost every available inch of deck space is covered with crates, boxes, small army wagons. Because of this maximum load, the ship is rolling more than it should on a comparatively calm sea.

It is almost impossible to sleep. I slide about my bunk like a dried pea in a pod. This evening, even Sela swallowed one of the Dramamine tablets he had sneered at earlier. I didn't have the heart to remark on his greenish pallor. Me? I feel fine.

January 4, 1953 Hit a gale in the wee hours. The first wave that hit the afterdeck sounded like a cannon volley. This must be first cousin to the storm we supposedly missed yesterday when we changed course and shifted slightly to the south. Everything not secured went careening about like New Year's Eve at a boiler factory. Even Hikmet seems to realize that everything is not smooth sailing. After the initial shock of feeling the ship dip away 25 to 35 degrees (Sela measured), she returned to her usual placid self. She simply holds tight until her equilibrium returns.

Since we are following the Gulf Stream, the air is comparatively warm and very humid.

January 5, 1953 Today was "typical cruising weather." I basked (no overcoat) in the sun of the upper deck. The ocean seems infinite, tremendously beautiful. It leaves one calm and refreshed.

The chief cook waylaid us in the passageway, invited us on a tour of the ship. We did the boiler room and adjoining areas: the power plant, the oil furnaces, the engine which rotates the propeller shaft. Difficult for me to describe, as it was explained in Greek with many gestures.

January 6, 1953 Being 11 months old today, Hikmet appeared at breakfast in her pink nylon dress, sweater, and hair ribbon. Anything for diversion. Also, I am trying to correct the impression that she's a "boy baby."

She now looks quite feminine, I think. Although even in overalls she manages to charm sweets, apples, oranges, and other edibles from the crew. She puckers her lips with a most audible smack, winks, and waves by-by as a thank-you.

Another magnificent day. The cloud formations are enchanting: wispy fingers through which the hidden sun glances. Pale blue puffs of cloud hang low along the horizon. High above are foggy gray fragments constantly changing, with an occasional sea gull in silhouette. I've never really watched a sea gull in flight before. They swoop and glide and then float almost motionlessly as if moved by the merest breath of wind. Sheer poetry in flight.

January 7, 1953 Wind and rain. Ideal for long, lazy conversations. The conversations in reality are long but not lazy. Great effort is put forth to make oneself understood and the results are often hilarious. After-dinner table topics tonight ranged from the weather report from the weatherman (always a preliminary) to bikini bathing suits to world currency to the superiority of Greek and Turkish food over American, to labor union problems....

The Second Captain, whom we all call "Adonis" because of his unmarried status and charming good looks, has accumulated a vast amount of empirical knowledge, having lived "a full life" in the Greek Royal Navy, to quote his own words. In articulate eloquence, he runs a close second to the Turkish gentleman. The latter bears a remarkable resemblance to movie idol Adolph Menjou, with his dapper mustache and beard, silk ascot tie and cosmopolitan air. He usually holds forth the longest.

January 8, 1953 We are approximately halfway to Gibraltar. Adonis, the second captain, says he can smell the Mediterranean. "Wonderful smell most of all," he claims. On such a fine sailing day as this, we make all of twelve knots an hour. The weather is gorgeous, both in my opinion and the second captain's, and we are skimming right along.

January 9, 1953 Today and tonight we are passing the Azores. The islands rise like gray ghosts along the horizon. After seeing nothing but the ocean for over a week, I can imagine how the seamen of yore must have exulted over the sight of land. But alas, just passersby, we!

It has been marvelous the past few days; the sea is calm with only our own waves to break the still. Today, the main deck is suddenly becoming animated. Passengers from below, whom we seldom see, stroll up and down the broad cargo hatches, and deck hands are busily hammering and splashing paint.

I exchanged a few words in Turkish with a below-deck passenger, a Greek born in Turkey. My Turkish is progressing very slowly, but I think I could order a full meal in Turkish — if one were to be had. Actually, the food aboard ship, with a few exceptions, is really pleasing to my palate.

Dinner tonight, however, proved to be one exception: extremely salty white fish fried in batter and served with garlic cream sauce. Very pungent, to say the least. I consumed most of it in self-defense. We were all breathing strong garlic fumes everywhere, much to Hikmet's displeasure and our amusement.

January 10, 1953 Our fabulous fair weather has passed from view with the Azores. We are now rocking on the cradle of the deep, with a strong wind whistling off the starboard side.

There is something romantic about a ship on the high seas in such weather, especially a cargo freighter manned by Greek sailors. Homeric overtones. Unlike Ulysses' men, however, they see their families not in twenty years, but every two or three months. They are manly and bold and some are indeed handsome – loud laughers and boisterous talkers. It is fascinating to watch them talk; half their speech is manual, with a lot of hand waving and many hand gestures.

January 11, 1953 Wind, rain, and more gray weather. Sela and I take turns napping with Hikmet, so today I was free to while away the afternoon playing Canasta with the second captain and the Turkish gentleman. Having misplaced his glasses, the T. G. was forced to read the canasta score with his monocle. I suspect he'd been waiting for just such an opportunity. What aplomb! And in these surroundings! Like the proverbial Englishman who, in the depths of the Congo, always had afternoon tea and dressed formally for dinner.

January 12, 1953 Violent gastritis today. The food must have been too heavy for my delicate (!) constitution. On the bright side, it's always a luxurious feeling to dine from a tray while lolling in bed.

The breeze from the porthole is fresh and invigorating; it gently flutters Hikmet's diapers draped over the porthole cover to dry. I carefully measure out the soap powder for each hand washing in our cabin basin, so that our supply will last until Istanbul.

January 13, 1953 Overslept this morning. Missed a glimpse of a monastery on the tip of the coast of Portugal. The weather has cleared, along with my constitution, and we should be able to see Gibraltar tonight.

According to word received by wireless, a former captain of this ship has died. The Greek flag is now hanging half-mast off the aft end. Its stripes almost match the blue of the sea today.

The cook, who promised to show me the galley, has been tippling too much and is a trifle unsteady on his pins. Rumor has it that he was once third chef at the royal palace and the pastries he prepares for us are all named after the member of royalty whose favorites they were. So far, we have had Queen Mary's cake and Prince Paul's pastry.

January 14, 1953 Couldn't sleep last night, fortunately! At about one o'clock, we neared Gibraltar. From our porthole, on the starboard side, we could see the beacon on the African coast. As its beam swung across the water, there was scarcely a ripple from our ship. We seemed to glide along the coastline. The sea and sky were black and every star in the sky glittered like diamonds. All was still; even our engines quieted to a murmur. It was as if we were a phantom ship ghosting through the narrow strait.

Dawn cracked early and revealed specks along the horizon. When our sleepy eyes could focus, we were able to make out ships, scattered like chess pieces, moving imperceptibly. On our port side, the Sierra Nevadas rise through a mist sprinkled with sea gulls. We seem to be hugging the shore: the nearness to European soil is stimulating.

January 15, 1953 We were indeed hugging the shoreline last night; a big storm was reported to be swooping down in our direction. Many shipwrecks occur in this part of the Mediterranean, we're told. Rather than cutting straight across from Gibraltar to Genoa, our new course is veering sharply inland. Since noon today, however, the storm path has changed and we are reverting to the original course. A few moments of excitement there!

The farther into the Mediterranean, the greater the sea traffic. While I was engaged in rescuing Hikmet from falling off her bunk, Sela spotted part of the Spanish fleet. Also some two dozen of Franco's old, German-type planes.

While I was at my daily task of washing and wringing out Hikmet's diapers to dry above our porthole, the deck hand painting the bulkhead outside announced a group of American planes. Gazing skyward, he leaned toward the porthole to announce this; I leaned forward out of the porthole to listen — and smacked into his outstretched paintbrush! Fortunately the ship has gallons to spare. This morning, the crew is busily painting everywhere.

During every return trip through the Mediterranean, the ship is painted as a standard procedure. Now the men are working against time to finish before Genoa, and our ship is looking more respectable with every hour.

January 16, 1953 We are hemmed in by wet paint from the end of our passageway aft, so we spent part of the morning visiting in the pilot house. The second mate asked if I'd like to try a few turns at the wheel. Child's play! I thought to myself. (Fortunately to myself.) When he motioned for me to take over, I took a few turns too many and left an embarrassingly wide swerve in the ship's wake.

The biggest thrill of the day, though, was spotting the coast of France; Spain has been out of sight since yesterday.

This evening, Sela crooned Hikmet to sleep with one of his sleep-inducing Turkish lullabies. He tucked her in snugly in the lower bunk, using the wooden ladder to fence her in, and the two of us stumbled through the dark up to the pilothouse.

From this vantage point, we could see the lighthouse beacon near Cannes, then Cannes, and a half hour later the lights of Nice.

It's very hazy tonight along the coast. At first we were confused by the lights of a large fishing vessel out of Genoa. Our pilot flashed "Recognition" in International Code, but got no reply.

At this point, the first captain, whom we had met but two or three times, called up the speaking tube in an agitated tone of voice. He had heard Hikmet waking up, and was combing the ship for us. I drew the short straw to stay with Hikmet, so Sela got to spy the lights of Monte Carlo. He reported that one very bright light high above the others signaled the famed Casino. Sigh! So near and yet so far from this famous spot.

January 17, 1953 A frosty cold, clear morn. We are at this moment being tugged into the pier at Genoa. From our porthole, I can see mountains looming up just behind the town, an enormous stone granary, trolley tracks running alongside the quay, and port officials in bright, brass-buttoned uniforms. At last, I think I'm really getting excited!

The freighter will be in dock until evening, so we three, with Adonis as escort, will have an outing in Genoa! From the ship, we rambled up to the town in an antiquated Fiat taxi. Our plan was to buy a few postcards and a silk umbrella for Sela's father.

Our excursions are somewhat limited. Hikmet is getting to be a heavy armful to carry everywhere, since we don't have a baby cart of any kind; Sela and I continue to take turns carrying her. Both Sela and Adonis are shrewd bargainers and Adonis knows a smattering of Italian, so we all had a merry time shopping. On my own, I attended to having my shoes repaired and also bought a little souvenir. What a feeling of satisfaction it is to make oneself understood in a foreign language. On the whole, with the aid of paper and pencil, finger counting, shoulder-shrugging, and facial expressions, we managed very well indeed.

It was fun to watch Hikmet's reactions. She delighted in the workhorses lumbering along the twisting, cobble-stoned streets. She formed immediate attachments to certain people. One such person was the shopkeeper's mother, in the shop where we spent much time bargaining. Elderly as she was, she insisted on carrying Hikmet about and escorting us to several other shops.

Adonis treated us to hot chocolate and pastries in one of the pastry shops. It was wonderfully rich, too delicious for words.

As we walked about, we seemed to attract rather overmuch notice. I assumed it was Hikmet in her powder-blue snowsuit. When someone called attention to my red wool beret, I suddenly realized there was no other red hat in sight, and I felt very conspicuous. Also, it has a gold braided monogram on it; some people may think is a royal crest!

The shops are crammed with lovely things: jewelry of gold and silver, sweaters of soft angora wool, pure silk neckties, felt and velour hats, hand worked leather for which Genoa is well known. The prices are all in hundreds and thousands of liras, difficult to translate into American money. (Sela did the transactions.) The cab driver, for instance, who took us from town back to the pier, whisking us past the guards and depositing us three feet from our gangplank, demanded 400 liras. I gasped, but was told that at the rate of 6.3 liras to one American cent, the long ride cost about 65 cents!

January 18, 1953 I slept past breakfast this morning and was served toast and coffee in bed. My indolence cost me the sight of some famous places. Sela, always an early riser as "punctual as a tax collector," was kind enough to bring in up-to-the-minute reports: the isle of Capri on our port side, Corsica off the starboard, then Pianosa, and Monte Cristo. He reportedly could see a crater atop a now-defunct volcano on Monte Cristo. And now the open sea again....

January 19, 1953 Stromboli — the "volcano island of fire and raging passion," according to a recent and controversial Ingrid Bergman movie filmed there. We didn't see the volcano, but we did see the smoke from the fire, at any rate. From two miles away, the billowing, brownish-red smoke was visible, hanging over the crater. It erupts every ten minutes, I was told.

Through the pilot's glasses, the white and pink houses on the mountainside were quite distinct: flat-roofed and rectangular, square windowed, perched here and there in clumps of green. I think I spotted a cemetery on a wide, green terrace. This was the first bit of land where we could actually see signs of life.

The other islands in the Lipari group, jutting out of the water like so many jagged rocks, soon faded from view. Toward sundown, we approached Messina on the northeastern tip of Sicily. Lights were beginning to twinkle in the houses lying close to the hillsides. Dotting the waters of the strait were the tiny, homeward-bound fishing boats, oared by ant-sized fishermen.

The town of Reggio, lying almost opposite Messina, quickly disappeared in the twilight. Here I saw my first porpoise. I couldn't help shouting in glee as they flipped themselves into arcs and dived in and out of the water. What a delightful sight!

January 20, 1953 We are crossing the Ionian Sea today and the sunshine on the water is dazzling. Because our ship is over 300 tons, our pilot tells us, we are not closely following the northern coast of the Island of Peloponnesos and through the gulf to Corinth, but are taking a southern route through the Gulf of Lakonia and then up to Piraeus.

Hikmet is peacefully napping now after her daily shipboard walking exercise. Sometimes the crew try out different enticements to get her to take steps. There's a noticeable roll to the ship today and she's developing a real sailor's shamble. A unique handicap in learning to walk!

January 21, 1953 Cape Matapan and Cape Malea were nothing but blurs on the vague skyline. A gale came up during the night, blowing 40 miles an hour. The winds were from the northeast, fortunately diminished in strength by coming from the land and not the sea. Our speed was cut to seven miles an hour.

"Skullduggery afoot," quoth the Turkish Gentleman. He claims the engineers reduced the speed, not because of the storm but because they calculate arriving in Piraeus too late to unload any cargo, but not too late to enter the harbor. Since the crew can't work after five o'clock, and the harbor regulations don't allow ships to enter port after six o'clock, this would call for careful calculations. However, if his dark suspicions are true, who would blame the men for wanting to spend the first evening ashore?

We docked in Piraeus at six p.m. amid great tumult. From the pilothouse, Sela, Hikmet, and I witnessed part of the proceedings. The verbal communications took on a strident, more aggressive tone so we slipped quietly down to the second deck to watch. Apparently only one tugboat had been sent out to pilot us into port and the ensuing ten minutes were vociferous and vitriolic. The captain's voice was clearly audible above the shouts from shore, the tugboat horn blasts, whistles, and general din. Everyone seemed to be pulling in a different direction at once; it was nerve shattering but quite exciting.

When comparative calm descended, a boatload of customs and immigration officials came aboard, and the arena of action shifted to the officer's mess. Everything, apparently, got sorted out to everyone's satisfaction. Most of the below-decks passenger have surfaced, all smiles, waiting to disembark here....

January 22, 1953 This morning, we readied ourselves for "shore leave" and were instructed to descend the shaky gangplank tied to a waiting launch. We followed the lead to the launch and soon were off, chugging and yelling, to the opposite end of the port, passing a motley assortment of fishing boats and tankers, and three impressive British destroyers. The British seamen were industriously repairing and painting; a half dozen were lined up at attention, drilling.

We docked next to a garbage scow, scrambled across it, clambered up to the dock, walked through the huge Piraeus customs house salon, and out to the street side past a row of orange trees heavy with shiny fruit. We'd arranged to meet up with Adonis for coffee in a small sidewalk cafe; but the icy cold wind drove us inside to wait. The wooden floor was sprinkled with sawdust, the window lined with a row of wine bottles. We sat on rush-bottomed chairs and ordered coffee from the small boy in charge. He was serious, professional, sad-faced, and never smiled, even at Hikmet. When we stepped back out into the waterfront wind, my hat blew off and four little boys from nowhere chased it, earning a small gratuity.

With Adonis now as guide, we looked in a few shop windows before taking the subway to Athens. Here the train runs underground for only a short way; soon, we could see the Acropolis and the Parthenon high above us. Grass was growing about the ruins once the glory of Greece.

It was our good fortune to be invited to Adonis' home, an apartment on a side street in a residential section of "modern" Athens. Because we were chilled to the bone, the first thing I noticed about the apartment was that the parlor was unheated and our breath was hanging in the air. By American standards, the furnishings were circa 1880; by the standards here, I'm sure, they were considered very modern and "showy." (The bathroom boasted two American toilet fixtures.) The tapestries in the salon and dining room, as well as the oil paintings and vases in profusion, created an effect of luxurious warmth.

Certainly heartwarming, however, were the greetings by his aged grandmother, young-looking mother, and married sister. They were all wearing long, heavy woolen garments, I noticed. Someone brought in a portable kerosene heater, which took the chill off the room.

Again, language proved no barrier and we had a delightful time communicating in gestures and smiles over cognac, pastries, and coffee. Hikmet, of course, was the conversational focal point and the three ladies looked surprised as I changed her diapers in the corner. Up to that point they had been calling her "boy baby " in Greek, Adonis informed us. Misled, I dare say, by her corduroy overalls. After the refreshments and effusive good-byes, he escorted us via trolley back to the center of Athens, where we were on our own.

We stopped in a pastry shop for another coffee while furtively mapping a route back to the pier. Our furtiveness was of no avail. Everyone stared at us. Not just a sidelong glance, but often halting for an over-the-shoulder inspection. I found this very disconcerting, but it's evidently no breach of etiquette to stare at foreigners.

People seem to have an air of poverty and industry. Women scurry about the streets shopping for food, which seems to be very dear. Men and small boys line the sidewalks with their shoeshine kits, trays of rolls and bread, flowers, candies, and baskets of trinkets, always shouting their wares.

We, or rather Hikmet, bouncing up and down in her usual, uninhibited fashion, struck up another non-vocal conversation with an old woman on the return subway. Some of the suspicious glances directed toward us foreigners gradually turned to smiles. When a blind boy with crippled fingers came into our compartment playing a plaintive Greek tango on his accordion, the passengers silently passed paper drachmas to the boy's companion and resumed their conversations.

Nearing the customs house, we stopped to buy postcards at a street stall and witnessed an amusing trilingual interchange: Two officers from a Swedish ship were trying to buy cigarettes. In English, they questioned a man standing next to us, with no success. Sela intervened and asked this third man if he knew Turkish. He did; also Greek. So, the third man bargained with the seller in Greek, translated into Turkish to Sela, who relayed the information to the officers in English. They quickly bought their favorite brand and then strolled off, chatting happily in Swedish.

Back through the customs house then, across a garbage scow, and into the waiting launch, where we were almost drenched before pulling alongside our ship.

January 23, 1953 Our aft porthole presents an interesting spectacle. Since we are unloading Greek Army supplies, the dock is swarming with a lot of Greek soldiers, and a few American. A long line of military trucks keep moving up and carrying off the supplies. Some of the small Jeep wagons are being loaded onto the freight cars on the tracks just behind the trucks.

The winches fore and aft strain continuously. Each load in the rope nets is lifted from the hold by winch; there's a wheeze of steam, a rumble and whistle, then a deafening thud as the loads are swung over the side and dropped. From casual observation, the number of men shouting out the orders closely equals the number of men actually doing the work. Just beyond our ship is a most strikingly anachronistic scene. Beneath the shadow of a behemoth overhead crane, dodging gigantic American-made loading trucks, men are loading coal deposited by the previous freighter — not with scoop shovels and conveyor belts, or even hand-shovels, but with their bare hands. These workers, wearing cloths over their heads and shoulders, scoop the coal into large baskets by the handful, and carry the full baskets to the waiting trucks and horse-drawn carts. Some of the large pieces of coal are carried one at a time. Like ants moving a mountain.

This evening, an American Army major, his aide and his interpreter, all with the American Army mission here, dined with us aboard ship. They are here to check in the cargo. It is being delivered, they tell us, to the Mission and the Greek Army as part of the Mutual Defense Aid, Greece being a member of the North Atlantic Pact.

January 24, 1953 Fortune smiled today, with warm sun and no wind. Sela counted up our drachmas [45,000 = $3.00] and we set off again for Athens.

From the subway stop, we hiked up the long hill past the Acropolis, now a hollowed-out field where great broken stones lie tumbled about. We took a shortcut through a hillside park. In this discreet, sylvan grove of fir trees, utterly relaxed in the sunshine, I changed Hikmet's diaper, gave her baby biscuits and her bottle. Sela and I ate bread and cheese from the ship's pantry.

There were few other tourists about as we finished our climb to the Parthenon atop the hill. We wandered through the ruins in an atmosphere of quiet peace and serenity. Sounds of the city below were hushed. A tiny bird twittered as it hopped from stone to stone.

Faintly, we could hear the painstaking tapping of a workman's chisel on a new piece of marble. Skillful restoration work is in evidence here and there. One's imagination can readily envision the temples as they once must have been, with the temple's tall pillars rising in beautiful simplicity, unbroken lines of friezes picturing graceful Grecian scenes, six voluptuous Caryatides, vestal virgins draped in flowing garments. We spent two wonderful hours wandering among the antiquities, and reluctantly took the train back to Piraeus.

Oh, changing life and customs! From the historically sublime to the squalid, teeming life of the waterfront. The street vendors' shouts and cries seemed even louder now. The sellers squatted or sat cross-legged on the narrow sidewalks, displaying their mats and trays of celluloid combs, shoelaces, clothing, pastries, and plastic sunglasses. Pushcarts and donkey carts crowded the streets. The afternoon sunshine and balmy harbor breezes enlivened everyone.

For a short while, we followed a longhaired white goat being led by its master. Later on, we passed the pair at a sidewalk table; the villager was sipping his afternoon coffee with the goat tethered to his ankle.

January 25, 1953 The last of the army freight was unloaded during the night and at dawn we shifted to another pier. At lunch, one of the Greek agents astounded us by saying Piraeus claims to be "one of the most efficient ports for unloading cargo" in the world. He explained that the stevedores are paid not by the hour — in contrast to American unionized dock workers – but on a tonnage basis. In addition, bonuses are paid for maximum speed. These incentives compensate for the lack of up-to-date-equipment; the men, working in six-hour shifts, put forth maximum effort.

The temple dedicated to Athena standing in front of the Parthenon has had its entrance mostly replaced, also most of the marble steps. During the height of the Ottoman Empire, the Turks used this vantage point for their cannons, causing much damage.

The famous "Elgin" marbles were named after Lord Elgin, once ambassador to the Ottoman Turkish rulers in Greece. He was given consent to take what he wished, as the ruins then were neglected. One of the famous figures of the Caryatides, removed and now in a British Museum, has been duplicated to complete the original six at the Parthenon.

January 26, 1953 Up before the crack of dawn this morning. Immigration officers swarmed aboard at six o'clock to return our passports and reclaim our shore permits.

Now at nine o'clock, the docks are clear, the pilot has cast off — with a fresh pack of Chesterfield cigarettes in his pocket. We are sailing through the foggy, foggy dew into the Aegean Sea. Hundreds of seagulls have already settled in our wake to scavenge on refuse.

The Cyclades Islands on our starboard are dim, almost indiscernible. We passed Kaos at noon and between Euboea and Andros early in this afternoon.

At about two in the morning, the pilot says, we should reach Çanakkale, a small town on the Asiatic side of the Dardanelles. We'll stop at long enough to be cleared by the Turkish health authorities.

January 27, 1953 One month from the day we embarked in New York Harbor, we see Turkish land. Strong headwinds slowed us down so we didn't pass Çanakkale until dawn today. The Turkish steamer "Ankara," which left Piraeus almost twelve hours after us, sailed past this afternoon and will arrive in Istanbul long before we do. The sun shone through the clouds briefly, giving us a glimpse of a village in a gray-green valley.

All through dinner, the Turkish Gentleman bemoaned the fact that we wouldn't arrive during daylight. In his opinion, Istanbul has the most beautiful approach and skyline in the world. Lacking his wide travel experience, I can't share his disappointment. I find the night view enchanting.

The engines are slowing now to pick up our pilot. We are close enough to see the colored lights gleaming all along the Asiatic and European shores. We can make out the seven minarets of the Sultan Ahmed mosque and the four minarets of the Aya Sofia mosque. Their huge domes arch against the evening sky and their slender minarets gracefully point heavenward. ❦

1

ARRIVAL IN TÜRKÍYE

Letter to Spokane and Tulsa

Kadıköy/Istanbul

February 4, 1953

Dear Family and Friends,

I can hardly believe that we've been in Istanbul only one week! So much has happened since we took the motor launch from the ship to the customs house salon in Istanbul Harbor. It was raining and very late; we expected to arrive quietly and spend the first night in a hotel. But, not to be! The Istanbul branch of Sela's family had been expecting us all day; his two young uncles were waiting patiently for us in customs. There was little difficulty with our baggage, fortunately, and we were whisked off to meet the rest of the Istanbul relatives at his Aunt Saadet Uçar's house. (Aunt, I discover, is a graduate of the American Girls School here and speaks English fluently. What a great blessing for me!)

A Family Welcome in Istanbul

Returning after almost seven years of study abroad, with an American wife and child, was a Great Event in the family. We were greeted with many hugs, much kissing, and not a few tears of joy. Hikmet was admired by all, then carried off to bed. A young housemaid served us tiny cups of Turkish coffee on a silver tray, with tiny chocolates wrapped in silver foil. One small boy came in to welcome me traditionally by kissing my hand and raising it to his forehead. Sela says this graceful gesture is a mark of respect shown by children to adults, and by younger adults to their elders.

Sela and the relatives were afire with questions, as if seven years' abroad could be related in one short evening! Much later, with heads in a whirl, we said good night to everyone in the household and were shown to our bedroom, where the enormous woolen quilt and pillows had been heated with a long-handled, copper bedwarmer to take off the damp chill. In the soothing warmth, we immediately fell into a deep sleep.

Strange sounds awoke me next morning. I recognized a horse cart's rumbling and rattling down the cobble-stoned street outside the window, but not the mournful cries: "Sü-üt! Sü-üt!" It was the milkman who ladles out milk from his milk cans, Sela explained; he was chanting *Milk! Milk!* as he passed our door.

A Typical Breakfast in Istanbul

There is no central heating in this large apartment, it seems, except for a cooking stove in the kitchen and wood/coal stoves in the bathroom and long hall. Someone slipped in and carried off little Hikmet to bathe and feed her in the kitchen, so we were left to dress hurriedly and breakfast in the cozy alcove at one end of the hall. The silver breakfast tray held an array of small, crystal dishes:

1

black olives, green olives, white manda [water-buffalo] butter, salty white cheese, rich yellow cheese, quince marmalade, fig preserves in syrup, cherry preserves, clover honey, thick slices of bread still warm from the bakery. The strong black tea in small bell-shaped glasses was steaming and stimulating, to ready us for the day's excitements, whatever they might be.

Visiting Day in Kadıköy

It was Aunt Saadet's visiting day, so she was already preparing for visitors. The entire household — Aunt and her husband, her young son home from boarding school, her younger brother and his bride, a visiting cousin, an older widowed aunt, and the servant girl— all scurried about their various tasks of sending out for supplies, fetching fresh food from the market, roasting and grinding coffee beans, baking pastries, lining the chairs up along the wall for the visitors. The air was electric with excitement.

The news had spread fast, and soon neighbors and nearby relatives started drifting in, eager to meet the arrivals from America. When Aunt Saadet's mother, whom everyone calls Büyük Anne (Grandmother), rang the bell, there was a stir to plump up the pillows and straighten the covers on the divan by the sitting room window. I could see this was "the cozy corner," the place of honor reserved for the most venerable visitor. Grandmother was not only the most senior, Sela told me, she was the daughter of an *agha*, or old-time landowner. She seemed to take her position seriously.

As she entered, everyone stood to greet her. I shook hands with her, but the others kissed her hand and raised it to their foreheads. Everyone sat down only after she had arranged herself cross-legged on the divan and adjusted the black silk scarf covering her hair. The visitors took turns welcoming Sela back to Turkey, congratulating him on his university achievements, and on his wife and child. I heard many of the same expressions repeated over and over, which Sela, sitting next to me, quit translating after a while. The happy, animated conversation flowed around me in excited phrases, unintelligible but musical-sounding. I smiled at appropriate times, I hoped. The morning passed pleasantly, with many little cups of coffee served, and many little tea glasses filled and refilled. In due time, the visitors departed with more well-wishings and blessings.

A Lavish Family Lunch

For lunch, we were served creamy chicken-rice soup with lemon, green salad, tiny fresh anchovies fried in olive oil, rice pilav, minced meat steamed in grape leaves, vegetables simmered in olive oil, fruit compote. Every dish was delicious.

During the fish course, Grandmother, not only the most respected family member, but also the liveliest talker, fell silent. Aunt, sitting next to me, explained that her mother was anxious not to commit any breach of American etiquette, so she'd been observing my table manners. She'd just eaten a mouthful of fish bones and was waiting to see what I did with *my* fish bones first. As soon as I used my fork to remove a bone from my mouth and put it on the edge of my plate, she immediately did likewise — with a loud sigh of relief. Everyone burst out laughing.

Aunt confessed her mother was a great wit and it was difficult to get the best of her. This prompted an imp in me: I retaliated by raising my left arm above

2

my head and eating the next course with my right hand only. Grandmother, without hesitation, raised her arm as if she normally ate that way, and continued eating. Again, everyone laughed uproariously and we ended the meal in great, good humor.

Bathroom vs Toilet Terminology and Technology

I have already been introduced to several cultural institutions that warrant sharing with you arm-chair travelers back home. As any tourist in a strange country will advise you, among the first essential items to look up in your bilingual dictionary or phrase book are the words for bathroom and toilet. I've just learned that the English word bathroom or the Turkish word "banyo" [borrowed from French] simply means the room with the bathtub or shower. The Turkish words for toilet are "tuvalet" or "hela" [or "yuz numera," one hundred, sometimes written *00* on restroom doors in Istanbul].

This may seem somewhat confusing, but not *shocking,* as the initiation to an actual Turkish toilet is for a Westerner like me. It takes special adjusting to, the reason being that the little room contains no "throne" upon which to sit, but a kind of horse-shoe shaped ceramic trough with foot places to stand upon or squat over. It also contains, on the wall approximately one foot up from the trough, a water tap which automatically drains down into the trough.

And lastly, or actually firstly, outside the toilet door there are wooden clogs to slip on over one's house shoes while inside, standing on the foot rests. In Aunt Saadet's house, I have discovered, there is a Turkish toilet in one separate little room, and a Western "throne" in another. In addition, there's a French *bidet* in the bath room. Well, so much for this introduction to home hygiene and sanitation....

Exploring Mysterious Istanbul

On the other hand, my first tour of Istanbul yesterday was *not* particularly shocking. Before we left the U.S., I'd read a few available books about modern Turkey, and had pictured the city in my mind as crowded, dirty, teeming with people of every description. But it surpassed my expectations. It is totally fascinating!

From Aunt's house on the Asian side of the Bosphorus Strait, we set out early in the morning to cross to the European side in Uncle Avni's Buick. It was brand-new, one-of-a-kind, and certainly attracted a lot of attention! (Owning *any* car, it seems, is a tremendous luxury in Turkey.)

My first memorable impression of this side of Istanbul is a classic anachronism: a gas station attendant kneeling on a cloth on the grease rack saying his prayers. His head, wrapped in a white cloth, bowed up and down in complete oblivion to all the donkeys, horses, cars, taxis, and motor buses passing by. Here was a centuries-old tradition, unchanged in the throes of modernization.

We crossed over Galata Bridge, which spans the curved inlet of the Bosphorus called the Golden Horn, and left the car with a guard. We continued on foot through the narrow streets, following the crowds thronging to the vast Grand Bazaar, or Covered Market, entirely covered over by high, glass domes. One could easily become lost, I think, in its maze of twisting and turning alley-like passageways.

3

Shopkeepers lounge about in open doorways, enticing passersby to enter and browse. Occasionally, artisans can be seen at work in their shops, sitting high above on elevated work-shelves, patiently creating intricately tooled leather bags, filigreed silver brooches, carved wooden stools....

Everything imaginable is sold somewhere in the Bazaar, if one has patience and a good guide: antiques; Bursa silk, hand-knotted wool carpets, pastries, Turkish coffee, furniture, furs, embroidered house slippers, spices, uncut stones, glittering gold and gem-encrusted jewelry....

A constant undercurrent of noise is carried in from the streets outside. Donkey brays, car horns, and traffic whistles mingle with the haggling voices of merchants and customers. Occasionally, a drift of delicate flute music floats in. The senses are assaulted by this cacophony of sounds and titillated by the flamboyancy of colors, the bouquet of fragrant, pungent, spicy aromas. Because of its ever-changing contents, the Bazaar is unendingly exciting; walking through its narrow lanes and alleyways is like exploring the far edges of a medieval map, intriguing and mysterious. A perfect introduction to this city spanning Europe and Asia.

On this tantalizing note, I close with greetings to all, Anna Maria

---

Journal: I Go to the Dentist and Sela Goes Shopping We're staying an extra day or two in Istanbul so I can visit a dentist. It seems, alas, I have a tooth problem, despite a "thorough" check-up before we left Wyoming. (I suspect the little filling done in Worland wasn't properly disinfected.) But Aunt Saadet's family dentist is most kind and reassuring, explaining everything to me in fluent German. I find it quite a memory test to try to dredge up college German verbs and gender forms while sitting in a dental chair, experiencing probes and punctures. I comfort myself that this problem didn't flare up when we were still sailing on the high seas!

Sela spent the time shopping for a warm winter coat and hat for Hikmet. He found a ready-made, fuzzy wool outfit in which she looks like a small, brown teddy bear. Everyone in the household now calls her "Teddy Bear." ❦

Baby Hikmet, Istanbul 1953

2

VOYAGE TO SELA'S HOMETOWN

Journal: Farewells in Kadıköy It is the end of our two-week visit in Istanbul. Early in the morning, an assemblage of Istanbul relatives meet in front of Aunt Saadet and Uncle Avni's house in Kadıköy.

The younger uncles' wives have come to bid us farewell, bearing parcels of fresh cheese pastries, meatballs, and sweet rolls. Aunt Saadet has sent to the market for oranges, boxes of foil-wrapped chocolates, and other goodies for our trip to Sela's hometown.

When we do the kissing on both cheeks and goodbye hugging at the door, I am tearful at leaving all these kind women. It is especially hard to say goodbye to English-speaking Aunt Saadet, my bridge over unknown waters, but I am ready for the next adventure. The young uncles have arranged for another vehicle to transport our luggage, and we set off for the harbor, to board the Black Sea steamer.

So far, in addition to all the greetings and welcomings, leavetakings and farewells, a good deal of travel seems to consist of packing up/loading/unloading suitcases, footlockers, crates, and string bags. By the time we arrive at the harbor, the taxi with our luggage has already disgorged our load, and hamals [porters] appear out of nowhere to pick them up, strap the large items on their backs, and load everything onto the steamer. I am in another state of excitement, where it is hard to take in everything at once. ❦

Journal: Black Sea Steamer to Sürmene The few days on the steamer from Istanbul along the Black Sea coast to Trabzon are so much livelier than the weeks of sailing across the mid-Atlantic and the Mediterranean! Our main preoccupation, again, is tending to Hikmet's needs. Sela and I take turns playing with her inside in the cabin, and when the ship makes its scheduled stops al ong the way, we all walk with her on the windy deck to watch the goings-on. To her great delight, there's a flurry of activity and excitement at each port of call: cargo from Istanbul is unloaded and eastward-bound cargo is on-loaded; sea gulls swoop and shriek overhead; animated passengers come and go, some toting wicker baskets on their backs stuffed with fresh market produce, others carrying crates of squacking poultry, bedding, odd bundles.

We three sleep well each night, with the fresh sea air coming through our open porthole. ❦

Journal: A Family Welcome Enroute Finally, the steamer pulls into our port of call, Trabzon, and anchors in the shallow harbor at a considerable distance from the shore. The majority of passengers seem to be disembarking here. I watch them rush to the ship's railing, clamber overboard and down to the bottom rung of a rope ladder, and from thence into one of the small dinghies that have been steadily moving toward the steamer, to transport passengers ashore.

To my amazement, Sela seems to be in no hurry to leave ship. Instead, his eyes are glued on two dinghies coming towards us. They soon disgorge several dozen men who scramble *up* the ladder and rush into the ship's salon! These are male relatives, it quickly becomes apparent. They have driven two hours from Sela's hometown of Sürmene to meet the steamer, impatient to welcome him home after so many years abroad, arriving with his wife and child from America!

I've pored over Sela's photograph album so often I'm able to recognize some of the faces. I spot Sela's father, Mehmet Ali Malkoç, first of all. Now that we are meeting, I feel too overwhelmed to try to say anything. We hug, and Sela does all the talking. I know that Sela calls his father Baba, which is easy to remember, and I may call him Kayın Baba [Kayın for in-law]. Or I can simply call him "Baba." Somehow, when I think of calling someone else Father and Mother, I feel a kind of disloyalty to my own parents. I guess I can get used to this, telling myself they're not actually the same words. But I already feel warmly disposed toward him. Before Sela and I married in Tulsa, he had sent a letter with his blessings, along with a message to my mother assuring her he would cherish and protect me like his own daughters.

Sela's mother, Ayse Malkoç, will be my "Kayın Anne. He had also explained that I may simply call her Anne [ahn-neh]. Then, he confided that his mother probably will not like me. This shocked, in fact, rather outraged me. "Why is that?" I asked him. "She hasn't even *met* me!"

"That's just it," he responded. "She had picked out someone else for me to marry, a girl in town. It's kind of embarrassing." Embarrassing for all concerned, I think to myself. I try to put this thought out of my mind.

Sela takes baby Hikmet and motions me to follow him and his father out of the salon. Dozens of willing hands are carrying our suitcases, food parcels, string bags. I follow along to the ship's rail, hesitate briefly, descend backwards down the wobbly ladder, and step gingerly into the dinghy that takes us to shore.

Once on terra firma, Sela quickly passes Hikmet over to me and makes a beeline for his mother, who has been waiting for us on shore in the forefront of a group of women all wearing the same attire: long, black coats and black silk head scarves. I follow uncertainly, not sure how to greet my Kayın Anne: Shake her hand? Hug her? Although in Istanbul I'd seen younger women kissing their elders' hands to show respect, somehow I just can't bring myself to kiss anybody's hand. I don't seem to be ready for this custom, so I shake her hand and hug her. Her daughter Güher greets me with a hug and kisses: "Hos geldiniz, Yenge," [Welcome, sister-in-law] she says, and swoops up Hikmet with a big smile. I have learned the polite response: "Hos bulduk, Güher." We smile at each other, and walk with the women toward a large blue bus. The other women chatter away in happy voices. I hear the word "gelin" frequently and guess they must be referring to me, "the bride." I am silent, of course, understanding only a few words of Turkish, but I smile a lot.

When I look around for Sela, I recognize more faces from the album: another uncle, more cousins. The men folk have surrounded him, all laughing and shouting happily, hugging and kissing him on one cheek and then on the other. I

6

remembered Aunt Saadet's warning about kissing customs: Men and women never kiss in public, but men do greet each other by kissing on the cheek. (And they also hold hands walking down the street, I've noticed.)

Now the men all walk off together and I feel Sela is being taken away from me. He is probably far more westernized than his family realize, I think to myself, but now he's on home ground and he has to go along with the men. They all get into automobiles.

I am gently guided into the waiting bus with Güher and Hikmet, Kayın Anne and the other women. As the bus driver starts up the creaky vehicle and steers us down the street, my mother-in-law reaches into her coat pocket and pulls out a fresh lemon. Now and then she squeezes it and breathes in its sharp fragrance. She offers it to me for a sniff. This is to ward off car sickness on the winding, coastal road to Sürmene. ❧

Malkoç and Kıralı Families, Sürmene 1953

front row: Remzi Kirali, his four grandchildren, Mehmet Ali Malkoç
middle row: Behice Kirali and Ayse Malkoç (on either side, in black head scarves), groom Muammer & bride-to-be Nezihe (white corsage in center)
back row: Kıralı and Malkoç relatives

7

3

SÜRMENE ON THE BLACK SEA

Journal: A Family Welcome in Sürmene, February 13, 1953 By nightfall, our
"ladies' bus" reaches Sürmene and the men's separate automobiles pull up behind
us. We are in front of a tall, two-storied wooden house on the side of the Black
Sea coastal road we've just traversed from Trabzon. Male relatives come up to
me, introduce themselves and shake hands. Someone picks up Hikmet, others pick
up the luggage and show us the way up the steep, dark stairs of Sela's home.

The heavy door at the top of the stairs opens onto a long, high-ceilinged
corridor, with a shelf at the entrance for street shoes and house slippers. Güher
takes me on a tour of the house, opening various doors to the toilet, the bathroom,
the pantry, the kitchen, a bedroom, another bedroom, the family room, and a room
I'll call the parlor.

The first evening, we all have supper at the round table in the family
room: Baba, Kayın Anne, and Güher, all engaged in animated conversation with
Sela. Next to him, I am holding squirming, wriggling Hikmet, trying to feed her as
she grabs for the spoon and the porridge bowl. Sela says something to his family,
then turns to me. "Get me a glass of water," he says in English. All eyes are
focused on me.

I'm puzzled and shocked. Is this a *test*, I wonder? It is so out of character
for Sela to make such a demand, especially when he's just *sitting* there, and can
see I'm occupied with the hungry baby. In a low voice, I murmur: "Get your own
water!"

He translates my reply, and everyone roars with laughter. He had just
warned them what he was going to ask me — and how I would respond. "Now
you see," he tells them in Turkish, "I have an *American* wife!" 🍃

Journal: Remzi efendi's Dinner The next day is happy and leisurely. In the
evening, we are all invited to a family dinner across the road. This large house
facing the sea belongs to Remzi efendi, a relative of Kayın Anne. More
importantly, Remzi efendi is the father of fair-haired, blue-eyed Nezihe, the girl
whom Sela's brother Muammer wants to marry. Muammer will be taking leave
from the Navy soon, Sela says, and has arranged for an intermediary to pave the
way in asking for Nezihe's hand in marriage. It's not clear whether Remzi efendi
has given his consent yet. It's my impression that Remzi efendi is highly regarded
in the family.

We enter, and are welcomed by the host and his wife, Behice hanım,
standing with their shy daughter Nezihe and their younger children. Güher has
described Nezihe's mother as " smiling-faced" (according to my dictionary) and
sure enough, she is beaming at us. In fact, everyone is smiling, and overjoyed to

8

welcome Sela back home, together with his new family. A young girl carries Hikmet off, and Sela and I are left to walk on into in a long, high-ceilinged open salon with many rooms opening off from it, and at the far end, many windows facing the sandy seashore.

Sela and I sit at a long table with several dozen male relatives engrossed in happy, lively conversation. Behice hanım brings in a steaming tureen of lemon chicken soup and ladles it into the soup plates in front of us. Everyone begins the first course in leisurely fashion, savoring both the delicious soup and the family fellowship. Politely, I wait for our smiling hostess to come back and sit down at the table.

"Don't wait for Nezihe's mother," Sela says. "She's busy. All the women are busy; they'll eat later." Indeed, through the half-open kitchen door, I can see them bustling with pots and pans amidst clouds of steam, fragrant aromas, laughing chatter. After the soup , they bring out course after course of equally delicious dishes: rice pilav with black currents and pine nuts browned in butter; a roast leg of lamb; hot, steamed vegetables stuffed with rice and meat; squares of parsleyed white cheese pastry; rice wrapped and steamed in tender grapes leaves, served cold with olive oil and lemon wedges.

I fight off feelings of guilt because I'm the only female, and I'm sitting while Nezihe's mother and other relatives are serving me. "Relax," Sela tells me. "You and I are the guests of honor; this will happen to you only once here. Enjoy it!"

After a respite filled with more lively conversation and family reminiscing, we are served the traditional demitasse coffee. Then Sela's favorite dessert arrives: walnut baklava. This dessert of flakey, strudel-like pastry leaves is cut into diamond shapes and drenched with syrup. Literally, mouth-watering. As in the old fairy tales that describe a sultan's feast, I will say each delicious dish was prepared to perfection, and each course was more delicious than the last!

The preparation for some of the dishes must take hours and hours, I think. For a big dinner like this, I imagine the women in the neighboring households get together in advance to stuff and roll up the dozens of grape leaves for the sarma, and to roll out the dough into the paper-thin leaves for the many layers of baklava. It reminds me of the old-fashioned socializing at a quilting bee, and my mother's favorite adage: "Many hands make light work." ❧

*Journal: **Strolling in Sürmene*** The next morning, Sela and his father suggest going for a walk in the fresh sea air. "Where would you like to go?" they ask me.

"To the marketplace," I reply. That's my idea of the "essence" of a town. But Sela balks at my suggestion.

"Women don't go to the market here," he explains. "They don't shop like in America. Only very poor women, with no men in their family to help them."

"Well, who buys the groceries?" I wonder.

"Men do," he answers. "They handle the money." Still, to please me, he and his father ignore local tradition, and we three set off down the road toward the marketplace. Because it's not a market day, the square is empty: no vegetables or fruits are being brought down from the villages in the mountains. We walk on toward the center of town, near Baba's dry goods/hardware store, to have a look around. Sela explains that Baba is taking a few days off to visit with him.

We continue our leisurely stroll on the road back home. "Are there any other Americans around here?" I ask idly.

"No," Sela says. "You're the first around here. And they're all interested in *you*."

"How do you know?" I ask.

"Look up at the windows!" Sure enough, there are faces peering out of every house along the road.

On this chilly and damp morning, I'm wearing my winter stadium boots from Tulsa, a heavy, grey wool trench coat, a bright red wool tam, and thick wool gloves. Suddenly, I realize how differently I'm dressed. I try to view myself from a different perspective, through the onlookers' eyes. When Kayın Anne and Güher go out of the house, their custom is to wrap a long striped woolen shawl around their waist as a warm overskirt and another over their head and shoulders to completely envelope their top half. This seems to be their "everyday" dress then they leave the house.

To the people here, I must look like some being just landed from Mars! I keep these thoughts to myself as we continue our leisurely walk. My father-in-law doesn't seem the least bit embarrassed by my foreign garb. He's totally engaged in conversation with Sela, who seems to be thoroughly enjoying the scene. They're both wearing European-style woolen business suits and overcoats.

But I feel so terribly self-conscious. So out of place. Suddenly, being a foreigner seems such a responsibility, especially in a place like Sürmene where people have never seen an American woman, except perhaps in an American movie. I'm not *typical* enough to *represent* American women. How should I act? I feel so inadequate. I try to sort out my jumbled thoughts calmly. I 'm not ready to give up my "American-ness" — whatever that is — but I make up my mind to follow Aunt Saadet's admonitions about local customs as carefully as possible: I must be as polite as I know how, especially to elders. I must be observant, watching what people do on entering and leaving, addressing each other, how they eat at the table, and so on. I must ask lots of questions — as soon as I learn the words. And try to understand the answers. ❦

Journal: Sela Leaves for Erzurum   Despite Sela's teasing within the bosom of his family, it is good-natured and light-hearted. He seems so well-balanced and self-confident that his presence makes me feel secure. He explains things that are strange to me, and explains my strange habits to his family.

After only a few days of visits with family and relatives, now he's leaving to pay respects to his sister Sülhiye and brother-in-law Süleyman Atalı in Erzurum, a mountainous region far to the southeast. Although I know it's his family obligation, I am uneasy that he has to go. He assures me that he will be back for Muammer's wedding, and then take Hikmet and me to live in the oilfields. Wherever that is. ❦

Journal: Language Learning Is Continual and Never-Ending   When Sela leaves, his sister Güher becomes my mainstay. I am constantly asking her questions. She is patient and eager to have me learn the names of everything in the house.

"Yenge," she instructs, "Bu ne?" [What is this?] and I respond with the newly-learned words for faucet, stove, chimney, glass, cup, window, quilt. I always confuse the words towel [havlu] and carrot [havuç] and we have a good laugh together.

I'm trying to memorize her household vocabulary, and more words from my dictionary. I listen to the family playing with Hikmet, and to the words they are using with her. For me, it is all an endless language lesson.

In a sense, like Hikmet, I am starting with a clean slate. She's beginning to speak Turkish now, saying a few words I can recognize, like "su" for water and "amca" for uncle. To her, uncle is any adult male, including her grandfather. (He is trying to teach her to say, "Büyük baba"[grandfather] instead of "amca.") Before we arrived in Sürmene, she had had a vocabulary of several words in English, including "Dada," "teddy bear," and "ball." And, of course, she was calling me "Mama."

Now, however, whenever she calls for her "Mama," someone hurriedly brings her a bowl of warm porridge, that being the meaning of "mama" in Turkish. While she is sorting out this confusion, I think it best to take a back seat, linguistically speaking. She has so many attending her in the household, and little cousins across the street to play with her, she is never alone. It is only at nap time and bedtime, or when we are alone in the house, that I speak English with her. And I encourage her to call me "Anne," to avoid confusing others also. ❧

Journal: Visiting Day in Sürmene The days pass quickly. There is so much to see and learn about the rhythms of the house. Tomorrow, I am told, is Kayın Anne's Visiting Day. As I understand it, relatives and friends from the villages around will come to pay their respects, congratulate the family on Sela's return after seven years, and take a look at Hikmet and at me, the "new" bride.

In preparation, the family have hung up the carpets outside in the garden and have beaten them vigorously with rug beaters. There are no vacuum cleaners; all cleaning is done by hand, vigorously. I think there are other helpers brought in for this work.

Güher has swept the pine floors with a heavy, handle-less broom and then scrubbed them on her hands and knees with a soapy cloth. She has wiped down all surfaces with clean, damp cloths. Everything has been polished within an inch of its life. Everything is clean as a whistle for tomorrow....

Finally, today is Visiting Day! She and Güher have risen early, prepared cookies and rolls on huge trays, and sent them down to the municipal bake oven. While I am readying Hikmet and myself for the day, someone has already brought back the baking trays, and the fragrant smells from the kitchen are enticing. I peek in at the round, buttery cookies in powdered sugar, tiny rolled "cigarette" puff pastries, layered parsley-and-cheese pastries. The assorted pastries include something sweet and something salty for the guests.

Everyone seems to be in a the state of excitement and it's hard to get through breakfast and lunch. In the kitchen, the sweet and savory refreshments are arranged in mounds on serving trays. Tiny coffee cups and saucers are arranged near a small serving tray. A larger tray of tea glasses and saucers, a crystal bowl of sugar cubes, and a cup holding delicate silver tea spoons all sit awaiting the visitors.

Finally, the heavy iron door knocker on the enormous front door clanks loudly to announce the first callers. Kayın Anne and Güher greet them, one by one, and I timidly try to follow suit. None are strangers to the house; they change their street shoes for house slippers and file down the hall into the parlor, now lined with chairs around the walls.

I recall what Aunt Saadet told me about seating: The custom is to wait until your mother-in-law sits down first. But Kayın Anne sees me standing undecided, motions me to a chair: "Sit! Sit!" she tells me.

I watch as she makes the welcoming round in the room, now full of guests, stopping in front of each woman, asking each one the same questions. For me, it's a repetitive language drill:

"Hos geldiniz!" [Welcome!]
"Hos bulduk." [a polite response to "Welcome"]
"Nasılsınız?" [How are you?]
"Tesekkür ederim. Iyim. Siz nasılsınız?" [Thank you. I am well. How are you? And so she goes, around the room. Automatically, I memorize the drill.

After an interval of ten minutes or so, Güher serves a tiny cup of coffee to each guest. The custom of serving, I notice, is to start not with the order of arrival, but according to the visitor's age. The eldest is always served first.

In the kitchen, young girl relatives help out, cooking each serving of coffee separately in a cezve [djezve], a small metal coffee pot large enough to hold one or two servings, with a long handle to hold it over the fire. One demitasse of cold water, a heaping teaspoonful of freshly ground, powdery coffee, and one or two sugar cubes are stirred in and brought just to a boil — but never boiled — on the stove. The pot is then removed from the heat for a moment or two. This is repeated twice. The third time, a spoonful of foam is removed from the pot and put into the demitasse, then the hot coffee is poured from the pot to fill it up. Without the foam on top, it is not "real" Turkish coffee. ☕

Journal: Visiting the Neighbors in Sürmene After Kayın anne's visiting day, we pay a call on the nearby households on their visiting days. I try to remember the greeting formulas, and follow her example. We enter the parlor, greet all the women of the house, take seats. The lady or daughter of the house comes around the circle with a bottle of lemon cologne and sprinkles a few drops into our cupped hands. This is refreshing — and antiseptic.

My mother-in-law chats conversationally with each guest, asking after their health and the health of their family members, according to the polite formulas. I listen politely. Much of the conversation after that, I can tell, is Q and A about me, the "gelin."

Inevitably, the hostess or her helper brings out a silver tray holding a cup of Turkish coffee and a crystal dish of chocolates wrapped in bright foil, serving each guest in turn, beginning with the eldest. (In this small community, everyone seems to know everyone else's age.)

Sometimes I become bored with the conversations going on around me and unwrap my chocolate to see if I can recognize a word — any word — on the slip of paper inside, which I imagine are wise sayings like the inserts in Chinese fortune cookies. At one point, the lady sitting next to Kayın Anne observed: "Look! The bride is reading!"

I shook my head, but Kayın Anne wanted to show me off, I think, perhaps to show that I was able to do *something*. "Read! Read!" she gestured.

This is not difficult, I think, since the new Turkish alphabet, like English, is written in the Latin alphabet. [When Atatürk became president of the new Turkish Republic, he changed over the Turkish writing system from Arabic script to the Latin alphabet. Unlike the complicated *spelling* of English, however, modern Turkish is an almost perfect phonemic fit when written in the Latin alphabet: each written letter represents one and only one sound in the Turkish language. The sounds/letters system are explained quite simply in my dictionary.]

So, I looked at each word in the proverb, and pronounced it carefully. "Güzel! Güzel!" [Very nice! Very nice!] the ladies all murmur. I haven't learned negative verb forms yet, to be able to tell them I don't *understand* the words, I can only *pronounce* them. I think they wouldn't believe I can read a word aloud and not know what it means.

Kayın Anne seems quite proud of my "reading." [A highly intelligent woman, she herself is actually illiterate. Like most other women of her generation, she was never sent to school, although her father was well-to-do and her brother was well-educated — as were her much younger half-sister Saadet and half-brothers Süleyman and Özcan in Istanbul. I think she is trying to learn to read now.]

The tea is served, and the conversation moves on. At a silent signal from Kayın Anne, we stand up and slowly take our leave, with more polite phrases as we go out the door.

Among our first return visits is a call on the large and friendly family next door, who seem happy and light-hearted. Güher sometimes takes Hikmet and me to visit them, and the daughters make delicious coffee for me. It's a pleasant change of scene, walking up a little hill and around a bend of trees to their house.

So far, my attempts to get someone in the house to go with me for a longer walk have been discouraged. Either they're too busy with their tasks, or they're not at all interested. And I'm definitely not encouraged to go out for a walk by myself. Apparently, women just don't go walking solo. As a matter of fact, I always see them in groups, or accompanied by a male family member, and they're always headed to someone's house. ❦

Journal: Famous Fish from the Black Sea The preparation of, and adjustment to, Turkish cooking, is a subject that could fill volumes. I frequently volunteer to help with cooking chores, but the response is always negative: "Misafir!" My dictionary tells me this means "guest" so I content myself with taking care of Hikmet, doing our hand laundry, and looking up words in my dictionary. Every day is an intensive language lesson.

One afternoon, there is a great to-do at the door when someone brings in a large tray of fresh "hamsi." These are small sardine-sized fish, apparently a

13

Black Sea favorite. Kayın Anne and Güher sit down to clean each little fish, one at a time. When I reach out to help, it's again: "Misafir!" So I watch them, and listen to Güher sing a local song about hamsi:

Hamsi koydum, ta-ta-tavaya. [*I put a little fish in the pa-a-an*]
Sıçra da gitti ha-ha-havaya. [*It jumped out into the air-air-air*]
Gitti de gelmez, o kız buraya! [*That girl, she left, and won't return*] ....

I observe Kayın Anne dip the hamsi in flour and salt, and sure enough, she fries them in a pan, letting them sizzle briefly in olive oil. She then clamps a heavy, flat lid on top; it fits exactly over the large pan, so she can flip them over to fry on the other side. She is deft at this.

We eat the hamsi for supper and they are truly a delicacy. "Eat! Eat!" says Kayın Anne. I hesitate over the larger bones, and observe others leaving them on the edge of their plates. I follow suit and indulge myself, feeling a little guilty, knowing how much work it took to prepare this seasonal treat.

"Look, Yenge has eaten a lot!" exclaims Güher, in a pleased voice. I haven't the heart— or vocabulary — to say that the pile of bones on my plate represents only a portion of what I have actually eaten. The smaller bones were so tender and delicious, I chewed them all up. ❧

Journal: A Black Sea Dessert It is fascinating to watch Kayın Anne prepare many different kinds of food. One morning I am surprised to see her chopping up a large pumpkin from the vegetable garden. She is hacking it into pieces with a good-sized hatchet,. "Bal kabak," she says as she whacks away. My dictionary tells me this is a kind of "honey pumpkin."

She puts the small chunks into an enormous pan and simmers them slowly in syrup until they are almost translucent, then arranges them on a large tray to cool. Güher has already shelled and ground up fresh hazelnuts with the mortar and pestle and sprinkles the nuts over the cooled pumpkin pieces. When she brings the dessert to the supper table, a dollop of clotted cream adorns each serving. "Very nice!" I tell her appreciatively. ❧

Journal: Turkish Coffee and Turkish Tea Of course, I love the little cups of coffee, cooked according to one's personal specification: "very sweet," "medium sweet," "not very sweet." The first time, I indicated I wanted "no sugar" and everyone at the supper table winced. I quickly realized the strong brew did need some sweetening, so now I say "medium sweet."

I find I am also adjusting to the strength of the local tea, especially the black tea from Kayın Anne's tea garden. Güher pours a small amount of steeped tea from a little porcelain teapot into a bell-shaped tea glass sitting on a crystal saucer. [The little teapot has been steeping atop the huge tea kettle on the hazelnut stove.] She then fills up the rest of the tea glass with boiling water from the kettle, and serves the glass on a tray. There is a sugar cube or two on the tea saucer, and a tiny silver spoon for stirring.

This family-style tea arrangement seems to be based on the same principle as the more elaborate and elegant samovar, which has a holder for the tea pot on top of its charcoal-filled chimney in the center of the urn. The little pot, filled with tea leaves and boiling water, sits steeping while the charcoal embers within the chimney heat the water around it in the belly of the urn. When it reaches boiling point, the tea-maker partially fills the small tea glass with steeped tea, and then, by turning on the samovar's spigot, fills it up with boiling water.

Relevant facts: As with braziers and hot water heaters in the bathroom that also use charcoal embers, samovars require careful airing of the room to safeguard against the noxious, potentially fatal carbon monoxide fumes given off by the charcoal. ❦

*Journal: **The Ubiquitous Leek Goes to Market*** I've always liked a variety of vegetables — served hot or room temperature — but here many vegetables are cooked in olive oil and served cold. For me, these cold vegetable dishes require a slow adjustment. I think I understand the advantages here: the cooking can be done in advance, the dishes keep well in the cold weather, and they do not require refrigeration. Yesterday, for instance, Kayın Anne boiled broad beans in water and a little olive oil, then added finely diced potatoes, carrots, and tiny green peas to cook slowly in the pot. When she served the cooled dish, she poured more olive oil on top and cut wedges of fresh lemons for the platter. Everyone relished the dish, and sopped up the juices with chunks of fresh bread.

Leeks, with their yard-long, green stalks and white, bulbous ends, are another vegetable Kayın Anne often cooks in olive oil and serves cold. In these parts, they seem to be a very popular vegetable indeed. Today is market day, for instance, and I can see a group of village women walking on the road below, carrying great loads of fresh leeks in wicker baskets strapped to their backs. From my window vantage point high above them, I see only the tops of their bobbing baskets as the women walk along, chatting and laughing.

I am struck by the illusion of an undulating mass of thickly meshed, verdant green vegetation moving en masse down the road; I'm compelled to create my first sentence in Turkish. Quickly I consult my dictionary and call Güher to the window: "Güher! Bak! Bahçe yüriyor!" ["Look! Garden walking!"] Already, I hear Güher quoting my linguistic achievement to the family. ❦

*Journal: **Cooking and Heating with Hazelnut Shells*** This evening, I am beginning to appreciate the ingenuity of the tinsmith who created the strange stove in the family room. But, I admit everything here is strange to me, and I am continually comparing things here with their equivalents at home back in America. In my mind, everything *there* seems quite superior in comparison to things *here*. I wonder if this is a natural reaction. I think I must get over this negativeness and take things as they are, without a constant comparing. Otherwise, how will I ever be happy here?

But, I digress. I think my father, a mechanically gifted man, would especially appreciate this stove. It is four feet high, oval-shaped, made of sheet metal, with a little front door for adding fuel. Its top is big enough to hold the large tea kettle, with room to spare for a small pan. At the moment, it is toasting fresh hazelnuts for us to munch on with our tea. Inside the little stove, hazelnut shells (from the Hazelnut Cooperative down the hill) are burning brightly. The shells give off a quick, intense heat and leave only a powdery white ash. At the same time, the stove and its chimney warm the whole room.

"Not designed for burning coal or long-lasting logs," I can just hear Papa marveling, "but efficiently designed for this clean, free fuel!" ❦

Journal: Laundry Day in Sürmene Today is laundry day, when I will discover the secret behind the spotless whiteness of the household's bed clothes and table linens.

Early in the morning, Baba fires up the tall copper boiler in the terrazo-floored bathroom before he goes off to his store. Güher and Anne bring in wide, heavy copper washing pans, put them down on the bathroom floor, and fill them with steaming hot water and some kind of castile soap. They agitate/beat the clothes vigorously with large wooden sticks, which they use also to lift the heavy items out for rinsing. They pour water off into the open drain on the floor; it goes into a small brook running next to the house and down the hillside.

On sunny days, like today, they hang the laundry outside; on rainy days, they hang it under the rafters in the attic. Güher shows me how to pull down the heavy wood ladder to the attic by yanking on a rope that hangs from the ceiling.

I, also, wash my hand laundry and Hikmet's things in the bathroom. Güher demonstrates how to wring diapers as dry as possible before hanging them on the lines under the attic rafters. The air is usually very damp up there, so the laundry takes a long time to dry and we end up draping it behind the "hazelnut stove." ❦

Journal: Hikmet's First Steps At times when the stove is unlit in the family room, Hikmet practices walking, holding on along the edge of the sofa and chairs. This morning, my mother-in-law holds Hikmet's hand and encourages her to take a step on her own. My father-in-law sits several feet away, coaxing her toward him. "Come here, Hikmet, come here!" he gestures and smiles at her.

Today, she slowly lets go of her Baba Anne's hands, and toddles the few steps to reach her Büyük Baba's. There is joy in the household over her first steps.

Prophetically, when Baba had sent Sela his blessings on our marriage in Tulsa, he had assumed we would, sooner or later, have children. He wrote something to this effect: "When the time comes, let your first child be named 'Hikmet.' It means Allah's omniscience, which has brought you two together from such different worlds."

Now Hikmet has arrived from the other side of the world, and takes her first steps to her doting grandfather. He is her "name-giver." ❦

Journal: Baby Needs a New Pair of Shoes Now that Hikmet is walking, she needs shoes with firmer soles, in place of the knitted booties she's been crawling about in. I look up the words for "small" and "shoe" and approach Güher, who is so patient with my language struggles. She quickly catches on to my request, and relays it to Baba, who smiles and nods in agreement.

I wait for some sign that I am to bundle up Hikmet and set off for a shoe store. But, no. The next evening, Baba brings home a parcel from the shoemaker next to his dry goods emporium: in it are three pairs of delicately stitched little leather shoes. I am to choose a pair. I try them on Hikmet and we all decide the white kid lace-ups are the best fit. I thank Baba, and ask about the price. "Para?"

[Money?] He shakes his head and waves away the idea. I thank him again. "Thank you, Baba!" I say.

I try the same approach when I need a stamp to mail a letter to my mother: I look up the word for stamp and show the letter to Güher. Perhaps this will mean an adventurous outing to the post office! But, again, no. Güher simply gives the letter to Baba as he leaves for work the next morning. "Thank you, Baba!" I tell him. He smiles and waves goodbye with my letter in his hand. ❦

Journal: Winter Weather on the Black Sea: Cold and Damp The rooms in this house, as in Aunt Saadet's house in Istanbul, are unheated except when the hazelnut stove is fired up for a brief spell, or the charcoal-burning mangal [brazier] is brought in to take the chill off a room. The rooms are dank, and I notice that everyone wears several layers of woolen clothing. Coming from the warmer climate of Tulsa, Oklahoma, where we didn't wear heavy clothing, I'm at a loss here; my wardrobe seems so unsuitable. In any case, were I to find a clothing store, I would have to wait until Sela earned enough to afford winter clothing. But to date, I haven't seen any ready-made clothing at all. I guess, like Hikmet's shoes, everything is hand-made.

At bedtime, Güher shouts out an alarm: "Dikkat! Dikkat!" [Look out! Look out!] as she brings in a charcoal-burning bedwarmer, holding it carefully by its long handle. This antique contraption is a copper pan with a slotted lid clamped onto a wooden handle; it is full of glowing red embers. She carefully moves it between the cold, damp sheets while I hold Hikmet out of the way. We wait until she slowly removes the warmer and leaves the room. At her signal, we quickly slide into bed to relish the toasty warmth that is eventually replaced by our body heat.

Several nights ago, Kayın Anne brought in a heavy wool sweater for Hikmet to wear in bed. It felt so coarse and scratchy, it made me itch to look at it. I shook my head, "No, thank you." I couldn't explain that Hikmet was used to sleeping in soft cotton vests and nightgowns. She frowned and took the sweater away.

I have noticed that in this cold weather, a number of the neighbor children coming in to play with Hikmet have had colds and runny noses. Yesterday, Hikmet seemed to have picked up her first cold, and perhaps a little fever. Now, I think perhaps she should have worn Baba Anne's bed sweater, over her regular nightgown.

Today, she is definitely running a fever, which worries me. "Hot!" I indicate to Kayın Anne, showing her Hikmet's forehead. I try to indicate my concern to Anne. She makes an herb tea with honey. Hikmet sips a little, but makes a face and shakes her head.

"Hot! Doctor?" I say. Anne looks worried but undecided. When Baba comes home from work, I meet him at the door with Hikmet. I hold her out to him, to feel her temperature. "Doctor! Please!" I tell him.

After one quick touch of her forehead, he immediately goes out to find an available doctor, returning at length with a young man carrying a leather bag. He checks Hikmet with his stethoscope and thermometer, then looks at her throat, where the problem seems to be. He confers with Baba, takes out a box of tablets.

"New medicine." he says. Kayın Anne joins the discussion. They look at me. I nod agreement, and the doctor explains the dosage. Baba Anne administers it, and Baba and Güher take turns walking Hikmet about the house until she falls asleep. I pray the new medicine works.

This morning, after Hikmet's medication, Kayın Anne brings out a little woolen sweater she's been busily knitting. It is as soft as eiderdown, and just fits Hikmet. "Thank you, Anne," I say. She nods, with a smile. ❦

Journal: Who Does the Work in the Garden? Today is a bright and sunny day and I take Hikmet outside for a walk about the garden. She seems to be recuperating well. Kayın Baba is cultivating the rich dark soil around the grove of tangerine trees; he seems embarrassed about the hoeing and wants to communicate something to me. Waving the spade about, he points to himself and says something. Then he says: "America?" I remembered what Sela told me about gardening being considered "women's work" in Turkey. I don't understand what's he's saying, but I smile and nod my head.

[Much later, Muammer explains that Baba wanted me to know he loves to garden, even if it's considered "women's work." Ironically, I think, such heavy gardening is usually done by men in America, but my mother does it because she loves it. She's been growing fruits and vegetables for our family for years. A large part of our winter diet included the tomatoes, green beans, beets, peaches, apricots, pears, and berries she preserved in glass jars; also the carrots, potatoes, onions, apples, and squash stored in the root cellar; as well as the crocks of sauer kraut she pickled from the garden cabbage. But my father, who always worked long hours in his repair garage to make ends meet during the Great Depression, never gardened in his life. So much for men's and women's work loads, I think to myself.] ❦

Journal: Wedding Preparations Everyone hopes Nezihe's father will acquiesce and give her hand in marriage to Muammer. Apparently, traditional marriage arrangements are moving ahead optimistically. Nezihe has shown me her hope chest full of exquisitely embroidered sets of table cloths and napkins, lace-edged bath and hand towels, spidery lace doilies of many sizes and shapes. She has also made silk night gowns and blouses, with embroidered trousseau cases to hold them all. These are all examples of her skills in sewing, tatting, crocheting, lace-making, knitting.

As fortune would have it, Muammer's naval ship had been stationed on temporary duty in Norfolk, Virginia, where he was able to shop for the silks and satins on Nezihe's wedding list. He sent on the packages, and now neighborhood seamstresses are busy making a white satin wedding gown. Two dozen tiny covered buttons with tiny loop fasteners cinch in the wasp waist; the skirt falls in voluminous folds. It is a dream dress.

Meanwhile, Muammer is doing his best to meet the rest of his future father-in-law's stipulations. These include, as far as I can understand, a pair of diamond earrings, a number of gold pieces on a gold chain, and a bridal bracelet. All of which are like money in the bank, I guess — or, more old-fashionedly — a dowry from the husband. I think Nezihe's father provides furniture for the

18

bedroom, etc. but apparently this varies from family to family and region to region.

In preparation for the wedding, Kayın Anne, Nezihe, and several other female relatives are going on a shopping trip to Trabzon. I am urged to join them. Güher, as usual, stays home to baby-sit Hikmet.

Kayın Anne's main objective is a specific goldsmith's shop; my guess is, it's owned by relatives. The shop window fairly glitters with gold jewelry of exquisite workmanship: rows of delicate bracelets and bangles, shelves of earrings for pierced and unpierced ears, draped chains of all lengths and linkages. Contrary to the old expression, everything here that glitters *is* almost purely gold. Some jewelers' marks are as high as 22 carats.

Anne seems to be intent on large gold coins. [I learn later some of them are to be made into "Trabzon bride's bracelets."] She points to a three-inch cuff of finely woven mesh, fastened with a clever clasp, that has been fashioned from these coins. The jeweler measures Nezihe's wrist, and then my wrist also, but I am not aware of the significance of this.

In fact, there is always so much going on around me, of which I am totally uncomprehending, that I live in a state of suspended comprehension. Later, I tell myself, I'll try to look that up in my dictionary. Or, some day, I'll ask Sela to explain that in English.

In the meantime, I'm glad to see Muammer, who has just arrived and has been making family visits, I gather. I am doubly glad to see him since he speaks some English, and I'm hoping he can translate what is happening. Today, I ask him when Sela will be coming back. Before answering, he discusses something with Anne, then tells me that Sela won't be here for the wedding. He and Anne point out the date on the wall calendar. We all nod in agreement that I will wait with Hikmet until after the wedding.

Now Muammer is caught up in the drama of his marriage proposal. From what I gather, he has many meetings with Nezihe's father, Remzi efendi, to convince him in person of his eligibility.

I understand Muammer and Nezihe had lived in these same houses across the road from each other as children. When Muammer reached high school age, he was sent off to a naval training institute to be trained in electronics, and then went into the Navy.

When he finally decided it was time to get married, he wrote telling his mother of his intentions. She sent him photos of several eligible girls in Sürmene, and out of the group of pictures, he picked Nezihe's. Subsequently, the two sets of parents had serious discussions concerning such a marriage between their families. Was Muammer a suitable husband for their daughter? And vice versa, would Nezihe be a suitable wife for their son? And so on.

Nezihe, of course, has also seen Muammer's photos, and she agrees to accept him. So, in a way, this is — and isn't — an arranged marriage. [They are actually second or third cousins, I learn much later, and had played together when very young, but hadn't seen each other since childhood.] Insallah, God willing, Remzi efendi will give his blessing. ❦

Journal: Is This a Betrothal or a Wedding? Today, March 18, 1953, Güher and her mother are wearing their best dresses. They indicate that I should ready myself and Hikmet, too. There is an air of excitement in the house. The Malkoç family — Baba, Anne, Muammer, Güher, Hikmet and I — emerge from the house to join the Kiralıs — Remzi efendi, Behice hanım, Nezihe, and her younger siblings in their home.

I note that Nezihe is wearing a new, two-piece wool suit, not the beautiful satin wedding dress I was expecting. So, this is not the wedding? I've looked up the words for engagement [nishan] and marriage [nikâh] but I get them mixed up in my mind. Well, this is not the time for a language lesson, I decide, and wait with great curiosity.

We all stand in attendance in the front parlor, and witness a ceremony presided over by an official seated at a small table. He places a large book of records on the table in front of him. Nezihe sits on a chair near him, Muammer sits next to her. Both look pale and tense. Neither looks at the other or speaks. The official reads from the book, and asks questions of one, and then the other; they respond in turn. It all seems like civil marriage vows to me.

They rise, sign the record book, and shake hands all around. The photographer takes group pictures of everyone looking as serious and somber as the bridal couple. Nezihe is spirited out of the room, leaving Muammer behind.

We are all served tall, narrow glasses of a ceremonial beverage made of red rock sugar and water, to drink to the couple's health. Then we're treated to a festive meal prepared in advance: sarma, zucchini dolma, white beans in olive oil and lemon, cold chicken slices, white cheese, black olives, a variety of börek, humus [chick peas pureed with sesame oil], and the perennial favorite desert, baklava [squares of thin pastry leaves drenched in syrup and walnuts]. ❦

Journal: This Is a Wedding! After lunch, Güher takes me into the room where Nezihe has changed into the white satin gown. Family members come in and out to fuss over her: one powders her nose, another puts crème on her flawless skin. Her mother comes in to adjust the already perfect folds in her dress; someone else rearranges her bridal crown of silk roses, white marabou, and dangling silver threads entwined in the bridal veil. The whole effect is utterly fetching.

In addition, of course, Nezihe is wearing her wedding jewelry: the four enormous gold coins on the heavy gold chain, the sparkling diamond ear rings, the gold wrist watch, and the gold mesh bridal bracelet, which arrived just in time. To my surprise, I received one also, and have been instructed to wear it, to indicate I'm also a "Trabzon bride."

At a signal from her mother, Nezihe rises in all her splendor and departs with her entourage. In fact, we all cross the road and enter a newly-constructed house adjacent to the Malkoç house, which is larger and spacious enough for the bridal festivities. ❦

Journal: The Women's Celebration The vast room we enter in this new wood-frame house is bare and unpainted. Electric light from the open kitchen

20

illuminates one corner, where the bride's chair is placed. She sits there in state, while the women guests come one by one to congratulate her and express their wishes for a long and happy marriage. [Later, I learn one of the more poetic expressions: "May you always sleep with your heads on one pillow."]

In another corner of the room, two women bring out an enormous copper tray, tinned because it is used for serving food, and place it on a large trestle. Someone else comes out, sprinkles something like flour on the tray. Yet another person pours what looks like hot syrup onto the flour, forming a ribbon around the edge of the tray. In the dim light, the tray and its contents are a total mystery to me.

In the meantime, a local fiddler has set up in a brightly lighted outer room, and is energetically sawing away on an old, wooden, two-stringed violin. He rests his instrument on one knee, dragging a bow across the strings and singing impromptu verses in a strident voice.

The lively music entices the women and young girls from their food preparations in the kitchen; they begin to drift in and circle around the tray, linking hands and moving to the lively Black Sea tunes. Kayın Anne takes my hand and pulls me forward into the dancing circle. She can out-dance them all, I think, as I try to follow her lead. It takes me some time to get coordinated with the beat — listening to the music and watching the dancers' feet — before I realize the women are also making swooping movements at the tray as they dance around it. I vaguely follow suit, waving my elbows without comprehending the purpose of these motions. In the dim light, I'm still absorbed in watching their feet.

The fiddler, energized by the happy dancers, sings one rollicking verse after another. I can tell he's composing them for the audience as I recognize some of the names. At the end of each verse, the dancers shout in delight, which, of course, stimulates the musician to outdo himself, even to making up a verse for "the bride who came from across the sea." I can catch the rhyming words, but the only one I understand is "Amerika."

At some point, Kayın Anne slips into the kitchen, comes out bearing a platter heaped with that she indicates is pismaniye [pishmaniye]. She gestures for me to try a small portion. When I taste the light-colored, powdery-looking shreds, the answer to the mystery of the "Floured Tray Dance" dawns on me: This has been a kind of taffy pull!

Then, I recall seeing this stringy-looking confection in Istanbul; Aunt Saadet had explained it's made by kneading and pulling heavy syrup into strands, which become threadlike as they're worked into flour. The long strands are sprinkled with finely ground pistachio nuts and cut into chunks. Pismaniye literally melts in your mouth. 🍃

Journal: The Men's Celebration The fiddler takes a well-deserved break in the wedding music for a glass of lemonade. During the lull, I ask Kayın Anne about the groom: "Muammer?"

"The men are over there," she indicates, pointing across the road near Remzi efendi's house, where male festivities are going on full blast in another house. Who knows what refreshments they're having! I hear that some are drinking raki — the strong, clear Turkish alcohol that tastes of licorice and turns milky white when diluted with water. If so, I imagine they're kicking up some really wild Black Sea dances. But Hikmet and I retire before long, and the bride returns to her father's home for the night. ❦

Journal: The Wedding Tour It's midmorning the next day and everyone is getting ready for more festivities. From the window, I see Baba escorting the bride from her father's house across the road. Again, she's wearing all her wedding finery and Muammer is standing by a taxi festooned with red and blue bridal procession streamers. Kayın Anne gestures, "Go! Go!" So I join the wedding party in the taxi, as she takes Güher and Hikmet into the big blue bus following behind us, full of chattering female relatives and happy frolicking children.

It's a gloriously sunshiny day for a ride along the coastal road, and the Black Sea is reflecting the brilliant blueness of the sky. People shout and cheer our procession; we roll royally along in an easterly direction, as far as the small town of Of [which rhymes with loaf]. The driver announces we are 16 kilometers from Sürmene. Büyük Baba nods and we turn back.

On our return, people are on the lookout for us, barricading the road, flourishing clubs and sticks, and demanding forfeits from the new father-in-law. Baba has little bags full of coins ready for this traditional wedding ransom: tiny, one-kurush pieces smaller than one cent and worth about one mill — a tenth of a cent, so small, in fact, they are no longer in use.

We fling the coins out the window, little boys scramble for them, and the barricades are lifted with wild cheers from the crowd.

As we reach the outskirts of town, the wife of the regional Gendarme Kommandant comes running out of her house and down the hill. She is brandishing a pistol and demanding ransom. I fling out the last of my coins toward the "Pistol Lady." She waves in acknowledgement and fires off a round of real bullets into the air with a dramatic flourish.

Finally we arrive back at the Malkoç house. Baba ceremoniously escorts his newest daughter-in-law into the now-beribboned parlor that serves as the bridal suite. Nezihe's heavy walnut bedroom furniture has been magically installed, a richly embroidered satin yorgan [traditional quilt] covers the bed, and a matching satin case for the Koran hangs in a place of honor on the wall.

The imam [priest] enters the bridal chamber, Nezihe and Muammer follow. When he reads the wedding prayers to them, I think now they are truly married. ❦

22

Wedding Group, Sürmene 1953

Nezihe & Muammar Malkoç

A & H, Nezihe, Muammer, and Güher

Journal: Not a Honeymoon Leaving the house to the newlyweds, the family goes house across the road to spend the night at Remzi efendi's — which, like an inn, is full of happy overnight guests and good food.

After breakfast the following morning, however, everyone returns to Baba's house, where the bride has already dressed in her bridal outfit, for the third time. She and Muammer are waiting for the photographer to take wedding pictures. In one group picture with Güher and Hikmet, I blink as the photographer presses the bulb and ignites the flash. Baby Hikmet is reaching for the sparkling silver threads on Nezihe's veil.

Muammer's leave is up in a few days, which means he returns to his naval base. He will have to leave Nezihe behind to wait, like me, for word on travel arrangements to the oil camp. I am given to understand that Sela has gone to the oilfields and is "looking for a place for us to live." I am to wait until Muammer can come back for Nezihe, and, at the same time, escort Hikmet and me to Istanbul. From there we will take a train on to Batman, the nearest station to Raman Dagi. I mark the promised day on the family's wall calendar.

[In reality, I am to learn much later, Erzurum was suffering severe snowstorms. All roads were closed and telephone lines were down. Sela not only couldn't come back to collect Hikmet and me, he missed his beloved brother Muammer's wedding.] ❧

Journal: A Very Different Wedding in Trabzon I sense that Kayın Anne has been concerned that I may be bored and unhappy, and she tries to find diversions for me. She is very good at communicating through gestures while repeating simple commands or basic words. So, it didn't take me long to understand that I

23

was to get ready to go out with her and Güher would stay at home with Hikmet. I did as I was told, of course, and followed her outside and into a car waiting to take us to Trabzon. I was full of curiosity during the two-hour ride.

We arrived at a downtown theater, where a poster in front advertised "Amerikan Filim" with Esther Williams in a swimming pool. I recalled the only movies I'd seen in the Istanbul cinemas were Turkish films, and figured this must be a special event. "Güzel! Güzel!" [Very nice! Beautiful!] I said to Kayın Anne, repeating this many times to express my appreciation over her effort to entertain me. Truth be told, my tastes run more toward swashbuckling Douglas Fairbanks, Jr. and debonair Ronald Coleman, but I admit it was fun to see Esther Williams in Trabzon.

And there were more treats in store for me. Unfortunately, my dictionary was too heavy to tote around, so I couldn't look up the words Kayın Anne was using to explain where we were going after the matinee. Like everything else happening in my life at the time, I literally "didn't know what I was getting into." Without question, I followed her into a taxi that took us to a large, sprawling, multi-level gray stone house.

[Muammer later explained that his grandfather — Kayın Anne's father, an architect/constructor — had built this house for his third wife and family, but he was always good to *all* his various grandchildren, including Sela and his older brother Sabri, the grandsons of his first wife. Because there was no high school in Sürmene then, the two brothers came to live in the grandfather's house while they attended Trabzon High School.]

Kayın Anne greeted some members of the household as we entered and climbed up the wide stone stairs to the first floor. They all seemed to know her. The doors to the large salon were wide open, allowing busy helpers to bring in more chairs to line around the walls, and eventually fill the entire room. This must be a wedding, I surmised.

Kayın Anne smiled, nodded to several women, and gestured to empty seats in the center of the room. She settled down into a waiting mode, looking perfectly happy to sit, like all the other guests, and wait in silence. Surrounded thus by about one hundred women, I eventually ran out of empty spaces to stare at politely. Short of closing my eyes, and actually falling asleep, where could I direct my gaze? I settled on the frieze running around the high plaster ceiling, examining and analyzing the motifs in its floral design: one tendril, a bud, and two squiggly lines; then another tendril, two flowers and one squiggly line....

An hour passed in silence. Far below us, we could hear the heavy wooden street doors open slowly, a scurry of feet, a murmur and then a gasp from the guests, as the bridal couple appeared at the salon doors: the bride, elegant in white silk gown, stood clutching the bridegroom's arm. My heart went out to the young bride, but more to the young groom, who had to brave the crowd of staring women. With some difficulty, the pair made their way through the crowded room to the bridal suite, right off the salon.

When the groom opened the doors to the bed chamber, Kayın Anne and I had a clear view of the whole room; spang in the middle was a huge, carved walnut bed expansively covered with an elaborately hand-quilted and pearl-embroidered satin yorgan of a lovely peach color. Silken cases, all hand-stitched, from the same gorgeous satin as the coverlet, lay on the head pillows, holding silk lingerie and pajamas. Lavishly scattered about were more peach-colored satin cushions. Except for the velvet Koran case hanging on the wall, the bridal suite resembled a dream boudoir for a Hollywood movie queen. Before we could take in all this sumptuous luxury, the doors shut on the bridal couple. Only few minutes later, they opened again as the groom exited quietly, disappeared downstairs. The bride then emerged, to sit in our midst and be admired (and appraised) by all the guests.

Kayın Anne whispered that this bride was not as beautiful as "our bride," and I agreed, but this one, we noticed, was wearing *two* gold mesh bracelets, and *six* large gold coins on a heavy chain. Our comparisons were abruptly cut short with a noisy clearing of chairs from the center of the salon and we had to re-seat ourselves. From somewhere, a phonograph started a tango. Shortly, I felt a gentle nudge from Kayın Anne, and gradually realized that the charming lady of the house was standing before me. She was saying, "Wollen sie tanzen?"

What is this? Am I in a dream? She's speaking German, and she's asking me to *dance?* I take a deep breath to clear my head. There's a sharper nudge on my elbow. "Get up! Get up" Kayın Anne is whispering and gesturing. I see that she's smiling, as if pleased that our hostess is honoring me with the first dance. Apparently, it would be a rudeness to refuse her. *When in Rome*, I remind myself, and smile as I rise to the occasion.

On the cleared dance floor, the hostess and I dip and sway to the strains of "La Cumparsita." I try to engage in polite small talk but her German conversation confuses my feet. I can't believe I'm actually dancing the tango *with a woman*. I think she's telling me she's the wife of a diplomatic consul and has been in Germany, but I'm not sure I really understand what she's saying. In a dream-like state, I look around, become aware of other women on the dance floor. They look quite sophisticated in fashionable Parisian styles, all doing the tango. And no head scarves in sight. *This is not a dream*, I keep telling myself. *Definitely, this is not Sürmene*!

Much to my relief, the tango stops and the action moves into the adjoining hall. Kayın Anne and I follow the crowd, to watch the arrival of the wedding musicians. They set themselves up in a corner and begin to play music for the newlywed bride — the groom being elsewhere with the men. As if on cue, the lovely bride initiates the traditional festivities by floating into a willowy and graceful harem dance. When she finishes with a delicate flourish of her veils, the onlookers applaud appreciatively.

The musicians next strike up a familiar tune, and the women who'd paired off for the tango all join hands for a traditional Black Sea circle dance. They've barely circled around once, however, when there's a sudden commotion below. Doors open and close and the sound of heavy voices and hearty laughter drifts up the stairs. This signals the arrival of the men guests, coming up to have their dinner in the salon. Frantically, the women all dash about for abandoned head scarves to cover their hair before the men reach the top of the stairs. [Although some 25 years earlier, President Atatürk had legally abolished face veils, no self-respecting woman around here goes about with her hair uncovered in the presence of men — with the exception of her husband and family members.]

I, too, tie on my flowered silk kerchief and follow Kayın Anne, who'd kept her black silk head covering on all the time. With the other women, we file down a secondary stone staircase to an annex off the great stone kitchen. There, at the enormous stone hearth, household servants ladle out vast quantities of steaming rice pilav, stuffed grape leaves, and aromatic roast lamb for all the hungry ladies. Kayın Anne and I join in with gusto. After the wedding feast, she pays gracious respects and felicitations to the bride, wishing her long life and happiness. I try to echo as best I can, and smile a lot. We depart in the taxi waiting to take us back to Sürmene. ❦

Journal: A Bitter Disappointment Time seems to pass more and more slowly. I have been counting off the weeks on the "page-a-day" wall calendar in the family room, looking forward to the promised day when Muammer will take Nezihe away to wherever he is to be stationed. Also, I've been given to understand, he will escort Hikmet and me as far as Istanbul. From there, we are to take a train southeast to Sela's camp at Raman.

This morning, there are only a few days left before "the day" and I see the family holding some kind of important discussion. It concerns me, obviously. They avoid looking at me and are focused on the wall calendar. Kayın Anne shakes her head and turns over many pages on the little calendar. She seems to be saying that I will not be leaving for Istanbul on "the day." She seems to be saying that some other relative will be going on business to Istanbul. In one month? Two months? Longer? Are they saying Hikmet and I can wait until then? And Nezihe will be traveling at an even later date? I don't want to believe my ears. I am stunned. My heart sinks. I struggle to hide my disappointment, for fear I'll burst into tears in front of everyone.

I leave the room and look for a place to escape. Hikmet is napping in our bedroom. The only refuge I can find is the high-ceilinged pantry at the end of the hall, the food storage with its shelves of preserved garden produce. As I step inside and close the door, the tears begin to flow. I find myself staring through a mist at the tall glass jars of Kayın Anne's ruby quince preserves, golden figs in syrup, crimson tomato paste. Their vivid, vibrant colors are a blur in front of my eyes. Dimly, I hear the family going about their daily life in other parts of the house, and feel utterly detached. I weep and weep. I cannot stop myself....

Time passes. I hear Hikmet waking up from her nap. Güher enters the bedroom; they laugh happily together. Later, I hear Nezihe coming in from her parents' house, asking Anne for the latest news of Muammer. She asks about me. I hear all of this through my tears....

At some point, it must dawn on them I haven't been seen for hours. Doors open and close. I hear Kayın Anne telling Nezihe's little sister to look in the garden. I hear Nebahat returning shortly with a negative response. I hear her going to check with the neighbors, returning with another negative response.

There is more scurrying around, but I do not budge from my spot. I have given myself over to spasms of weeping, venting feelings of frustration, anger, helplessness over my fate. How many more weeks of waiting, I wonder? I sit down in the chair by the narrow pantry window. Today, the Black Sea, like me, is so dark, so cheerless.

I sit pondering my situation, reminding myself of what I already know: the family is doing their best to make me feel welcome, happy, comfortable. Everyone is so good to me, so loving and sweet to Hikmet. I *appreciate* all their efforts. I struggle with my emotions; my feelings are so mixed-up. I *want* to be polite. I *want* to show that I am not ungrateful. But, my inner voice argues, I traveled from the other side of the world to live with Sela, not to be left here without him!

Here, I am like an infant: not able to speak my own language to anyone, not able to express my thoughts, not able to understand what people are saying. I don't know what they are *deciding* about me. I am totally *dependent*. I feel like a *nothing*. I weep on and on….

It is sweet Nezihe who finally thinks to look in the pantry. She opens the door, finds me gazing out the window with red and swollen eyes. She murmurs a few words that sound consoling, slips out to report to the family. I'm sure it is Baba who goes out that afternoon to the post office and sends a telegram to Sela. The next morning, he shows me a telegram from Sela. When I find the words in my dictionary, the gist is: "Send immediately." A dark cloud lifts at once.

In a calmer mood, I recall a childhood memory when I was about three. Before my baby brother was born, my two older brothers and I were all "farmed out" with relatives and I stayed with my cousin Lucile on her farm. At first, I loved Aunt Ann's house, loved playing with my same-age cousin, but then, mysteriously, I began to lose my appetite, refuse my favorite foods, refuse all food. Aunt Ann must have telephoned Mama, because she arrived the next morning. Magically, the moment I heard my mother's familiar voice at the front gate, I revived. Once again, I was happy and hungry, and all was well in my world. ❧

4

RETURN TO ISTANBUL

Journal: A Predeparture Letter to Sela Arrangements were made for my travel to Raman Camp. On the evening before departing from Sürmene, when I had put Hikmet to bed for the night and gathered all my belongings and thoughts together, I sat down on the bed with pen and paper and poured out my heart to Sela. Now that I was "escaping" from this provincial place, I just let the words and thoughts flow freely and unchecked in a tumult of pent-up feelings. It was, I felt, necessary that he know what had been going on in my head while I had been trying to learn the language, follow etiquette rules and family routines, and generally adjust to the life of the household for the two months I was left in the hometown.
A Silent Resistance to the Status Quo
I realized, first of all, that I was in a state of inner rebellion against some of the local customs. I told Sela, for one thing, that while I respected his parents, I resented being forced into the family hierarchy in which I could never be "myself," but always and only a minor member.

This was in such contrast to my own family's emphasis on independence as I was growing up during the Great Depression of the 1930's and the second World War. Like many families, we were poor. But, unlike many others, we weren't on welfare. We "scraped along." My parents were amazingly resourceful, full of Horatio Alger-like pluck and determination. always persevering despite adversities. They were my role models for developing self-confidence, high expectations, and a strong desire to improve one's lot in life through hard work and education.

All this was too much to try explaining to Sela in a letter. I simply wrote that I hated being "dependent" on his father for everything. I couldn't go to the market and buy a new pair of shoes for Hikmet, or buy a stamp for a letter to send to my mother. I couldn't even receive a letter in the mail, one that was addressed to me alone — Sela's last letter to me in Sürmene had been enclosed in a letter to his father. This seemed to be the final straw for me. I felt totally robbed of my own "selfness," robbed of my own identity as a person.

When I'd filled the second side of the small sheet of paper, I was forced to stop. I debated, briefly, whether or not to send the letter. It was so unhappy, so negative. But, I reminded myself, they were my true feelings. I quickly licked the flap of the envelope, sealed it securely, and addressed it to Sela at Raman camp. The next morning, with only the slightest of qualms, I gave it to Baba. He walked it to the post office before our bus arrived for Trabzon.

[That was the only letter I ever wrote with such misgivings about mailing it. And, Sela was to tell me after I arrived at the camp, he never kept the letter. In fact, he went on to confess, he never keeps any of my letters. "Why should I?" he asked. "You're here now, and that's all I want!"] ❦

28

Letter from Sela

My Sweetheart!

Haven't heard from you for ages! I guess it's because of my address. How is Hikmet? According to Father's telegram she had a bad cough. I am worrying too much about you both.

You should be in Istanbul by today. How was the sea? I hope you didn't get seasick. You see how much I worry. Some nights I can't sleep at all. It's getting to be a habit for me and next day I can hardly keep my eyes open.

Have you inquired at the American College for Girls about a job? If not, maybe Orhan can help you.

Have you decided to come here? You better, darling. I don't think you should stay there with Saadet teyze very long; two weeks is more than enough. Every week on Saturday there is an express train that will take you straight here. You don't have to change trains at all. I will be at the station when you darlings arrive.

I have not received any salary here yet, but I will soon. I hope. As soon as I can, I will send some money. I am just fine, and healthy. The only worry I have is you alone.

Please give my warm regards to Saadet teyze, Avni dayı, Süleyman dayı, Özcan dayı, Büyük Anne, and so forth. Will write again. I do love you very much. Your SM

Another Cultural Conflict

PS: Just received and read your letter from Sürmene, three or four times, one after another. I couldn't believe my eyes, but I guess it's true. I expected this, but it came too soon. As you write, there is not even one nice word in it, not even a small itty bitty love.

I knew that you were not happy in Sürmene, but what can I do, darling? I thought I had played my cards right, not to hurt anybody. I must have not done this right. It seems that you are angry just because I enclosed my letter to you with my father's letter. I can not explain this in a letter, but if I did not have any reason, I would not do this.

You must have lost your mind, saying that my father comes above all else. Do you think I would have married you and taken you here if it was so? I told you I was going to come and get you as soon as possible when I left you in Sürmene.

I cannot explain my feelings about you and other things, and besides, I don't want to cry in the office, writing this letter. I would look odd. I think it's better you come here and talk things over. You will be all right then. Now today is the 8th of April; there is an express train leaving from Istanbul on the 18th. Make a reservation for a sleeper when you get this letter. I will send some money by telegram later this week.

Kiss Hikmet for me. I hope she is all right now. Love, Sela

Letter to Family and Friends

Aunt Saadet's house, Kadıköy/Istanbul
April 24, 1953

Dear Brownfields and Other Dear Hearts,

I am at back in Istanbul, a kind of jumping-off place for me, halfway to Raman Camp. This will bring you up to date, at least, on welcome celebrations, relatives, and general enlightenments. So, settle back and relax whilst I share my latest experiences and take you on a vicarious tour from Sürmene on the Black Sea back to Istanbul, enroute to Raman Camp.

My heart being where my husband is, I was more than eager to leave Sürmene, despite the valiant attempts his family made toward my happiness. After two months of Ottoman Empire atmosphere, the novelty palled and the life for me became quite unbearable without Sela around.

My previous contention that "people are people" hasn't changed. I grew fond of the family and many of the neighbors there. Rather, it was the rigid adherence to customs now outmoded, to my way of thinking, that I found personally incompatible. Even the younger generation exposed to "modern views" are compelled to follow customs that haven't changed even with Atatürk, who outlawed the custom of the veil, I understand. But here, women cover still their faces when passing strange men on the street, for one thing; no decent woman goes down the street with head uncovered, for another. This was not expected of me, however, since everyone around here knew I was a foreigner, although I do wear a kerchief or a wool tam, because the weather is cold this time of year.

Older people must be given unlimited respect, even though (in my opinion) it may sometimes be undeserved. Women are always subservient to men and are protected from outsiders, at times to the extent of segregation when male visitors come to call. The women and girls must simply leave the room.

The bridegroom brings his bride to his father's house, where the father, or his father, rules supreme. This seems to be a custom rising out of economic necessity, which I can understand; from what I've seen, this seems to result in a harmonious family organization. But as for myself, after ten years of being more or less self-sufficient — working as a shipyard welder during the War and then working my way through college — such a situation would be unbearable for me.

Sela's father, a rare and understanding man, took no offense at my tearful reactions to the possibility of a prolonged stay in Sürmene (after having already waited patiently for two months). Since women do not travel alone, Baba quietly arranged for brother-in-law Muammer to escort Hikmet and me back to Istanbul to wait further word from Sela.

Farewells in Sürmene

Departure time was delayed somewhat, but eventually confirmed. Finally, the day before Hikmet and I were set to leave Sürmene, Sela's mother indicated we were to go visiting. She was dressed in a long, black, French wool crepe coat and black silk headscarf, wrapped carefully to hide all her beautiful, waist-length hair the color of dark gold silk.

She took me to say goodbye to all the relatives and neighbors, going from house to house in the neighborhood, sometimes climbing steep and winding

30

stone steps to huge, almost inaccessible homes above the main street (which is actually the road that runs through town and all along the coast).

I remember the house we visited last. It was the weekly visiting day for the lady of the house, and so the large room set aside for this day was already crowded with women. Many came from the various hill villages near Sürmene. To me, their lives seem monotonous and their worlds small. My departure seemed to be of great interest to them. Although I was a foreigner, not only in nationality but religion, I was never made to feel unacceptable through their words or actions. I think this is one of the rules of hospitality here, and I cringe when I think of how foreigners are sometimes received in America.

As custom requires, I said goodbye to each woman, starting with the oldest and working my way around the room. As a rule, a younger woman will kiss the hand of an elder and then raise it to touch her forehead, but I settled for handshaking and a kiss on both cheeks. The farewells were quite touching.

Departure from Sürmene, and The Black Sea Bed Roll

Arrivals and farewells are, indeed, taken very seriously. At this early morning leave-taking, the family and neighbors gathered about the relative's autobus. My mother-in-law and others were already shedding tears. I think the tears were for Baby Hikmet because everyone, including the venerable Remzi efendi, had learned to say "teddy bear," "ball," and "no-no." (This comprises Hikmet's English vocabulary at present.)

Hikmet and I were ready, together with a heavy footlocker, two suitcases, the traveling typewriter, and Güher's freshly-cooked cheese pastries in a string bag. At the last minute, Sela's mother went back into the house for a mysterious addition.

Both Sela's parents emerged shortly, bearing wide pieces of heavy white cloth and twine ropes. They seemed to be engaged in some kind of ceremony by the side of the road in front of their house, first placing the white protective cloths on the flat ground, then carefully laying down the twine ropes across the cloths, and a thin, woven wool rug lengthwise on the ropes. Atop the ropes, they carefully placed a large mattress stuffed with goat's wool, indicating this was for Sela and me, and the smaller mattress was for Hikmet. Atop the mattresses, they placed a lavender taffeta yorgan [quilted coverlet] with matching pillows, then three large copper cooking pots wrapped in embroidered bath towels. With the coordinated effort of strong young relatives simultaneously rolling up the sides of the mattress and pulling on the ropes beneath the carpet and mattress, this impossibly bulky bundle was pulled tighter and tighter into a long but narrower bedroll. The cleverly looped ropes on top became handles for toting the roll.

It was puzzling, but I decided that sending the daughter-in-law off with a bedroll must be a Black Sea custom. I tried to look appreciative, all the while wondering about managing this on the train. I expressed many thank-you's, repeatedly.

The same stalwart relatives tossed the bedroll atop the creaking bus and lashed it down. Somehow they found enough space, even though the roof was already loaded with a chicken coop, wicker baskets of tangerines, long green leeks, cabbages, and crates of fresh eggs for market in Trabzon. Heaven protect this load, was my silent prayer!

There were more farewells, hugs, and kisses, and I boarded the bus with Baby Hikmet. Baba would be escorting us as far as Trabzon; Muammer and Remzi efendi would accompany us by steamer all the way to Istanbul. There Aunt Saadet's household would put us up until we were ready for the next part of our journey, by train, to the oil fields where Sela would be waiting.

From Sürmene to Trabzon by Bus

A taxi makes it from Sürmene to Trabzon in less than an hour; by bus it's two torturous hours. The narrow dirt highway runs perilously close to the Black Sea, swooping up and down again in treacherous hairpin curves, around sudden hills, sometimes three and four in succession. From time to time, it seems as if the bus will be catapulted off into space, to be dashed on the wave-washed cliffs below. For all that, it is a dramatically beautiful seacoast route.

On leaving Sürmene, the weather was mild. Gardens and fields along the roadside were being readied for spring planting. Apparently, it is women's work to cultivate the vegetable patches with crude tools, but I often saw an entire family of men — once, a long row of twenty men and boys — working side by side, slowly but surely turning over the rich soil in a huge field.

I saw many evenly-lined groves of hazelnut trees, meticulously planted and cared for, all along the Black Sea coast. A chief export crop.

We frequently ran into — almost literally — village women toting wicker baskets of firewood to market. Turbaned and bearded old men would coax their scrawny donkeys off to the side of the road as our bus passed. Young boys herding sheep and goats were most distinctively attired in sheepherders' capes. Somehow, the sheepskin is turned with the fleece side inside and the stiff corners are folded over to fit their shoulders. This seems to be a great and practical protection against cold, rain, and strong winds.

We spent a pleasant afternoon in the seaport town of Trabzon (in ancient times a Greek colony, the capital of a medieval empire known as Trebizond). This hillside town runs downward to the harbor, with ancient stone steps leading to even more ancient stone quays. Muammer tells me the new pier was built with post-war Marshall Plan aid.

Close to midnight, a contingent of Trabzon relatives gathered to escort us to the pier and arranged for the waiting hamals [porters] to transfer all our baggage to the launches. We were thus transported to the S.S. Istanbul, lying a mile out in the harbor. Sela's father carried the sleeping Hikmet, the "flower of his household," safely on board.

From Trabzon to Istanbul by Steamer

My father-in-law brought us to a large, communal cabin for women and children off the central area below deck. I pushed open the door and found myself in the midst of a busy scene: mothers nursing infants, changing diapers, feeding crying children. There seemed to be little privacy inside or out; whenever anyone opened the door, we were all open to public view. Male passengers, congregating and passing the time of day in the smoking area outside, stared curiously and directly into our cabin. After the cloistered atmosphere of the past several months in Sürmene, I suddenly felt quite vulnerable to stares from strange men. (I miss my sense of privacy more and more. I haven't expressed this to anyone; in my dictionary I can't even find an appropriate word equivalent for "privacy.")

Even more unsettling, I couldn't find our designated place in the cabin. All the dormitory-style iron bunk beds seemed already occupied, with no place left to even sit down. So I stood, perplexed, holding Hikmet and not knowing quite what to do. Also trying, unsuccessfully it turned out, to hide my feelings of dismay. Father-in-law took in the situation, gestured me to wait, and quickly disappeared up the stairs.

He came back shortly with another ticket, picked up Hikmet, strode forward to the upper deck, spoke to a cabin steward who took us to a private cabin — a first-class suite. The difference in accommodations was dramatic. Our suite, finished in ivory enamel woodwork, had a dressing table with two crystal lamps, an ivory telephone, and — most elegant of all — a private lavatory/toilet.

Since the only way I can express appreciation is "Tesekkür ederim," [Thank you], I repeated this many times over, with feeling. In a traditionally paternal gesture of kissing my eyes and Baby Hikmet's, he wished us a good journey in Allah's care and left us, to return to Sürmene.

That evening, in their cabin on the deck below, Muammer and Remsi efendi feasted on the delicacies in Güher's food parcel, while Hikmet and I dined in the formal dining room on the upper deck (meals being included in the first class ticket). That is, we dined there for our first meal. Blonde, blue-eyed Baby Hikmet attracted so much attention flirting outrageously with the stewards, that for the remainder of the voyage I asked to have our meals served in our stateroom.

This Black Sea voyage was calm. The only times I realized we were moving was when I heard the whistles from the pilot boats in the ports of call along the way. Hikmet and I went out on deck to watch crates of eggs, barrels of hazelnuts, crates of live chickens, bales of wool, and fresh vegetables being on-loaded for market in Istanbul.

A crowing rooster woke us early the last morning, so by the time we glided into the Bosphorus, all of us were packed and ready at the railing. We watched the shore line gradually grow nearer and nearer until we could see the famous Byzantine fortresses guarding either side of the narrow strait. Muammer spotted a lone automobile that seemed to be following our progress; it stopped at the narrowest vantage point and we recognized Aunt Saadet and Uncle Avni waving valiantly. In great excitement, we waved back, they hopped into their car, and sped off. By the time our steamer docked, they were waiting for us at the gangplank with reinforcements. My heart leaped up.

Return Arrival in Istanbul

Sela's youngest brother, Orhan, was also waiting at the dock; he'd cut classes from medical school to welcome us and carry Hikmet down the gangplank. Several other Istanbul relatives were there to arrange for the baggage, always a matter of great concern.

The next leg of this trip was by car ferry across the Bosphorus, from the European side to Kadıköy on the Asian side, where Aunt Saadet lives. Someone was dispatched to the Haydarpasha train station to arrange for our train tickets to Batman, which would be the last leg of the trip for Hikmet and me. At the house, Aunt Saadet and Uncle Avni's household were all eagerly waiting to greet us. There was much rejoicing to see Hikmet again, who is the "flower of the household" here, too. She was promptly whisked off to be bathed and fed and pampered.

As faithfully as I could, I conveyed greetings from the Sürmene relatives and friends. I've learned a lot of Turkish names now; they sound musical to me, and often have poetic meanings. I've tried to learn the kinship titles as well: For example, your husband's brother [Kayın birader] is a different brother-in-law from your sister's husband [eniste]; and your father's sister [hala] is a different aunt from your mother's sister [teyze]. Sela calls his mother's half-sister Saadet Teyze, so I do, too.

I will continue this edification after Hikmet and I complete the last leg of our travel to Raman Camp. In the meantime, greetings to all!

Love, Anna Maria

Journal: Aunt Saadet and Uncle Avni's House in Kadıköy The night Hikmet and I arrived in Istanbul, Uncle Avni sent someone to the post office to send a telegram to Batman, letting Sela know of our safe arrival. His last letter came in response to my bitter note from Sürmene, and I've already written him a short but happier letter.

The heaviness in my heart has lifted. Because the atmosphere in this house is so dramatically different from Sürmene, I feel like a bird out of a cage. Not only can I speak English with Aunt Saadet, who has a hearty sense of humor, the general atmosphere of the whole household is livelier. When Uncle Avni offered me a glass of beer at dinner tonight, and a cigarette after dinner, I felt like an emancipated woman.

Back in Sürmene, for a woman to smoke at all, much less in the presence of an older person — especially a man — was really ayıp, [shameful] some kind of depravity. It's not the cigarettes, per se, but the general attitude that I privately object to — allowing men to smoke, but forbidding women to. Ah, well, I'm enjoying life in Istanbul now.

All the relatives here are eager to learn how I'd fared in Sürmene. Aunt Saadet sat next to me at dinner this evening, and translated for me. Everyone wanted news of the family there. They asked after each family member, one by one. They wanted to know details of Muammer's wedding: How was the bride's dress? According to the marriage agreement, demanded by the bride's father, what did the groom give the bride? A Black Sea bracelet, a gold wrist watch, diamond earrings, four gold pieces on a gold chain, I reported. I pointed these out in the newly-weds' handsome wedding portrait.

Eventually, the conversation veered to other topics and Aunt Saadet stopped translating. At such times, I amuse myself listening to music playing on the radio while family and visitors carry on lively conversations. I can recognize the rapid-fire news broadcasts as such, but can't make out the words, except a place name now and then. It's still all one long stream of speech sounds to me.

After dinner, the table was cleared. With a mischievous wink at me, Aunt Saadet stood up and motioned for us women to join her; the men remained seated, to smoke and have their after-dinner coffee at the dinner table.

We followed Aunt into the small parlor adjoining the dining room, and sat down. Aha, I thought, we'll have our coffee here. Yes, but first, she pulled a silk cord to close the heavy velvet draperies on either side of the long salon. This immediately and effectively enclosed us in another space entirely. Aunt opened up the mahogany gramophone in the corner, selected a record from a collection on the shelf, placed the record on the disc, wound up the machine, swung the needle arm in place. Then, within the privacy of the velvet curtains, and with another mischievous wink, she began to gyrate gracefully and sinuously to the rhythmic strains of the harem dance music emerging from the corner. ❦

Letter from Sela

Raman Petrol Kampı
April 13, 1953

My Schatzi!

Received Uncle's telegram yesterday, and your letter from Istanbul today. I was worrying about you both concerning the sea travel. I am glad that you have already made appointments to visit Robert College and the American Consulate. I am going to send you some money by telegram today. I am expecting you on the express arriving here on the 21st of this month.

Raman Camp is quite nice now. It had been raining in the last ten days, but now the weather is getting to be nice and warm. They say it will get a little warmer yet. I am not working very hard since there is not much work around here for me. I am just waiting for you to come with open arms. There is nothing else to write. Please give my best regards to everyone there.

Just be patient, darling. Everything will be all right in a few years. I love you. Kiss Hikmet for me. Your Sela
PS: Things You Have to Bring With:
1. The waffle iron
2. The iron
3. Pressure cooker (if you have room for it). We may use it.
4. All my books that are related with petroleum industry. They are in the trunks at Süleyman's office. The keys of those trunks are with Orhan.
5. My sport jacket which I left in Sürmene
6. All your summer clothing (It's going to get warm around here.)
7. We can find milk for Hikmet here, but just in case, get a can of powdered milk.
8. Save 50 lira from the money I am going to send, to spend on the train for food.
9. After all your needs, if there is money left, buy me a pair of brown shoes, number 42. Orhan will help you shop.

Be good. Sela

Journal: More Exploring in Istanbul The past week has been delightful. Hikmet and I did much visiting and I saw "Gone With the Wind. "

I also went back to the dentist, with whom I'd spoken in German only two months before. Now I couldn't think of one German word, only the few Turkish words I've learned came to mind. Dr. Mehmet, in the meantime, has been picking up considerable English over the short-wave radio. The fact that so many people know English here is a deterrent to my learning Turkish, but I'm struggling on.

I've had many lengthy conversations with Orhan, who inherited the job of escorting me when Muammer reported back to the Navy. I say lengthy, because with my scanty Turkish, Orhan has to do all the talking. I think people have to be very clever to understand foreigners. Fortunately, O. is very clever.

In Beyoglu, on the European side of Istanbul, where the most elegant shops are located, we went looking for shoes for Hikmet. I found a pair of little pink leather oxfords in a shop selling ready-made shoes. I also found a weighty Turkish-English dictionary in a bookstore crammed with multi-lingual dictionaries. I love dictionaries, the language learner's best friend!

We went out along the beautiful Bosphorus to the famous Robert College for an English teaching interview. In case Sela does his military service in this area, I need to find a job. I now have some idea of how and where to apply. It would be a wonderful situation here.

We then visited a less famous mosque, simply called Yeni Cami [New Mosque], at the end of the Galata Bridge where Uncle Avni has a service station and gasoline depot.

From the outside, the mosque looked dark and unimposing. Upon entering, I felt we left not only our shoes at the heavily curtained doorway outside, but also the twentieth century.

The cold stone floors inside were carpeted with numerous large carpets, old and new, running the length of the mosque floor. The vast central space was broken only by columns rising to the top of the dome. An enormous crystal chandelier in the center glinted against light from the stained glass windows high above, its reflections on the gold and mosaic ceiling creating an impression of infinite height, and a feeling of being pulled upward.

The few people who had drifted in during the early afternoon went through their prayers kneeling and rising noiselessly, the silence broken only by a hodja [religious teacher] chanting from the Koran in a clear and resonant voice. It was memorable first mosque experience.

Today, on a visit to relatives in the Kadıköy district, I glimpsed a young muezzin in the Yeni Cami minaret calling people to prayer, turning first toward Mecca, then facing toward each of the alternate directions. His strong, clear voice rose above all the din of rattley horse carts, gypsy hucksters' cries, streetcar trolleys, and floated into the atmosphere. ❦

5

KURTALAN EXPRESS TO BATMAN

Letter to Family and Friends

Raman Camp
May 4, 1953

Dear Brownfields and Other Gentle Readers:

This will bring you up to date after leaving Istanbul.... In brief, after reporting in to his government office in Ankara, Sela went to Raman Dagi camp to begin work, at last, as a petroleum engineer! He sent a series of telegrams to his father and to Istanbul relatives about my travel arrangements to Raman. His brother Muammer was delegated to escort Hikmet and me to Istanbul, where we visited happily for two weeks.

In preparation for our train trip on the Kurtalan Express, the male relatives went to the train station for tickets, to the market for fresh fruit, bottled water, baklava. The women of the household baked börek [cheese pastries], köfte [minced meat patties], and other delectables. They packed the mouth-watering treats into a basket for our ongoing journey.

On the evening Hikmet and I departed, I said my thank-you's and farewells to warm-hearted Aunt Saadet, her younger brothers' wives, Hüsnüye and Sevim, the matriarchal Grandmother, a widowed Yenge [aunt by marriage], and Fatma, the girl from the village who took care of Hikmet. We all shed a few tears at the door.

The entourage to the train station included brother-in-law Orhan carrying the sleeping Hikmet, and Aunt Saadet's brothers Süleyman and Özcan Kıralı, carrying my suitcases and trusty typewriter. [I must digress here to say that when we arrived in Turkey, it irked Sela to have to call these dashing young fellows — who are younger than he is — "uncle," since they are the children of his grandfather's third wife, who is Saadet's mother. The grandfather had only one wife at a time, I should add, but that's another story.] Now back to the train....

Once again, kindly Uncle Avni directed loading operations for my departure. It took four strong porters from the marketplace to carry the trunk and the footlockers we'd left in storage when we went to Sürmene, plus the famous Black Sea bedroll full of copper pans, etc., a gift from my parents-in-law. Along with the wicker basket, parcels, and string bags loaded with beverages and treats, we were all stowed away into Uncle Avni's famous Buick and an auxiliary taxi, then driven to the nearby Haydarpasha train station. There, two porters carried off the bedroll, and others roped the baggage to their backs and toted it all to the baggage train. It took them several trips.

At the station platform, I expressed my grateful thank you's to Uncle Avni and Orhan, who reluctantly handed over the still-sleeping Hikmet. Now

Süleyman and Özcan escorted us to our compartment and made it clear through many gestures, and some French expressions, that the WC [toilet] was next to our compartment, the dining car was the next carriage, I could have room service, but I was *not* to open the door to anyone, except the conductor. After all, I was a young lady traveling unescorted! As if the train were full of traveling scalawags, I thought to myself.

Aunt Saadet had told me this elegant train was originally designed as an extension of the famous Orient Express; it runs thrice weekly from Istanbul to the small town of Kurtalan in the far southeastern region of Turkey near Lake Van, a journey of two and a half days. To her young brothers, apparently, Kurtalan is off the edge of the civilized map. *"Kurtalan!"* they muttered, and just shook their heads. But to me, *Kurtalan* sounded exotic and adventurous. Of course, I was clinging to assurances that Sela would be waiting at the end of the line, wherever it was…. There were more thank-you's and farewells, the whistle shrilled, and the Kurtalan Express rolled off in a cloud of steam. I waved from our compartment window until the figures on the platform became tinier and tinier, then passed out of sight.

So, there we were, Hikmet and I, in a second-class sleeper with a washbasin, and the WC conveniently located next door. Such luxury! The conductor quickly made up our berths and the two of us were soon sleeping to the clickety-clack of the rocking train wheels. In the morning, I rang for tea and yogurt and we breakfasted on the rolls and cheese pastries, fruit, and bonbons.

That day, and the next, passed pleasantly and without mishap. We had light meals and naps in our compartment, enjoyed dinner served elegantly on white linen in the dining car. From time to time, we took little walks through the adjacent cars, and played an endless game of "Look! Look!" out the compartment window. Hikmet was enchanted with the passing landscape, as was I. Once, I thought I saw a camel. By the time I put on my glasses for a good look, it was only a speck on the horizon, but my patient scanning was rewarded, for later I saw dozens of camels grazing in mixed company with many animals of the Anatolian region: cows, sheep, horses, goats, oxen, and water buffalo.

Kurdish Sheepherders and Farmers

Many of the herders and farmers in this part of southern Turkey are Kurds, I've been told. They have an ancient, biblical look: the men wear long trousers somewhat like baggy jodhpurs, layers of upper garments, cloths wrapped turban-style around their heads to protect against the relentless sun. The women wear brightly colored, cotton print salvar [baggy pantaloons gathered at the ankles], and long, flowing head scarves. The little girls, dressed much their mothers, seem like picturesque dolls.

At twilight of the third day, the train pulled into the Batman Station in the wake of a whirling dust storm. It did, indeed, look like an outpost near the end of the line, with a few small shops and what I guessed were some small refinery buildings. Loud blasts of military music were coming from one of the new constructions. [I was told later they were testing the sound amplifier in the new Company theater. And, no, it was not a musical welcome for us!]

On the station platform, Sela was the first person I spied, looking overjoyed, and quite at home in this new location. He was flanked on either side by old university friends Hasan Göker and Mustafa Solim. [They were all classmates at U of Washington, Hasan was our best man when Sela and I married in Tulsa, and now they're engineers at the refinery.] What a heart-warming welcome to see their smiling faces!

In no time at all, they helped Sela transfer everything into the Company Jeep, wished us good luck in our new home, and waved bye-bye to Hikmet. Sela bundled us in and took over the wheel, for the last leg of the long journey to our new home in Raman Camp....

Now, with love to all, Anna Maria

Raman Dagi Camp 1945

39

6

LIFE IN RAMAN DAGI CAMP

Journal: Our New Home in the Concrete Barracks "Dag/dagi" means mountain in Turkish. As a native of Washington State with its rugged, heavily forested Cascade Mountains, Raman Dagı to me seems more like a tired old hill, without the trace of a tree. "All cut down for firewood long ago," Sela says. The only vegetation on Raman Mountain is an occasional scraggly bush, and sparse grass which the continuously grazing sheep and goats keep cropped off.

On our first ride up here from the train station, horses in the fields shied away from our unfamiliar vehicle. We passed several farmers plowing in the arid, rocky fields, one walking behind his ox hitched to a wooden plow, another pulling the wooden plow himself. They turned to stare curiously at our Jeep chugging along the road. I couldn't help staring back. They looked like pictures from the Old Testament.

The bumpy Raman road winds upward around the treeless mountain for some twenty kilometers; on this first trip, it seemed endless. Finally, an oil derrick came into view, and then the smell of petroleum permeated the air. "Here is the camp!" Sela announced. "And there is our lojman!" [housing unit]

He was pointing to the first of several one-story buildings constructed of gray concrete blocks, each with a wide veranda running the length of the building. The engineers and the camp manager, he went on to explain, are allotted one space each in the first lojman, technicians live in the adjacent one, with the rest of the work force in the two additional buildings. Altogether, these are the men running the drilling and pumping operations on Raman Mountain.

Our Allotted Space in the Lojman

The entryway to our "space" is large enough to accommodate a shelf for work boots/house slippers, hooks for work clothing, trunks, and a table that can hold an electric hotplate for boiling tea water, or for making coffee.

Two inner doors open off the entryway. The first door opens into a spacious, wooden-floored living/sleeping/family room, with a built-in closet and wide casement windows. The room is spacious enough for a large bed (or several twin size), a small table, several chairs, a wardrobe and/or clothes chest. The clean and functional wooden furniture, all made in the camp workshop, is unpainted, Sela says, because of the "steep price of imported paint."

The other entryway door opens into the concrete-floored bathroom containing a single electric light bulb dangling from the high ceiling, with a chain to pull it on and off, a western-style toilet, a simple shower contraption, a water tank with its own heater, and a tiny porcelain washbasin.

Tap Water from the Tigris

The small stream of water from the bathroom faucet is piped up from the Tigris River. Any water remaining in the basin overnight, I notice, leaves a rich, dark brown sediment in the bottom. Even so, a refinery chemist told us, this tap water still tests purer, "fewer microbes floating around," than the fresh drinking water brought up by donkey back from the neighboring village. Ironically, our drinking water *looks* crystal clear.

An added amenity for each building is the service of a janitor or "house boy." Yusuf 's tasks, for instance, include sweeping down the verandah each day; sluicing buckets of water on the concrete to cool it; and keeping a constant lookout for yellow spiders, centipedes, scorpions, and other poisonous creatures in the central camp area where the children play. He runs occasional errands down the path to the mess hall, carrying trays of special pastries the wives prepare to be baked in the mess hall oven. He's always on call for emergencies during the day.

At night, an anonymous watchman patrols the perimeters of the camp, tramping heavily and swinging his flashlight to and fro to chase off stray donkeys, the only marauders I'm aware of to date. ❦

Letter to Family and Friends

Raman Petrol Kampı
May 20, 1953

Dear Brownfields and all,

My present life in Raman Camp is a lazy one, and by comparative standards here, a luxurious one. We have electricity, hot running water, a small oil stove, a shower of sorts, a short wave radio, and a telephone — essential for Sela's communication with the refinery down in Batman and the other camps in the field. In addition, we share a mess hall which serves our meals three times a day, and a washhouse where we send bed linens and work clothes to be laundered.

The villagers living in the village just over the hill have none of these aforementioned amenities, except, perhaps, electricity. They live in small square houses made of baked mud blocks. From time to time, I remind myself of this, to keep things in perspective.

A number of (most of?) the men living in the lojmans have a wife and small children living with them. The mothers of some young bachelors occasionally come to visit. They mend, sew, knit, attend to the tea brewing, coffee making, and other light housekeeping tasks.

The camp housing faces the middle of the camp site, in a rough semi-circle comprised of four units of apartments with five apartments to each unit. The road up from Batman enters the camp through a cluster of warehouses, garages, and machine shops, then runs along in back of the units all the way to the mess hall and laundry facilities at the other end of the camp clearing. Somewhat removed from these buildings is the school house. It serves the children in the camp as well as the children from the village on the other side of the hill.

From our apartment windows, I can see the surrounding hills fall away into a wide valley leveling into a broad plain, and still farther away, a rim of the Bitlis Mountains. From this distance, the fields below us look like a relief map with brown, green, and yellow patches. I understand much of the land is good wheat land. I've read that under the post-WWII Truman Plan, tractors are loaned out and the results are "gratifying," but I've not seen a tractor around here yet.

Never have I seen such indescribably gorgeous sunsets.

Hikmet is flourishing on this bracing mountain air, and has learned one Turkish word for every English word she already knows, roughly a dozen, all told. We pick wild flowers on the hill, and watch the pack donkeys wandering up and down the camp trails.

I'm enjoying this life to the utmost. While it lasts. Sela, presumably, won't go into compulsory military service until fall, and his six months' training will give me a chance to teach English in Istanbul or maybe Ankara. After that, he says, he'll be sent back to the oil fields to finish his Army time, since there's a great shortage of engineers here. This is a promising outlook for us right now.

I trust this letter reaches you all in equally happy moods. Please write. I'm not homesick, believe me, but I do like to refresh my memory once in a while. And if there are unanswered questions on the local rainfall in August (zero), politics in Anatolia (confusing), or Turkish meatball recipes (delicious), I shall try to oblige.

PS: Thought you would like to know that I just saw the Tigris River.

Jaunt to Hasan Keyf on the Tigris River

Sela had an official visitor in the camp, and Hikmet and I were invited along on their tour this afternoon. We drove past the last oil rigs on the hill and looked down the valley at the Tigris, a chocolate-brown ribbon winding along close to a gray limestone cliff on one side.

Our destination was the famous Hasan Keyf archeological site, actually now a village of several hundred souls, lying across the river on the other side. We could see a minaret and a tumbled down bridge [built by the benevolent Seljuk prince Kara Aslan, in 1114, I was later told]. We could also see steps carved into the face of the limestone; they lead from rooms carved under the top of the cliff all the way down to the river's edge. I was told this provided the cliff dwellers protection, and enabled them to get water from the river during times of siege. The trip down and across the river by the old "Noah's ark" wooden ferry takes two hours or more and will have to wait for another time.

I thought I had experienced the ultimate (or worst) in road travel, but today I learned that sheep trails are also called "roads." Only a Jeep could navigate them, and one has a feeling of dangerous adventure while jouncing over open and uninhabited countryside. We stopped to pick a few wildflowers on the way. When we arrived home in a cloud of dust, sleepy Hikmet had a wilted buttercup still clutched in one hand.

The last Jeep for the day is going down to Batman shortly and the driver will post this letter. Our very best to everyone at home — home being anywhere in the States.

Love, A

Raman Dagi Pump and Oil Tanks 1953

View of Hasan Keyf and Ancient Bridge 1953

Letter to Tulsa Friends

Raman Petrol Kampı
Must be the 28th of May, 1953

Dear Brownfields/Rakestraw,

Can't think of any way to thank you all for the *Life* subscription. One copy came via Sürmene; already it's going the rounds. Even the bachelor engineers who can't read English like to look at "the pretty pictures" [women].

43

They, too, are very grateful. I might add that by the time the magazine has been read by all, it's pretty dog-eared.

Now please tell me: Who's had what, who's done what, where, how, and why? The fact that we've changed addresses umpteen times accounts for no mail?

The more I sit and reflect, the more sentimental I get. So please shake hands with everybody for me. And regards from Sela, who's out in the field playing volleyball "to relax."

The Inimitable A
PS: In sharing this missive, please add this:
Bayan Anna Maria Malkoç
Bay Selahattin Malkoç elile *[at the home of]*
Raman Petrol Kampı, Batman, Turkey

Journal: News of Bill's Breakdown We received news that our good friend Bill had gone from Tulsa to New York after a break-up with his wife Doe. According to his father, he went to the Big City to "discover" himself and try his fortune as a writer. Intense, intelligent, idealistic, isolated — and, I suspect, eating poorly and drinking heavily — he fell ill. Friends from Tulsa fetched him back home. We've just received word that he is now recovering his health and well-being. ❦

Letter to Bill Brownfield

Raman Petrol Kampı
July 13 or so, 1953

Dear William "The Unpredictable,"

Sela just brought the mail in, but teething Hikmet has already chewed up the envelope with your parents' address on it, so I'm trusting to the astuteness of the Tulsa Post Office to forward this to you....

After I started this letter, Sela went back to Garzan camp to check up on things, and Hikmet and I walked over to the American tool pusher John Shirley's house at the other edge of the camp to visit his wife, Alice hanım. She always answers my questions about local customs and is my "fountain of information." We enjoyed fresh lemonade in the shade while her husband, "Texas John," was having a discussion with visiting engineers about packers and other drilling matters.

We've returned home now, Hikmet is napping in her little bed, and I'm really in the letter-writing mood. So, back to you and your cryptic note. The postmark indicates you're in New York City. You say you were looking for more than a mundane life, something on a higher plane, and "thought and thought yourself into a peck of trouble." I'm so sorry about your troubles, Bill!

You're so intellectually intense, burning out your brains searching for the deepest meaning of life, yearning for a life above and beyond the "ordinary and commonplace." What can I say to you? Perhaps I shouldn't be subjective at a time like this, but I've always had to settle for a "mundane life" myself, mainly because of economic reasons. I'm thinking about my year in Chicago right now, going to

44

school, and working part time in the Hyde Park telephone office. And in New York for one semester, I was the receptionist/"odds-and-ends girl" in a Mid-eastern oil company office, coincidentally.

And now, you don't think it's ever "ordinary and commonplace" in Raman Camp, Bill? Here it's oil, oil, oil! The smell is everywhere. And nowhere to go to escape it. Interminably, the men discuss drilling and "fishing" for things dropped down the pipes or whatever. And interminably, the women gossip about the other women, who ditto.

Yes, in answer to your kindly question, I do trade around for books from the English-speaking engineers to read, but they're all American Westerns or horrible dime detective stories.

And yet, I must tell you, Bill, there's the loveliest time at sundown every day, when little Hikmet and I rest on the cooling concrete veranda and have a glass of tea together with our neighbor, Shaziye hanım. We sit on the wooden bench and gaze far off at the delicate colors of the never-the-same sunset. I am moved at the magnificence. I gaze at the horizon stretching away southward to the Bitlis Mountains and the even more distant Syrian ranges, taking in all the purplish mists and rolling hills, grayish green plains and valleys that change with every view. It gives me such a feeling of remoteness. And peace.

Sela never takes me down the valley to Batman that one of us doesn't say, "Wouldn't Bill enjoy this!" You're an important part of our lives, Bill. And if, as you say, nothing ever comes from your pen in the way of a world-shaking publication (though I believe it *will*), you've already got a priceless gift — that of truly befriending people. For example, look what you did for our mutual friend Angh Ki Moe, who was so lonely in Tulsa and homesick for Burma. And your ex, Doe, who was so lacking in self-confidence. And Sela, who was a stranger in a strange land.

Sela says if you were a tool pusher with simple tastes, you could come here, to the tune of $1,000 per month and expenses, and see what this life's all about. Mind you, it has its limitations, but the more life I see around here, the more remains to be seen, I realize, so I never seem to stand still. Just last week, I heard about a Yezidi village half-way down the mountain. Some people call them "devil-worshipers." My research into this is going slowly, but I shall report my findings, if any.

Now, Bill, I'm getting slightly off track here, and will stop. Besides, there's a mouse in the cupboard that I have to make up my mind about. Don't worry about not writing. I'll be dropping you a note now and then, whenever the muse is upon me.

Love to you all, Anna Maria

Journal: The Raman Camp Mess Hall All the residents of the camp eat in the mess hall, a cavernous, barn-like structure holding three or four rows of long mess tables flanked with benches. Three times a day, the mess hall workers carry enormous trays loaded with plates of food to our tables.

Breakfast consists of hot tea; pide (flat bread baked in the Batman town oven and trucked up early every morning); white cheese; salty black olives; some kind of quince or lemon marmalade; an occasional soft-boiled egg.

Lunch and dinner always include chunks of standard, regulation loaf bread, pilav [rice] at least once a day; also legumes in some form — lentils or green string beans, cooked plain or cooked with mutton, or cooked and served cold with olive oil. Or, dried kidney beans cooked and served cold with olive oil; or lima beans, ditto.

Rather often, we have lamb (mutton, really) stewed with vegetables. Once in a while, we're treated to chicken. It may be stewed with tomatoes, or noodles, or boiled and served cold with lemon. Sometimes we have boiled or mashed potatoes, sometimes stuffed green peppers, or stuffed tomatoes, or stuffed eggplant, or stuffed squash, depending on the season.

Like the other diners, I miss home cooking. Frankly, sometimes my spirits flag and I lose enthusiasm for the camp food because the dishes are often floating in oil and mutton fat, which I avoid after my bout with hepatitis long ago. Then I remind myself that I don't have to do any cooking! This automatically lifts my spirits.

In actual fact, I couldn't cook if I wished, since there are no grocery stores east of Diyarbakir, with the exception of several hole-in-the-wall shops down near the train station, selling staples. What I've found so far are mostly Turkish state monopoly products: white flour, granulated sugar, black tea, all sold in bulk; green beans, tomato paste, fish, all in tin cans; a kind of castile soap cut into bars; and wooden matches. I plan to continue my market research when the opportunity arises.

While I try to keep my negative feelings about the mess hall food to myself, not everyone does. Our neighbor Fritz, a geologist from Germany, is famously outspoken. One day recently, he strode in from Garzan camp, wearing his black leather trench coat, looking extremely hungry.

"See that coat? He must have been S.S. [*Schutzstaffel*] in the War," muttered Sela. "The Nazi special police all wore black leather coats."

Fritz strode over to a seat at the next table, picked up a lunch plate, took a sniff, and growled, "Fasulye! Gott in Himmel! Immer fasulye!" [Beans! God in Heaven! Always beans!] He slammed the plate down, turned on his heel, and strode back out.

"I hope his supply of imported cheese and crackers holds out," Sela snickered, rather unsympathetically. ❦

Journal: A Visitor's Cryptic Comments on Camp Life Sometimes we linger at the mess hall table for a coffee, and chat with whomever is visiting. Recently, Sela's old school friend Parisa, an enormously tall, good-humored geologist, stopped by on a rare visit to Raman. He and Sela had studied in Germany together and always love to joke when they see each other.

"Merhaba, Selahattin bey!" he boomed as he walked in and sat down. "Imagine finding a world traveler like you, speaking three languages, living here in Raman Camp! Tell me, how can you bear life so far from Istanbul, our true center of culture?"

"Merhaba, Parisa bey!" Sela responded. "Welcome to the hospitality of Raman Petrol Camp! And may I ask how an educated gentleman with three degrees like yourself, can exist in an uncivilized place like Garzan Camp?"

"Ah," Parisa replied, "how can I live there, you ask? You should see the place that I came from!" There was great laughter at this sophisticated witticism, because everyone knew he was proud of coming from Of, a very tiny town east of Sürmene. Then he grew quiet, and said, "Seriously, we joke, but how about Anna Maria? We don't hear her complaining!" He turned and addressed me, "How is it that you, coming from America, can stand to live in this camp?"

"Ah, Parisa bey," I replied in the same vein, "the secret is that before I came here, I stayed in Sürmene for two months. Now, I'm like a bird out of a cage!" ❦

Journal: The Raman Camp Wash House Concerning laundry, I take a cue from my neighbors. I hand wash my own laundry and hang it discretely in the bathroom; I hang Hikmet's diapers on a clothesline in front of our door (there's one in front of each unit). Unlike the atmosphere in Sürmene on the Black Sea, the air here is devoid of moisture, so the laundry dries quickly.

All sheets, towels, and work clothing are sent to the camp wash house; toting the laundry bags is one of Yusuf's tasks. I'm told that one of the engineers devised a commercial-sized washing machine that runs on electricity. The wash women from the village launder everything, iron and fold it, and see that it is returned to the rightful owner. Their system seems to run smoothly according to their own three-category ID system. Turkish names seem to pose no problem. So far, Sela hasn't lost a shirt or sock. For the American who's been here a long time, they mark his laundry bag "Ingiliz" [English or British], because they know he speaks English. But I happened to see the visiting UN geologist's bag, and I guess they weren't sure how to pigeonhole him. They marked it simply "Gâvur" [gyah voor], meaning non-believer, non-Moslem. Apparently in the mind of the laundry marker, any other (non-Ingiliz) foreigner is a gâvur, synonymous with foreigner. I think the word is usually used as a pejorative. ❦

Journal: My Camp Neighbor Sühendan hanım In the mornings after breakfast in the mess hall, I do laundry and light housekeeping. Now and then, Hikmet and I go for walks around the camp, but most often she plays on the wide concrete verandah in front of our door with Ferhan, the little girl next door.

Ferhan's mother, Sühendan hanım, one of my first friends in Raman Camp, is my model for hospitality. Tall, dark-haired, with a serenely oval face, she has a calmness about her I find soothing.

Whenever she invites me over for a cup of coffee, which is often, it is always a treat. I enjoy watching her cook the coffee, holding the cezve [long-handled coffee pot] over the small spirit stove installed in their entryway. The blue flame shoots out like magic from under the cooking ring.

Although we camp residents usually eat our meals together in the mess hall, Sühendan often prepares "extra" dishes at home on her little stove. She cleverly manages to get the houseboy, who lives in the village over the hill, to bring her fresh vegetables from home, and gets occasional supplies from the hole-in-the-wall shops by the train station in Batman. She says her husband, Mehmet Baytan, whom she fondly refers to as "Pasha," likes special home-cooked dishes now and then. [Pasha, the military term for "General," sometimes is used jokingly for the head of a household, or for someone who is autocratic and dictatorial.]

Sühendan hanım's Pasha is a tall, affable, fun-loving engineer from Adana. I understand he'd served in the Turkish Air Force and then was sent to train in San Antonio, Texas. This has given him an ineffable air of urbanity. ❦

Journal: What Is the Key to English? One afternoon, Sühendan hanım took me to pay a call on a neighbor's elderly mother-in-law. This is a required courtesy whenever a neighbor's mother or mother-in-law comes for a visit; the other women take turns preparing afternoon refreshments to entertain her. Somehow, they gracefully exclude me from these obligations since I'm still very much a "foreigner." When I asked Sela about this, he said, "Don't worry about it. You'll have your turn when you learn the ropes."

Today's visitor, partially bedridden with arthritis, was curious and eager to meet the "foreigner." Probably her first encounter with one, I thought to myself. I'm sorry I haven't learned enough Turkish yet to talk to her; I hope I don't shock her too much.

When I walked in with Sühendan hanım, she immediately sat bolt upright and took a good look. "Hmm." she muttered. "Hos geldin." [Welcome.]

"Hos bulduk," I responded, and shook hands. I down sat on a chair beside her bed.

To be polite, she didn't direct her questions to me at first, but at Sühendan: "What does she speak?" When Sühendan answered, "Ingiliz," the woman turned to me and asked in Turkish, "What is that in English?" She was pointing to the door.

"Door," I answered in English.

"Hm, *door*!" she repeated thoughtfully, then pointed to the bed.

"Bed."

"Hm, *bed*!" she repeated more thoughtfully. She seemed to trying to work out some kind of a sound-correlation or a syllable-correspondence system. "*Door. Bed.* English is easy!" she declared in Turkish, then paused to test her theory. Pointing to different objects, she asked: "What is that? That? That?"

"Window," I answered. "Pencil. Paper. Wrist watch."

I admired her inquiring mind and her attempt to discover a language-learning key, but she wasn't going to find any easy system to match up English words with Turkish, as I knew only too well. I was sorry to disappoint her. ❦

Journal: My Camp Neighbor Alice hanım Sela walked Hikmet and me over to the single house in the compound one day to meet John Shirley, the tool pusher from Texas. [The drilling rig supervisor as well as the most experienced drilling expert around, Mr. Shirley rates special accommodations.] Sela seems to have great respect for him.

John's wife, Alice — another handsome, dark-eyed beauty — had just come in by train from Istanbul with her school-age daughter Hilda and her little daughter Mary, Hikmet's age.

I was overjoyed to meet Alice hanım because she speaks English and can explain many mysteries to me, also because she's friendly, intelligent, and outspoken. When I first arrived at Raman Camp, Alice was kind and helpful. And interesting. I thoroughly enjoy her company and learn a lot about local customs from her.

During the school year, Alice stays in her apartment in Ankara, and Hilda goes to Dame de Sion, a private French Catholic boarding school in Istanbul. By taking the Ankara-Istanbul overnight train, Alice is able to see Hilda often. And from time to time, Mr. S. goes up to Ankara or Istanbul. During the summer months, Alice brings her daughters to stay in Raman.

I find her generous and hospitable. From time to time, she invites the other wives to tea or thirst-quenching lemonade — *with ice cubes* — in her garden gazebo. She always brings out special refreshments to delight her guests.

Sühendan hanım, who has been here longest perhaps, knows Alice hanım well and also enjoys her company. But not all of the other neighbor women do, apparently. When visiting the camp manager's wife recently, I caught a glimmer of their gossiping. From the few words I could understand, I gathered the talk was about Alice hanım. It sounded negative and I wanted to say: "If you don't like Alice hanım, why do you go there for tea? And eat her imported cookies? And drink her lemonade with ice cubes!" But since I can't express any of these thoughts, I keep them to myself.

To me, in the scorching summer heat of this dusty, treeless cluster of concrete blocks atop a remote mountain near the edge of the map, Alice hanım's hospitality is like a breeze from an oasis in the desert. And, in my opinion, to speak unkindly of someone who has shared her ice cubes from the only home refrigerator east of Diyarbakir is hypocritical and undeserving of her gracious hospitality. ❦

Journal: Recreation at the Camp: Movies and Visiting Once in a blue moon, it's Movie Night in the camp. The camp manager arranges for the Company's projectionist to bring his equipment and movie reels from the refinery's little movie theater in Batman and set it up after dinner. The mess hall rapidly fills up with workers, wives, elderly relatives, and children of all ages. The lights are dimmed and the reel flickers into life. For a brief time here in the bare, bleak, and graceless building, all of us are carried away to the faraway worlds of our individual fantasies.

A Visit to the Village

Once, when time was hanging heavy, I mentioned that I'd like to visit someone. Sela talked it over with his usta [foreman] to find out who in his village would like have a visitor. Someone not intimidated by a foreigner, I imagine.

Yesterday, Sela duly informed me that Ahmet usta's wife was expecting Hikmet and me for a visit in the afternoon, and that Yusuf would escort us to the house, not far away on the other side of the hill.

I prepared a gift bag of chocolates from Diyarbakır. (From what I've learned about gift-giving, one should never visit a house for the first time empty-handed.) I found a suitable sun hat for Hikmet and put on a modest cotton dress with sleeves down to the elbow. (In this respect, my main models for appropriate dress at the camp are Sühendan hanım and Alice hanım.)

Ahmet usta's wife, whose name sounded like *Durdaneh*, greeted us at the open door with a smile and led us inside her refreshingly cool, thick-walled adobe house. I nudged Hikmet to present the package of sweets to our hostess, which she accepted with more smiles. We sat on the divan that seemed to be recessed into the wall. It was covered with a snow-white cotton cloth, embroidered with bright flowers.

Without appearing to stare, I observed that the floor was earthen, hard-packed and smooth. The electric light bulb hanging on a wire from the ceiling was more or less similar to the one in our "space." Everything seemed to be extremely neat and tidy. I could appreciate the effort it took to achieve this cleanliness, guessing that the only source of water was probably the village well.

Durdaneh hanım excused herself and disappeared into a back room. At times like this, I talk to Hikmet in English, about what we can observe of the life around us. "Look," I pointed out, "there are flowers everywhere: a silk rose in the vase, flowered patterns on the cushions, embroidered flowers on the doilies, velvet tulips on the wall-hanging." Where flowers fail to grow in the environment, I thought to myself, people compensate by creating their own artistic expressions.

Shortly, Durdaneh hanım reappeared with a cup of fragrant coffee on a tray, with a foil-wrapped chocolate for Hikmet. The coffee was cooked, I guessed by the faint hissing noise, on a spirit burner like my neighbor Sühendan hanım's.

We chatted for a time — that is, she talked, and I nodded in agreement. Or, she asked simple questions that I could answer simply in a word or two. She had the advantage of being bilingual in Kurdish and Turkish; I felt she could sympathize with my linguistic handicaps.

Hikmet played with her little dolly while our hostess served us lemonade, along with sweet and savory cookies. There must be a communal oven in the village where the women have such special confections baked, or perhaps there *is* no village oven, I idly conjectured. Perhaps Ahmet usta arranged to have a tray of the cookies taken down when the camp truck made its regular run to the Batman town oven. In any case, I know that nothing here is "ready-made" or easily available. Such sweets are indeed luxuries to be savored as special treats.

Actually, this kind of formal visit is a rarity for me. After light housekeeping chores, I usually spend my time tending to Hikmet, mending, writing letters, reading, and of course, visiting my close neighbors in the other units. I consider every visit with them to be a social occasion, as well as a Turkish language lesson at the same time. 🐝

Journal: Hikmet and the Teddy Bear   Now and then, there are even more exciting events at the camps, such as the morning Sela invited Hikmet and me along on a Jeep ride to check on the pump operation at Garzan Camp. Our former neighbors Fritz the German geologist, and his wife Sigrid, a trained dentist, looked happy to see us visitors. And I was happy to see Sigrid, especially. When Fritz was assigned to Garzan camp, I missed her. Not only because she speaks English, but because she has an unfailingly calm and even disposition, in spite of the often wearying camp life. And is full of resourceful and practical ideas.

Sigrid and I were chatting away by the side of the road when the camp cook came out of the cookhouse, carrying the camp mascot in his arms. "Hikmet! Look! See what we have here!" he called out, and carefully deposited a small, light brown bear cub on the ground. It was exactly the same color as Hikmet's wooly winter coat. When it stood up on its hind legs, it was exactly the same height as the 18-month-old little girl.

Although the two young creatures were standing some 50 feet apart, they seemed to make instant, magnetic eye contact. It was a spell-binding moment. We were all holding our breaths instinctively. "Teddy bear!" shouted Hikmet. With little arms outstretched, she started toddling toward the cub — which was already running on all fours toward Hikmet. It was an amazing sight to see them meet halfway in a dramatic bear hug. We watched without breathing.

Instantly, Hikmet must have sensed something strange about this teddy bear. She started to cry, and struggled to free herself, prompting the cub to hug harder. The men rushed up to separate the pair, and the cook took the cub back to its leash in the screened kitchen. Sela soothed Hikmet, who seemed to suffer no traumatic reactions.

…. Later that fall, Sigrid told us that the bear cub had grown into such a destructive, dangerous pest they had to send it away to the Ankara Zoo. She visited it there once, she said, and found it pining away in a bleak, treeless, concrete enclosure. It seemed to recognize her voice. On her next visit, it was gone. 🐝

Journal: A Visit to a New Baby in Batman   My neighbor Sühendan hanım invited Hikmet and me along on a ride down the mountain to Batman yesterday. Her good-humored husband, Pasha, had to check a piece of equipment at the old refinery, he told me in English. He was dropping us off so Sühendan could congratulate his foreman's family on their new baby. Without waiting for details, I hopped into the van with Hikmet. I was happy to be taking a ride anywhere off the mountain top, and we all set off down the dirt road to Batman in merry spirits.

Pasha pulled up in front of a small house not far from the old refinery. He escorted us to the house, greeted the woman opening the door, then, saying he would pick us up on his return, left. The lady of the house seemed to know Sühendan hanım, who explained that Hikmet and I were her neighbors in Raman Camp. The woman nodded and ushered us in with a warm smile.

As we entered, Sühendan unobtrusively placed a small, wrapped gift into her hand. I realized to my embarrassment that this was a gift-giving occasion and I had come "dry-handed." Sühendan caught the distressed look on my face, whispered "Okay, okay!" — her one word of English — to let me know a gift was not expected of me.

We were introduced around the circle of other women already seated in the room. They, like our hostess, were wearing long, draped, white head coverings and flowered cotton salvars. They all seemed quietly polite and friendly. ("Smiling-faced" is the Turkish expression.)

Telling Fortunes from the Coffee Cup

Even Sühendan wasn't following much of their conversation, I noticed. Although my Turkish is woefully limited, I soon realized the other women were not speaking Turkish, but Kurdish. Despite these language blocks, we all enjoyed sipping the strong, sweet coffee our smiling hostess was bringing out to us, one at a time.

Sühendan finished her coffee. She placed the saucer upside down over the cup, held the two tightly together, and quickly flipped them over so the upside down cup would drain any remaining grounds into the saucer, which was now on the bottom. She set it aside until it cooled. This, I knew from many visits to our neighbors at the camp, was a signal she would like to have her fortune told, if anyone in the room were inclined to do so.

One of the women quickly obliged. She sat down next to Sühendan and picked up the now-cooled cup. Turning it round and round with a practiced air, she looked for meaningful patterns and symbols in the thick dregs at the bottom, interpreting whatever she saw. A fish was good fortune, she divined. A deer would bring good news, a cluster of dots indicated money, and so on. From time to time, Sühendan would nod at the fortune teller. At the finish, she gave a pleased little chuckle. "Insallah!" [God willing]

"Insallah!" echoed the other woman.

I politely turned down the offer to have my cup read, knowing I wouldn't have understood a word. Unfortunately. But I was quite happy playing patty-cake with Hikmet on my lap, and observing the social exchanges.

At this point, a little girl came out of the inner room with an announcement to alert all the women. A younger model of our hostess, quite obviously her daughter, now entered the room carrying a small bundle swathed tightly in fine white cotton. Carefully, she placed it in a kind of bassinette in the corner and sat down next to it. This, I gathered, was the new baby and it was now on view.

Sure enough, the other women rose in turns to take a look into the bassinette and murmur something that sounded like "Masallah," a kind of blessing to protect the baby from harm. At Sühendan's nod, I followed her with Hikmet to take a peek. Inside the basket, we saw a tiny face with wee, closed eyes. It was wrapped all around like a miniature mummy, with nothing moving except the new mother's hand gently nudging the crib to and fro.

After a time, the same little girl came out with a large piece of snow-white cheese-cloth. This, the young mother carefully draped over the sleeping infant's bed, then she turned to answer questions from the older women.

Diyarbakır Fly Bite

Idly, I watched the sunlight from the window shining behind the new mother's pretty head. One ray of light struck a white circle on her cheek about the size of a 25-kurush coin [or a 25-cent piece]. The circle was perfectly smooth and shiny. There was a similar mark on the little girl in the house and I wondered if it was some kind of local tattooing.

I sat there, uncomprehendingly, amidst the conversations in Kurdish flowing about me, letting my mind wander idly as I often do when the language barriers are up. I recalled seeing facial tattoos and other oddities down at the train station, a junction for meandering tribal groups.... Several women with blue tattooing between their eyebrows, passing through.... And several women in black robes, with eye windows of black mesh in their head veils, most likely wives of the camel caravan drivers from parts south.... Then the man in the marketplace with no nose. Did he lose it from a feuding knife slash? Or leprosy?... And the nomadic tribes traveling with their sheep and round, black leather tents.... One recollection led to another ....

My private musings ended abruptly when Sühendan indicated it was time to thank our hostess and leave. Pasha's Jeep was at the door.

On the ride back to Raman Camp, I asked about the "round white circles on the face." Not knowing the word for tattoo, I struggled without my bilingual dictionary to describe what I'd seen to Pasha. "Sounds like 'Diyarbakır fly bite,'" he said, cryptically.

"Very bad," Sühendan added, which only heightened the mystery for me.

At home that evening, Sela shook his head at my question. "I'm a Black Sea man, myself," he responded. "We don't have Diyarbakır flies in Sürmene."

A very long time later, one of the Company doctors studying English explained this certain variety of fly is found in the hot, dry southern regions around Diyarbakır and Aleppo. The insect "bites" and lays its eggs in the wound it makes. This is not fatally poisonous, but the wound festers a long time while the eggs are developing. When the infection heals, it leaves a characteristically round scar of healed skin tissue. My new dictionary also terms it "Aleppo or Diyarbakır boil or carbuncle."

I thought back to the swaddled baby and the pretty mother with the white tattoo, carefully draping the white muslin over her baby's crib. ☙

Letter to Tulsa Friends

Raman Petrol Kampı
August 13, 1953

Dear Bill,

With the complicated filing system I have, I don't have your father's address anymore. The file gets so crammed with Sela's and my letters that we jot down pertinent new items and file the old letters in the wastebasket. I thought I'd made a note of the address but hadn't. Sorry!

We just heard from Aung Ki Moe: General Delivery, Billings, Mont. He is so happy he got a job through your father, and is evidently doing well. The

Howards and Days prove themselves incorrigible non-correspondents, still. However, life goes on in Tulsa, I dare say.

Hikmet and I got back last week from visiting family and friends in Ankara. We stayed in Alice hanım's comfortable Ankara apartment and spent two weeks of generally luxurious relaxation: afternoon tea and lemon ice in sidewalk cafes; a delicious cafe garden dinner; and taxi excursions through the modern new section of the city with its magnificent, park-like boulevards.

Job hunting was only incidental. A teaching job this winter in Ankara is practically certain, if I want to teach a general science course — mainly elementary mathematics and biology. Ironically enough, these courses were my near downfall in school, so they're sending me a textbook to look over. Only yesterday, I learned that Ankara College (Ankara Koleji) is not a college, but a secondary school that has a preparatory year in English, then teaches most lessons after that in English. I feel more hopeful, as apparently they're short of English-speaking science teachers.

Back here at the camp, I'm tutoring in English two new pupils, since my first pupil, Hilda, went back to boarding school. (She and her little sister Mary spend summers here with their mother, Alice hanım.)

But as for my new pupils, they are also neighbors — Osman bey, the supply agent for the camp and his teen-age daughter, Hamiyet. In his spare time, Osman bey has written two volumes of poetry and is working on a novel now, I think. Lo, a kindred spirit in the wilderness! I wish I knew enough Turkish to understand his poems.

This life has its comparative high points, you see. And to prove to you that I am able to acclimate, I must say that my recent taste of city life in Ankara utterly *thrilled* me: book stores, libraries, theaters, parks, restaurant food. All these I had become "unused" to. Of necessity, one learns to content oneself with very little!

Your books came yesterday. I meant to be a miser and ration myself to, say, a book a week, but I've already read two! *Day of the Locust* is wonderful; I'd never read Nathaniel West. What a discovery. And *The Castaway* I must read again. At the first reading, I was in sheer terror, not totally comprehending because the symbolism is so challenging One reading is not enough. Eventually, when I've done with them, I will pass the books on to a few other English readers here in camp, who will also much appreciate them.

So, we all thank you, Bill. Second-hand greetings from Sela. He's up the hill at the rigs, slaving away over a hot oil well. And here's a buss from the wee beastie.

Love to all in Tulsa, A

7

DUTY CALLS IN ANKARA

Journal: Military Service and A Divorce of Convenience After six months in the oil camp, Sela received notice to report for compulsory military service in Ankara. He took the train up to the capital, and found a semi-basement apartment near Ankara College for Hikmet and me. It has a bit of garden in the front, and back doors opening onto a small garden. The owner is a quiet, sedate judge who lives on the second (top) floor with his small family; another family lives on the first (second) floor, above us.

Sela has been in contact with friends with foreign wives, to learn about their military service experiences. Although I am registered in his hometown official records office and have a certified registration booklet, officially I am still a "foreigner" here.

One friend had heard of a case several years ago when a Turk in California, married to an American movie starlet, was called up for his compulsory military service. He learned that with a foreign wife, he would not be eligible to serve as a commissioned officer for a term of 18 months (plus a small salary). Instead, he would be obliged to serve as a private for 36 months, (with only a meager "cigarette stipend"). His clever strategy was to divorce his wife for the duration, then remarry her after completing his required, but shorter service, as a second lieutenant.

Sela consulted with attorney friends who'd all heard of the case. They advised him that we each needed to have an attorney and a witness. Other friends volunteered to help out. Because I didn't know the language, it was decided that I could meet with a court official (the judge, I believe) beforehand to present "my case."

At the appointment time, Sela took me to the official's office, acting as my interpreter (and using a pseudonym). He didn't look at all nervous, but I felt cold and shaky inside. The judge asked me a number of routine questions which Sela translated perfunctorily. Then he asked the key question: "What is the reason for divorce?"

I'd been coached to respond with "irreconcilable differences." By way of explanation, I added: "My husband changed when he arrived here. I don't understand what's going on now. I'm not happy." In silence, the judge wrote down my responses as Sela translated them. Shaking his head resignedly, he signed and stamped the document. Our official divorce would be duly noted in the official documents registration office in Sela's hometown. The procedure didn't seem to take long for the judge. He handed over the signed document to Sela, then quite impulsively, burst out: "Tell me, what kind of man *is* her husband? What kind of man would marry this young woman, and bring her all the way from her home to Turkey, and then treat her unkindly?"

Although my language was extremely limited, somehow, at that moment, amazingly, I understood the words that the judge was saying. I looked over at Sela. His face had turned color, and he was shaking his head, as if he simply couldn't answer the last question. I'm sure my own face had gone quite pale. We solemnly thanked the compassionate judge, and quickly left the room.

Afterward, long after that morning and after some months had passed, we discussed the divorce proceedings. Sela confessed that he had really been on pins and needles that morning, especially when he saw our landlord (who is also a judge) going into the next office! But apparently, we passed by his open door without attracting his notice.

Fortunately, Sela drew lots to serve his military duty in Ankara, so he'll be able to take a bus into town to see us on his leave days. What good luck! Many fellows get sent to outlying border regions and other far-flung spots. ❦

Military Service, Ankara 1953   *Ankara College*

Journal: Teaching at Ankara College   During his first six months' military service, Sela had explained, he would receive no pay, so I should find a job teaching English. Initially, I had some qualms about this idea, having had no real teacher-training to speak of, only one summer course (plus the experience of studying college German, a semester of French, and several in Spanish). The alternative, he suggested, was staying with his family in Sürmene, where Hikmet and I would always be welcome.

I agreed to the teaching. Again, to use one of my Papa's nautical terms, I was going to have to steer my little sailing ship through strange waters and I didn't "know the ropes." But Sela was my steadfast compass. He had asked one of his friends to make an appointment for me, arranged with his brother Orhan to baby-sit with Hikmet for the day, and mailed me clear instructions on how to get to the school.

It was a 15-minute brisk walk on a crisp, fall morning. Following Sela's simple directions, I passed through the pleasant residential neighborhood, turned

56

down the busy avenue where the school was situated, strode through the main gate and entrance, and found the headmistress waiting for me in her office.

Miss Marion Nosser, I was told, was a young graduate of the University of Chicago when she was appointed by Atatürk himself to start up a "cottage school." The new president of Turkey was envisioning a comprehensive school where children could learn English at an early age, and later French or German as additional foreign languages. He borrowed the term college [kolej].

This was in the mid-30s, I guess, and the school has grown considerably since then. Now there are several dozen English-speaking teachers, mostly from England, several from Scotland, Ireland, Australia, Canada, and a few from the US. Ankara College [Ankara Koleji] is referred to as an English-medium state-supported/ tuition school. The entrance exams are highly competitive, the tuition is high, the waiting list is long.

And Miss Nosser, now gray-haired and austere-looking after 20 years of service, has an aura that immediately commanded my respect. She welcomed me warmly, introduced me to some of the other teachers, and gave me a copy of Professor Gatenby's textbook for English lessons. According to the semester's schedule, teachers are expected to follow the syllabus set out for each term, so that everyone covers the same lesson material on the same day, and assigns the same homework as their colleagues. Quizzes and tests are given to all classes on the same day.

I have been assigned to the "prep" level of the middle school, where the 12-year-old pupils study mostly basic English sentence structures and grammar. They learn simple question forms, for example, and practice a lot of question-answer drills. They seem to learn mostly by rote. I feel inadequate, but I am going to do my best. ☙

Journal: My First Cooking Lesson in Ankara   Until the apartment Sela had found for us in Yenisehir [the "new part" of Ankara] was ready for occupancy, Hikmet and I stayed in Ali Dramalı's apartment. (Ali bey is Sela's friend and former Raman Camp chief.) On the morning I was to be interviewed at Ankara Kolej, brother-in-law Orhan arrived early at the apartment to babysit Hikmet.

This meant planning an evening meal — my first in Turkey — before leaving for school. The simplest thing that came to mind was lentil soup: there was, conveniently, a bag of lentils and some onions in Ali bey's kitchen, and this was one of the few soups I knew how to cook. I carefully measured out and rinsed the lentils and left them to soak.

When I returned that afternoon, I rinsed the lentils again, cut up yellow onions and added them with a dash of salt, and let it all simmer slowly until properly tender. It had a hearty and satisfying flavor, I thought. At dinner time, I set the table, ladled out a big plate for Orhan, and smaller bowls for myself and Hikmet. We each had a big slice of fresh bakery bread on the side. This was our supper.

Orhan dug in with great enthusiasm, slowed down after several spoonfuls, then asked a question that I took to mean: "Yenge, is this your first lentil soup?"

"Hayir! [No!]" I replied proudly. "Amerika çok!" [Many, many! Much, much!] On a student's budget, lentils were always cheap, nourishing, and filling.

He took another spoonful, paused again, and asked: "Yenge, begging your pardon, are these lentils clean?"

I quickly looked up the word for "clean" in the dictionary and nodded, pointing to the kitchen faucet. "Hmm," he muttered, and got up to look at the bag of lentils in the cupboard. He poured out a quarter cupful on a tray and brought it over to show me. I could tell this was going to be some kind of demonstration.

Starting from one edge of the tray, he slowly and methodically sifted through the little brown legumes, from time to time carefully pushing aside what appeared to be tiny white specks. As he sorted intently, he piled up a lot of these specks. "Look," he said, pointing. On close inspection, I could see that the specks were, in fact, tiny white *stones*.

"Look," he pointed to his soup plate. There, on its rim, was a small pile of the stones. "Clean!" he said in a commanding tone, pointing to the tray.

"OK," I nodded, to show I understood this new meaning of the verb "to clean." I often recall Orhan's graphic demonstration, which applies not only to legumes, but to rice and any other dried food stuff. I take care to look things over carefully, and pick out any tiny foreign objects before washing and cooking. ❦

Letter to Bill's Father in Tulsa

Süleyman Sırrı Street, Ankara
January 10, 1954

Dear Mr. Brownfield,

What a kind muse inspired your gift of the *Atlantic*, one of my favorite journals! It gives me the sort of intellectual stimulation I need, especially after teaching children all day long. I can't thank you enough!

Sela, Hikmet, and I have been here in Ankara since September. Sela is finally in the Army in officer's training, which ends in May. He may finish his following year's duty in the oil fields, as there seems to be a surplus of officers and a dearth of engineers. Fortunately, his school is near Ankara, and he comes home some weekends.

I am teaching English and science in English at Ankara College. It has a kindergarten and elementary school, with separate boys' and girls' classes in middle school through senior high (more on a junior college level). It was founded by Atatürk himself; the dedicated headmistress who is now my boss was appointed by him personally.

Seniha Atalı, Sela's young relative from Sürmene, lives with me and takes wonderful care of Hikmet while I teach at the school. I also teach evening classes for adults at the Turkish-American Association. [This is a bicultural center supported in part by the U.S. Information Agency in Washington DC.] And I have private students now and then. There's no spare time at all, but I'm happy that teaching keeps us out of the red, since Sela gets no salary at all in basic training,

I feel very bad that we've neglected Bill all this time, but I've got to grind away until summer vacation. Then I hope to do plenty of letter writing.

58

Could you or Mrs. Brownfield please drop a little note just to let us know how Bill is doing? We wish he'd come here for a visit. It might be just what he needs.

Our very best to you all, most sincerely,
Anna Maria Malkoç

Seniha & Baby Hikmet

Anna Maria & Baby Hikmet

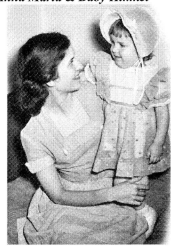

Letter to Family and Friends

Ankara Koleji, Ankara
March 16, 1954

Dear Family and Friends, Greetings!

Spring has risen, and so have I, at long last! Although to rise to the task of answering this monumental pile of letters leaves me somewhat fainthearted. In all truth, I meant to keep my New Year's resolution to answer each letter personally. But, as you may have divined from my pure and gloriously polished language (typing excepted), I've been teaching English in Ankara! I have classes at Ankara College from 8:30 a.m. until four p.m. every afternoon and half-days on Saturdays; adult classes three evenings a week; and a private student six hours a week. Plus all the homework to check, which I don't like to think of now, this being vacation week.

My newest blessing is Seniha, Sela's sister's teen-aged step-daughter. (It took me a while with my scant Turkish to figure this out.) She arrived from Erzurum to help with Hikmet, and takes wonderful care of her while I teach.

It's a lovely spring day today, perfect for spring cleaning. Seniha has been diligently scrubbing the apartment and I've been "de-winterizing" all the moth-balled clothing in the bath tub. [Yes, there are washing machines in existence, if you have a really luxurious life style.]

59

A Typical Two-Year-Old's Conversation

At the moment, two-year-old Hikmet is seated atop a mound of cushions at the coffee table, eating rice pilav and stewed figs. She is telling Seniha how much she loves eight-year-old Sema, a new private pupil who comes every day during vacation; Sema's mother is a Turkish teacher at Ankara Koleji.

H: I love Sema. Do you love Sema?

S: Yes, we all love Sema.

H: I do not love Mustafa amca. ("Uncle" Mustafa is Sema's dignified father.)

S: Why not, little darling?

H: [Long pause] I don't like his lap.

S: But he gave you some chocolates, little darling.

H: [Another long pause] Oh, I *love* Mustafa amca!

Of course, little darling's mouth is full of figs, and my powers of translation are stretched to capacity, so some of this conversation is left to my imagination to fill out. But Hikmet is now reaching the stage where she not only speaks accentless Turkish — natural for children — but knows words I haven't heard of yet.

Early this morning, for example, she and Seniha were speaking together:

H: Dear Seniha abla [elder sister], what are you doing?

S: Making the fire, my dear little Hikmet. (We have a huge, pot-bellied, cast-iron stove in the center living area that heats all the smaller rooms opening from it; it's our "central heating unit.")

H: Oh, are you making the fire?

S: Yes, my little everything. (I'm listening carefully to the verb forms.)

H: What have you in your hand, dear Seniha abla?

S: Kindling, my dear little Hikmet. (I had learned that essential word when I went to buy stove wood at the market last week, but promptly forgot it. I asked her to repeat.)

A: What did you say that was, Hikmet? (I always speak to her in English; she always understands me, but answers in Turkish.)

H: I beg your pardon, mother dear?

A: What is that, Hikmet? (I point again.)

H: It's kindling, mother dear! Don't you know? *Wood!*

By the time Seniha and I stop laughing, I've forgotten the word again and she has to write it down for me. And so it goes.

Trouble with the Water Works

Time has elapsed.... Our landlady, gesticulating wildly, just came in with Yusuf, the apartment handyman. (Every apartment house hires a janitor to attend to the coal deliveries and building maintenance, as well as regular chores and errands: carrying out the ashes, buying fresh bread daily from the bread store, mailing letters at the post office, etc.)

Yusuf immediately checked out the small wood-burning stove in the bathroom, with its unhappily-connected pipes. Although modest in size, this cast-iron stove fires up the tall, copper boiler sitting atop it and provides us with hot water for our baths and laundry (which Seniha and I do in the bathtub). For the past few weeks, unfortunately, we've been troubled with great clouds of steam from the boiler. Appropriate enough for a Turkish bath, you might say, but not when it's accompanied by blinding smoke from wet wood.... Happily, Yusuf has now fixed everything that was amiss. Unhappily, however, he has left in his wake a deluge of soot and ashes in the bathroom and in the adjoining Turkish toilet....

More Specifics on White-Tiled Telephone Booths

Oh, dear, this brings up a subject I promised long ago to elaborate upon, but have hitherto lacked the courage to tackle, as it requires a delicate approach. I've taken a casual poll of visitors from here and there, 99% of whom report failure in explaining Turkish toilets to folks back home. This may be due to a lack of sufficiently elegant euphemisms. I have worked out the following instructions for ladies; gentlemen will have to fend for themselves:

Before entering the Turkish toilet, slip on the wooden toilet clogs provided at the door. Now, imagine yourself in a white-tiled telephone booth with nothing in it but lo, a lonely water tap — and no telephone.

In the middle of the floor is a slightly raised section with foot indentations for placing your feet, (and facing the door, ladies). On the side wall down near the floor, there will be a water faucet for both washing and sluicing away. Keeping in mind there is no place to *sit*, be aware that the key verb here is *squat*. Also, that all water drains down a rather large-sized drainage [sewer] hole in the floor near the rear wall....

Fortunately, we also have a bathroom with a "throne" which permits the luxury of sitting rather than squatting. In genteel whispers, we direct guests to the Turkish or the French facility — also called English or American, depending on the visitor's nationality. "Turkish or English?" I murmured politely to the little English girl who came to Hikmet's birthday party recently. "English, if you please," she whispered back. One must be internationally alert.

A Coffee Shortage

And speaking of international crises, how's the coffee situation back home? We had a dearth of coffee here recently, which almost brought about a collapse in the general morale of the teachers at Ankara College. We feel a need for a strong stimulant during recesses, to cope with, well, just to *cope*! The underlying reason for the cornering of the coffee market, I was given to understand, was the deep and dark maneuverings of the Opposition Party here.

I received this impression from the young hamal whom I usually find in the market to carry my groceries and kindling. You may have guessed that a hamal is a basket carrier or porter, who totes a very large wicker basket strapped to his back for a living. My first thought was "How medieval," but, lacking a grocery cart or anyone else to help me carry home the week's supplies, I welcomed his services and thought the price of a silver ten-kurush coin well worth it. Note on currency value: This would buy a number of loaves of bread, the staff of life here.

Learning to Shop in the Marketplace

Oh, that you might behold these marketing expeditions! There are the regular open-air markets, of course, that flourish daily, but I shall now relate of a bi-weekly market day, or pazar (whence the word bazaar). Once a week, I manage to go before morning classes on Wednesdays, or after classes on Saturday afternoons. I take the list of fruits and vegetables Seniha writes out for me, and set off with a string bag on my arm for fresh bread. [So much for your typical

Frenchman on a bicycle with a long loaf under his arm; I take a clean string bag, and shank's mare.]

My neighborhood pazar is several blocks down the little tree-lined street. On the way, I decipher Seniha's list and run over whatever new phrases I've acquired during the past week. If I feel nonchalant, I may stop at the first row of vegetables and "have a go at it." [Unconsciously, I seem to be acquiring a lot of British English from my teaching colleagues.]

Sometimes, if I feel really "in first form," I wander causally up and down the lanes where the produce is laid out on tables. I cock an ear for prices being quoted to the local residents. First, I inquire of two or three sellers what they're asking for, say, oranges, and then I descend upon a fourth. I try to offer a price about a fourth of what the first seller asked and then go back up the price scale. (I've been told to never pay the first asking price.) If you think this is a complicated way doing the weekly shopping, you're quite, quite right! I'm no good at bargaining at all.

This is where the young basket carrier comes in handy. He usually knows where the best fruits and vegetables are, who is selling old eggs, and how much to pay for spinach this week — spinach being a very temperamental sort of vegetable. [All the fruits and vegetables, I should note, are grown with no artificial fertilizers, and are picked when sun-ripened, so their flavor is naturally delicious.]

When we return home, his tall wicker basket is loaded down with tangerines, lemons, apples, oranges, radishes, parsley, potatoes, cauliflower, cabbages, and whatever other winter vegetables are in season, plus the usual stalks of leeks dangling over the top. In addition to his usual fee, I pick out several choice pieces of fruit for himself....

Again, the Leeks!

Hikmet and I have turned into great leek eaters. I've learned to take a pinch of salt, a handful of rinsed rice, a couple of white onions, and several stalks of chopped leeks. Then I add a little olive oil, put on the lid on the pressure cooker and let it steam for about 20 minutes. Note: This dish may turn out like several other things I might mention. "You have to get used to it."

Later, the next day.... My regular private pupil arrived for his English lesson; Dr. Hatipoglu is a pediatrician preparing to go to New York for a year's special training. Very conveniently for us, Hikmet and I can get typhoid shots, or whatever we need for whatever may be floating around.

Spring has gone behind a rain cloud this morning, and here I am with Hikmet and her three little friends, ready to set off for the local train to the zoo. But what's a rain shower or two compared to a cageful of live monkeys and a real elephant? The zoo is next to the famous model farm designed by Atatürk.

Well, more next time, whenever that may be. Greetings from the Chief Türk — who only comes home on weekends to flex his new Army muscles. Also from Little Darling and me.

Our very best to all! A

Journal: An Engagement Party in Ankara On one fortunate occasion, Sela and I were invited to the engagement party of Ibrahim, a young man who had worked at the Raman camp when we were there. It was fortunate because that weekend Sela had leave from military duty and we could actually go together.

The family of the bride-to-be were Armenian Turks, as were many of the guests; this made it especially interesting for me, since Alice hanım, my dear neighbor from Raman Camp, also Armenian, was one of the guests. We sat down together on chairs lining the entire perimeter of the long salon. In an aside, Alice whispered that the prospective bride's father owns a popular night club in Ankara and the musicians already ensconced in one corner were from his club. As they played old favorites for the crowd, they bantered good-naturedly back and forth with the guests. They all seemed to know each other well.

Sela was chatting away with several school friends he hadn't seen in years; this is always happening to him out in public. There were even parents of some of my Ankara College pupils, who recognized me from the last parent-teachers' meeting. The young bride-to-be told me she'd recently graduated from Ankara College herself.

It seemed quite possible, if you chatted long enough, to find some kind of connection with the person sitting at your elbow: same neighbors, hometown, relatives, or relatives of relatives, Army service, school friends. At any rate, everyone was conversing in high spirits by the time the sumptuous buffet table was ready. The lady of the house and mother of the bride-to-be was busy seeing to it that everyone had enough to eat and drink. I admired her dynamic energy.

A Former Night Club Dancer

I also admired her fashionable hairdo and elegant brocade cocktail dress, both in the latest Parisian style. As I sat taking in these details from the corner of my eye, I saw our attractive hostess gave a nod to the musicians to strike up traditional harem dance (belly dance) music. From some hidden pocket in her dress, she pulled out a voluminous, diaphanous chiffon scarf to wave as she gyrated slowly and sinuously to the beat of the musician's tambourines.

This was a shock for me, fresh from Sürmene where women danced only in front of women. (Or for their husbands.) I gave Sela a quick nudge, but he didn't seem at all surprised. "She used to be a night club dancer," he whispered. "In her younger days."

Who Pays the Piper?

I watched in fascination as our hostess danced in front each male guest, pausing and gyrating to the accelerated tempo, until the guest pressed a bill into her outstretched hand. The money magically disappeared somewhere in her brocade bodice, but not before I'd glimpsed the denominations: ten, twenty, fifty, one hundred lira bills. I gasped. My entire monthly salary was only 700 liras!

Sela was laughing uproariously along with the crowd as the dancer approached one male guest waving a tempting handful of bills at her. He waved, but would not relinquish the money.

The musicians increased their tempo, the dancer gyrated in ever more sinuous twistings until she achieved a marvelous snake-like back-bend. At this point, the tempter relented and gave the dancer her due. "Everybody knows he's a rich tightwad," murmured Alice.

It struck me then that the dancer had slowly been making her way around the end of the drawing room, and would soon be in front of Sela. "Alice," I whispered desperately, "Sela has only five liras in his pocket! What should he do?"

"Don't worry," she whispered back. "Everybody knows Malkoç is in the Army. She won't stop by him!" And she didn't — only winked at him as she danced by.

On the way home after dinner, I asked Sela why, if her husband was indeed such a wealthy nightclub owner, the hostess was dancing for money.

"The money wasn't for herself," he explained. "It was for the musicians. She just likes to dance!" ❦

Letter to Bill

Süleyman Sırrı Street, Ankara
March 17, 1954
Dear Bill,

To say that your latest letter elated me is to *understate!* (That's my close association with my British colleagues and their understating!) How could I have let this much time go by without sending felicitations and congratulations! What luck, Bill! What wonderful luck!

As I recall, when your letter came about a month ago, I'd just been thinking about a common and unfortunate recurrence in my life: meeting interesting people just as I'm about to journey off. Kathryn was a point in mind. I'd barely said "Hello" to her before I had to say "Goodbye," when we left Tulsa.

At any rate, blessings on you both, and best wishes for a rich and eventful adventure in your marriage. Predestined for you, I'm sure.

Also, I must tell you the book arrived, for which I thank you profusely. The story I like best so far is about the whale. (Yes, I know it's for Hikmet, but she can wait!) It's a priceless book. If she grows up with an imaginative mind to appreciate it, I could hardly ask for more.

Yes, would you kindly send the last letter around to the existing group? I dare say Mary Fitzgerald — now Mrs. John C. Guilfoyle — would see to it that Rosalie would make mimeograph copies, as usual? Rosalie, by the way, sent a lively and newsy letter recently, so also did Aung Ki Moe, and Mimi. Please give them our love.

As always, A

Journal: Ordering Coal for the Winter Our apartment is a nice fifteen-minute walk to school, and only ten minutes to the open-air market where I am learning to shop for fresh food. On certain mornings, I make time to do the shopping and have it carried home with me before I set off for school.

Seniha helps me make out my shopping list, pronouncing the words carefully so I can spell and memorize them. Sometimes her Black Sea accent confuses me so I check the dictionary — which I neglected to do on the morning I went off to the neighborhood coal depot office to order our ration of winter coal.

Sela had already registered me at our new address and explained the procedure for ordering a load of coal, so I had the required amount of liras and the official permit in hand as I entered the little office. Several men were standing about drinking tea and smoking cigarettes. I approached the man behind the desk and politely said good morning.

He responded politely and asked what I would like. I assumed it was already obvious: "Chomur, lutfen," [Coal, please] I said, and handed him the permit. At my response, all three men stopped in their tracks. I repeated myself and handed him the money for one load, as designated on the paper. Now, the men were all smiling.

"Chomur?" The man at the desk put down his pen and stared at me. "Afedersiniz, hanım efendi. Amerikalı mısınız?" [Excuse me, madame, are you American?]

"Yes," I nodded.

"Ah.... Afedersiniz, hanım efendi, Türkçe nerede ogrendiniz?" [Excuse me, madame. Where did you learn Turkish?] he inquired quietly.

"Sürmene," I answered. The other men were all really smiling now, probably, I thought, at the idea of an American woman in that provincial Black Sea town.

The man at the desk pointed to the piles of coal outside his back window, and shook his head. "*Ch*omur degil. *K*omur, hanım efendi." [It's not czhoal; it's coal, madame.] He calmly deposited my money in a box, wrote out a receipt showing the delivery date, at which time it will be dumped in back of our apartment building, then stored in the coal room.

I thanked him politely. He stood up and bowed politely as he handed me the receipt. I made a mental note as I walked out, always to check my dictionary, especially for the standard pronunciation. ❧

Journal: Bargaining in the Market Place Usually, my shopping forays are pleasant adventures, and educational. Now I know where to buy tea glasses and a big tea kettle. I have observed some vendors provide sacks made of newspaper for staples such as sugar, rice, dried beans; some fastidious shoppers bring their own plastic bags for these items. Or glass jars for pickles from the large crocks. And most shoppers carry some kind of crocheted string bag for their purchases; I have several.

I'm learning the names for root vegetables and greens, and seasonal produce like apples, pears and quinces. Also citrus fruits shipped up from the Mediterranean coast.

I'm also learning to handle the money and do the arithmetic in my head. Basically, the Turkish coins are easy: the currency is based on a metric system and corresponds to U.S. dollars. One lira is the equivalent of 100 kurush [very tiny brass coins scarcely in use any more], a five-kurush coin which I think of as a nickel, a ten-kurush piece that must have some silver in it and looks like a dime, and a 25-kurush piece the size of a quarter. There is no 50-kurush coin, but there is a 2 1/2-kurush coin, brass with a hole in the center, that throws me off when counting in Turkish. (I'm training myself to do this because my natural tendency is to count in English.)

Last market day was a significant experience in buying radishes.

Some bright red radishes on a vendor's table caught my eye. The small scrap of paper on the top bunch was marked *5 K*. As I fumbled for a five-kurush coin, another customer came up next to me.

"How many kurush?" the man asked the seller, pointing to the adjacent carrots, marked *10 K*. The seller picked up a large bunch, and I listened carefully.

"Ten kurush, sir," he declared.

"Two and a half kurush," the buyer countered nonchalantly. They began haggling, good naturedly.

"Eight," the seller laughed.

Without losing a beat, the customer said: "Three kurush."

"Seven and a half, sir."

The customer compromised. "Five kurush?"

"Tamam." [All right] By now other customers were lining up and the seller was anxious to finish this transaction. "Five kurush, bey efendi." Coins exchanged hands and apparently everyone was happy.

Now it was my turn, for the radishes. "Please," I said pointing, and gave him a 25-kurush piece from my coin purse. The seller picked out a nice bunch and dropped several coins, including a holed coin, into my outstretched hand. For a long moment I stood there, coins in hand, doing my mental counting in Turkish. The man must have thought I was unhappy with the change, and dropped several more small coins into my hand! Was this a kind of silent, passive haggling? How much easier, I thought to myself. I really hate having to bargain for anything.

Sometimes, after classes on Saturday afternoons, Seniha, Hikmet and I all go grocery shopping together, which is more enjoyable, and with less mental anguish. ❦

Journal: More English Teaching, More Friends The long and demanding school year at Ankara Koleji finally ended. I have learned a lot about teaching and made many new friends among the teaching staff, especially Helen Sorhus from Canada and Molly Emre from England. But, everyone, without exception, is friendly and helpful to one other, and our paths continuously intersect in Ankara. I feel fortunate to have these friends.

When I wanted to find a doctor for a check-up, friend Mollie recommended her physician, Dr. Kent, who speaks English (having trained in London). Later, I came down with a severe case of summer dysentery and went back to Dr. Kent. At first he feared amoebic dysentery, said to be incurable, but his medication eventually cured my case. I was weak for some time, but recovered and was able to look for an easier teaching job. There is no shortage!

Friends from Ankara Koleji steered me to the Georgetown Program, or GELP for short, [Georgetown University English Language Program], where they were hiring native speakers of American English to teach pronunciation classes using their new teaching material. The GELP linguists have been writing (quite non-traditional) lessons for teaching English to groups of selected Turkish Air Force personnel, agriculturists, and other professionals preparing to be sent for training in the U.S. Some of the more traditional teachers are reluctant to adopt their methodology (called "mim-mem" for mimicry and memorization) in which the students have to listen and repeat until the patterns become ingrained. The approach seems to work well with some of the students, but not all.

From time to time, we locally-hired Americans attend seminars taught by the linguists and teacher-trainers sent by the U.S. Information Agency in Washington, DC.

To supplement the summer earnings from the morning classes, I joined several other colleagues who were also teaching evening classes for adults at the Turkish-American Association. This is another challenge in life! I find in many ways it's easier for me to teach adults than children. And, here again, to my good fortune, I've made more new friends: Marion Türker, a wonderfully kind and helpful executive secretary in the office, and Edith Oyhon, an experienced teacher who gives me useful pointers. Their husbands are also doing their military service, so we have a strong common bond.

Edith and another teacher, Ann Whitlock, have introduced me to their friend Elizabeth Brown across the street from the Center. Elizabeth, who is expecting, says she's got "cabin fever" staying at home with her small daughter, so she's happy whenever we can drop by for coffee. Dan, her husband, is a news correspondent at the American Embassy.

Someday I hope to see my friend Perihan Turgay, a young attorney at MTA [the Mining and Metallurgy Institute that gave Sela scholarships to study in Germany and the US.] When I came up from Raman Camp with Hikmet last summer, Perihan hanım and Alice hanım treated me to a delicious dinner at Bomonti, a garden night club owned by one of Alice's friends. It was a delightful night out! ❦

Letter to Bill and Kathryn

Süleyman Sırrı Street, Ankara
November 12, 1954

Dear Bill and Kathryn,

What good news! I couldn't wish greater happiness to two nicer people! Well, well, Kathryn! You and me in the same month! There's something so special about the first one. I remember feeling like the Queen of the May,

My sister sent me Dr. Reade's words of wisdom in his book *Natural Childbirth*. I'm doing my old exercises again, taking vitamins, and going to a top-notch English-speaking obstetrician here in Ankara.

I left the Kolej at the end of the school year. The evening course which I'm teaching now is at the Turkish American Association; it ends in January. We're hoping Sela will finish his military service back in the oil fields. He'll then have an income while I'm not working. He's here now, and all is well, although we had to arrange a "divorce of convenience." A most complicated situation....

Hikmet Becomes Bilingual

Hikmet is flourishing, as usual. She wants to know where Uncle Bill is, what a ship is, and if America is near Istanbul. Our present conversations are almost entirely in English. She started speaking English recently when Helen

Sorhus, a teacher from Canada, stayed with us for a month. One day, I asked Helen, who doesn't speak a word of Turkish, how she managed to get along with Hikmet when I was off teaching classes. (Hikmet understands me in English, but always answers in Turkish.)

"Very nicely," Helen said. "We both speak English, of course." So, it was during Helen's visit that Hikmet, perforce, became bilingual. Her Turkish, at age two and a half, is fluent — judging by her playmates' language skills. Now her spoken English is also progressing rapidly. Sela suggests hiring her out as an interpreter, so we could retire.

Life in the Capital

Ankara is lovely in the autumn. Municipal gardeners are preparing all the parks and children's playgrounds for the winter. Each season brings out different flower bed arrangements all along the length of Atatürk Boulevard, which runs several miles from the main shopping center in Ulus down in the old part of the city, up to the crest of the hill near the President's Palace. The boulevard is like one long, slim tree-lined park, with brightly colored asters and zinnias and brilliant scarlet flowers trailing in clusters. The leaves from the poplar trees are hosed down and raked up tidily. This must be Turkey's cleanest metropolis.

The view of Ankara from the crest outlines the hills encircling it, and emphasizes the fact that it lies in a natural basin. A smoky, bluish haze rises over the city. [Sela says it's the coal smoke from all the heating stoves using soft coal.]

I now teach only five hours a day and life seems leisurely and pleasant. Hikmet and I go walking in the mornings and late afternoons. I think of all the frantic clock-watching I'd gotten used to; now I just smile and relax. There's still time for sewing, bridge now and then, and visiting — which is a social must, to a certain extent, even for me. And once in a while, too, something intellectually exciting. Last week, a private student of mine, the husband of an opera singer, gave me tickets to "Tosca," sung in Turkish at the National Opera House. Several scenes I thought were really excellent, and I could understand a snatch of Turkish now and then! That was a peculiar feeling, suddenly comprehending the words in a familiar aria whose lyrics are always sung in a strange language.

Sorry to cut this short, but lunch hour is up — only an hour and a half! I'm enclosing a picture of Hikmet.

I do miss those hair-splitting, brain-cracking bull sessions we used to have in Tulsa, with your pot of miner's coffee and cauldron of bean soup, Bill.

"Deepest and truest" greetings from Sela, and a hand-blown kiss from Hikmet. My best to all.

As always, A

Letter from Sela

Raman Petrol Kampı
January 1, 1955

My Dearest,

First of all, my best for a Happy New Year. I hope to live with you happily for many, many, many more years!

Today is the seventh day after I left Ankara. It seems to me a year, and I miss you so much! I dream about you and Hikmet. How did you celebrate New Year up there? I hope you had a good time. We gathered in a room with 24 persons and sang and drank. On the other hand, the ladies gathered in another room and had fun, I guess.

My work here is not started yet. My pay will be 17 liras net per day. According to my calculations, I will be able to send you 600 a month easily, I think that should be enough for you to live on. So please don't try to sign more private students; you should take it easy now.

How is Hikmet? I sure miss her! How is Seniha? I hope she is happy and getting along fine. Please don't leave her at home alone any more than possible. You can't ever tell what might happen and we are responsible for her.

Rifat came and saw you, naturally. If he has already not left for Raman, give him the following books from the trunk underneath our dressing table, also a typewritten paper about "pressure-gauge" or "bottom-hole pressure bomb" for measuring the bottom hole pressure of a well. (It might be in a book or folder as a loose-leaf or bound booklet). The titles to look for are: *Reservoir Engineering* (3 books) and a production engineering manual (green).

Say hello to Elizabeth and Daniel Brown, Edith and others, please. In closing, kiss Hikmet for me twice and say hello to Seniha. Please take care of yourself. I love you.

Only yours, Sela

Letter from Sela

Raman Petrol Kampı
January 26, 1955

My Dear Schatzi,

With the exception of this week, I have been writing to you every week and you haven't answered any of my letters. I worry and worry. Today I decided to send a telegram. I received a letter from brother Sabri with some pictures that he had taken during his stay in Ankara. I am sending you those pictures.

How is the weather in Ankara? Are you going to have enough coal supply? Sometime around March, you will have to pay 55 liras more to the landlord; I probably will be there by that time.

I am fine, not doing too much. I only worry about you. In closing, my love to Hikmet. With my best love, Sela

Letter from Mother in Spokane

Route 4, Box 188, Spokane
January 29, 1955

Dear Anna Maria,
    Got your letter this week.... Joyce is at the Deaconess Hospital, expecting any time. The new babies are all fine (Camilla's, Nona's, Rosemary's). You will get announcements from them all, so it'll be a surprise!
    Since Uncle J.B. passed away last summer, Aunt Mill is planning to come here the last of March. She will live here with me and maybe visit her family once a year on trips, so I'm getting ready to have her room done over....
    Have heard from Dr. Eber at the Sacred Heart Hospital. That is, he called me with the help of another doctor (he is certainly no English speaker over the telephone.) Then I went up to see what his hours are and left some home-baked cookies for him. He's an interne in Pediatrics, and his Turkish name has been shortened to Dr. Eber for convenience. I called our Dr. Smith, who has patients at Sacred Heart; he promised to extend a hand to Dr. Eber. As soon as things simmer down a little, we will bring him out here for a family visit.
    Had a letter from Mike, he's back in Korea from a furlough in Japan. One line in his letter was censored! He is now a corporal for his fine work on amphibian tracks. We are in a jittery state here at the Filter Center.

Our regards to all of your family. With love, Ma

Letter from Sela

Raman Petrol Kampı
January 31, 1955

My Dearest,
    I received your nice last letter last night, which you had written right after receiving my telegram.... I sent you 500 liras by telegram yesterday and will come to Ankara around the end of next month. I won't be receiving any money, in Ankara, but we probably will manage. There is not much news around here, only that Alice hanım, our neighbor Mrs. Boynton, Mübeccel hanım and Nesrin hanım send their regards. Rıfat asks if Hikmet is still keeping up with her jokes.

With all my love, Your Sela

Journal: My Batman Neighbors Meral and Mübeccel   I often miss my old friends in the States, and I also miss my newer friends in Batman, wondering how they're getting along out there in the boondocks.
    I think of the new bride Meral, wife of Selahattin Özkan. Of all of Sela's school friends, Özkan dates back the furthest: they went to high school together in Trabzon and studied together in Germany, also in Queens College in Flushing

NY. When Özkan became officially engaged to Meral in Ankara, he brought her to our apartment here for dinner — on a weekend when Sela had leave — so "we could all get a good look at her."

Meral was daintily pretty, sweet, and shy. Also very nervous to be out with her fiancé, the tall, dark, and handsome Özkan. [Dating does not seem to be a custom here at all.] After they married, he brought her to Batman and we became neighbors. Now, several years later, she's prettier than ever, and not quite so shy!

Mustafa Solim, who was at UW and at Tulsa U, is another old friend who married and brought his bride to Batman. His wife, Mübeccel, is also pretty and sweet, but I think she has enough spunk to hold her own with Mustafa, who's a less intimidating personality than the dashing Özkan.

I look forward to seeing these dear friends once again when we go back to Raman. ☙

Raman Oil Derrick

Letter from Sela

Raman Kampı
February 6, 1955

Anna Maria Darling,

Received your letter yesterday when I came back from Reshan Camp. The well over there is lost because a drill pipe got stuck.

I do worry about you so much. How is your coal supply? Will it be enough for the rest of the winter? Take care of yourself and don't catch cold!

I am glad that you can go to the opera, and that you bought a tricycle for Hikmet's birthday. Today is her birthday! All I can do is say Happy Birthday, Hikmet! I miss her so much, darling.

I don't need anything you could send from Ankara at the moment.

Hasan, Bezmen, Hulusi, Abdi, and the new director of the Company are coming to Raman today. I guess there is going to be a big gathering here in a week. Please let me know when I should come to Ankara, so I can let the office know, and can reserve a place on the plane or train.

Özkan's wife, Meral, is in Ankara now. She is also going to give birth around the 15th of March, so Özkan and I will be coming to Ankara around the same time. I conveyed your regards to everyone and everybody says hello from here.

Isn't it nice that Camilla and Nona are fine and already had their kids? Are you thinking for a name for ours? Think about it and let me know. I am giving the opportunity to you; you name this one, will you?

Give my regards to everyone. Kiss Hikmet for me.

With my deep love, yours alone, Sela

Journal: Names When Sela and I married, his father sent his blessings, along with a name for our first born: "Hikmet."

I was surprised at this, but Sela said it was the custom. "If, and when, we do have a child," I had asked him, "how does your father know what it will be?"

"It's a name for a girl *or* a boy," he said, and continued to translate the letter. His father had explained that the name means "divine omniscience" and wrote: "Whoever would have known that Selahattin, born in Sürmene, would meet and marry Anna Maria, born in Spokane, on the other side of the world? Only God would have known!" ❧

Letter from Sela

Raman Petrol Kampı
February 19, 1955

My Dearest,

I am a little late in answering your letter this week. Hasan will let you know about the goings on around here…. Tell him about my coming to Ankara; whenever you want me to come, he will arrange it, and let me know by wireless.

I am thinking of leaving here Sunday the 27th for Ankara. If you think it's the right time, please let Hasan know so that he could arrange my coming to Ankara on Company business. Özkan will be leaving for Ankara next week. He will stop by to see you.

Alice hanım is in Ankara now. She is ill. If you could see her, I think she would appreciate it. How are Hikmet and Seniha? Say hello to everyone for me. Hope to see you soon, darling. I love you. Sela

---

Journal: Cemile Arrives in Ankara Sela took the plane up to Ankara and hurried to Dr. Kent's small clinic where my friends had brought me early in the morning. I was resting in the two-bed ward, resigned to going through the event alone, when Sela suddenly appeared in the doorway in his new brown suit, looking handsomer than ever.

He sat down quietly and held my hand. The patient in the other bed, an elderly woman waiting for gall bladder surgery, was clearly curious about the two of us. Her staring got on my nerves; apparently, staring is not considered rude. It was hard for me to ignore her, but Sela greeted her politely and respectfully.

We continued to chat in low voices about all the news from the camp. Every time there was a contraction, I would give his hand a little squeeze. Finally, "It's time to go upstairs," I whispered. I didn't want to wait for the nurse, but got out of bed and headed for the door.

"She's not ready, sir," the elderly woman advised Sela, who was trying to catch up with me. "She's not making any noise!"

The nurses brought me upstairs, and Cemile arrived not long thereafter, much to my room-mate's surprise when she found out later. Sela could stay only long enough to settle up things at the clinic, and to check in with Seniha and Hikmet at the apartment before taking the train back to Batman.

Friends saw to it that Cemile and I were discharged from the clinic and escorted home in style, checked to see that Seniha was coping with groceries, kindling, and coal for the heating stove, and that Hikmet was OK. Somehow, all these arrangements were quietly "taken care of" and I never had to worry.

It was only during Sela's military training, when I had to pay for food, wood and coal, shoes for Hikmet, and rent out of a teaching salary of 700 liras, that I was forced to count every kurush. Now I can relax…. ❦

Hikmet Holding Baby Cemile 1955

Letter to Tulsa Friends

Süleyman Sırrı Street, Ankara
March 16, 1955

Dear Bill and Kathryn,

Have you yet, or haven't you? *We* have! A girl, born March 5! Her name is Cemile [Jem ee leh] and it means lovely or beautiful in old Turkish. She looks quite like Hikmet, with plump cheeks, but dark hair, just to be charmingly different. I fairly exude mother love and vitality. It's wonderful having *two* daughters.

Sela thinks so, too. He was here for a week, and left again for Raman Camp in very high spirits. He'll be back in May to assume civilian status, thank God, and will have several weeks leave here before returning to Raman. I'll probably stay here and teach until October. It's so hot at the camp in the summer.

Hasan Göker dropped in last night with the news that Mustafa Solim is also the father of a daughter. I asked Hasan if the new father was passing out cigars. Seems Mustafa was so befuddled that Hasan had to hand *him* one!

So, you find us all well and happy, especially Hikmet, who is thrilled to bits over the baby. She sings her "Rockabye Baby" and then switches over to a Turkish lullaby. And, no, my Turkish isn't anywhere near Hikmet's level, but she sweetly obliges me by interpreting any new words. Will have pictures of the family taken soon as possible. Next dispatch will cover details of a wedding, I hope. With this mysterious and tantalizing promise, I close. As always, A

Letter from Mother in Spokane

Route 4, Box 188, Spokane
March 25, 1955

Dear Sela and Anna Maria,

This is just a line to admit the new girl into the family. We are all so very thrilled that Hikmet has a sister.

The little girl cousins here – Teresa, Christina, Martha Ann, Janene — get along beautifully when they play together. They know Hikmet by her pictures and are well aware that she is "across the ocean, up in Turkey."

So our love to you all, from us all. Mother *Marie Harms Jones*

Letter from Sela

Raman Petrol Kampı
March 27, 1955

My Dearest,

Received two lovely letters from you yesterday, thank you. I am glad that you are getting along all right and that Cemile and Hikmet and Seniha are all fine.

I caught an awful cold the other day, but I am getting better everyday and feel fine already.

74

When I wrote that it would be a good idea if you came down to Raman, I meant sometime in May. I will come up around the 25th of April to get my discharge papers from the Army anyway. When I come, we will get officially remarried. Then we will come down together.

I will take Seniha back to Erzurum, I guess, if we can't find somebody to send her with. I got a letter from my father the other day. It seems that Sülhiye is going to be all alone, and they need Seniha quite badly to help around the house in Erzurum. [Seniha is Sülhiye's step-daughter.] So we have to send her there as soon as possible. The way it looks, I may have to take her myself.

Of course, we will take some of the good furniture with us when we leave Ankara for Raman. I will describe the house at Raman Camp to you:

Luxury Camp Furniture (Relatively Speaking)

Starting with the kitchen, there is a sink with cold and warm water faucets, one table, four chairs (like the ones we have for our dinner table, but a little cheaper), a nice china closet with silverware drawers, a cabinet, a six-foot Frigidaire, an oil stove, two serving stands, shelves, and a screened cabinet.

In the big bedroom, there is a nice rug on the floor, a big chrome-plated bed for two (even three), completely furnished with sheets, mattress, and blankets, a clothes closet, a clothes hanger stand, a table with magazine stands, a table lamp, and a chest of drawers.

In the living room, there is a divan with two shelves on one side, complete with cushions, an oil stove, an old standing lamp, three arm chairs, two coffee tables, shelves for books, and a floor rug.

In the small bedroom, there is only a bed and mattress. In the bathroom, there is a water heater and other miscellaneous equipment. As you know, in front of the house there is a veranda.

When I come to Ankara, I will take a 10-15 day vacation and will arrange moving the shipment of the stuff we will take down with us. It's a good idea subleasing the apartment, if you can do it.

Re-Marriage Plans

Since I won't be in Ankara before the 25th, it would be a good idea if you talk to Perihan hanım [our lawyer friend] about arrangements to get married again. Maybe Hasan would talk to her, if you can't. [Perihan speaks no English and my Turkish is inadequate.] What I am afraid of is that it might take a long time, and we must leave Ankara before the 10th of May. The Company doesn't want me to stay away from the oil field any longer because Rifat [Sela's counterpart in the refinery] may be going to the U.S. for training in reservoir engineering sometime during the next month.

Say hello to everyone for me, darling. I love you very, very much. Your Sela
PS: We will have lots of space in our trunks, don't worry.

Sela, Checking on the Pumping Operations

8

A SAD RETURN TO RAMAN

Journal: Problems Have Resolutions, Eventually Before leaving Ankara, I went to the American Embassy to register Cemile on my passport. The desk clerk, Naciye hanım, filled in the usual information, and I told her about Sela's military service and the divorce. Since we had legally divorced, the clerk explained, Cemile cannot be registered as our legitimate child. She was sympathetic with my situation, but could offer no helpful suggestions. My heart sank.

I pondered this dilemma as I walked back to the apartment, then decided to leave it to fate. There were other things more pressing at home: Hikmet was running a high fever. I went to a neighbor with a telephone and called a friend who knew an English-speaking doctor, the most popular baby doctor among foreign wives in Ankara at the time. He was kind enough to stop in after office hours to check on Hikmet, and assured me she did not have diphtheria. Rather, she had a case of tonsillitis, for which he prescribed medication.

While the doctor was there, I asked him to please check Cemile too, because every evening she seemed to cry in such distress. He gave her a general looking-over and said, "She looks very healthy, masallah. [God bless her.] You're just nervous. You American women are all nervous!" He smiled at his own witticism, though I tried to tell him I wasn't nervous when I was tending to her, I was very relaxed. But who was I to argue with a renowned pediatrician?

To my great relief, Hikmet soon recovered with the prescribed medication. Then a relative came to escort sweet Seniha on the train to Erzurum. We were all so sad to say goodbye. I don't know what I would have done without her willing help all those months.

Next, Sela arrived from Raman, we packed up our few belongings, left a few meager pieces of furniture to the next renters. Unlike leavetakings from Sürmene and Istanbul, there was no fanfare at our departure, but we were happy to be going "home" to the camp! Now that Sela has finally completed his military service, it promises be a new beginning for the four of us. ❧

Letter to Spokane and Tulsa

Raman Petrol Kampı
May 27, 1955

Dear Family and Friends:

What strange changes have been brought about in our lives! I'm back in Raman, as you see.

As field production engineer, Sela was offered the single house in the camp for us to live in, recently vacated by the chief tool pusher from Texas. Situated on the edge of the camp area, it's the only *house* here: four rooms, an immense kitchen with a refrigerator, and a shaded rose arbor in a small front garden. Ironically, life has its little compensations.

Losing Cemile

Three weeks have passed since we came back to settle into our new life here, and this is the first day I felt I am able to sit down to write the sad news.

Our return from Ankara had the saddest of beginnings.

On our very first night in the house, we unpacked our suitcases and put Hikmet to bed in her new little bedroom.

Then Cemile starting crying as if in great pain. It was such a strange sound, we sent the night watchman to fetch the camp doctor, who lives over in the first row of apartments about a city block away. Cemile cried out again, strangely, went limp, then into a coma.

Dr. Nevzat bey, a new medical school graduate with no field experience, came strolling over, took a look at the baby, then ran back for his medical bag. This took another 15 to 20 minutes. He gave her an injection to stimulate her heart, but it was obviously to no avail. She was gone in a matter of minutes. Just like that.

Sela took care of all of the arrangements, which were "very simple," he said, but which I didn't understand at all. We cried together until dawn. And I really don't understand the problem with Cemile at all, either. Something to do with glands that gradually disappear as infants grow older, another doctor surmised later.

At first, I fought back a lot of useless anger: at the young, inexperienced camp doctor's inability to help in a hopeless situation, at the pediatrician in Ankara who had checked Cemile there and pooh-poohed my complaint, at myself for not being more insistent that there really was a problem with her.

And then, in retrospect, I realize it may have been the strong medicine I took to cure my terrible dysentery last summer that affected the baby. I realized then that probably nothing could have saved her. I try to keep all these dark feelings to myself and look at it as "kismet."

Sela is quietly philosophical, and comforting. Three-year-old Hikmet had barely hardly gotten used to having a baby sister, and missed her for only a very short time. She says Cemile "is sleeping in heaven" and goes off to play with the other children in the camp.

I had never realized that a little baby of two months would leave such a void in one's heart. I cannot bear to look at other babies here. I have to keep busy with other things.

Teaching at the Refinery

Some time has passed, and Sela is finally officially out of the Army, thank heaven! At the moment, he has a crew busy pumping oil down the mountainside to the old refinery in Batman. The new refinery there will be finished within the year, and what was once a mud-hutted village on the train line is becoming a little boom town.

Americans from the Parsons Company in California, hired by TPAO (the Turkish Petroleum Company) to construct the new refinery, are training men by the dozens to operate it. And guess what! I'm also hired by the Company, to teach English classes! A driver will take me down to Batman and back — a half-hour

78

Jeep jaunt each way, for an hour's class. In preparation, I wrote to the Turkish-American Association in Ankara (where I taught last year) and they kindly sent lesson materials to adapt for my classes. The refinery office is making copies for each lesson.

I had imagined that teaching English to the untrained refinery workers might be a big challenge. But just how big a bite I'd bitten off — and might be more than I could chew — became clear the moment I was escorted into the huge, concrete garage designated for the English lessons.

The first thing I saw was an enormous blackboard painted standard dark green, some large chunks of chalk, and several flannel dust cloths placed in readiness at the front of the garage. Some 60 or 70 men sat in rows of benches facing the door, most looking ill at ease, and none holding notebook, paper, or pencil.

The refinery engineers introduced themselves and talked to the group about the course, then introduced me as their teacher.

I was acutely aware that it was not the local custom for men to speak to strange women, let alone to a non-Moslem foreigner. Choosing my words as carefully as I knew how, I introduced myself as the English teacher, and started on the first page of the lesson material. It was immediately obvious that I needed the microphone they handed me: it was a long way to project one's voice to the back of the garage, where the TPAO director and other officials from the head office in Ankara were sitting in vigilant attendance. I also realized that I needed the aid of the quiet translator patiently standing by. He proved to be more or less bilingual, and absolutely *essential*.

Momentarily ignoring my own feelings of inadequacy, my heart went out to these men willing to face such a linguistic challenge. I'm guessing most are local Kurds, have had only the slightest amount of schooling, perhaps read Turkish with difficulty. I hope I can help them learn some English. I'm going to do my best. This teaching period is for three months, long enough for the refinery supervisors to "spot the workers with more potential," Sela says.

In any case, I think simply working at the refinery is opening up new worlds to these farmers and herders, for whom a Jeep is still a novelty. (And I personally can't complain, since I'm being paid a pretty penny; it will go into my fund for opening up new travel opportunities to Spokane!)

Because there's an overflow of requests for English lessons, and time drags heavily at the camp up here, Sela has handpicked five men to have English lessons in our enormous kitchen, including several engineers who plan to go the States for training. So I'm going to begin evening classes for them three times a week. When the weather is nice, we'll have the lessons outside in the little rose arbor.

Sela's Birthday Party

Instead of having an English session last night, we celebrated Sela's birthday. The men all sat outside in the patio/gazebo playing bezique (a popular card game resembling pinochle, but more complicated). We women sat inside in the cool front room. A dozen children, including Hikmet, ran hither and yon.

Ayten hanım, the doctor's wife, had baked a cake; that is, she mixed it up and sent it to be baked in the mess hall oven. We had beer that Sela brought in from his trip to the Army draft board in Kurtalan, and ice cream I made in our real refrigerator. Luckily, it was strongly flavored with vanilla to overcome the goat milk smell. (I suspect that Halil, the water boy commissioned to bring us cow's milk from the village, had run short again, and filled up the bottle with goats' milk. It's a smell I couldn't stand in childhood and I've never gotten used to it.)

Hikmet and a collection of little neighbor girls — Ferhan, Ruhan, and Ilknur — have just arrived from an afternoon of meandering around camp, and are now finishing off the remains of the birthday cake in the kitchen. They're singing "Uskudar," the song Eartha Kitt popularized in the States. Hikmet knows all the words; the others are humming the melody.

What a wonderful time she has here, picking wild red poppies, taking rides with Sela to the rigs on the hill, talking to the camp watchman, chasing the baby donkeys, visiting the other women here. She comes home with her pockets crammed with dried raisins, white cheese, bread, chocolate, sour plums, and other tidbits. Sometimes I find a fresh egg in her sunbonnet.

Now, I'm sorry to stop this lengthy and delayed letter, because then I must start writing an exam for my first class at the refinery.

Until next time, please pass along our best to one and all. And write!

Love, A

Journal: Acclimatizing to Kurdish Wedding Music Although I've been in Turkey for two years now, life is still strange and mysterious in myriad ways. I recall how different it was in Sürmene on the Black Sea, compared to life in Aunt Saadet's house in Istanbul, and then again, here in Raman Camp! I feel I've barely scratched the surface of my existence here. I'm still struggling to comprehend Turkish, let alone Kurdish, the local language the villagers speak.

As a surprise one evening recently, Sela drove Hikmet and me down to Batman. We were to meet families of the Parsons Company engineers from California (who have been hired by the Turkish government to build the new TPAO refinery). While the new housing development is being constructed, they're living in makeshift quarters somewhat like Raman Camp, but they all seemed happily adjusting to local conditions. This was my first meeting with the Parsons people and I was impressed with their congeniality.

Not long after, a group of the Parsons executives and their wives drove up from Batman at attend a local wedding in the Raman schoolhouse. As this was an official courtesy invitation, to be equally courteous, we all went.

By the time we entered, the chairs lined up around the long hall were filling up fast with entire families dressed in their best. The musicians were already assembled at the end of the hall, playing lively tunes on stringed instruments, reedy pipes, and a big bass drum. The atmosphere was happy and festive, with lots of excited children running about underfoot.

Sela made all the official introductions for our group. I took a seat next to Opal Kaye, one of the Parson wives, and we watched the musicians as we chatted. She'd been music superintendent for schools in her hometown in California, she told me.

80

I was curious. "As a music teacher, Opal, how do you like this Kurdish wedding music?"

"When are they going to *start?*" she asked.

"They've been playing for some time," I whispered.

"Oh," she said in her gentle, apologetic voice. "I thought they were tuning up!" Like language, music is something else requiring a new ear. ❦

Letter from Mother in Spokane

Route 4, Box 188, Spokane
June 8, 1955

Dear Anna Maria,

Just a line to let you know that we all had your letter of May 11. Some how, we just couldn't sit down and answer sooner. I think the girls all felt as bad as I did about losing little Cemile. Even if we had never seen her, she was one of the family and we all loved her as one of the youngest group. I'm very glad that she was one of us all, and loved as such a one. No matter how short or long a life is, it should be counted by the love and consideration of people nearest to it. Otherwise, there is nothing.

The whole family wants to send Sela and you a word of sympathy. The boys too, although they don't seem to be able to say it, but they do feel it. Tell Sela that, please do.

David, Aaron, and Wally are busy building their houses. Pete is home to stay, working at the shop and puttering around the place, not "engaged" yet.

Aunt Mill is delayed coming here; something is very wrong with Rita's health.

Will write again soon. With love, Ma

Journal: A Trip to Diyarbakır and My Hero on a Big White Horse At first light one recent morning, the senior field engineer from the refinery rumbled up to Raman oil camp in the company station wagon. Abdi bey announced that he and Sela had company business in Diyarbakır, and because they would be returning the same day, little Hikmet and I were invited along for a "change of scenery."

Riding down the winding mountain road in the early dawn, we passed an occasional still-sleeping village nestled against low hills, surrounded by long stretches of flat, brown fields. Some areas under cultivation — what I would call "scrabble farming" —were demarcated here and there by wobbly rows of light-colored stones to indicate ownership.

We crossed the broad plain and neared the bend of the Tigris River just as the rose-colored rays of the sun dawned across the landscape, illuminating flocks of white sheep grazing along the dark green riverbanks. Their silvery, tinkling bells resounded sweetly in the morning air.

We drove through a gate of the ancient city walls, stopped at a tiny pastry shop for a typical Diyarbakır breakfast: strong black tea in bell-shaped glasses, syrupy apricot jam, salty black olives, juicy watermelon slices, slabs of salty white cheese, and thick slices of traditional bread, still warm and fragrant from the city bakery oven.

Next stop was the Company's guest house, where Hikmet and I were left off, along with a tray of fresh simits [sesame rolls] and instructions to Aslan, the tea maker on duty, to bring us hot tea, coffee or lemonade, as we desired.

We two were the only guests on this sunshiny spring morning. Aslan, a friendly and hospitable fellow, invited Hikmet for a walk-about in the flowering garden. They discovered ripe mulberry bushes, practiced how to pick the soft red berries without crushing them. Aslan obligingly found a small paper sack for Hikmet to fill it up and take home.

While they were absorbed in this delicate and painstaking pastime, I found a comfortable nook to settle down near fragrantly blooming jasmine, one eye on my book, another on the two berry pickers. The morning passed pleasantly. Abdi bey and Sela finished their business in town, we had lunch together at a hotel restaurant, and set off for home in a relaxed and rested mood.

As usual, Abdi bey drove and Sela sat next to him in the front seat, quietly discussing oil rigs and pipeline situations at the Raman location. Hikmet snoozed on her pillow in the back seat next to me, while I took in the scenery unfolding before us. We were passing the curving bend of the Tigris, where the narrow dirt road straightens out westward through the treeless countryside, when my eye was drawn to a solitary plane tree. It stood, a stark sentinel, at the edge of a rocky field. Abdi bey waved his hand in its direction, announcing in the manner of a tour guide: "Local bandits call that the 'Lone Tree.'"

Scarcely were the words out of his mouth when *Thunk! Thunk! Thunk!* One of the rear tires went flat. "Oh-oh," he muttered, pulling over to the side of the road. "I'm afraid we have no spare."

"Don't worry!" said Sela. Without a second's hesitation, he climbed out and set off at a lope for the nearest village, several kilometers back down the road we had just come along. We watched his running figure as it quickly moved down the road and disappeared from view. The realization then hit me: Abdi bey, little Hikmet, and I were all alone in the middle of nowhere....

"Well, Anna Maria, don't worry about the bandits," said Abdi bey, in an effort to reassure me. "They're only interested in money. They never harm women or children."

That thought had not as yet entered my mind, but now that it had, it lingered....

"I'm hungry," said Hikmet, pulling out her sack of mulberries. She politely offered them first to Abdi bey, who politely declined. "Okay, one mulberry for you, Mother, one mulberry for me..." She began a counting game with the berries. Time passed slowly. The sun began to sink behind the hills.

Two sheepherders materialized from the shadowy scrub brush on the other side of the road. Abdi bey meandered over to them. In the still air, their voices carried clearly and I could hear him, in his kindly, gruff way, introducing himself and asking after the well-being of the men. How were they? Were they in good health? And how were their families? (Sela had once explained a conversational courtesy about *family*: a man would not ask how another man's *wife* is; he would ask how his *family* is.)

82

"Have you children?" Abdi bey asked the older of the two men.

"I have, sir," the shepherd replied. He sounded pretty matter of fact.

"How many?"

"Nine, but several died." Now he sounded philosophical; it was the will of Allah, after all.

Abdi bey commiserated with the man, wished good health upon his head. He continued his polite small talk. "How many boys? How many girls?"

"All boys, mister." responded the shepherd, staunchly. "We don't count the girls."

The younger man, listening silently, pulled a crude, foot-long steel knife out of his leather shoulder bag. From where I was standing, the blade looked heavy, menacingly sharp, and I felt a flash of fear simply at the sight of it.

He reached into the bag again, pulling out a large loaf of village bread. Silently, he sliced off a chunk and offered it to us. Knowing this was their daily sustenance, I was quite touched, and politely refused for myself and Hikmet, still nibbling away at her mulberries. But Abdi bey, always courteous and sensitive to local custom, accepted a piece. Now and then, he chewed away at the bread as he continued his conversation with the two men.

Daylight was waning. Time crawled along at a slow pace. Little Hikmet's curiosity, in the meantime, had led her to wander about to look at "interesting insects" and "unusual rocks" in the ditches on either side, and then back into the middle of the dusty road. It was she who first spotted her father in the hazy distance.

"Oh! Look way down there!" she shouted proudly. "It's Daddy! On a big white horse!" Sure enough, there was Sela, looking more heroic than ever, astride a large plow horse. He was followed by the local village muhtar [headman] and a motley procession of men and boys on foot behind him. He slowed the horse down and dismounted by the station wagon.

At this point, Abdi bey stepped forward to greet the village crowd who had so immediately come to our rescue.

Simultaneously, a large army truck pulled up from the other direction and disgorged a half-dozen gendarmes. These regional police officers had been alerted by the muhtar and were ready, their spokesman announced, to assist the "engineers from the refinery." Instantly, the quiet, dusty road was aswarm with uniformed men moving about, one issuing orders, the others carrying out orders. In no time flat, the flat was fixed!

Hikmet and I stood at one side, quietly observing, as Abdi bey and Sela formally thanked the gendarmes, the village muhtar, and all our rescuers, individually; the shepherds and their sheep had long since melted into the darkening shadows.

We four travelers happily piled into the repaired vehicle, waved more goodbyes, and drove off to Raman Mountain.

It was late that night when we finally got back to camp. What a relief to wash the mulberries from Hikmet's face and hands and tuck the sleepy child into bed. What a relief to be *home*, safe and sound.

"And thanks!" I murmured gratefully to my hero. "Thanks for the change of scenery!" ❦

Raman Petrol Kampı
July 14, 1955

Dear Camilla,

Your letter and pictures came today. Hikmet was so thrilled about the children: "Who is this? This? And this? Is his name Andrew? Where is Janene?" She always recognizes "Grandmother" and talks about her constantly.

Travel Plans for Mama

Sela and I spend a lot of time discussing plans for Mama's trip here. I get so excited myself I don't know where to start in.

First, a word about freighters. They're undependable as far as departure is concerned, because of their loading, unloading schedules, etc. Pretty risky. We were marooned an extra two weeks in New York, remember, which cost us a borrowed $200, living frugally. That was Fugazy, a Turkish agency.

About the time of year, another word. Winter ocean travel may not be bad, but the winter weather here is lousy. It gets cold, and travel is hard. It may snow in up here. Around March, it starts to loosen up. April, I think, would be a nice time to arrive, but I'm not sure about the weather while getting to Turkey. Up to April, Istanbul is cold and damp. Miserable weather. Worse than Seattle.

Here the climate is about like Spokane, but much, much hotter in the summer. Last week it was 104 Fahrenheit, and going up every day. When it gets too hot, the storks take off for cooler parts; that's how we know about the weather changes. Spring and fall are the nicest traveling times in Turkey, but I'm no authority about the weather on the bounding main. (It was bounding, sure enough, in January when we were on the Mediterranean!)

Don't know much about tourist restrictions re bringing things into Turkey. but there are only several things that I yearn for. Some bras (the Turkish word sütyen translates loosely as milk bag, and how apt!); nylon panties; and Max Factor makeup. Also, costume jewelry: rhinestones for pierced ears are the rage. Plastic playing cards. Bobby pins. But these things are not really important, and I'm just rambling on….

Failing as a Daughter-in-Law

A side note about Sela's family. This is personal, Camilla; you probably ought to skip this paragraph when reading it out aloud. Sela's mother is extremely nervous sometimes; they say this is the case with people who have diabetes. (?) I never quite made it back to Sürmene, you notice. And all the times Sela's father came to stay with us in Ankara, he never said thank you. Of course, I know he's "not supposed to!"

The last visit was for two weeks, before Cemile was born. I was teaching from nine to five, had private students at night, was seven months pregnant, and had to supervise the food. Frankly, I'm really a poor cook and I can't eat heavy, fried foods, or lots of salt. Young Seniha, a teen-ager, had to do all the cooking, and of course, she can't cook like her mother yet! The food wasn't very palatable, I'm afraid, for Sela's father.

Once I tried to make a cup of Turkish coffee because Seniha was busy with Hikmet. I boiled it up in the little saucepan like miner's coffee, poured it into a demitasse cup, put it on a little tray with a doily, and brought it to him. I watched his face while he took his first sip. "OK?" I asked. He smiled, shook his head, said something that I took to mean that if his daughter had made it, it would not be acceptable but since I was learning, he would accept my effort....

The first pot of tea I made for him was equally embarrassing. Like the coffee ritual, I had observed but never really practiced the necessary steps in making tea. I filled up a tea glass from a pot of tea that I not only had not allowed to steep, I'd used water that had never come to a boil. The result was as if I'd simply turned on the warm water tap and let it run over a few dry tea leaves. I'm really a failure at Turkish refreshments.

He left one morning, while I was off teaching. I'm sure he missed home cooking!

Feeling at Home in My Own Home

Mind you, I respect him tremendously because he's Sela's father, but that was the only time Sela and I really quarreled. What Sela didn't understand — poor Sela, he was in the middle — was my feeling about having "my" home. It's really "our" home, but I think of it sometimes as "mine" in relation to Turkish homes in general. At the time, I was working hard to earn money for the rent, the food, everything, since Sela wasn't getting a salary in the Army. And trying to adjust to yogurt, Turkish verbs, leaving my street shoes at the door, and all those things everywhere else. But in my own house, I have a need to feel mistress of my own domain. Sela is really "the boss" in important decisions, but you see what I mean, I hope.

The thing was, I felt like a stranger in someone else's home whenever Sela's father was there. I hope he never knows this, because I'm sure he would be hurt, but that's the way I *feel*. If he didn't take everything as his due, he'd be welcome to everything I earned. Oh, well, you know me and my emotions. I'll get over it. I just have to let off steam now and then. And, I guess I have to make a greater effort to adjust to customs.

Anyway, enough of that. Mama will want to bring a special gift for them, which would be very nice. I'll ask Sela what would be appropriate. He says, "We'll load your mother up when she comes for a visit!" He's down at the Batman refinery tonight at a meeting of long faces. They're all that way because they didn't strike oil at the last drilling location. He looks happiest, of course, when he comes home covered with it.

What to Send from America?

I keep reading your letter over, Camilla, and many thanks for your kind offer. I'll say no thanks on the hats; I wore a hat only once, to a foreign affairs high tea in Ankara. No home permanents either, thanks; now I'm braiding my hair up, mostly. But, if as a special favor, you could sew or buy a dress for Seniha, I'd be really happy. She's about Cousin Lucile's size. Nothing sheer, open-necked or short-sleeved. Maybe maroon or burgundy color, in nylon. It's very popular here, you know. She'd be thrilled to death! She worked so hard for us in Ankara, taking care of Hikmet and the house while I was working days and evenings. I can never really repay her.

Someday, though, I hope to repay *you*!

The Night Watchman

Hikmet has just been watered and bedded down — again — and is clutching her "pink doll." A cool, petrol-scented breeze is blowing over the mountain, the nearest rig is pumping away at a mighty rate, and the dratted donkeys are at it again in back of our kitchen storeroom.

Otherwise, all is quiet except for the night watchman crunching his way down the gravel path in front of our house. He's a Yezidi, my driver tells me. This is an off-branch of dissenting Moslems who supposedly "worship Satan around a bonfire." (I don't know how true this is, at all.) He wears baggy white pants, a turban sometimes, carries a long hickory stick, and twirls black handlebar mustaches. His appearance scares me, but Hikmet thinks he's "very nice."

He's not much of a watchman, if you ask me. I guess he's only concerned with two-legged intruders in the camp, because cows, sheep, goats, mountain goats, and donkeys roam in and out of the little front garden, willy-nilly. Not to mention the ubiquitous chickens, cats, and scavenger camp dogs. There are now no grape vine leaves remaining, except on the gazebo roof. And the real rose bush planted by my predecessor, Alice hanım? Vanished, alas.

Well, enough of that! I have to look up something for class tomorrow: Do you "blow" a relief valve or "open" it?

Until next time, our best to one and all. Your loving sister, A

Letter to Sister in Spokane

Raman Petrol Kampı
August 9, 1955

Dear Camilla,

I just re-read your last letter. Yes, we finally got the things. I could kiss Cousin Lucile. It's just what I need! The doll house is put away 'til winter and will Hikmet be excited! She's just the age now to appreciate it.

You mentioned vitamin capsules: they would be wonderful, and as soon as possible. Also, if there is an available calcium tablet on the market. Could you ask Dr. Smith? Sometimes cow's milk is scarce, and it's mixed with goat's milk. Then it's unpalatable to me. I mean it's *really* smelly.

Sela is busy at the rig on the hill. I'm busy with more classes 'til December. Hikmet is off with Mehmet the houseboy to visit the shoemaker in the village over the hill. This camp life eats up the shoe leather; he turns out a new pair of sandals a month for her!

Here's another request: For some used dress patterns and an old dress catalogue. My neighbors here sew like mad and my old patterns (vintage 1948-50) are getting worn out. Basic dress styles, so they can be altered: size 12 - 16.

Also a good maternity suit pattern in size 18 for my friend and neighbor, Sühendan hanım. They'll all be so pleased. I'll write later about reimbursement.

…. Hikmet is back from the village with a new pair of sandals and a balloon! She says "Thank you for the pants, Aunt Camilla!" Now she's off again.

Time to get ready for lunch and classes.... Love to one and all. And a kiss for little Andy Paul.

Your loving sister, Anna Maria

Letter to Sister in Spokane

Raman Petrol Kampı
September 8, 1955

Dear Camilla,

Thanks for sending the patterns for my neighbors, and by airmail! Boat mail is cheaper, of course, but dismally slow.

Little Hikmet is buzzing around, and I can hardly concentrate. She's riding her tricycle all around the mulberry bush in the kitchen garden, backwards, and it's slightly nerve wracking. She's chattering about the pictures you sent, and asks about Marty and all her other cousins. "Do they speak English?" she asks, and says hello to Andy Paul. How I'd love to see them all....

Now, she's found a pal in the garden, so quiet reigns for a moment! I'm still grinding out the English lessons for the last group of trainees in the refinery. Since the oil industry is a new one in Turkey, there are no trained men available to work in the field, and the American refinery construction people are having a hard time training men without a basic knowledge of English.

Remember Hasan and Mustafa? They're down there instructing in English, too. It's discouraging at times, but I do admire the men for making such an effort to learn. It isn't easy. *I know!*

Sela just came down the hill for lunch, so I close for today. He says to say Hello, please. Hikmet is back and says Hello, again. Give our love to everyone. Hastily, A

Letter to Family and Friends

Raman Petrol Kampı
November 19, 1955

Dear Brownfields, the Near and Dear, and the Here and There:
Weather Report and Marital Mishmash of the Malkoç Menage

We'll skip the weather in order to clarify any cryptic remarks you all may have observed in the not too recent letters. Now, how shall I begin? Very simply, I guess. Sela and I finally got remarried!

First a brief flashback, and then the Big Event. In order for Sela to be eligible for an officer's commission while doing his military service, and serve only 18 months instead of 36, which wouldn't be possible if he were married to a foreigner, we had to get a divorce.

Now, the pay for an army officer here is meager: none for the first six months, and then only enough for the rent and bare basics. Still, in comparison to a regular soldier's stipend, it's infinitely more to be desired. The regular Turkish soldier's life would make a buck private's in the U.S. Army look princely, but this is a simplistic comparison. So, we got a divorce, quite painlessly, thus carrying out the letter of the law, if not exactly the spirit.

After six month's basic military training, Sela was commissioned and spent the remainder of his military service in the oil fields, since there are only a handful of petroleum engineers at work in the newly-formed Turkish Petroleum Company. He came back up to Ankara for his official discharge and we all returned to the Raman camp together.

He immediately started procedures to get re-married. All this kind of official correspondence has to go to the hometown official documents and birth registration office, in his case, to Sürmene, where it must be proved that both parties are unmarried. This is an effective precautionary measure against bigamy.

For some reason, Sela's papers had been transferred to another village, and the clerk there evidently decided it would be less work for him if he just said the whole procedure was not possible, since we had been legally divorced. To straighten this out took four months of telegrams, letters, affidavits, reports from the doctor that Sela was languishing, and trips to and from Beshiri, the local county seat. Last week, he Jeeped off to Diyarbakır where he must have lost his head in the bright lights. [In reality, it's one of the oldest walled cities in the world that is still flourishing.]

He returned triumphantly bearing among other things, precious nylon stockings — imagine *finding* them! Also a case of fresh lemons from Adana and beverages: many bottles of raki, cognac, and vodka (which blends nicely with pomegranate juice); a gold wedding ring for himself because he had never had one; and a stylishly large, magenta alexandrite ring with a delicate gold setting for me. This really lifted my jaded spirits.

Finally, the Marriage Clerk!

The following day, in the teeth of a three-day rain storm, he set off once again, this time for Beshiri, to bring back the provincial marriage clerk. After a hearty dinner in the mess hall, Ahmet bey settled his two-hundred-odd pounds in our one and only easy chair, rustled through the marriage book, pasted in our passport-style pictures, and began reading through the officially required statements, questions, and answers.

With all the strange voices in the house, little Hikmet woke up and came to the front room. She stood in the doorway to watch people standing up and sitting down at intervals. [When answering the clerk's questions, protocol requires that you rise and stand respectfully.] The question-answer period seemed interminable.

"What is everybody doing, jumping all around?" she asked in a polite whisper.

"Shh, your father and I are getting married again," I whispered back.

At length, we and our witnesses all signed the marriage records book, and shook hands to finalize the ceremony. Finally!

Celebrating our Second Wedding

The celebration was on the following evening. Never was there such a party here, I'm sure. Because of the continuing heavy rain, none of the Americans invited from Batman braved the trip up the hill, so it was strictly local. Halfway through the evening, the guests were festooned with crepe paper streamers, the salad and sandwiches I'd slaved over — I'd made at least a gallon of mayonnaise — were fast disappearing, Sela's famous punch was living up to its reputation, and the camp comedian gave in to public demand and started the dancing.

Oh, these wild Turkish dances! An impromptu competition began to determine who could kick the meanest leg, and Sela won out every time! During breathing intermission, everyone waltzed to a tape recorder, courtesy of an engineer just back from Germany. Sela waltzed, jitterbugged, polkaed, and even dashed through a couple of Mexican hat dances. taking turns with all of the wives. He cuts such a romantic figure. You see why I married him not once, but *twice*?

So now we're living happily even after. And such excitement to come! I'm quitting my refinery English classes early in December and taking Hikmet to Amman, Jordan, where I've been invited to spend Christmas with some friends there. Insallah! Then we'll go to Ankara to wait for the arrival of my mother and another little Malkoç in March. I'm "pulling the days with a rope" as the Turkish saying goes.

Sela sends his best as always, and Hikmet says, "Hello to everyone in America."

Your loving sister, Anna Maria
PS: We're moving down to the town of Batman, to the new Company housing units. Very nice, more room, and better for Sela's work, he says, since he drives to the other camps frequently now. I'll miss our garden and privacy here. You can write us at:
Selahattin Malkoç
TPAO Sitesi, Batman
Turkey
PS on Camilla's copy: We're very anxious to know if you've gotten Mama's ticket yet. Let us know right away? The patterns finally arrived and we paid customs here, so they'll be sent from Istanbul any day. All the women are very happy, and thank you! What's Andy Paul doing now?

Keep us posted. Love to everyone. A

Journal: Visas and Passport Laws My request for a visa to Amman, Jordan was turned down: "Not essential travel." This is due to the present government limitations on travel abroad, to prevent people taking large amounts of gold out of the country, I assume.

Ironically, my mother is also having a hard time trying to get a passport to travel to Turkey. To the best of my knowledge, it's all because my father, who was born in England, entered California by way of Australia without a passport sometime in the early 1900's. According to genealogists, this was not considered a matter of any consequence at the time.

When the first World War broke out, however, all male British subjects were called home to enlist. For reasons known only to him, my father stayed put. [It is my assumption that he had neither the strong emotional ties — he had been sent at an early age to live with a married sister in South Africa when his father died — nor the travel money to return to his old home in England, which, in any case, no longer existed]. But, whatever the case, instead of returning to Great Britain, he settled down to work in Spokane, Washington and married my mother around 1918.

During this time, I understand, U.S. law held that wives of foreigners were also considered aliens, since their citizenship was forfeited at the time of marriage and they automatically assumed their husband's citizenship. Aliens, and their spouses, therefore, were subject to deportation. This law held for anyone who had married before 1920, when the law was repealed.

Papa never spoke to us children about any of these details. We all thought he was born in San Francisco. It was only after he died in 1949 that Mama told me this much of his story, and she didn't tell my siblings much, if anything at all, about it. More water under the family bridge.... 🐢>

Batman Sitesi Housing Construction 1956

9

A RELUCTANT MOVE DOWN TO BATMAN

Journal: We Move Down to Batman, November 26, 1955 The TPAO housing development has completed a row of three single houses for executives and a Guest House, and a row of four four-unit apartment buildings facing them across the street. Also a small hospital, a theater, and a school. Additional rows of apartment buildings are going up on the adjacent streets. It is referred to as "The Site"[sit eh].

The new concrete buildings stand starkly gray on the grassless, treeless building lots. The unfinished streets are dusty in dry weather, and muddy when it rains. In excessively rainy weather, the mud becomes so thick and gooey it mires vehicles and sucks the shoes off one's feet. An element of nature to reckon with.

Initially, I was disinclined to leave the single house at Raman Camp, with its enormous kitchen, flower garden, and rose arbor. I enjoyed the relative privacy and serenity it afforded, while still being part of the camp life. But I also accepted that it was important for Sela to be more centrally located to the new refinery and the other oil camps. "We have to put in our bid for one of the 16 apartments on the first street," he said excitedly. "They're going to draw lots, and they're already fighting over who's going to live across from who!" [*They* meaning the other employees who would be our neighbors.]

People come and go, I thought. Who knows how long it will be before your neighbor decides to move, for whatever reason? And new people arrive? I guess I'm more flexible than most folks about living arrangements. I had no preferences, personally. So we ended up in an apartment on the ground floor, what I would call the first floor, on the end corner of the street, kitty corner from the Guest House. It has two bedrooms, an L-shaped living room/dining room, a kitchen, bathroom, toilet, and hallway, with storage rooms in the basement. The walls are white-washed. The floors are terrazo concrete, with floor drains in the kitchen and bathroom so they can be sluiced down in hot weather. Everything is simple, functional, no frills.

Our neighbors across the hall are Dr. Cemil, his wife, Esen hanım, and a son, Hasan, a year older than Hikmet. We were all happy to meet each other.

The custom here requires a call on the new neighbors, to welcome them, and to offer best wishes for their new home. So, one by one, we meet all our incoming neighbors as they arrive and settle into the site. ❦

Journal: My American Neighbors across the Street Though they're here only for the duration of the refinery construction project, the wives of the Parsons Company engineers from California seem well settled into their living accommodations, and have quietly formed a kind of sub-community of their own. Two of the executives' families are living in the newly constructed single houses across the street, several are living in our row of apartment houses, and one couple is living in a small trailer house that can be hauled off to other sites, if need be.

Several of the American women — Opal Kaye, Alice Pierce, Arlene Horning — are trained school teachers. They've set up a schedule for their children using the Calvert Home School program, and it seems to be working well.

This morning I was invited for coffee at Alice's house across the street so Hikmet could play with her daughter Leslie. When Alice opened the door, Hikmet stood transfixed on the threshold. "Oh, Mrs. Pierce!" she exclaimed ecstatically, "Your house smells *beautiful*!" Her sensitive nose detected the fragrances of Palmolive dish detergent, Rinso laundry soap, and Jergens hand lotion.

For a very long time, I was not aware that one reason the Parsons Construction personnel and the UN consultants seem to cope as well as they do, so far from their comfortable U.S. homes, is because they are allowed to bring in, or have shipped in, many home amenities including foodstuffs, beverages, and household supplies. This must alleviate many cravings, and compensate for things they left behind when they came to this remote outpost.

But I confess I'm not overly curious, or even truly envious. Although I, like these other Americans, am a foreigner in Turkey, my plane of existence is so different from theirs. I'm here on a more permanent basis, trying to adjust to the culture, while theirs is a temporary sojourn on the periphery.

One day, a Parsons engineer commented: "We Americans are actually doubly foreign here; even the Turks seem to be "outsiders" in this region of Kurdish villages."

My present level of Turkish is still so inadequate I can't even begin to think about learning the local language, alas. I notice that some of the new TPAO engineers' brides are picking up Kurdish words to use in the marketplace, and are trying to talk with the villagers who come selling fresh eggs and produce door to door. I do admire them. ❦

Letter from Mother in Spokane

Route 4, Box 188, Spokane
December 5, 1955

Dear Anna Maria and all,

Camilla just got your letter. Rosemary is writing, I'm sending her the letter with your new address.

I'm still dickering with the U.S. clerk of court. I can get a delayed birth certificate for myself, but to get a posthumous copy of one for Dad is another thing. This business of getting married before 1920, when the law of citizenship by marriage was changed, makes it pretty hard. Aaron has a German lawyer friend (Richart Mundt) busy on it; he does that for some of the German Lodge members. I'll know in a couple more weeks if I can get the visa.

It would have been very easy to settle on Camilla, or some of the boys and family, to visit you. No trouble at all. Why don't you write me and tell me to postpone the trip until next year? That would save a lot of explanation and argument with the family here, so set on their own ideas, not realizing what the real drawback is.

In the meantime, if Aaron's search turns out OK, I'll let you know at once. Moral to the story: Always be aboveboard.

My very best to Sela. He sounds like a mighty nice person. Also, tell lil' Hikmet hello. More next time. Ma

PS: I'm very busy. Have typed last month's shop statements only as far as *H*. We have been really busy here.

Letter to Sister in Spokane

TPAO Sitesi, Batman
January 16, 1956

Dear Camilla,

That letter with the gingersnap was delicious. Yum! Yum! And Hikmet admired the picture no end! She's sending one she made for Grandmother. To be painfully truthful, she made "something," which I turned upside down and guessed was a Christmas tree. So she put decorations on it.

As you've noticed from the address, we no longer live up the mountain at Raman Camp; we've moved down to the new housing complex. It's not paved or landscaped around here yet. I'll try to send you a picture.

Tutoring in the Site

And, yes, I have been wishing hard for an electric blender, the kind with a glass container. Right now, I'm tutoring an American neighbor's son who's going back to high school in Oklahoma next year, so I'll be reimbursed in coin of their realm. It won't be much but it should cover the cost of the blender.

Sela says he would be very happy if he had a heavy sport shirt, size 15 and 1/2, sleeve 33), something washable but slightly "flashy" in blue. Of all the things I'd like personally, I can only think of bras. I've mended and patched til the poor things won't hold up any more. I was just given 25 smackarinos, which I'm hoarding as small payment, and don't know whether to forward it, or save it for Mama. I know all these "small" requests add up, and I feel like a destitute, deserted islander. We're far from destitute; it's just that I can't really retaliate in kind. If it's any compensation at all, rest assured Mama will have a royal time here. You know Sela, he's no miser!

For her trip, Mama should have small pox, tetanus, typhus, and typhoid shots. We weren't checked, but they're a good idea, especially the typhoid. And all shots should be recorded on a World Health Organization card, in case it's required in ports of call on the way.

I'm waiting anxiously for your vitamin capsules. My blood count is back up to normal, and I think I can quit the vitamin shots I'm taking, as soon as I get a report from my doctor in Ankara.

Please thank Nona for the Dr. Spock's book. Bless her heart! When Hikmet had a slight touch of the croup recently, we looked it up, found out what to do, and were we relieved!

93

I've probably forgotten numerous news, with all the excitement coming up. Hikmet wishes you and Andy Paul and Uncle Wally were here.

Love to all, A

Letter to Mother in Spokane

TPAO Sitesi, Batman
January 30, 1956

Dear Mama,

Sorry I didn't get in my happy birthday wish on time. I was so swamped that day, it would have taken super-human effort.

Life in the Site

The bridge and canasta playing American ladies in our new neighborhood dropped in for an afternoon session, plus children, plus several other neighbors who happened by. It all went off very pleasantly, and I felt gratified when the Americans complimented me on the date-nut bars. (They all bake with American stuff, but I was lucky to find the Syrian dates and Black Sea walnuts in a hole-in-the-wall shop in the village.)

And they thought the sugared doughnut balls were too delicious for words! Sela hasn't had a doughnut cutter made for me yet, so I had just made doughnut balls. When they didn't cook in the middle, I broke them in two and deep-fried them a bit more. They were very peculiar looking, so to camouflage them, I dipped them in lemon-flavored, seven-minute boiled frosting. Everyone wanted the recipe!

Our last maid left after only a couple of weeks. Her husband, sadly, just got out of the Army because he's gone blind. He won't let her work, but keeps her at home to cook, etc. I guess he figures his second wife can earn enough in the wash house here in the housing units to support the ménage. Having more than one wife is illegal, officially, but the village imam [priest] performs a religious ceremony that seems to take care of any scruples people around here might have. Happens every once in a while in villages, I understand. We sure miss her and the fascinating blue tattoo on her forehead. With luck, we'll have a girl starting next month, but it's hard to find one who's suitable and willing to adapt to our household. I hope we can find one soon; doing the laundry in the bath tub and sweeping with a handle-less broom is getting me in the lower back. Sela sweeps up for me now and then, bless him.

More Tutoring

A neighbor boy who's on school vacation comes for English and science lessons every day; an engineer comes for English every other day. Also, Hikmet's little pals come to play, and neighbor ladies — some Turkish, some American — with time on their hands come to call at tea time.

When we first moved down here from Raman camp, like most of our neighbors we were getting meals from the mess hall, since food is hard to find on a regular basis. Now that I've learned more about the marketplace in Batman, I shop for rice, bulgur [cracked wheat], spaghetti, dried legumes, seasonal

94

vegetables and fruit, chicken or lamb. I try to whip up three meals a day out of whatever's available.

Well, that covers our daily routine here pretty well. We're waiting to hear from you about your plans. Have you gotten passage yet? Sela wants to be with Hikmet and me in Ankara the last of March, but he also wants to save part of his vacation time for when you do come. Friends are going to let us use their empty apartment for two months in Ankara and we'll be there until the end of April. At any rate, Sela will meet you whenever you do arrive.

Which reminds me, I do hope Camilla sent me directions about those vitamin capsules for anemia. My supply ran out again and I have to change brands. Some aren't coming into the country any more because of the currency exchange, so I have to take whatever I can get.

There's such a peaceful scene here at home tonight. Sela is reading an old *Pocket Book*, Hikmet is asleep with her pink dolly from her Aunt Joyce, and three books from her "brothers and sisters in America" under her pillow. The new book from Camilla is on top.

This afternoon, she entertained the two American children from the next apartment house. After their tea party, the young guests washed all the plastic dishes under her careful supervision. And one child was allowed to look at her very precious *Mother Goose* book. I think Hikmet plays well together with all the children. My only complaint is that she mimics the two American children next door unconsciously, speaking Turkish the way they do with an Oklahoma accent. Ironic, isn't it, that she was born in Tulsa! Here I struggle self-consciously with my Turkish pronunciation and Hikmet can imitate accents so easily....

By the by, have the surprises for you and Camilla gotten there yet? Let me know! Give one and all our very best. Write us soon, Mama.

Your loving daughter, Anna Maria

Letter to Sister in Spokane

TPAO Sitesi, Batman
February 15, 1956

Dear Camilla,

This is your Happy Birthday letter! I always seem to slip up on everybody's birthday. I feel so ashamed I can't remember all my little Jones nephews and nieces, when everyone was so sweet about Hikmet's fourth birthday.

I wish you could see how proud she is whenever a card comes in the mail. Last week, the card from Janene was passed around; whoever dropped in got to touch the angel's pink feather, just once. But she wouldn't allow the lock of hair in Andy Paul's card to be touched, only looked at! It's exactly the same color as her hair now, maybe a little redder.

We always go through the list of all the cousins whenever we hear from one. "Now, where is Marty? How big is she now? What is Terry doing? Do they have little brothers and sisters? Does Janene eat yogurt?" Her first remark when she saw Andy Paul's picture was, "Oh, he's so sweet! I want to eat him up!

Uncooked!" As you might imagine, the first two are common phrases of endearment, translated; the last is her own expression.

Speaking of cards, I'd made a remark recently to neighbors that in the States, one could find a card for every occasion. Then along came Mama's cards to prove the point: A "Valentine for Daughter & Her Husband," and one "For Granddaughter." Hikmet arranged them on the hall table to be admired by all.

I was disappointed to hear Mama hasn't cleared up that passport business yet. I hope you all are keeping after it. I think she'd truly have the time of her life traveling here. Especially since she's never had a chance to travel any farther than Pocatello, Idaho.

Nafiye's Customs

We finally found a girl, Nafiye [Nah fee yeh], from a nearby village to do housework and watch Hikmet when my students come for English lessons: She's very bright, clean, and willing.

I asked her about coming with us to Ankara next month for the baby, but probably her family won't let her go because she'd be staying under a stranger's roof, not her father's.

Nafiye wanted to know all about Ankara, though, and added that naturally I'd be in bed for 40 days after the baby. I just laughed.

Later, I asked my neighbor Sühendan hanım about this childbirth custom. She chuckled and said they don't actually stay in bed all that time; they rest a lot in fancy night gowns and bed jackets, under satin quilts, etc. If relatives aren't available to come and help out, the new mothers get up to do their housework, but don't leave the house. The idea of resting up is fine, but to me it seems tied up with traditional swaddling, blue bead charms to keep off the evil eye, another superstition I still find strange....

Daily Household Activities in Batman

More interruptions.... Just for fun, I'll tell you what I've done in the past two hours:

- Hikmet has been staying in with a sniffly nose. When she woke up from her nap, I told her about the dancing bear I saw in the market this morning.

- The house boy for this apartment house brought in my grocery order from the market, including five kilos of flour — in bulk, very messy.

- Yasmin, the little girl from two doors down, came to play with Hikmet. I had to find house slippers to fit her.

- Suat Basaran's wife, Martha, my newly arrived American neighbor down the next street, stopped in. I put on the tea kettle for tea and baked some cinnamon rolls which had been rising, not very successfully.

- Hasan Göker — from UW in Seattle, remember? — came in looking for some yogurt for a friend with the flu [the friend's my evening student, coincidentally]. I'm finally learning to make fresh yogurt and it's delicious. Very good for convalescents.

- Sela came in from Raman and took Martha home in the Jeep.

- I lit the bathroom water heater to take a delayed shower because I spilled olive oil down my front while putting the flour away.

But enough of today's happenings! Maybe we'll play bridge tonight. I'm a "desperation fourth," and join in only when they can't find anyone else to make up a bridge table. Sela, on the other hand, is a very popular player and, according to the latest poll, the best around here. Now Hikmet says "Hello to everyone!"

Love to all, and from Sela, too, Anna Maria

Letter from Mother in Spokane

Route 4, Box 188, Spokane
March 12, 1956

Dear Anna Maria,

You have a letter coming, this is just a note. Aaron went to hear this Turkish newspaper woman speak, see enclosed clipping... Now I'm waiting to hear more about my passport. Haven't hear from Mr. Brown's secretary, Miss Bish, since Feb. She's supposed to be working on it.

Lucile was here on a short visit, left some lovely hand-made little girls' dresses, different sizes. What shall I do with them? Is the duty so high?

More anon. Ma

[Following are excerpts from the article in *Spokesman-Review, March 13, 1956.* The speaker, whose father published a leading newspaper in Istanbul, was born in Turkey and educated in France and the United States.]

"Middle East's Role Stressed: Turkish Newspaper Woman Speaks"

The strategic importance of the Middle East — the connecting link between Asia, Europe and Africa — was stressed by Miss Ismet Sanli, newspaper woman and lecturer in Spokane last night.

The average American, Miss Sanli said, probably does not know that the United States produces and supplies 53 percent of the world's oil and yet has 25 per cent of all proven oil resources.

And the average American probably does not know that the Middle East provides 35 per cent of the world's oil — and has 60 per cent of all proven resources.... The lecturer said Middle East nations have always been under some type of imperial or colonial rule; these nations are now awakening in statehood, independence and sovereignty....

"Naturally, these people are still backward and there is a large percentage of illiteracy. There is jealousy among the states, instability in governments and suspicion of the motives of the west. If proper guidance and leadership would be asserted by the West in the area at this time, much future good could be done."....
end of article

Timur Arrives in Ankara

telegram from Maltepe/Ankara/Turkey
to Spokane, Washington
March 25, 1956

GRANDMOTHER UNCLES AUNTS SISTER BROTHERS COUSINS
NEPHEWS NIECES STOP WE ARE CELEBRATING ARRIVAL OF TIMUR
STOP HAPPY DAYS STOP MOTHER.

Welcoming Baby Timur, Ankara 1955

Letter from Mother in Spokane

Route 4, Box 188, Spokane
April 3, 1956

Dear Anna Maria and all,

Don't know if you got my last letter.

We got the telegram celebrating the arrival of Timur. Hope everything is all right. We think and talk about you constantly. Have Lucile's exquisite hand-made dresses arrived?

Had a snapshot from Mike when he was in the USN hospital in California, where he had an appendectomy and an infection. Oddly enough, he says he had a ball: "no work, no nothing" for a month off.

Everyone here sends you best wishes. Your letters are passed from hand to hand and your stamps go to the oddest places. Some stamp enthusiast is always popping up. Oh yes, met a young fellow on my team at the Filter Center.

He said, quote: "I worked at the NY APO, and people are really crazy. They send air mail to Turkey! We know the letters go out on camel back way into

98

the interior. Why bother with air mail?" unquote. Found out he was handling our mail! Heh, heh!

Our very best to Sela, Hikmet, and Timur, and yourself.

Love, Ma

Letter to Mother in Spokane

Semsi bey's apartment in Ankara
April 8, 1956

Dear Mama,
    Your letter was forwarded from Batman.
    Hikmet was so happy over the Easter card. She's starting the paper doll stage right now. Keeps me busy finding things for her to do now that I'm cooped up for a spell in our friend's apartment here in Ankara. Luckily the landlady's children are so nice. They take her out for walks and play with her.
    Timur hit the nine pound mark yesterday. We took him in a taxi to the hospital for circumcision a few days ago. Glad it's over with. The custom in these parts is to wait until some age over five or so, and celebrate with a big party. Barbaric, if you ask me, but I recall Aunt Ann's adage: "Every one to his own taste, said the old lady as she kissed the cow!"
    Anyway, I'm fine, thanks to that load of vitamins from Camilla. We're all blooming, in fact, in spite of not having a cleaning woman now. Sela helps me with the laundry and housework, otherwise I'd be swamped. These coal stoves are messy, what with ashes, wood, kindling, etc. Remember the wood stove in the kitchen on Third Avenue during the Depression?
    We have visitors in dribbles, and things are never at a standstill. I'll be glad to get back to our own apartment in Batman with all the conveniences — mainly oil heat, hot water, and an electric range. Our generous friend Semsi bey's apartment here is scantily furnished, as it's just for temporary visits when he and his wife Esma hanım come up to Ankara from Batman.
    You asked about books. Wonderful! I'd love all the used *Pocket Books* you have. None are coming into the country now because of the currency exchange (or lack thereof). Whenever I come up to Ankara, I collect old books from friends and pass them along when I finish.
    As you can imagine, there's not much home entertainment in Batman, so how about a deck of plastic playing cards for Sela, the master bridge player? He'd be "tickled pink."

Your loving daughter, Anna Maria

Letter to Mother in Spokane

Dr. Kent's Clinic, Ankara
April 15, 1956

Dear Mama,

The other day my friend Eleanor Senyurek brought me your cable celebrating Timur's arrival. He's doing just fine and so am I, although I haven't seen him since Tuesday, when I had to have an appendectomy!

Yes, my appendix burst in the middle of the night and Sela had to take me back to the clinic. They couldn't knock me out because of low blood pressure. (Or problems with the anesthesia apparatus.) I'm lucky I'm here in a hospital, with a good doctor.

And good friends! Sela spread the word and everybody offered to take Timur. An American woman I'd met once a year ago added to the collection of powdered milk for Timur's formula, which is not available on the market now.

Hikmet is staying with her little pals, and "has lollypops and ice cream everyday." Friends even take care of Sela, who always copes well!

It's very quiet in the hospital now. The nurses are all saying their prayers because it's Ramazan, the month of fasting from sunrise to sunset. They're all very good to me, and pop in and out with other patients' visitors they think I'd like to talk to. It's a very congenial institution here. Private and small.

Well, give my love to everybody. Hope we can take Timur's picture soon. He's a different looking one, all right!

Your loving daughter, Anna Maria

Letter to Tulsa Friends

Dr. Kent's Clinic, Ankara
April 18, 1956

Dear Brownfields et al,

We have a son! Healthy and plump, named Timur, from Timurlenk, of Turkish fame. We liked the sound. And it's Old Turkish for "iron," a strong name. He was born March 25 with much ease, though impatient and howling, at my doctor's clinic in Ankara.

This clinic was originally a three-story apartment house, with French doors dividing some rooms. Relatives of the patient in the adjacent room asked us to please be quiet, their father was dying. I thought I was actually being quite quiet, but try hushing up a new-born! On later reflection, I thought how poetically symbolic: Death and Birth, on different sides of the door.

At any rate, Baby Timur weighed in at four kilos, and 50 centimeters. Quick, the slide rule!

In an Emergency, Sela Takes Over

Being astute readers, you all may be wondering at the date and address above. Yes, I'm back in my doctor's clinic. Three weeks after Timur arrived, my appendix burst In the middle of the night. Very dramatic and very scary.

100

Sela telephoned friend Edith Oyhan, who rallied friends Marion and Eloise to pick up baby Timur and four-year-old Hikmet. Edith, a knowledgeable pharmacist herself, sat up the rest of the night with me in the clinic, cooling my brow with lemon cologne, and keeping an eye out for peritonitis. Fortunately, I healed without complications.

We were doing so well, too, staying at a friend's vacant apartment. Sela was getting up early every morning to mop the terrazo floors, bring me breakfast on a tray with a fresh flower, make breakfast for Hikmet, wash Timur's laundry in the tiny washing machine, and hang it to dry in the garden.

I could hear him discussing soap powders and rinsing procedures with the concerned neighbor ladies over the back fence. They were probably immensely shocked — and amazed — to see a *man* in a *business suit* doing all these things, and so *efficiently*. Yes, and all before dropping Hikmet off with a friend on the way to his office.

Well, Dr. Kent says I'm doing terrifically and may go back to the little apartment tomorrow. Timur and Hikmet are being cared for by a host of friends here. At such times, my faith in the goodness of human beings is renewed.

Dr. Kent also says we can return to Raman after May 1. Write to us:
Bay Selahattin Malkoç
TPAO
Batman, Turkey
I trust you'll pass this along? Sentimental best wishes to all, and much love, A
PS: Yes, Sela is "the same." Perhaps even more so. Rises nobly to every occasion and looks especially masterful smoking a celebratory cigar.

Letter to Mother in Spokane

TPAO Sitesi, Batman
May 27, 1956

Dear Mama,

Your letter of April 3 came yesterday, forwarded from Ankara. Also, the magnificent Mother's Day card came in the same folder. How could I have forgotten the day again this year? Thank you, Mama. It's on my dressing table and is admired in passing by all the ladies who come in to peek at baby Timur.

I was sorry to hear about Mike's appendectomy in Twenty Nine Palms Army Base. What a coincidence! If you send his address, I'll try to write.

Gradually things are getting straightened out here and I'll have lots of extra time. When I'm not teaching again, that is. Timur is so easy to take care of, he's no problem at all. He had a slight cold or some kind of bug the other day, but it lasted no time at all. He was on a diet of rice water and apple powder — a very good German preparation — and a bit of yogurt now and then. Really effective. All the women in the next apartment building vie to see who can hold him when I visit them.

If this typing is incoherent again, it's because three of Hikmet's little girl friends are here, and I'm trying to keep up with their Turkish, and type this letter in English.

Shopping in Diyarbakır

Had a chance to go to Diyarbakır on the morning train last week with Nazire hanım and her husband, Hasan bey, the camp manager in Raman. (I left Hikmet with one kind neighbor and Timur with another). We had to do some shopping for dress material and silver for friends. Also, I had a checkup at the doctor's; she says everything's ship-shape.

In my opinion, it's worth a trip here just to go shopping in Diyarbakır. This ancient walled city was once a junction for camel caravans from Adana, Antalya, and Iskenderun on the Mediterranean Sea; also from Iran, Iraq, Syria, and other parts south. Then it evolved into an important railroad junction for passengers and freight trains, and added a small airstrip for planes bringing passengers and mail from Ankara. Because of its movie house, several small hotels, numerous men's coffee houses, pastry shops, and bustling open market, the field engineers here jokingly refer to it as the Paris of Southeastern Turkey.

Yes, a shopping excursion to Diyarbakır *is* really something to write home about! We three shoppers arrived and had breakfast near the train station: börek [puff pastry with white cheese and fennel] and glasses of very black tea, strong enough to stimulate us for the rigors of shopping. We swatted through clouds of flies hovering over the fruit stalls and meat stands and made our way to a special shop in the silversmiths' street. The shop owner ordered lemonade and offered us cigarettes while we made our selection of silver items (gifts for various upcoming wedding and circumcision celebrations). Bargaining in this shop was simple; we'd been there several times before and were "good customers." Usually the price is hiked way up for foreigners, and it takes finesse to unhike it.

From the silversmiths' shop, we began our next search along a dry goods street crammed with shops selling bolts of woolens for men's suits, cotton prints for women's salvars, plain cottons for children's clothing, machine-made lace for curtains, and so on. We had had no luck finding the dress material we wanted, though we stopped in every shop on the street. (The lemonade sellers had gotten to recognize us: we were plied with beverages in every shop we stopped in.)

The shop keeper at the last place, another "good friend" of Hasan bey, sent his helper out to scour the little stores on the next street for us, graciously offering us tea, lemonade, and coffee while we waited and chatted. The helper finally came back with exactly what we had been looking for, located in his brother-in-law's store. By lunch time, my eyeballs were floating.

We ate at the Turistik Palas Hotel, where well-trained waiters serve my two favorites: delicious wiener schnitzel and crème caramel.

And where, during this season, I always spy a camel or two passing nearby. This time, though, it was not a caravan, just four of the patient beasts plodding along the sidewalk, bearing full saddle bags and spindly logs for some treeless destination east of Diyarbakır.

Managed to telephone our old UW school friend Zeki Beyaz. (He's the engineer engaged to Joyce Kirk from Spokane, remember?) He's doing his military service in the area, and sounded fine.

Bought a handsome bathrobe of blue, black, and gray stripes in Turkish toweling for Sela's birthday. These robes are wonderfully luxurious and very practical. Even Timur has a little caped bath robe.

102

Bought a food bucket for the meals we order from the mess hall. Since it's made of copper, I had it tinned right there at the back of the shop. (I've learned you can't put food in anything copper for fear of copper poisoning; you have to have the copper covered with tin.) The tinsmiths do a thriving business, as copper is commonly used to make cooking vessels. [I think there are copper mines in the region.]

Found a long, brass, cylindrical coffee grinder. Now we can have freshly ground coffee — if we can find the coffee beans to grind, that is, during the current coffee bean shortage.

Picked up walnuts and vodka for Sela's party, and crammed everything into the suitcases just in time to catch the evening express from Ankara. Sela gallantly pretended not to notice how heavily the bags were loaded when he met us at the Batman train station, and never said a word when I figured up the shopping expenses, even though there was an obvious discrepancy. He knows how I love surprises, but I've never been able to surprise him yet. And I didn't!

Not a Surprise Birthday Party

Last night before the party, when I emerged in my party dress, he wished himself a happy birthday! By the way, he got all the cards and was much pleased to think that you all remember him — his birthday, that is.

Thinking that only a few people would show up, we were surprised that 50 neighbors dropped in! There were mad dashes to borrow chairs and glasses, and squeeze extra lemons for the vodka refreshment. Nafiye stayed late, and brought her little brother to help. Ali wrestled with the chairs and the lemon squeezer, and watched to see if anyone admired his wreaths of morning glories, dandelions, and poppies. Sela took the two home early with part of the birthday cake the Guest House cook had ordered for me (from the Raman camp kitchen).

All in all, it was a quiet party that went a bit lame in the middle. This usually happens when everybody doesn't speak the same language, but at least people got to meet each other. As I've mentioned, the TPAO Site keeps growing!

Afterward, there was a lot of potato salad, sandwiches, and deviled eggs left over in the refrigerator, so Sela invited the bachelor engineers and geologists from Raman and Garzan camps to finish it up tonight. At the moment, they're all playing bridge furiously, amidst a flurry of little coffee cups, raki glasses, and pistachio shells. The living room looks like a regular Turkish coffee house, but with a woman's touch.

Well, it's time for me to break out the walnut-fig bars I made fresh today. I swear these fellows smell it all the way over to the last camp when the oven's baking! It's a little tin bee-hive oven with two racks that sits over the electric hot plate. I've already managed a leg of lamb, and even an applesauce cake in it.

Nothing ever goes stale around here, even the failures I've turned out. It took many tears of frustration to work out a successful recipe using yogurt but now I'm "famous" for my waffles.

Later…. Timur has been burped and put to bed for the night. Hikmet, clutching her Pussy Cat doll and her favorite *Mother Goose* book, is "chasing rabbits." And I quit! Your loving daughter, Anna Maria

A, Baby T, H, Water Tanks, New Apartments

Letter to Mother in Spokane

TPAO Sitesi, Batman
May 30, 1956

Dear Mama,

After great deliberation (with remuneration later), here is my list:

1. A good, substantial food grinder. I'm going to start doing our own cooking again soon. It's hard to cook easy dishes without ground meat for meat loaf, meatballs, stuffed peppers, etc.

2. An electric refrigerator ice cream freezer that fits into an ice cube tray. (This Company refrigerator is a GE) The one in the magazine costs about $20.00.

3. A rust-proof, durable flour sifter.

4. A set of aluminum measuring cups and spoons.

5. Rubber bands for Hikmet's hair.

6. Several dozen cup hooks.

7. A skirt hanger. Our closet is very small and I try to utilize space.

8. Ten place mats, heavy, practical, for the dining room table, in bright yellow.

9. Plastic bags, large size. Whenever I bake, I send something up to one of the camps where life gets a bit dreary, and I never get the bags back.

10. One or two pairs of earrings for Nafiye (pierced ears) A Woolworth's necklace would make her the belle of the village.

If you can't manage everything, OK. Rubber Bands are most important. But please remember I appreciate everything you send. Hikmet and I open each package slowly, I take out a hairpin and untie the knots "just like Grandmother did!" It drives her frantic, just like it did me. Such a delicious frenzy of anticipation. She saves the ribbons to dress up her dolls, and cuts up the paper with her scissors — not that she lacks for little toys, thanks to everyone's generosity. (I hide the new ones and dole them out at appropriate occasions.)

Sela sends his best regards. Your loving daughter, Anna Maria

PS: I hope you pass along my letters to the Neighbor Ladies of the Rimrock. I think of them all whenever I open their beautiful book of American Indian tribes. I always let visiting children look at it if their hands are clean!

PPS: Here's another one worth a nickel: Nafiye says the reason I shed hair (which I seem to do every summer) is because "Timur recognizes me." Did Grossmutter ever have a superstition about shedding hair?

PPPS: Please tell that fellow on your Filter Center team, who works in the post office and saves stamps: Yes, air mail does go all the way to Diyarbakır, and then it's sent by train from there. Camels don't carry any mail. Or any male, either. The camel drivers I've seen usually walk! Well, that's my pun for the day. A

Letter to Family and Friends

TPAO Sitesi, Batman
July 11, 1956

Dear Brownfields and All: Good morning!

There's a lull around here this morning for some reason. Oh, yes: no lessons!

Timur has just finished off his morning farina and milk, and Hikmet is out playing with girl friends Yasemin from next door and Leslie from across the street.

H. just breezed in and out with her bathrobe and bathing suit to go swimming with "the big girls." There's a new concrete pool with diving board across the road, next to the tennis court under construction. Oh, this housing development is looking up!

Trachoma, an Ancient Pestilence

We all had a shocking jolt last week end when I took the twelve-year-old brother of Nafiye, our house maid, on the train to Diyarbakır to see about getting glasses for him, he was squinting so.

The Diyarbakır eye doctor took one look at Ali's eyes, quickly washed his hands and instruments — scrubbed them with alcohol, in fact — and said: "Don't let him in your house!" I must have looked startled, so he added, "Trachoma!"

Not knowing much about trachoma, except that it was a disease causing blindness, this scared the wits out of me. My second thought was, how heartless of the doctor to say that in front of the child.

[One of my first impressions of the Batman train station was seeing raggedy children milling around the tracks, begging money from the passengers. One small boy, walking with a tall stick and hanging onto an older boy's arm, had a rag bandaged around his eyes, oblivious to the black horse flies settling on his face. Flies seemed to be swarming everywhere, in fact: around the food and fruit stalls, and over the meat hanging above the butchers' stands at the end of the station.

Historically, I believe, trachoma was prevalent in these parts, although Batman seems to be pretty well rid of it now because of the government

105

campaigns and free treatment. It's carried by dust and flies, I'm told, and is most contagious during the first week or so of contact.]

The day after returning from Diyarbakır, our entire household trooped down to the doctor in the new little TPAO hospital. He okayed all of us; Ali is being treated with medications. Such a pity. He and his sister Nafiye do odd jobs to help their mother, who used to do our laundry, now works in the wash house.

It will be even more of a struggle for Ali to get any more schooling, I guess. It's heartbreaking to see the children in these remote villages. One wonders how they survive. The mortality rate, I've been told, is high.

Government Projects Improve the Regions

Some small villages have no running water, electricity, schools, or money for medical attention — even if there were any facilities or doctors. The government projects under way, like the TPAO refinery here in Batman, offer employment; mostly unskilled labor employing local villagers. The projects build their own roads, establish their own electricity, water supply, medical services, schools, clinics. So they must make a tremendous difference in the local standards of living. Everyone in the area directly or indirectly benefits.

Goodbye to Our Parsons Neighbors

Last week, the Guest House had a farewell dinner in honor of some American engineers who are finishing their contracts. One by one, the men sent out by Ralph Parsons Construction Company in California are turning their jobs over to the TPAO engineers. I'm sad to see each family go; they've all been good neighbors.

Also last week, the petroleum pipeline to Garzan camp was completed. In a sacrificial ceremony, the local imam slaughtered a lamb over the new pipeline, to insure its long life and good luck. When that camp gets underway in regular production, Sela will be driving back and forth to Garzan every day.

….This letter has been all day in the writing! We've just finished dinner: green peppers stuffed with rice, "Albanian style" cubed liver sautéed with onions and tomatoes, and yogurt with cucumber and garlic. (I've been trying out my neighbors' recipes.)

The children are now fast asleep and it's time for Sela and me to have our evening cup of coffee and a quiet moment before bed. My favorite radio program, "Turkish Music on Western Instruments is playing: harp, zither, violins, piano, and an occasional light drum. Altogether a lovely evening.

And a lovely goodnight to everyone! A

Journal: The Company Guest House Prior to TPAO, as far as I know, there were no overnight accommodations suitable for high-ranking visitors and official government guests on tours of the petroleum fields east of Diyarbakır. The construction plans for the TPAO Batman Site, therefore, included a guest house that would provide temporary lodging and appropriate accommodations.

The present Guest House fulfills another essential function for the refinery executives, UN consultants, petroleum engineers, geologists, chemists, and other highly trained specialists who live in the Site: it serves as a social meeting place, as well as a restaurant for dining and dancing on Saturday nights and special holidays. In short, the Guest House provides an opportunity to dress up and feel "civilized" out here in this extremely remote area so far removed from the nation's capital. It's wonderful for the morale.

Additionally, for me personally, attending the functions at the Guest House is always an occasion to learn polite Turkish expressions and observe social customs.

On very special occasions, the director's wife holds an afternoon tea, or several women join in hosting their visiting day, at the Guest House. 🍂

Letter to Tulsa Friends

TPAO Sitesi, Batman
July 12, 1956

Dear Brownfields and all,

Do you realize it's nearly four years since we left Tulsa? We're anxious to hear of your family, the wee and not so wee ones. And don't spend half the letter explaining why you haven't written. Just let's hear what you've been doing all this time. How are your parents, Bill?

And what's the word from Aung Ki Moe? Did he go back to Burma?

So far, there's no hope of our coming back to the States soon. The Company plans had been to send their engineers back in rotation for more training, but the economy here has nearly hit rock-bottom. Perhaps we can visit on our own in a year or so. Just a thought in the back of my mind.

When an American neighbor departed last week, she gave me a copy of *Master of the World,* the bloodcurdling, gruesome story of Tamerlane [Timurlenk]. I pray Baby Timur won't follow in the footsteps of the book's hero! (We chose the name because we liked the sound, and it means "iron" in Old Turkish..) But, hark! He calls.

And I must also extract Hikmet from the bathtub where she's "learning to swim."

Please give our best to all. Much love, A and S

Letter to Sister in Spokane

TPAO Sitesi, Batman
July 23, 1956

Dear Camilla,

Have you seen Joyce Kirk yet? She flew home to Spokane last month when her father died. Saw her fiancé Zeki in Diyarbakir last week. (Remember him from U of W?) He's fine, but pining for Joyce, I guess. He has tentative plans to leave here when his military service ends.

Seems like I had so much on my mind but with all these interruptions I forget. This morning, I weighed Timur in at 19 pounds. He'll be four months, day after tomorrow. He's the easiest baby to take care of! Now he's lying on the floor, kicking up and rolling around....

Well, that's enough of that subject. All babies are cute. Speaking of cute things, never saw anything like Cousin Lucile's handwork. I've put the little dresses all away for Xmas and next spring since Hikmet will grow into them about the time her present wardrobe falls off her. Besides, she'll swoon. Just purely swoon. And so will all the other mothers. I try to be modest about my Sewing Cousin, but once in a while, I have to brag a little in self-defense in front of these artistic handwork experts who do exquisitely fine hem-stitching, embroidering, tatting, crocheting, lace-making, and of course, marvelous knitting.

And I've put the precious little doll away for now. We'll wait to see what the next one will be....

He/she should arrive — have you recovered from shock? — sometime after Hikmet's birthday. But I'm not sure of the date, so hush! Sela took me for a check-up at the hospital in Diyarbakır last week. I had gotten too upset, worrying about all this trachoma business, also tired out from doing the laundry in the bathtub, carrying the heavy enameled buckets out to the garden, etc. But I'm all right now, and going strong on those pink and blue vitamin capsules you sent me.

Each year we say, "Maybe next year a trip to Spokane." What I'm trying to work out now is some plan of earning the fare. The main thing is to find a suitable woman to live with us for the next year or so. Nafiye, our present helper, comes only days and can't manage babies *and* housework. Otherwise, I could be teaching regular classes. I've given up lessons because it's sometimes a little too much, with everything else. Sela thinks there's a vague possibility of being sent, but the rumors come and go. I'd want to stay for at least a half year, and work if possible.

I've almost given up Mama's trip in despair. Has she given up? Entirely? She hasn't mentioned it for so long, I can't bear to ask her again.

Hikmet asks "How big is Andy Paul?" She also wants you to know that she can turn on her own bath water. She practices swimming in our big bathtub, and sometimes takes three "baths" a day with her pal Yasemin to "cool off."

I'm grateful and marvel at the change in her since we came back from Ankara. What a spoiled brat she was then. With everyone agog over little Timur, ignoring her, and expecting her to sit ladylike on velvet chairs, and then saying in her presence, "She's jealous, of course, isn't she?" — who wouldn't be! But she's her old self again and is wonderful with Timur. Right now she's keen on her *"Humpty Dumpty"* magazines. Also her *Alice in Wonderland* book, although most of it's beyond her.

Our new neighbor Avis, wife of a new geologist, is fresh from teaching primary school in California; she says Hikmet is "very advanced for her age." This is, ahem, as Mama says, just between you and me. Anyway, that's Hikmet up to date.

Your loving sister, Anna Maria
PS: Hello to everyone!

Journal: Washboards Are a Boon

Here in the Site, our standard of living is relatively very high, compared to the local villagers' life. You may find it odd that we have the seeming luxury of household help, for example, and yet we lack modern necessities like a washing machine (a hugely expensive, imported luxury here). On the other hand, we are blessed with a plentiful fresh water supply from the Site reservoirs.

From time to time, we find young maids willing to scrub and do housework, but unfortunately for me, they usually end up going back to their villages to be married. For a while, an older woman we called Badji teyze came in especially to do the washing, in the bathtub as I do, but it just wore her out. In all conscience, I couldn't ask her to do any more laundry. She took care of Timmy while I did it.

Laundry is an eternal chore, a regular routine: I soak the clothes in the bathtub in soapy water, then scrub and rinse in several clear waters. (With my new little washboard, the scrubbing is much easier.) I carry the rinsed clothes in buckets to hang on the clothesline outside, where they drip dry.

I rinse the baby's diapers, then soak them in soapy water overnight in a special enameled bucket; next day I scrub them in fresh soapy water, then rinse numerous times in fresh water. Most of the time, the sun is so bright and strong that the diapers and sheets bleach themselves to a snowy whiteness.

This scrubbing-rinsing-carrying routine has become, in a way, a kind of calisthenics, and seems to have strengthened my back muscles. Also kept me in small dress sizes. ❦

Letter to Mother in Spokane

TPAO Sitesi, Batman
August 7, 1956

Dear Mama,

Mike wrote us a couple of weeks ago. After waiting so eagerly to hear from him, Sela got too excited and tore the address off! So, would you please forward Hikmet's letter? Also, I'd like Mike's address again, thanks.

When I bought a food bucket in Diyarbakır in May, I think I never explained it very well. It's a set of three/four tinned copper pans, six inches in diameter. They nest one on top of another, and fit onto two vertical bars that act as holders with a handle on top; the pans slide up or down, to be filled or washed, as necessary. This traveling food box [sefer tase] is a convenient arrangement to transport cooked food, and each apartment house's janitor/houseboy is responsible for delivering the lunch and dinner meals [cooked in the Company's kitchen down near the refinery and sent up to the Site]. It's a well-organized system.

However, I find the mess hall food always floating in oil, and too starchy for me, so we discontinued ordering it. Which meant I had to start cooking again. Unfortunately, right after this decision, there are new price cuts and strict price ceilings, so no garden produce came in from Diyarbakır or Adana for several weeks. I had to search hard to find foodstuffs to cook.

Then, when a shipment finally did come into the train station, Wow! Pow! Fist fights in the market place! Sela and one of the doctors braved the melee and came back with this season's first watermelons. These melons, by the way, are said to grow to phenomenal size; they say one donkey can carry only two!

But we're luckier than most families who don't depend on the mess hall food. Since Sela now drives to supervise the Raman, Garzan, and Reshan operations every day, he occasionally picks up fresh produce, also fresh butter, chickens, and meat. And, fortunately for me, he doesn't insist on having a three-course meal at night, each on a different plate, like some men here do. These Turkish dishes are wonderfully delicious, but require hours and hours of preparation. Every dish, they say, has to go through at least two cooking stages.

Well, Hikmet and pal have just left to deliver a message down the street. Yasemin was singing a little French ditty, and Hikmet was telling her about "Tom the Chimney Sweep and the Water Babies." It's hard to concentrate when they're here; I get too fascinated listening.

Now it's Timur's time to shine. He drank pear juice and vitamin drops from Hikmet's silver cup this morning. He thrives on everything. Last time I weighed him, a couple of weeks ago, he hit 19 pounds.

I sent a tiny parcel off with a traveling engineer, and hope you get it. Some "needle lace" doilies for Lucile and Aunt Edna, Also something for your kitty. Bath time for Timmy boy now. Our best to all.

Your loving daughter, Anna Maria

Letter to Tulsa Friends

TPAO Sitesi, Batman
August 29, 1956

Dear Brownfields and all,

Such a rewarding letter from you! Sela had me read it to him while he rested his feet from driving to Reshan camp. Over a bottle of beer from Beshiri. A lovely evening it was, too.

Right now, a trip to the States is my favorite topic of conversation. At night I have a recurring dream that I'm in a hamburger joint full of delicious hamburgers, vanilla malted milk shakes, and shrimp cocktails on ice, and the best part of the dream is that I own the joint!

But seriously, if I do manage the trip, I mean to meander a bit and stop through Tulsa. Every once in a while, Sela lifts a cryptic eyebrow and mutters "Who knows? They may send me, too." But it's mostly muttering.

The real reason for my sudden aspiration is that my mother can't clear up her citizenship status, and the family want to give me her ticket money for a trip to Spokane. Plus, I would like to have a thorough medical checkup Stateside. I think it would be reassuring after the last one in Diyarbakir. Will keep you-all posted.

Love, Anna Maria
PS from Sela:

Well, Bill, in your last letter you were blaming me about "not writing a few lines" in one of Anna Maria's letters. Honestly, I have been very lazy about writing letters, isn't that terrible. As I understand, you and Al are running an exploration co. All I can say is: Good luck!!

My work here at the moment is district field production engineer. Here, that is in Batman, there is a 7500 bbls refinery built by Parson Co. and completed about a year ago. Raman oilfield is about 14 miles up the hill from Batman. This field is already developed and producing about 7000 bbls 20 gravity crude oil from 14 wells. The wells are pumping wells. There is another field, called Garzan, about 30 miles from Batman. This field is under development and we have been putting up pumping units there now.

Garzan oilfield is smaller than Raman but has a better quality oil (27 gravity AP0). Since there are only 6 petroleum engineers in Turkey, they make us do all sorts of engineering jobs. For instance, when I came here first, I worked in the drilling department, production department, building department, etc. At the moment I am supposed to be field production engineer, but I haven't been doing any engineering work at all. I run around all day to supervise the work in a Jeep on the dirt roads and bumpy roads which break your back. Well, that's life, I guess.

About my going to the States: There is a rumor but it's not certain yet. I sure would like to see my old pals like you and the others. Sam

PPS Later, Sela quit his letter writing when he was called last night at 9:30 for a conference, referred to as a "Raise-you-twenny-five." They're supposed to help clear the air and benefit the overworked nerves.

Hikmet's Tonsillectomy in Diyarbakır

PPPS: Much, much later.

Sorry this letter didn't get off per schedule. I had to take Hikmet on the train to Diyarbakır to have her chronically ailing tonsils taken out.

God, how I dreaded it! The one time I really have qualms about living way out here is whenever it's a health crisis.

It seems that gas or any general anesthetic is not too satisfactory in such cases here, so they gave her local shots. If you can picture it, the two doctors were wearing medical masks, dark red rubber aprons and long, dark red rubber gloves. They looked horrifically medieval.

And they wouldn't let me stay in the room so Hikmet could at least *see* me. I waited outside her door, sweated out her screaming. Well, mercifully, it was quick, with apparently no long-lasting after-effects. We stayed overnight and a day in the hospital; I slept in a cot by her side. Friends took us to the train, and Sela met us at the Batman station. All in all, she's been a good little patient, recovering fast and picking up weight.

She really does take after her father! Right now she's out in the side yard with her little shovel and bucket, digging holes in the ground....

How I'd love a picture of the Brownfields, Days. and Stewarts. Can't wait to see all your little darlings. Please give our love to the Biebers in their boarding house. Such nostalgia creeps over me at times!

As always, A

Letter from Mother in Spokane

Route 4, Box 188, Spokane
September 19, 1956

Dear Anna Maria and all,

Just a mere line about the Big News. Wonderful! Well, you'll get along all right, no matter where you're at. Remember your Grandmother Harms on the old homestead, when she had the 10 little Harmses, one after another, and no electric gadgets to help with the work, either.

Anyways, hope everything will go along all right. It has to, with Sela at the helm, and you following orders. Ahem, are you good at following orders, or do you always have to have it your way?

David has a question about the ice cream maker: what is your current? AC or DC? Is the blender he sent OK?

More later, Ma

Journal: My Neighbor Senol   Her name means Be happy, joyful. Like my neighbor Sühendan hanım, Senol [Shenol] has long, dark hair and dark brown eyes, with a beautiful smile that lights up her face. She comes from Maras [Marash], a hot, dry region of Anatolia.

Senol's husband, Said [sa eet] Shahankaya, was one of Sela's schoolmates in Germany. The marriage between Said and Senol was "arranged" by their families. They are distantly related, I understand, and this keeps land holdings within the family. When Senol arrived here by train, she was newly married, only 15, shy, and away from home for the first time. But like most other girls in her region, she was already trained in all the housewifely arts.

Soon after Senol arrived in Batman, Sühendan hanım sent word that several of us neighbors would like to pay her an afternoon welcoming call. This custom of giving advance notice allowed her some time to prepare refreshments, such as they might be on short notice in Batman.

It was a hot day, well over 100 degrees Fahrenheit, when we three neighbors arrived. The curtains in Senol's apartment were drawn against the sun but the air in the apartment was stifling.

We sat down on the settee and the new bride sat facing us. One by one in turn, we politely exchanged greetings with our shy hostess and inquired after her health, her family's well-being, and so on.

After these polite formalities, she slipped into the kitchen to prepare a cup of coffee for Sühendan hanım, the oldest among us. She served the fragrant coffee in a delicate porcelain cup and saucer on a silver tray, with a sugary fruit confection from a silver bowl — all wedding presents, I surmised.

She returned to the kitchen to repeat the process for me, the next eldest present, and then Meral hanım, the youngest. We sipped our coffee slowly, and chatted about life in the Site. When the conversation lagged, she asked, in a timid voice, if we would like to be cooled off "Maras style." Of course, we were all curious and eager for a new experience.

112

Cooling Off, Maras Style

Senol excused herself from the room, and we next heard a lot of water splashing in the bathtub. Lots and lots of water. Then silence. Soon she returned, carrying an enormous bath towel that apparently had been soaked in cold water and wrung out by hand. Fascinated, we watched as she stood in front of Sühendan hanım, let the damp towel unfurl to the floor, then grasped it firmly by two corners with an upward movement, and gave it a tremendously powerful snap and flip.

Tiny drops of water from the towel sprayed out upon Sühendan hanım and all about her head. "Ah!" she exclaimed ecstatically. "Ah, guzel!" [Beautiful! Wonderful!] Meral and I could hardly wait to experience this blissfully cooling moment.

Alas, in the stifling dry heat, the droplets from the towel evaporated "as quickly as the time it takes to tell this story," and our attention soon drifted to other Maras customs, cooking recipes, and life in general. ❦

Letter to Mother in Spokane

TPAO Sitesi, Batman
September 26, 1956

Dear Mama,

There's so much excitement around here that I don't know where to begin. Your letter and Joyce's came this morning, so naturally I had to stop flittering about and sit down with a coffee to enjoy them. Joyce always writes the nicest, newsiest letters. Well, this ought to be pretty newsy too.

Working up to the climax, I'll start with Hikmet. She's gained two pounds since she had her tonsils out. And has the old roses back in her cheeks again. Timmy was six moths old yesterday, and celebrated by cutting his first tooth. He's 21 pounds now and doing famously. Happy as a bug in his "new" play pen. He looks like Hikmet, except not so blond.

Well, I'm gradually running out of incidental news bits.... In the last letter to Camilla, I mentioned the possibility of spending this Christmas and the next few months at Rocky Acres. What about that?

In Camilla's letter, I suggested certain conditions under which I could come. Now it seems — although it hasn't been verified yet — that Sela will be sent to the States for a six-month training trip in December. This would make everything easier, since he'll be getting a salary and could send us enough for expenses. I've been writing for information on passports, also what kind of affidavit I'd need from you. (By Turkish law I have to leave on a Turkish passport and be sponsored by my family in the States.) I'll let you know more later.

Sela has been under a lot of work pressure since and he's now alone in his department. He usually drives to the Raman camp in the mornings (15 miles) and over to Garzan in the afternoons (about 30). The roads have been improved somewhat, but they still make the old Sunset Highway look like a smooth, super speedway.

Now, Mama, what's this about your advice to follow orders from Sela? You know that I can't stand "taking orders" from *anyone* — unless it's paid

113

employment, that is. But don't worry. I couldn't stand anyone who would "take orders" from me, either. In spite of all Sela's household accomplishments, which are absolutely unheard of here (he shows off while feeding Timur his bottle, for example), nobody calls him henpecked. They wouldn't dare. No, he's just noble by nature. My good fortune!

Hikmet, who is wearing her leather boots, prancing up and down the dirt piles by the road grader, and eating pistachios at the moment, says to please tell Auntie Joyce that the flowers on the letter were "very pretty, and thank you."

I hope you write your reactions soon to the trip idea. and hello to everybody.

Your loving daughter, Anna Maria

10

A TRIP WITH TWO CHILDREN

Letter to Mother in Spokane

TPAO Sitesi, Batman
October 11, 1956

Dear Mama,

Well, it was good to get your letter! I've been thinking things over, and every once in a while I get faint-hearted: too many difficulties with passports, money, traveling conditions.... Would there be somebody available to help me out for a couple of weeks? For laundry, watching Timmy, etc. Naturally, I'm spoiled having help here — when help is available, that is. It's the one compensation to life in the boondocks.

Now, Hikmet's no problem; in fact, she's often a big help, but Timmy takes attention, so I'm hoping you or Camilla can conscript some unencumbered temporary helper for me.

We had a bit of excitement recently. Celal Bayar, the President of Turkey, stopped through here on a general tour of inspection, and for a couple of days there were flags floating and a passle of soldiers and important-looking dignitaries meandering about. I got only a glimpse when the procession entered the Guest House down the street.

Everything here is just fine. Hikmet is fatter and sassier than ever. Timur has his second tooth. These pictures were taken in June; you can see he's much like Hikmet, sitting there on her "Ottoman empire."

Your loving daughter, Anna Maria

Letter to Mother in Spokane

TPAO Sitesi, Batman
October 17, 1956

Dear Mama,

Flash! Sela jut got this info from friends in Ankara. Sit down quick and write the following to the Turkish Consulate, Los Angeles, Calif. Air mail, registered, so you know they got it:

I, Marie Harms Jones, guarantee to provide all expenses for my daughter, Anna Maria Malkoç

and her children, Hikmet and Timur, for the entire length of their stay in the United States.

Now, you should type this with two copies (three pages all together) and have it notarized when you sign them. Then write another letter stating that I would like to visit you with Hikmet and Timur for approximately a year (to give me lots of leeway) beginning in December 1956. Send the three notarized letters with the cover letter to the Consulate.

. As you see, six weeks isn't very long to get all this done, so you have to include a stamped, self-addressed airmail envelope to the Consulate for their answer. When you get it, register it airmail to me immediately. Everything will start after we get your letter, with copies. Thank you for doing all this, Mama.

About the money, it would do me a lot more good there. Sela's getting our tickets here with Turkish lira, so that's all right.

Did you get the pictures? Our housing development looks pretty bleak from certain angles, but they're frantically laying sidewalks and asphalting the roads before the fall rains set in. By next year, everything should look green and grassy.... Things are going smoothly. Timmy held up his bottle to drink today, a big thrill for Hikmet. She's outside now, scrabbling about in the aforementioned asphalt.

Sela sends his regards. Your loving daughter, Anna Maria

Letter from Mother in Spokane

Route 4, Box 188, Spokane
November 7, 1956

Dear Anna Maria,

Just mailed my second set of notarized pages with a letter, and self-addressed stamped airmail envelope to Turkish Consulate, Wash. DC. Made phone calls to LA yesterday, concluded the LA set went astray. A Filter Center friend in U.S. Immigration office gave me the DC address, so I sent the notarized sheets and letter to the Turkish Embassy, Wash DC. Expect return delivery notice by 13th or 14th. Will send you airmail answer when it gets back here. If I write you with the shop address, means we haven't heard definitely yet. Hate to have you open a regular airmail and find nothing definite. If I get it, I'll send it in a long striped envelope, so you'll know at once. We expect it will work out all right.

Now that the election is over with, maybe Ike will buckle down to business.

Haven't heard from Mike in the Marines; he is in the Amphibian Tracks, you know. Everything is on the jumpy side. Don't worry about the money. We can manage. The family is progressing nicely with Camilla and Joyce, so far; now we're waiting for Rosemary and Nona. As Pete says, "little house angels are fine!" He's busy making baby cribs in his free time.

Our best regards to Sela. Mom

116

Journal: Note on Sponsorship Letters   None of us understood the correct procedures or addresses for obtaining the sponsorship required — which, it seems, is not the work of embassies, but rather of their consulates. Mama's letters were mis-sent to Washington DC, and apparently the "lost" set sent to LA were re-routed from the LA Consulate on to the nearest Turkish Consulate dealing with such requests, which was in Chicago.

The Turkish Consulate in Chicago returned the papers to Mama, requesting certification by the County Clerk in Spokane. They also requested a financial statement from her bank.

Eventually, after this exasperating routing and rerouting, all the proper papers arrived, were processed and approved, and sent on to Batman. ❧

Letter to Tulsa Friends

TPAO Sitesi, Batman
November 13, 1956

Dear Brownfields,

First, the books came some time past, and I never thanked you, did I? In fact, I've read them all now, except *The Universe and Dr. Einstein*, which I'm going to start during the next mental lull. Aldous Huxley was just what I'd been needing, something refreshing and chewy. Many, many thanks!

Travel plans are shaping up, and I think my visa papers will come through in time for me to make it home for Christmas. Or as soon thereafter as possible. Sela keeps saying I should take the polar flight to the States, which would land me in Seattle, an hour from Spokane. His trip's off, incidentally. Maybe next year.

But I keep saying that it would be much easier to stop through Tulsa with just Hikmet and Timur, than it would be to stop through on the way back with *three*. And I can't imagine a trip to the States without a tour through Tulsa! So, how are you all fixed for an extra room for about a week the middle of December? If that's not convenient, let me know. I'll post you on the time as soon as I can make plane reservations.

In the meantime, I'm busy cleaning house and practicing packing. Our Nafiye had to go back to her village, which left me up a creek. The word was out, so we finally found another maid.

Emine, Our New Blessing

My newest helper is Emine [eh mee neh], a girl from a nearby village who now lives with us. Barely five feet tall, long black braids, sparkling brown eyes, and a pure gold front tooth. She does the laundry, baskets of it, and twinkles about the house like a little bird. I marvel at our present good fortune: I would be wearing out in little pieces without Emine. I really miss her when she goes off now and then to visit her family in the village.

Emine's nephew, Mehmet, who takes care of somebody's horse down the road, comes in the morning and afternoons, between chasing, watering and feeding the horse, and watches Timmy. Sometimes, walking slowly, they go after the local newspaper or the daily loaf of bread at the little store around the corner. They enjoy the sunshine together.

117

Like Nafiye before her, Emine is learning about modern luxuries such as clothes pins and WCs. And she speaks little Turkish. Since I speak no Kurdish, we started off with a powerful two-word vocabulary: "OK!" and "Sonra!" which means later. When you give this some thought, you'll realize that along with voice inflection, facial and manual gestures, the possible connotations are numerous.

I also have some difficulty remembering Emine's praying times. She has to stop whatever she's doing, wash her hands and feet, take out her little prayer rug and readjust her head scarf to make sure all her hair is covered. Apparently they don't tell time by a clock in her village; it's up to me to learn her prayer schedule.

Sela's still busy, going from here to the various camps. Now that cold weather's setting in, he's back to wearing those old blue ski pajamas as underwear, the ones he wore as a dancing girl at Alan and Deanie's Halloween party in Tulsa. I've mended and re-mended them, until they're something of an institution now.

Nothing spectacular going on around here. Will save all the little oddments for an enormous pot of coffee and some "imported" Turkish cigarettes for you. The smell doesn't bother me at all anymore.

Give our best to all. Write soon.

Expectantly, A

Letter from Mother in Spokane

Route 4, Box 188, Spokane
December 20, 1956

Dear Sela,

This is a special greeting to you from all of us here. We do wish that we could see you and shake hands and say "Howdy!" But we do think of you when the family is all together, and we sit and talk and exchange news. We are all here but Mike, and he is still in the Marines, based in Twenty Nine Palms, California right now.

We hope Anna Maria and the little ones can come, but we are holding our breath till we hear. If and when the world gets better, we may all visit together as we'd like to.

In the meantime, it's been said many times, many ways, but again Merry Christmas and a Happy New Year to you.

Mom

Journal: Canceling the Tulsa Stopover At the last minute, I had to change plans for a stopover in Tulsa; the travel arrangements were simply too complicated, and time was too rushed.

I still have hopes for visiting the Brownfields and other old school friends on the return trip. 🐦

118

Ethelbert* and Marie Harms Jones Family, Spokane 1956

back row: John, Wallie, Timur, Pete, Mike, Aaron, David
middle row: Joyce, Camilla, Marie Harms Jones, Anna Maria, Nona, Rosemary
front row: Marty, Wendy, Andy, Chrissy, Hikmet, Terry, Katy, Johnny, Janene

Families at time of photo:

David Jones & Rosemary Nason Jones = Janene
John Harms Jones & Joyce McBride Jones = Martha Ann, John Curtis, Wendy
Anna Maria Jones Malkoç & Selahattin Malkoç = Hikmet, Timur
Aaron Jones & Nona Pacek = Teresa, Christine, Kathleen
Camilla Jones Phillipson & Wallace Phillipson = Andrew Paul
Simeon Peter Jones = *unmarried*
Michael Harris Jones = *unmarried*

Letter to Tulsa Friends

Route 4, Box 188, Spokane
January 2, 1957

Dear Brownfields, and all: Greetings and Happy New Year!

I finally made it to Spokane! It's taken me all this time to recover, so if you've wondered why the silence, chalk it up to travel fatigue.

The SAS Polar Route to Grandmother's House

It was a lovely Saturday afternoon, December 22, when Hikmet, Timur, and I took off from the International Airport in Ankara. The Scandinavian Air Lines plane was loaded with children and families being evacuated from Cairo, enroute to Europe. There was a lot of crying. Hikmet joined in, to my surprise, but

119

not because she had the jitters. She just suddenly realized she was leaving her Daddy, and she wanted to go right back to Batman. What a decision: Santa Claus at Grandmother's, or Daddy at Batman.... Santa won.

So, because the front seat baby basket was already occupied, I held Timmy all the way to Vienna. Try eating a filet mignon left-handed sometime, with a large infant balanced in the other arm. Finally, I simply picked it up and ate it in my fingers. *No one is watching*, I told myself, *and I'm really hungry!*

Luxury Stopover in Copenhagen

We flew over Belgrade and landed for short stops in Stuttgart and Vienna late that night, staying on the plane, of course. I was feeling shackled to the seat by the time we arrived for a forced layover in Copenhagen at about two a.m. Timmy and Hikmet were alert and bright-eyed as we waited at the Scandinavian airlines office to arrange for a hotel room, compliments of SAS.

Three of the women passengers from Istanbul were in a group with us, and because they knew only Turkish, I had to help them with their various problems: lost luggage, reservations, hotel arrangements. I didn't mind doing it, personally, but they certainly weren't very helpful in return. I learned a lesson there, all right: be self-sufficient, and never depend on other people to give you a hand when you travel. They may not!

Our room in the Hotel Europa was wonderful, the cleanest I've ever seen. Positively everything was disinfected. And the furniture was lovely: simple, but functional and graceful.

We three slept like logs under crisp, white, feather comforters and were served an enormous breakfast by a very efficient and sweet chambermaid. It was heavenly! When I saw the huge tray, I felt transported: hot sweet rolls, fruit juice, fresh butter, fruit jellies, cheeses galore, fresh cow's milk for Hikmet and for Timmy's bottle, whipped cream for my coffee.

After we checked back at the SAS desk for a flight up-date, the hotel sent up a German nanny to babysit with Timur and Hikmet, so the Turkish ladies and I could go shopping — mostly window shopping. Luckily, everyone I approached spoke English, and the shops were sparkling and magical with Christmas decorations. Later, I just had to take Hikmet for a walk. For a change, she was almost speechless. We both fell in love with beautiful Copenhagen.

About eight thirty that evening, we took off for Strongfjord, the last stop on the Polar Route and three hours out from Copenhagen. Timmy was snoozing in his basket, Hikmet was asleep beside me, so I watched the wind swirling snow about the plane while we refueled. It was terribly cold and dark for hours and hours. Eventually, we were told to set our watches back nine hours and were served a delicious breakfast. Later on, we had another delicious "breakfast."

Radioing the Radar Base

We saw the sunrise sometime in the afternoon.. Then later along the way, the SAS pilot came back to announce we would be passing over an American radar station. He asked me (*Me!*) if I would be kind enough to say a few words to the men stationed there. "We always do this," he explained. "They would love to hear a feminine American voice wishing them Merry Christmas." Since there were no other American women aboard, unencumbered or otherwise, I simply had to oblige. Up in the cockpit, the co-pilot held Timmy and his bottle while I

120

adjusted the head set and gave the call signal, talked for a minute or two, and signed off with *"Roger and Over,"* according to instructions. It was a thrilling moment to realize this call signal was actually connecting us to someone far below our airplane, on terra firma.

In response to my greetings, the American voice on the radio told me he'd talked to no one but Eskimos for almost a year. The only time he and the other men stationed there spoke English with any outsiders was with the planes flying over — such as the short conversation we were having. Now, that's *real* isolation, to my way of thinking. More isolated than Raman Mountain!

Arrival in the USA

After another long twilight nap, we glided into the LA International Airport on Monday morning at 10 a.m. California time [8 p.m. Ankara time]. Ah, the sunshine, the glorious, golden sunshine! I wanted to peel off multiple layers of heavy winter clothing on the spot.

Watching Hikmet, clutching Timmy on my left arm, holding assorted string bags, and guiding the last of the Turkish ladies (who shall remain nameless), I despaired of ever getting through the long lines at the U.S. Immigration and Customs gates. Diplomatic visa holders were first, then State Department personnel, then ordinary citizens, and aliens last. When it was my turn, I spoke up and explained that my Turkish friend didn't speak English and was lost without me as her interpreter, so they let allowed her to go through with the children and me. When we finally all reached the exit gates, "my friend" rushed on ahead toward her tall, stalwart son waiting at the gate. Off she went — without a backward glance at the three of us bogged down with hand baggage. Oh, the ingratitude, I thought to myself!

I was fading fast, with just enough pep to make it to the United Airlines desk. Thank God, in nothing flat, an attendant showed up with a baby stroller, told Hikmet where to buy an ice-cream cone with her dime, and confirmed our reservations on the next plane. I attended to Timmy first. Then, I made a telephone call to the mother of the helpful American Embassy clerk in Ankara, and relayed her daughter's sweet Christmas message. Next I rounded up Hikmet, who was talking to another little girl. "Are you going to America, too?" In Hikmet's mind, we wouldn't be in America until we reached Grandmother's.

At one p.m., our connecting plane took off for a short flight to Reno. There we waited desperately until six p.m. for the next connection to Spokane. I kept thinking, Oh, Lord, let us just måke it to the next stop! That turned out to be Pendleton, Oregon.

Fogged In Over Spokane Airport Christmas Eve

On the last lap of this adventurous Polar Route trip, we flew into a thick fog, right over the Spokane air field, circling for an hour over several dozen Jones and Phillipson relatives waving frantically and praying for us to land. Alas, it was impossible in that fog.

The most feasible connection to Spokane was by train, our pilot was informed, so he flew down to Pendleton to land, 15 minutes before the local "milk" train was due. With the help of two good Samaritans, the children and I managed to board the train, and spent the rest of the night in the coach car. [That was a fortunate decision: for the next week, no planes landed or took off in Spokane.]

At the Spokane train station, we piled into a waiting Checker Cab. I knew this was the taxi company my mother has a running account with, whenever she needs a ride into town. When the driver asked, "Where to?" I asked him if he knew Rimrock Drive above Indian Canyon. "Oh, yes! You must be Mrs. Jones's daughter from Turkey!" he exclaimed. "Welcome to Spokane!" That was the most spectacular part of our arrival in Spokane. The edge had really been dulled.

Arriving in Spokane on Christmas Morning

"Please honk the horn!" I told the driver, as he pulled up to the house on Route 4. It was now Tuesday, nine a.m., Christmas Day.

Mama opened the front door, gasped at the three of us there in her doorway, but recovered quickly. From her apron pocket, she pulled a tiny gilt bugle and blew a couple of sharp blasts, rousing the nearest families and neighbors. Throughout the morning, my brothers' little Joneses and my sister's little Phillipsons continued to arrive. All told, there were ten little cousins to greet Hikmet (the oldest of my mother's grandchildren) and Timur (the youngest). Mama was so proud of "the whole kit and caboodle."

Santa's Repeat Performance

After a lunch of many delectable potluck dishes, my brothers Michael and Aaron quietly excused themselves from the table. Shortly thereafter, we heard the sounds of Santa's sleigh bells and a noisy clatter on the roof. Then a red-suited, white-bearded Santa Claus burst open the front door with a "Ho! Ho! Ho!" and a gunnysack full of presents over his shoulder.

I thought Mike's dramatic sound effects on the roof, and Aaron's "Ho! Ho! Ho!"'s were quite convincing. Hikmet was awestruck by the whole scenario. She couldn't take her eyes off Santa as he dramatically emptied his bag of presents, gave his theatrical spiel, and made an equally dramatic exit.

"Well, Hikmet, what did you think of Santa?" Mama asked her.

Hikmet was in a state of puzzlement. "Grandmother, his hands were meat," she responded, (translating from the Turkish word for flesh) "but his face was *cloth!*" Never nonplussed, Mama explained the cloth was to keep his whiskers tidy and out of the soup. This explanation seemed to satisfy Hikmet. And in an hour or so, she'd stopped saying "Grandmother" and was calling her "Grandma" like her little cousins.

At some point the telephone rang, someone wanting to talk to me. "It might be Bob Briley, the reporter," Mama murmured, "for a telephone interview. As a volunteer at the Civil Defense Filter Center, Mama had met a lot of volunteers from the newspaper and radio stations. (I dare say they all knew about The Daughter in Turkey.)

The caller was indeed "Reporter Bob" at the local newspaper, with pretty standard questions about where I'd been living, how the trip was, and so on. I told him one travel highlight was my conversation in the SAS cockpit flying over Greenland. While I'd been manipulating the radio transmitter in the cockpit, I was rather nervous, but while being interviewed on the telephone in Spokane, I didn't feel nervous at all; my energy was at such a low ebb I didn't feel much of

122

anything. I did tell him I'd learned a new lesson on this trip: never travel with anything you can't carry yourself. And I spared him the details.

Later, dear Aunt Ann telephoned 70 miles away from the wheat ranch in Wilbur, saying she was thrilled to hear me on the radio. By that time I was sound asleep and dead to the world.

The whole Christmas holiday has been so festive that Hikmet stopped being excited after a while. Everyone seems surprised — they shouldn't be after my letters on the subject — that she speaks English with no Turkish accent. And that she won't speak Turkish to them. In fact, no one's gotten one word of Turkish out of her. I've always taught her it's rude to speak in a language if others present don't understand it, but it's the wrong time to be taking my training to heart!

Things have calmed down a bit. My youngest brother, Mike, on leave from Twenty Nine Palms Marine Base with his brand new sergeant stripes, has just left. There will be a slight lull until next Sunday when sweet Aunt Camilla, widow of a "hellfire-and-brimstone" German Lutheran minister, comes from Nebraska to stay with my mother. Mama says, "That will purify some of this atmosphere."

Timmy has an appointment with the pediatrician this afternoon. I've already had my check-up; the obstetrician reassures me all is well and I have an excellent blood count.

Oh, what a giddy round! Tomorrow, my three sisters-in-law: Rosemary, Joyce, and Nona, are coming here for tea and/or Turkish coffee, Turkish delight, Izmir figs, and Turkish cigarettes. I've saved a pair of silver earrings and a piece of lacework for each. I should have brought another suitcase of trinkets; they're flying like feathers in the wind!

It's a rather isolated area here on Route 4, and we have few neighbors except for Jones family members up the hill and down the road. Things are a sometimes a bit dull, so it's lovely to get a letter now and then. I think it also brightens the mailman's day…. This address is:
Mrs. Selahattin Malkoç
Route 4, Box 188
Spokane 16, Washington, USA

My very best to everyone, and will try to keep you all posted. Love, A
PS for Dear Brownfields:

I feel so awful about having left you all up in the air, I don't know how to ask you to forgive me. We waited and waited in Batman for Timur's visa papers, and I got more and more frantic. As soon as they came, we left the very next morning for Diyarbakır/Ankara, and such a mess! As you see, I just made it home for Christmas, in a state of near collapse. Don't know when I'll be going back to Batman. Not until I can keep track of three, that's for sure. Anyway, it will definitely be through Tulsa.

Please tell everyone how disappointed I was. I hope to see them all later.

Sela sent greetings. You can imagine how much he'd have liked to come, too. A

Journal: Watch Out for Teethers! Safely ensconced in my mother's home, and reassured by the family obstetrician, I'm waiting for the next Malkoç.

The Turkish saying is: "When the apple is ripe, it will fall from the tree." So we're all patient, and I am happy to be visiting my family here in the meantime.

Hikmet is learning to play with her "dozen cousins" and has learned all the words to the Mouseketeers' television theme song, which had mystified her when she first saw the other children singing along. Of course, she misses her Baba, but otherwise, she's one happy child.

Timmy is teething now and toddling everywhere. Not much hair yet, but he looks very collegiate in blue corduroy pants, tee shirt, and sneakers. These rubber-soled shoes are aptly named: he has an absolutely silent foot-fall.

Yesterday, he toddled into the kitchen, where Mama was washing dishes. She always hums little tunes while gazing out the window, admiring her fruit trees. "When I wash dishes, I'm in a world of my own thoughts," she says.

With his painfully erupting teeth, however, little Timmy has only one thought these days: something, *anything*, to gum on. He must have spied Mama's bare legs under her cotton house dress — right at his eye level — and silently toddled over to gnaw on her pale calf.

I heard Mama's piercing scream way out where I was hanging up laundry in the garden. "Why, I shot *straight up!*" she told me.

Eventually, Timmy stopped crying when we found him a teething ring to soothe his gums, Mama relaxed, and we all had a good laugh. The tooth marks disappeared in a few days.

We've arranged for neighbor Yvonne Dean to take care of Timmy when I go to the hospital. With her day-care service in her home, she's "the mothers' angel" of the neighborhood. So I'm reassured on that score. My overnight bag is ready, and I ask myself each morning, "Is today the day?" ❦

Journal: Kâmuran Arrives in Spokane Biologically speaking, the birth signal is often in the dead of night, with its own unique scenario. Picture this, if you can:

I awaken, bolt upright, like a character in a silent film. I get dressed, pick up my bag, and tiptoe over to brother Pete, sound asleep in the next bedroom. "OK, Pete, time to go! And don't talk," I whisper. I don't want to disturb Mama, sleeping in her bedroom downstairs.

Pete and I have thoroughly discussed the routine: He's to drive me to St. Luke's Hospital, where we were all born, coincidentally. The agreement is simple: he's to drop me off at the front desk, and he doesn't have to wait around — he's a young bachelor and has a squeamish side.

We tiptoe single file down the narrow stairs in the dark. "Are you OK, Pete?" I whisper. "Yeah," he mumbles as we make our way through the pitch-black living room.

Mama's voice pierces the dark. "Is it time to go?" She turns on the lights. She is already dressed and wearing her winter coat and scarf. By now, brother Pete has reached the front door, is pulling on his snow jacket and wool cap.

"Pete, are you *sure* you're ready to go?" I ask him, stifling a hysterical laugh. I mustn't startle him into a state of panic, I think to myself, because he's got to drive us all the way downtown and across the Spokane River on icy, snowy roads. After a long moment of silence, he looks down at his plaid shorts, realizes he's forgotten to put on his pants!

To shorten this long story, we all survive the agonizingly slow and hazardous ride to St. Luke's Hospital, of course. Baby Kâmuran arrives in her own sweet time, and with none of the complications we'd been worried about. Mama sends a telegram to Sela in Batman, announcing the good news....

Before leaving the hospital several days later, I thanked the stern head nurse. Although she never softened or cracked a smile, she gave me a compliment I cherish: "Wish all my patients were as good!" She had no idea how much I appreciated that hospital stay. Real luxury! ❦

Letter from Sela

TPAO Sitesi, Batman
April 24, 1957

My Dearest Schatzi!

How is Kâmuran doing? How are you and the kids?

Thought to write you a short letter tonight since I felt kind of lonesome. Hope you make it soon. It's getting awfully quiet around here without you. I don't think I can take it any longer than two-three months more.

It's been raining around here awfully hard; we can't do much work. Rifat came back yesterday from Ankara, so I can go to Diyarbakır to see the dentist.

Everybody around here is asking about you, and when you're coming back. I hope you are doing all right and not getting too tired taking care of Kâmuran and Timur.

Did he start to walk yet?

Is big darling Hikmet behaving nicely for her lonesome daddy?

Halit's wife, Nimet hanım, wants to know whether you could please bring her one durable, good quality panty girdle size 28, white; one slip size 32 white; and one bra size 36, also white. If you can bring them, her brother-in-law in New York will send you dollars to pay for them. Let me know how much you need, so they can send you the money order.

Give my best to Mom, Camilla, John, Michael, Peter, Aaron, and David. Everybody you know here sends regards. Give Hikmet a big hug around the neck.

Your loving Sela
PS: You wanted the words to "Üsküdar" so I wrote it on the enclosed paper. Sorry I can't translate this right now. [Eartha Kitt is making this song famous in the U.S.]

125

Letter to Tulsa Friends

Route 4, Box 188, Spokane
June 8, 1957

Dear Brownfields and all,

    You might know I lost my address book again! Last time I had it was during a family gathering with fourteen little things toddling/crawling around, not counting anyone older than Hikmet. Then I ran across that magazine you sent, Bill, with your address printed on it!

    I just wrote Sela, setting the date to leave here directly for Tulsa August 15, and leaving Tulsa a week later. Is that OK? Will you have room for us? How about a crib and/or playpen for Timmy? I don't think our visit will be *too* rough on you. I just had a wonderful time visiting an old school friend in Seattle: no nights on the town, children in bed at an early hour. We enjoyed just talking a lot. Now I'm all primed for questions about Turkey!

    Sela will write to friends in Ankara, who have friends in a travel agency, to get our tickets. (Everybody doing favors for friends and family, that's the way it's done over there.)

    He writes that he's very lonesome, he's busy playing poker, and rearranging the furniture, although he doesn't like the "abstract effect" he's created. Funny, the whole building being concrete! (My pun for the day.)

    Except for the fact that Sela's there, of course, I do dread going back, just a little. Sigh! Not because I'll miss everything here, but mainly because of the dreary gossiping and almost total lack of intellectual stimulation there. Even though I'm always "busy," I do feel the need for a little mental friction now and then.

    In the meantime, I'm enjoying life here and now. It's beautiful. As is life with you two, too, I trust....

Now, Timmy has just waked up, so adieu with love, A

Letter to Tulsa Friends

Route 4, Box 188, Spokane
July 1, 1957

Dear Brownfields and all,

    My Aunt Birdie just flew back to Alaska, which was saddening, and now I seem to have a cold in my back. But this morning, the mailman drove by with your letter and it helped lift my spirits!

    The strangest thing also came in the mail: the Turkish Consulate finally returned my Turkish passport, with Kâmuran's name now included, and they also included her photograph. However they did it is beyond me. I didn't send any photos because they hadn't mentioned that pictures of the baby were required, although I had inquired if they were necessary. The "new" photo they affixed is an old one of Hikmet at the same tender age! There is a family resemblance, but it

126

stops at the hairline. You may remember that Hikmet was as bald as Winston Churchill; Kâmuran has a delicate cap of dark auburn hair.

And I owe 52 cents on back postage! Well, I hope to have this all unsnarled by departure time. I must stop now. There's a sinkful of dishes in the kitchen waiting for me, and it's blowing up a rain on the laundry line....

Looking forward to seeing you all in Tulsa! Domestically yours, A

Letter from Ankara College Friend

33 East 83rd Street, New York City
August 14, 1957

Dear Anna Maria,

Assume you'd not received my letter before your last card on the 9th. Can I get a reservation for you? If so, let me know what kind of accommodations you'd want in way of beds, etc. Also about meeting you.

I can go over to Newark if you tell me the line and flight number. La Guardia or Idlewilde would have been much better than Newark, but don't suppose you can change that now.

I don't imagine you would want to come to dinner on Sat. after you arrive, but what about Sunday? You'll go mad staying in a hotel room all that time and the kids would misbehave. Between you, Hikmet and me, we could keep them happy long enough for dinner.

Let me know about the hotel and meeting you. Now that I have a two-and-a-half month old nephew, babies don't scare me as much. They aren't really bone china.

Love, Barb *[Barbara Chidsey, a teaching colleague from Ankara College]*

127

11

RETURN WITH THREE CHILDREN

Letter to Tulsa Friends

TPAO Sitesi, Batman
September 1, 1957

Dear Brownfields and all,

We made it home! A long letter follows soon, I hope, full of thanks for the wonderful, wonderful visit with you all in Tulsa.

We stayed only two days in Ankara; the baby's diapers hardly got a chance to dry before the last lap. (My daily pun) Everyone is fine, no accidents.

Sela says Hello! Hello! (Twice is for emphasis.) All is well here. *Very well*. East or West, Home is *Best*.

Love, A

Letter to Spokane and Tulsa

TPAO Sitesi, Batman
September 3, 1957

Dear Family, and Friends in Tulsa: Announcing Our Arrival!

To all those concerned, and to all our dear armchair travelers, here we are! The return trip was hectic, but happily mis-hapless and full of the old adventurousness that I love.

Flying Spokane to Tulsa

To begin with, I was full of butterflies, leaving Spokane. Saying goodbye, which I hate, was part of it; the rest was due to worrying. Hikmet was quite upset about leaving Grandmother and her domain; she later became a bit airsick. And I forgot the Dramamine!

The two-hour wait in Denver wasn't bad, but the stewardess who checked us at plane change seemed a trifle perturbed that we were traveling "alone." (This was nothing to the reaction from the Tulsa-to-New York stewardess: "What? Three children? All the way to New York? *Oh, no!*" I spared her any further travel details. To her surprise, she had no trouble from us at all.)

Actually, the flight to Tulsa would have been relatively restful except that the plane was late to depart, and we had to wait until after 8 p.m. for dinner. The children and I were the very last to be served, and then there was no milk on the plane!

On arrival in Tulsa, I did feel a bit haggard, and must have looked even more so, because our old friend Brownfield didn't even recognize me. K. and T.

were being carried off the plane by two kind strangers, which may have added to the confusion. At any rate, we had a fine time in Tulsa, seeing old friends and renewing acquaintances. When I think of how wonderful people are to us, I feel humbly grateful in spirit.

Nine days later, rejuvenated in both the spirit and the flesh, we set off for New York. On this flight, I felt sorrier for this stewardess than she for me. There were more than a dozen children under twelve, mostly babies, and several little boys going alone. Somehow, we all managed, and when we circled over New York City for the landing, I found myself really enjoying the thrill.

Stopover in New York

We came down in Newark, and there was our good friend Barbara Chidsey from Ankara Koleji, who had come over from upper Manhattan to meet us. Such efficiency! She grabbed all the bags, I had baby Kâmuran and the miscellaneous, Timmy trotted along waving his little red cookie bucket, and Hikmet nonchalantly brought up the rear with her doll and trappings. Can't you just picture us? We did look picturesque.

Our baggage was dispatched with swift dispatch, and we boarded the coach for New York City and the Tudor Hotel on East 42nd. Hikmet seemed disappointed that the sky scrapers didn't, actually, but she was quite impressed with the Lincoln Tunnel under the Hudson River. Arrival at the hotel was what I'd feared: the reception clerk wanted to give us a room at twice the price of the estimate, but our guardian angel Barbara bravely held her ground. She helped escort us to a minutely-sized room with twin beds on the sixteenth floor.

After showers, baths, and a supper of canned baby food and milk I'd brought from Tulsa to spare me a shopping trip in New York, Kâmuran dozed off in an empty bottom dresser drawer, and Timmy fell instantly asleep on a bed. Hikmet and I perched near the corner window and snacked on travel treats. "Oh, Mother, there's a whole city shining in your eyes!" she marveled, seeing the reflection in my glasses. Rain was splattering the streets below, mist was drifting about the top of the Chrysler building near us, the beacon on the Empire State building played in and out of the fog and blackness, the street lights, neon signs, and traffic lights glittered in the rain. It was all like Christmas under an umbrella.

The next day we were invited to lunch at Barbara's, in an historical, reconstructed Dutch farmhouse built in 1825 when there was nothing around East 83rd but meadowlands. Her one-bedroom apartment had its own entrance leading down from the street, with a black wrought iron gate and old stone steps. The kitchen was completely closed into the wall; you opened the door and there was a tiny sink, surface range, refrigerator, and built-ins. Amazing to see such a delicious dinner being concocted in such a Lilliputian space, but I did say Barbara was efficient, didn't I? And how I relished that baked ham!

Back at the hotel that evening, a friend of a friend in Ankara came by to see us. We exchanged news about our mutual friend, and had a delightful time of it, with ham and cheese on rye and a bottle of good beer, while I sat on a chair in the bathroom doorway to keep an eye on the children, and our guest perched with surprising dignity atop the you-know-what.

Idlewilde International Airport

We spent a restful night and awoke to a torrent of rain, lightening, and wind. Having acquired a wary weather eye from long experience with Turkish flight changes and postponements due to inclemency, I automatically picked up the phone and called the International Airport. I should live so long.

"Weather? What weather? Lady, our flight schedules have nothing to do with the weather!" I felt foolish but relieved.

Guardian Angel Barbara's friend Polly had checked up on baggage and called me with detailed instructions: Be there three hours early to check in overweight luggage; it can go airfreight on the same plane at half the price of overweight. So we checked out pronto, and were all in a dither to get to Idlewilde International before the deadline. The cab driver who was to take us to the East-side terminal, where we were to change to an airlines coach, which would take us to the airport, where we would take another cab to the Scandinavian Airlines — are you following? — knocked the fare down and took us all the way out!

It was a lovely ride all the way through Brooklyn, and by that time the sun was shining merrily. The baggage was neatly dispatched, and not exorbitantly. One SAS stewardess took Baby Kâmuran into the office and relieved me of all the hand baggage while everything was being cleared through.

Spending that three hours in the airport reminded me of the old riddle about the farmer with the goose, the fox, and the bag of corn: The farmer had to cross the river and could take only two loads at a time. He couldn't take the fox first, because the goose would eat the corn, and he couldn't take the corn first, because the fox would eat the goose, and so on. While I made little foraging trips, etc., I would leave either Baby Kâmuran or Timmy with Hikmet on a bench, but not both. It took downright ingenuity, if I do say so. Especially trying to fish a dime out of my pocket for the lavatory, with Timmy clutching my skirt or Kâmuran dangling on one arm. And those automatic coin-slot toilet doors are tricky. You get closed out if you're not quick on the trigger, and there you are, out of luck, and out of a dime!

Snoozing across the Atlantic

At zero hour, we were escorted ahead of the other passengers by an entourage of ticket agents, stewardesses, and helping hands. I thought back on all my strenuous practice sessions on Rural Route 4 carrying a loaded flight bag, a loaded tote bag and Baby Kâmuran, with Timmy and Hikmet carrying their own tiny tote bags down the road a quarter of a mile to visit my sister-in-law. Here at Idlewilde, I ended up carrying only the baby!

We sat in three seats across the front, all on the same side, and Kâmuran had a wall bassinet. There had been an error, oh joy, and another basket had been hooked to the wall across the aisle, in front of two empty seats. Timmy slept there all night. Hikmet curled up on a blanket at my feet under Kâmuran, and I stretched out on our three seats. Timmy kept bobbing up for water, and Hikmet's feet kept relaxing out into the aisle. (We were right next to the lavatories and this constituted a traffic hazard.)

In spite of all this, I managed several delicious cat naps. Breakfast was delicious, too. Sumptuous and almost more than I, in my "starved" condition, could eat. Then we were in Copenhagen.

130

A Change of Planes and Three Stops to Ankara

"All right, children, here we go." Like a little old firehouse horse put out to pasture but still alert to the fire bell, Timmy grabbed his cookie bucket, Hikmet clutched her Mary-doll, and we debarked with Baby Kâmuran to change planes. The hour of fresh sunshine was revivifying, and though we didn't leave the terminal, we got a good glimpse of beautiful Copenhagen on takeoff. The children slept through the stop at Stuttgart, but we all scrambled off for a walk about the Vienna airport.

From Vienna we flew straight on to Istanbul, where we stopped for less than an hour, though it seemed ages because we had to stay on the plane and the air circulation system was cut off. It was terribly hot. Hikmet and I unpacked our little silk souvenir fans and fanned furiously. The hour or so on to Ankara was a busy one, tidying up the children and getting ready. By now, it was nearly 11:00 p.m. We'd been aloft since 4:30 p.m. the day before, and where did all that extra miscellaneous come from? I frantically stuffed airplane souvenirs into flight bags and for the last time rallied the children round. "OK, children, here we go!"

Sela was there at the Ankara Air Terminal door, grinning like a Cheshire cat — with faithful friends Marion and Turhan Türker waiting to see that we were taken care of immediately at the customs desk. The officials opened one bag full of spent diapers and let it go at that. All the while, Hikmet was clutching my skirt, shy of Sela's glances on the other side of the railings. Her shyness soon wore off and she began a long account of Grandmother and her family in America which she hasn't stopped yet.

All of a sudden, I felt tired. I'd geared myself to hold up as far as Ankara, where I thought I would quietly curl up for about ten hours and do nothing but sleep. Hah! When we reached our old apartment — the friends who'd taken it after we left Ankara kindly let us use it while they were in Istanbul — all three children were still bright and chipper, looking like sleep was the last thing they needed. It was, sigh, 4:00 a.m. before they gave up and settled down in bed. By then it occurred to Sela: "Of course, they aren't sleepy! What time would it be in Spokane?"

Most of our Ankara friends were out of town to escape the heat, so our two days there were spent mostly trying to catch up on diapers and sleep. The morning we were to leave for Diyarbakır was the 30th of August, a beautiful day for a holiday. The crowded streets were decorated with gigantic paper lanterns and huge red flags with white crescents in honor of the visiting King of Afghanistan.

A Desperate Dash out to the Ankara Airport

We loaded our luggage on the sidewalk and sat down to wait patiently for Marion and Turhan in their golden Plymouth to take us back out to the airport. We speculated about the delay and gradually became concerned when they didn't show up. I got panicky, but Sela kept cool, of course, just bolted down the street to hail a taxi. We threw things into the trunk and the driver hastily roped it down.

It was a good half-hour drive to the airport and we had exactly 30 minutes. Greatly relieved to be on our way, we jolted along for a few minutes until the taxi suddenly jerked to a shuddering halt.

Out of gas! *Fate!* But in front of a gas station! *More* fate! The driver filled the tank, and cast about wildly for someone to take his money. All in

131

desperate silence. An eternity of five minutes passed before someone finally emerged to collect the gas money, and we hit the road again.

My main worry was catching that plane. I knew plane tickets were sold out days ahead, and trains are impossibly full this time of year. I was also concerned about our friends, always so punctual. I kept my mutterings in English, though. If we'd urged the driver to go any faster, I knew a blowout would be even more Fate.

Sela kept glancing back over his shoulder. "Aha! Here they come!" he shouted. We could see a tiny, golden glint speeding towards us on the long, flat road winding through the bare, brown hills. I was relieved that nothing really dire had befallen them; they'd been caught up in the holiday traffic snarl.

Our taxi rattled up to the terminal ramp only a few seconds in front of the Plymouth. Doors flew open, suitcases spilled out, I made a wild dash to the ticket desk, where they were paging us over the loudspeaker. Sela hurried off to check in the overweight baggage. He soon returned, strolling leisurely and calmly.

"Plane's late," he announced. Not the sort of travel situation for a weak heart, eh? We all sat down to sooth our jangled nerves with a glass of tea, to chat and wait. Finally, the plane was ready. In a much more relaxed frame of mind, we bid farewell to our friends and boarded the plane.

A Bumpy Flight to Diyarbakır, and the Post Train to Batman

This interior trip is one I've never liked to fly. It's always a small plane for the local flight, and flies low over the mountains of Anatolia. As usual, it was rough, and hot to boot.

When the plane stopped down in Elazığ for unloading and loading, we all had to remain in our seats, nearly perishing with the heat and no air conditioning inside the plane. Fortunately, the children slept almost the entire three and a half hours. Almost without exception, everyone else on the plane was upset, and busily involved with their airsickness bags. Sela and I exchanged glances and gritted our teeth. We couldn't afford to get airsick at this point, so we stuck it out, though it was really hard on our queasy stomachs.

Diyarbakır airport looked the same: hot, dusty, and full of flies, but it is our good fortune that TPAO has a clean, cool guest house in town where we could take over an empty room and nap in turns. Hikmet woke in time to see the holiday parade of soldiers marching down the street; we heard them winding up their festivities at the nearby military barracks. There's something thrilling about band music. The bravery of it, I guess, and in that heat.

At seven that evening, we were ready and waiting for the post train to chug into the Diyarbakır train station. Sela unloaded our baggage off the Company's pickup that had delivered us to the station, and tossed it all into a first-class compartment window. Unlike the Kurtalan Express, the post train is the equivalent of a slow milk train, so we whiled away the three hours to Batman juggling the luggage, watering and playing with the children, and munching on the apples we'd bought that morning in Ankara.

A Neighborly Welcome Home

What a motley crew we were, dusty and dirty, when we pulled into Batman Station and were greeted by what seemed like a huge crowd, but was really only a dozen close neighbors, who followed us all the way home to give us a "warm welcome." Of course, everyone wanted to take a good look at Baby Kâmuran, new to all, at Timur, no longer the baby of the household, and at Hikmet, who couldn't speak one word of Turkish anymore!

They all trooped into our living room and formed a half-circle. "Well," they asked in chorus, "How do you like it?"

I realized then they'd followed us in to get my reaction to the refurbished apartment. Sela had painted the living and dining room walls, had had the armchairs and divan recovered, and all the curtains washed and ironed. He "personally" had cleaned all the woodwork, "as well as the windows." The *piece de resistance* was a new end-table-bookshelf he 'd seen in an old *"Popular Science"* magazine — he'd gotten the camp carpenter to copy it (the sliding door actually slides!). All this, I was told, took several months of feverish activity. Our dear neighbors were happy to see me so pleased with the results.

"Oh, dear," I murmured later to Sela, "Won't the men all think you're really henpecked?"

"Who? *Me*?" he retorted. "*They're* the ones who are henpecked. They *say* they don't help their wives. Hah! They're lying. Just *lying!*"

Modern Marriage?

Now, this gives you a brief insight into marriage behind the scenes — in this Site, anyway — where all the young married couples affect to be very modern. The husbands [engineers, geologists, chemists, technicians] wouldn't be caught dead washing dishes, for fear of losing face. But when I had anemia, or when I get really busy with the children, Sela not only insists on washing the dishes, but leans out the kitchen window overlooking the sidewalk and shoots the breeze with friends passing by.

At any rate, our trip ended happily. It's good to be home again, where we dwell in comfort and the pleasure of having good friends and neighbors here and elsewhere. It's now eight o'clock by the night watchman's whistle, the children are nestled all snug in their beds, and all is well.

Much, much love to everyone, A

PS for Deanie: It was a delight to unpack. Bless you! Bless you all!

PPS for Bill: The *North American Indians* book arrived. Hikmet looks at it every nap time. It's magnificent and I thank you!

Emine and the children at our new apartment, 1957

Journal: My Batman Neighbor Ruhsar hanım Sela's boss, Suat Çalıslar, is a model of dignified decorum and propriety; his wife, Ruhsar hanım, is naturally elegant and poised. She's not only a beautiful dark-eyed brunette, she's my model for etiquette and formal Turkish. I observe the polite language she uses at official gatherings, and often ask her about perplexing customs. Her explanations, always perceptive and practical, are usually followed by a burst of laughter that puts me at ease. "Don't worry, Maria," she assures me, "you haven't broken any laws!" Her sense of humor and laugh remind me of Aunt Saadet. As a matter of fact, I discovered they were classmates at the American Girls School in Istanbul.

During a lull in the social life here, we decided to take up German conversation practice on a weekly basis. "We'll just have Kaffee, Tee, und Küchen."

"Und Klatsch" [gossip], added our German neighbor Hilda hanım, the mainstay of our conversation group. She likes the idea, especially since it doesn't include strict lessons or homework that she would have to check.

From time to time, my "name friend" Ançi has been able to join us and add fresh life to our vocabulary. (My words are limited to what I remember from College German 101.)

Unfortunately now, our weekly Kaffee Klatschen seems to be slowly losing momentum. Hilda hanım's son, Yilmaz, is getting married and moving to Ankara, and so our dear neighbor Hilda hanım, will be leaving. ❦

134

Mehmet Ali & Ayse Malkoç Family, Kutahya, 1957

back row: Muammer, Sabri, Güher. Selahattin, Orhan
front row: Ayse Kirali Malkoç, Mehmet Ali Malkoç

Families at time of photo:
Sabri & Seyyare Kursunoglu Malkoç = Sinan, Ilhan, Ayhan
Selahattin & Anna Maria Jones Malkoç = Hikmet, Cemile* , Timur
Sülhiye Malkoç Atalı & Süleyman Atalı = Seniha, Tulay, Ercan *in Erzurum*
Muammer & Nezihe Kirali Malkoç = Sirin, Serdar
Orhan Hasan Malkoç *unmarried*   Güher Malkoç *unmarried*

Journal: Sela's Parents Visit Batman In the fall, Mehmet Ali and Ayse Malkoç set out with youngest daughter Güher to visit their eldest son, Sabri, in Kutahya, where he's an agricultural engineer at the government sugar beet refinery. They actually had a kind of family reunion there; Sela was able to get away for a very short visit, and Orhan and Muammer joined them. With the exception of Sülhiye, who was unable to come from Erzurum, they were together with their five of their six children for the first time in some years.

They next visited their two sons in Batman, Selahattin and Muammer (who retired from the Navy, now works for TPAO). They stayed at Muammer and Nezihe's apartment, visited Sela's office in the petroleum refinery, and toured Raman Camp with him.

They spent a lot of time with the children and me, and were especially delighted with Hikmet. By now, she is able to carry on animated conversations on many topics with her beloved Büyük Baba and Büyük Anne.

Although Timmy is still in a more or less non-verbal stage, he was responsive to his grandparents and laughed happily all day long. Baby Kâmuran could only smile prettily, and sleep a lot during their visit.

According to the custom befitting a director's wife, Ruhsar hanım invited all the neighbor ladies on our street to meet Sela's mother, Ayse hanım. I think the highlight of her visit was this welcome tea in her honor. She seemed quietly pleased with all the respectful attention she received, and the heaps of compliments about her son Selahattin. ❦

On the Steps of Our New Apartment in TPAO Sitesi, 1957

Letter to Sister in Spokane

TPAO Sitesi, Batman
January 3, 1958

Dear Camilla and All,

Well, the holidays have come and gone. Hope you all have recovered!

A Different Kind of Christmas Tree in Batman

This year, we had a real-looking Christmas "tree." One of the men in Sela's department drove way off into the mountains and came back with a bit of a scrubby bush, bearing a few wizened red berries. From a distance, it looked somewhat like a very tiny Christmas tree. Sela had arranged this wonderful surprise.

As you may or may not know, trees are rare, and any vegetation is sparse in these parts. Goats and sheep graze off whatever they can find. Larger bushes and growth are cut down for firewood. There seems to be a superstition about trees attracting birds that eat the grain that the farmers plant. So farmers don't want trees around their fields, I've been told. There's supposed to be a large re-forestation project going on in some other parts of the country, but not around here.

Our neighbors across the street, the British UN petroleum consultant Mac (John) MacLeod and his wife Sylvia, along with engineer Yilmaz's mother, Hilda hanım, came over to help us decorate the "tree" with lights, balls, bells, and bits of tin foil. Hikmet and I punched out the Santa Claus mobile from the book you had

136

sent, and hung it up. I'd made gingerbread men and had saved some cocoa, so we had a real Christmas Eve party. By cocoa time, though, Hikmet was fast asleep.

But, oh, the next morning! I carried her half asleep into the living room to see the "tree" all ablaze, with packages under it. She was truly thrilled. And Timmy! Oh, my! He said, "Ahhhh!" and then, "Ball! Ball!" All in all, he was on quite good behavior. Only broke two.

Hikmet got a new bathrobe like Andy Paul's, her very own little bottle of lemon cologne, some "new" books, and a dress for her Mary doll. I had ordered a pair of gray-blue plaid flannel shirts for Timmy and Sela from the village tailor. Sela got a leather cigarette case and gloves, and I received some silver jewelry and scarves. Baby Kâmuran slept through it all, and will have to wait 'til next year.

We felt very festive and sat down to read all our Christmas cards again. Our neighbors stopped in to wish us Merry Christmas, and to see the "tree."

On New Year's Eve, the Company put on a party at the Guest House. There were paper lanterns, miles of used wireless tape draped in festoons, and strings of orange lights making everyone look ghostly. The overall effect was enchanting, however, and I had a lovely time. So did Sela; he won an eyelash curler in the raffle.

A Real Surprise Party

Speaking of parties, did I tell you about our 7th wedding anniversary? Last year it fell on the day the children and I left Ankara for Spokane, and I didn't remember it until we were on the plane. Of course, in all that travel rush, I didn't expect Sela to remember it, either.

This year, I arranged with the Guest House to bake a big cake. I made the lemon filling and boiled white frosting at home, and decorated it at the Guest House with flowers and the little bridal couple decoration from our first cake in Tulsa. I invited about 30 people, then plotted how to lure Sela to the surprise with an elaborate set of signals for everyone.

That evening, Emine giggled and nearly gave the game away, but she and the children dutifully ate dinner and went to bed early. I lit candles to glamorize the table, changed to a silk dress and asked Sela to wear a tie and jacket for our "special meal" (a new meatball recipe with green peas and rice). After dinner, I got out the cribbage board and started the game we'd just learned from our neighbors Sylvia and Mac. Then, without a word of explanation, I suddenly excused myself from the game, dashed across the street to the Guest House and had someone phone Sela to "pick up a package left at the Guest House." When he walked in to pick it up, he was really surprised to see all the smiling faces around the decorated cake on the table. First time he was ever taken in by a surprise party! Such are the happy excitements in our life here.

And Daily Life Continues

Changing the subject to a sad one, Aunt Saadet's husband, Avni Uçar, died of cancer last month. He was the kind uncle in Istanbul who was so good to us when we arrived in Istanbul. Could you please ask Mama to help represent the Jones family with a condolence card? (Aunt Saadet knows English well.) I think a card from you all would be much appreciated.

137

Address: Bayan Saadet Uçar, Eminonu Benzin Deposunda, Istanbul, Turkey. They own the service station at the end of Galata Bridge in the picture, and they get their mail there.

Nona's card came. Very nice family picture, thank you, Nona! Everyone looks at it admiringly, and picks out a favorite girl. So far, Terri, Christina, and Katie are running neck and neck and neck.

Baby Kâmuran has had very light measles. Not red measles, apparently, no fuss at all. So far, T. and H. haven't had a symptom. The TPAO doctor here says red measles are a different matter, though, and some children down in Batman village have died from complications.

Kâmuran is prancing around the playpen in her pink sleepers at the moment, with Hikmet's bathrobe floating over her shoulders. I just made her another sleeping bag. Now she's such a good sleeper! (Did I tell you I'm the proud owner of a brand new treadle Singer sewing machine from Diyarbakır?)

Timmy's a good sleeper too, after we let him cry it out for a while. All three are in bed nice and early every night. But teething is really throwing Kâmuran off; it seems they're all coming in within a very short time. Sigh….

About the post: I'm getting concerned about the crate that brother John shipped off to us when the children and I were leaving Spokane. My six-months' customs-free permission period after re-entry is nearly ended. Could he send a tracer? It's getting more and more difficult to receive packages through the customs.

And I haven't any books left for Orhan to study English. We're still hoping that he'll be transferred here to do his training. He's in Erzurum now with his father, who is not well. Orhan suspects appendicitis, but that's all we've heard.

Timmy Tries Out English

T. is surprising us by saying things in English: "Eyes, ears, nose, shots." He understands both English and Turkish. His total vocabulary production may be normal for his age, but it seems scanty in either language. He may be slower to talk than Hikmet, because she had so much stimulation and attention of so many adults, but we're just letting him take his own time while he sorts out the two language systems.

At the moment, he's sitting with young neighbor Mehmet, looking at a picture book. "Huh? Huh? Go-go?" [That's backward for dog, or any animal.] Timmy loves "talking" with Mehmet.

Hikmet Tries Out School

Last week was "Little Brother and Sister Visiting Day" at the elementary school down the street. Hikmet was invited to visit with Hasan, the seven-year-old across the hall. Being an only child, Hasan latches on to Hikmet, a year younger. He made his mother dig up his last year's black cotton school smock and launder a fresh white starched collar so she could wear it for the visit. " Oh, Hikmet, it's very becoming on you!" he said excitedly.

After the school visit, Hikmet came home chock-full of important information: toilet rules, who got their hands slapped with a ruler, and who "likes" whom. She was invited back "whenever the weather is nice." The older children's teacher was one of my "kitchen class" English students at Raman Camp, and also at the refinery. He evidently was practicing his English on Hikmet.

138

It's a foggy day today. Emine is showing Hikmet how to roast chestnuts on top of the oil heater. Timmy is wearing Sela's boots and riding his kiddy car. Baby Kâmuran is pushing herself in the stroller now, so you can imagine all the traffic inside. Plus the congestion of two laundry racks drying diapers by the dining room stove.

Up to now, it's been comparatively mild, but winter weather is setting in. We can see snow on Raman Mountain, and Sela says there's a storm in Garzan.

Well, I must get up and attend to things…. Greetings and hello to all again! Especially to Gracie and Rosemary.

Your loving sister, A
PS: It's bedtime already. Baby Kâmuran is already asleep in the yellow booties Elaine knitted her, and Timmy has fallen asleep with Hikmet's pussy-cat doll. He's so affectionate!

It's storybook hour for Hikmet. I can hear her brushing her teeth in readiness. She's wearing the pretty nightgown Cousin Lucile made her. A

Journal: My Batman Neighbor Sylvia Sylvia MacLeod and husband Mac (the UN petroleum engineering consultant from England) are middle-aged, tall, angular and poised, as I've always pictured well-traveled Britishers to be. I find them charming and intellectually stimulating.

I love to listen to their anecdotal reminiscing about where they've lived in other parts of the world. They seem to know how to make the best of things when life becomes difficult. They know how to search the local market for "make-do" amenities. In place of their traditional five o'clock gin-and-tonic "drinks," for example, they find state-produced vodka, and lemons from Antalya. They manage to carry on their daily habits even in Batman and their routine rarely varies: Sylvia always prepares five-o'clock tea for Mac when he comes in from the field, then they have drinks and a game of cribbage.

Mac has now taught cribbage to Charles Sternberg, his fellow UN petroleum consultant neighbor across the street. This week is a play-off for the cribbage championship. So far, Mac is ahead, with a tiny Union Jack on the board to mark his winning score. Alta has fashioned an equally tiny Stars and Stripes for Charles, who is lagging behind but unvanquished in spirit.

I admire Sylvia's resourcefulness at concocting "bits and pieces" for snacks at tea time, and English "boiled dinners" for their evening repasts. Cooking, reading, writing letters home to their twin daughters [one of whom, Jane, visited Batman] take up most of Sylvia's time. I suspect she's lonely during the daytime, and seems to find it difficult to strike up friendships with many people. I've grown fond of her. Like all of my other neighbors, she copes with life in this "outpost" in her own way. ❦

Journal: My Batman Neighbor Alta Alta Sternberg's husband Charles is a UN geologist whose famous father had written a textbook Sela and his classmates remembered from their university geology courses. Charles himself had studied at the U of Chicago, where Alta had studied art. They have no children. From somewhere enroute here, sweet, gentle Alta acquired a tiny white poodle named Vicki, trained to respond to commands in French only.

Alta's an accomplished artist and spends hours on her balcony sketching and painting scenes of the fields behind our apartment house row. Sometimes, we go on shopping tours in Diyarbakır, where her artistic eye is captivated by the rich, bright colors of the kilims [carpets that are woven, not knotted] from the villages in this region.

She was also captivated by the strange capes she'd seen worn by sheepherders in Turkey, and cajoled the houseboy into bargaining for one from a local shepherd. That evening she tried out her new acquisition and took Vicki for a stroll along our new sidewalk. The white and wooly poodle minced along after Alta wearing her white sheepskin cape. This naturally attracted the attention of the neighbor children playing in the street, as well as numerous passersby. *That* was a scene that should have been sketched.

I was embarrassed for her when I heard about it, but hated to dampen her artistic enthusiasm for this marvelously and naturally effective rain garment. I pondered whether to tell her it wasn't the custom for women to wear sheep herders' cloaks — only sheep herders wore them. Also, that the children had remarked she must be "a bit off."

"Tell her those shepherds might think she's mocking them," Sela suggested. So I did, whereupon she packed up the cape to wear to her heart's content back in the States. 🐦

Letter to Family and Friends

TPAO Sitesi, Batman
June 9, 1958

Dear Brownfields: Greetings to All!

I'm sitting at Hikmet's desk on the balcony watching the sun set, and for a wistful moment, wishing I might travel with it half way across the world....

But despite my wistfulness, I'm enjoying this lovely sunset here. The Batman River glistens against the far hills and everywhere the young poplar trees are a flourishing green. We now have asphalted streets, concrete sidewalks, and shrubby landscaping. The Company housing is looking more citified and elegant, especially since we are expecting President Celal Bayar and Prime Minister Adnan Menderes, plus a large entourage this week. This is in connection with an addition to the refinery.

Today I'm caught up with storing away winter clothes, blankets, rugs, etc. At the moment, it's so quiet and peaceful. Hikmet is promenading Baby Kâmuran in her dolly carriage up and down the sidewalk. (Oh bliss! No more muddy walkways in the rainy season!) Timur is promenading up and down by himself. All three are really blooming....

Trip to Tatvan

Sela's brother Orhan just spent a week with us, having taken the train from near the village of Mus [Moosh] in eastern Anatolia, where he's doing his government military service as an intern. On the ride to take him back to make train connections, Sela invited along Dr. Turhan hanım from Ankara, and the UN

140

consultant Mac MacLeod's daughter Jane, visiting from England. Petroleum engineer Melih Genca drove Orhan in a second vehicle.

Our two-station wagon convoy took Orhan to a town near Lake Van to catch his train back to Mus. That night we stayed in a rustic hotel in the small lakeside town of Ahlat, and roamed about the countryside the next morning. Most impressive was an enormous Selçuk graveyard [circa 11th century AD ?] full of tall headstones engraved in old Arabic script. Nearby stood the mausoleum of a Selçuk chieftain where, they say, pilgrims came to petition with special prayers. Each of the little marble windows under the dome of this shrine faces a different direction, with one looking out over the lake toward Mecca.

There were gorgeous wild flowers in bloom — hollyhocks and peonies – –and pomegranate trees with brilliant, fiery red blossoms. Hikmet discovered exotic land creatures: a huge land tortoise, and some amazingly pink and blue caterpillars. At a state-owned tea house on the Bitlis mountain road, we picnicked on flat bread fresh from the communal oven, boiled eggs, white goat cheese, vine-ripened tomatoes, and lemonade. In the fresh air, everything tasted deliciously flavorful.

While Sela was changing a flat tire, Turhan hanım and I dabbled our feet in a little brook meandering nearby; Hikmet discovered a crab in the water. Overhead, great flocks of magnificent birds were flying south: swallow-like birds with jet-black wings and pale pink backs, and birds resembling turquoise-and-gold parakeets. We spotted ordinary crows, eagles, and owls; buzzards on the telephone poles; mother storks feeding their young on the village roof tops.

It was altogether a lovely two-day outing. When we reached Batman the next afternoon, Sela stopped by the refinery to show us his brand new office. I was impressed to see his name above PRODUCTION CHIEF on the door, and the exploration maps on the walls with colored pins marking the various drilling sites. As a final, grand flourish, he ordered us all a round of coffee from Husein, the office tea and coffee maker on duty.

Once back home, we picked up Timur from the doctor's family across the hall and Kâmuran from the MacLeod's (who have ultra-strict, British ideas about child-rearing). Both children, we were told, had behaved "perfectly." And hadn't missed us at all!

Now Hikmet would like to say hello to everyone. She is going to type her name: HIKMET. I guess that ends this letter. Our best to all! A

Letter to Sister in Spokane

TPAO Sitesi, Batman
August 15, 1958

Dear Camilla,

We're all pert and sassy here, and hope you are too!

Sela is getting ready to take a two-month vacation, at long last. Since I already had a two-weeks' stay in Ankara with Kâmuran for check-ups, I'm staying here with T. and K. (Also I don't think we can afford it since transportation rates in some cases have doubled.) Sela and Hikmet will be gone only a couple of weeks — long enough to visit all the family in Sürmene and maybe find a girl who would come and be a mother's helper.

No spectacular news. Hikmet is learning to dog paddle with a pair of "water wings," dried gourds she acquired on a drive along the Tigris River. Some mornings, I put on my bathing suit and take a dip in the pool with her. T. and K. sit on the side lines and watch, fascinated and absolutely motionless. Odd for such a lively pair. I think they're awed by the Olympic-sized pool.

Hikmet Loves "The Odyssey"

I've been reading a new *Pocket Book* translation of Homer's *Odyssey*. Hikmet got so interested in my explanation of the story that she begged me to read it to her, and now she loves it! When it came to the scary scene where Cyclops was waiting at the mouth of the cave, counting all the sheep coming out and vowing to eat Odysseus if he could catch him amongst the animals, she was terrified. "Shall I stop reading?" I asked her. "No! No! Just read fast!" And she covered her ears until the end of that part. She also loves her *"Humpty Dumpty"* magazine, so it balances out.

Timmy can reach both pedals on the kiddy car now. He likes to take Kâmuran for rides on the back part. He's the sweetest boy! And Kâmuran is more winsome than ever. But I shouldn't rave on; I've got to do packing for Sela and Hikmet. She says, "How is Grandmother? What does Matt look like? How are all my other little cousins? Also my Aunt Camilla?" You're all fine, I trust. If you're busy, could somebody else write? If I don't get an answer to this, I'll have to send a telegram, out of perplexed anxiety.

Your loving sister, A

Journal: Hikmet's First Day at Primary School Sela has registered Hikmet at the Batman Primary School, which is still under construction by TPAO. They hired Atilla bey as Headmaster in charge of both levels.

My neighbors have told me about the school dress regulations: both boys and girls wear a black cotton smock buttoning down the front, with a white starched Peter Pan collar. Boys have short hair cuts; girls may have a white hair bow tying their hair back, but no other ornaments. Esen hanım across the hall volunteered to give me Hasan's smock since he's already outgrown it, with a collar to use as a pattern for six new collars (one for each day including Saturday, a half school day). I can buy starch at the market, and I had plenty of white muslin for the collars, left over from sewing bed sheets , saving me a trip to Diyarbakır.

On the first morning, Hikmet rushed through breakfast, eager to don her "new" uniform over her blouse and skirt, attach the collar, and "braid her hair like Ferhan's." She picked up her new schoolbag with handkerchief, pencil, eraser, writing tablet, and primer packed neatly inside, and flew out the door to join the flock of black-smocked boys and girls all headed for the schoolhouse. Some were holding hands, others were running or skipping, all happy to be starting school together.

I like the idea of the smocks to keep the children's clothes clean. Actually, the revered President Atatürk's plan to require school uniforms in public schools was a democratic policy, intended to "minimize socio-economic differences."

Atatürk also encouraged parents to send their girls to school as well as their boys. I think it's traditional in the villages for the girls to stay at home to do housework, cooking, and laundry while the boys and parents work in the fields.

This morning, the children looked about evenly divided, boys and girls. Headmaster Atilla bey says more village girls are being sent to school. A good sign! ❧

Nevbahar and Hikmet, First Day of School

Letter to Sister in Spokane

TPAO Sitesi, Batman
February 12, 1959

Dear Camilla,

This is a very special letter, so sit down with a nice cup of tea by the telephone and take a long, deep breath. Are you ready? I don't know how to start the Good News. Shall I say: Hikmet, Timur, and Kâmuran.... No.... Let's see, Sela and I have .... No....

Melike Arrives in Batman

Well, here it is: The Malkoç Family wish to inform all our beloved family and friends that we are now a family of six. SIX! Our newest addition is beautiful and her name is Melike [Me lee keh], which in my old Ottoman dictionary means empress, or wife of an emperor. She was born on February 9 at 1:30 a.m. and weighed 7 and 3/4 lbs. Plump cheeks, a Malkoç forehead like Hikmet's, and a nose like brother Mike's, we decided.

We tried to send Mama a poetic telegram to inform her of the latest jewel in her crown, but no telegrams can be sent now from Batman, and we couldn't get

143

through by phone to Diyarbakir to send one from there. I didn't say anything to you about expecting this time because I felt a bit pessimistic, and superstitious (?). But all went well.

We had made general arrangements with the Company midwife and the nurse at the little Company hospital two blocks down the street for "some time soon." And wouldn't you know it! The two women went to the movie house right after dinner, and Sela had to have them paged there. This, as you can imagine, is a most effective way of announcing the impending arrival. All the neighbor women were in a great stew, sitting through the movie, wondering what was going on at the Malkoç's. On the other hand, the upstairs neighbors hadn't gone to the movie and didn't have an inkling, until Hikmet spread the news at seven o'clock the next morning that baby Melike had arrived.

Meltem hanım, the midwife, and Nur hanım, the nurse, were an efficient team. Sela held my hand calmly; sometimes he laid his hand on my brow, which I found especially soothing. In addition to all this kind care and attention, I had the great good fortune of having neighbor Hessie Williams stand by — a registered nurse from Port Arthur, Texas! Now, dear Hessie drops in every day to give me a sponge bath, back rub, and fresh linen. She tends to the baby and chatters away in a delightful manner.

Sela is taking his vacation now, so he oversees this two-bedroom household. Luckily, we found a part-time maid willing to do the laundry. Our kind (and nurturing) neighbors swoop in bearing milk puddings, soups, lemon pies, yogurt, and other delicacies "for the nursing mother." Then they swoop out, taking Hikmet, Timur, and Kâmuran away for the day. They warm my heart!

At the moment, I'm lolling in bed and enjoying the fragrance of the wild narcissus Hikmet gathered from the field this morning. Bright April sunshine is coming through the window. It doesn't seem like winter at all.

Hikmet loves her birthday card! Thanks for your Valentine's cards, which just arrived.

Your loving sister, A

Journal: My Batman Neighbor Hessie   Hessie Williams is the wife of Phillip "Pete" Williams, the present UN/Caltex petroleum consultant at the refinery. At sixty, she has naturally curly white hair, beautifully bright brown eyes, and a happy chuckle. A loving wife and devoted mother, she misses her children and grandchildren in Texas dreadfully, but keeps up a cheerful front for her husband. She knows how much he has wanted to have this experience in Turkey before he finally retires "for real."

Like Alta, who lives next door to her, Hessie loves to go shopping in the Turkish markets, always on the lookout for gifts for her family. Her especial favorites are the copper and brass vessels. She spends hours burnishing them until they gleam, and fills them with field flowers, dried grasses, fruits and nuts. She recognizes them as works of art. Like Alta, she has an artist's eye.

Hessie endeared herself to me when Melike was born. She came over to help out Sela, and met the midwife and the nurse. Later, she wanted to express her

144

professional admiration to these "sisters under the skin," so she invited them to lunch. Also me, to be the interpreter. Unfortunately, I was late getting away from the house, and came in to find the two guests chatting in the living room. I apologized, contrite because they knew no English, and Hessie knew no Turkish. No need for apology, they said; they'd already had a nice talk with Hessie. "How is that possible?" I asked in Turkish. "What did you talk about?"

"Lots of things," Meltem hanım responded. Hessie had told them about a big house where she and her sisters lived with their mother and grandmother. Her father was an important man. Nur hanım added that Hessie also has many daughters and many sons, and they go to different schools.

I was amazed at their power of perception and intuition, and astounded that these two women were able to comprehend so much simply from Hessie's gestures and facial expressions. I excused myself, went into the kitchen to apologize to Hessie. She was busily stirring sauce, and humming happily.

"Child, don't worry! We had a nice time, talkin' away!" She loved being a good hostess, it was part of her Southern upbringing.

"What on earth did you talk about, Hessie?"

"Oh, I told them about where I lived as a child, you know, in a wonderful place out in the country. I was an only child, but there were always dogs and cats and horses around. We all loved animals." She chuckled as she reminisced. "My daddy was a doctor, and I wanted to be a doctor, too, like him. But you know, in those days in the South, ladies didn't go to medical school, so I went into nurses' training and worked in the maternity ward. Until I met Pete, that is. Then I married him and had two girls of my own!" She chuckled again at the memories.

All three women were happy at the thought that they had "bridged the conversation gap." Over lunch, our conversation moved on the other things even more enlightening — and factual. ❦

Letter to Tulsa Friends

TPAO Sitesi, Batman
February 19, 1959

Dear Brownfields and all,

We are happy to inform you of the arrival of the fourth young Malkoç! Melike was born February 9, plump, dark-haired, and healthy. Her name has a melodious ripple in Turkish [Mel ee kèh]. She was born here at home, and breezed into our lives on angels' wings. You see how ecstatic I still am? In attendance were the Company midwife and the nurse, our American neighbor who's a trained nurse, and Sela, who held my hand.

Every now and then, Sela discloses hidden depths. When I first knew him, he turned pale at the very thought of hospitals. But throughout this entire episode, he remained calm and collected. The excruciatingly funny part was his having to page the midwife at the movie, attended by most of the adult community, unless they're on night duty. Whenever the midwife gets summoned, it's a clear signal the stork is hovering.

The movie, incidentally, was "War and Peace" and everyone had to sit through hours of film with no progress reports, eaten up by curiosity!

Such is life in this remote community: births, deaths, marriages, train arrivals and departures make up the highlights of our lives.

Fortunately, we are all well and happy and most anxious to hear that you all are, too.

Much love, A

Letter from Mother in Spokane

Route 4, Box 188, Spokane
March 2, 1959

Dear Anna Maria,

Well, just have to get this into the mail. Too much goes along, too fast! To celebrate Little Melike's coming, I sent out a surprise alert and everyone was here. When I said I had An Important Announcement, the speculations were:

-Cousin Rita is coming from Nebraska.

-Mike is engaged.

-Ma is going to buy a car.

-Uncle Harris is going to sell the farm on the Columbia.

-Ma is going to elope.

-Somebody is pregnant again!

But I kept mum, not a word, until little Johnny, Wendy, Chrissy, Janene, and Andy came in. Martha Ann and Terri [the two oldest grandchildren] were prepared and presented your announcement. You should have seen the goggle eyes and dropped jaws. You sure bowled 'em over! Tell Hikmet she'll have to step lively if she has a sister like herself, with yellow braids and all. So the latest grandchild count is: Joyce 5, Nona 4, Rosemary 2, Camilla 2, Anna Maria 4. Makes it 17, doesn't it?

All the neighbors send a good word and are as you remember them. They would love to send you things, but that is so hard to do. I'd love to send you something but books seem to be the only thing that are no trouble. By the bye, did you get a small parcel of books for Hikmet? Sent them in December by parcel post; air mail would have been around $7.00 more than they're worth.

Now for a couple of news notes. Aunt Edith's stay at the hospital in Dec. and Jan. had us all in a state of nerves. She had some major operations for cancer. Very serious. She pulled through, though, and things seem to be all right now. We hope. You know how it is to have anything like that to battle with. She is back at the farm again, but must always be careful.

In December, we celebrated the adding of Baby Jeffrey (John and Joyce's) and Baby Stephanie (Aaron and Nona's) to the family, with very little to-do. Just two more beds and extra diapers when they're here.

When you went to the dentist here, what were the after-effects? There seems to be a lot to having bridgework done. Everyone I ask gives me long-winded experiences. I never realized that there is so much to dental work. Now, I look like something like Aunt Hanna Jane Brock and Kim Novak the movie star, but I don't *feel* like that!

146

Well, the Civil Defense Filter Center has finally closed up, and disappeared. I have a box of medals and citations, and some spare time, so what did I do? I started working at the Spokane Blood Bank with some of the neighborhood gals, every Saturday afternoon!

More anon. Ma

Letter to Family and Friends

TPAO Site, Batman
July 7, 1959

Dear Family and Friends: Greetings!

On a tray by my side is a bowl of fresh yogurt, a slice of fruit-nut cake and a glass of chilled cherry juice. Our new air cooler is wafting a delicious breeze from the living room, and on the shady side of the house outside, the houseboy is sluicing down the walls with buckets of water. The atmosphere is like an oasis practically in the middle of a desert!

Naime, our new helper, is playing with baby Melike in the shade of the balcony while the mid-day nappers Hikmet, Timur, and Kâmuran are gently dozing in their beds. A lovely feeling of contentment after a busy morning of laundry. Afterward, I may have a swim in the pool before lunch with Hikmet, who can now "frog paddle."

Three mornings a week I have an English class in the Guest House down the street: seven teen-agers in the neighborhood, who are home on vacation from private boarding schools in Ankara, Diyarbakır, and Talas. This summer session is a sort of trial run to see if I can manage this next year with a real course for some people here who desperately need to learn English for their work. I confess I'm not being altogether altruistic about this; I plan to put the proceeds into my "Trip to Grandmother's" fund.

Trip across the Tigris River to the Hasan Keyf Ruins

And of trips, I have a new one to report: the first family outing since last year — and the second trip to the Tigris River for me, with more excitement than the one six years ago. The newly arrived UN adviser, a visiting geologist from Israel, and a visiting guest from Texas had all expressed a great wish to see the famous Selçuk ruins at Hasan Keyf, so Sela invited them for a Sunday tour. Happily, there was room to spare in the station wagon and all of us family were invited along.

It was perfect weather for an uphill-and-down-dale jaunt on the bumpy road to the Tigris riverbanks. Today, several hundred people actually live here and there amongst the ruins, which include the remnants of a Roman marketplace. According to our visiting geologist, under the benevolent rule of the Selçuk Turks during the 13th century, this ancient village of Hasan Keyf was once a huge caravan junction with a population of 100,000. Amazing! On the river below, we could see the crumbling remnants of a collapsed Selçuk bridge, once an international transit route. High above, in the face of a sheer cliff of solid limestone, were tunneled-out stairways and lookout posts used by the inhabitants when they needed to fetch water from the river in times of siege.

We crossed the Tigris, I shudder to recall, in our loaded station wagon, on a dilapidated scow that barely afforded room for one vehicle and three men! The pilot stood at the prow and heaved at a rudder fashioned from an old log in the bow of the craft: it swiveled and served as the steering mechanism. Two extremely muscular men aided the pilot by poling the scow upstream until it headed into the current, then cleverly steering it about and thence into the onrushing down current. In this way, we were automatically carried downstream and across to the opposite landing. (Apologies if these terms are nautically incorrect or confusing to you true mariners.)

Be that as it may, we landed happily on the other bank, drove along the sandy shore until we found a spot to picnic, near a grove of pomegranate trees aflame with red-orange blossoms. This delightfully secluded place was hidden away under the brow of the limestone cliff, cool and green, with arching branches of wild apple trees shading us overhead. We lunched with gusto on fresh lettuce, cucumbers and green onions from our garden; white cheese, boiled eggs, tinned sardines, and fresh bread.... Alas, because somebody laid Baby Melike on top of the box containing my chocolate cake, it was totally overlooked.

Altogether, it was a delicious picnic. Our seclusion, however, had been an illusion. As we tidied up to leave, I looked about for stray litter, and through the foliage spotted a group of village women in long white head scarves and floral salvars, standing in the mouth of a cave, watching us picnickers. I do hope they had enjoyed observing us as much as we, in our imagined privacy, had enjoyed our Tigris riverbank picnic on their premises!

But no one on the jaunt had more fun than the lady from Texas. She was "simply thrilled to pieces and couldn't wait to tell the folks back home." During her stay, I invited her to tea one afternoon, together with Ruhsar hanım, the director's wife, Sylvia MacLeod from London, and Meral hanım, who speaks some English. I frosted little pink cakes and brewed Sürmene tea from special leaves Hikmet had picked in her grandmother's tea garden. Our guest was pleasantly surprised (as are most visitors) by the cosmopolitan atmosphere of the TPAO community.

Today, brother-in-law Muammer drove the children and me down to the train station to send Sela off to Diyarbakır; he'll take the evening plane to Ankara for a week's rounds of meetings and conferences at the head office. Let's hope he gets to have a little fun and exciting night life for a change. He was getting frazzled with the heavy field work, office work, and people dropping in at odd hours to discuss pump problems.

Although this is page 3, I continue with untrammeled spirits. Untrammeled, that is, because Louise, the Lady from Texas, has promised to mail these letters along with a packet of photographs collected from very generous friends. A camera, I should further explain, costs a small fortune, as does film, if and when you can get it. Mailing these letters with the pictures is also expensive, costing much more to mail from Turkey to the U.S. than vice versa. While I'm being candidly critical, please excuse the paper I'm using; paper products are extremely hard to come by right now.

148

Now, Ramazan the houseboy has just gone off to evening class at the elementary school down the street; he'll join the other Kurdish workers who are learning to read and write Turkish. I do admire their determination to learn!

Naime the maid has gone off down the road to her village, with a sack of dry bread and some squash from our garden.

It's the evening of a long day, and time to wind this up. Please send along our love to one and all.

Energetically yours, Anna Maria
PPS: If you want more details on ferrying across the Tigris, kindly send your inquiries to Sela. The more I think about it, the more phobic I get about river scows. A

Letter to Mother in Spokane

TPAO Sitesi, Batman
October 9, 1959

Dear Mama,

It's eight o'clock and the children are snug for the night: Naime and Hikmet in their top bunks, Timur and Kâmuran in the lowers, Melike in her crib.

Sad News about Sela's Father, Mehmet Ali Malkoç

Sela took off for Sürmene night before last, drove to Diyarbakır at midnight, hoteled there and drove seven hours to Elazığ, where he was to meet his older brother Sabri coming from Malatya, and then drive ten more hours to Sürmene, thus saving the one or two days by train. But they didn't make it in time. A wire just came announcing that his father's funeral was today. I guess he died while his sons were on the way. [There don't seem to be funeral homes here to hold the deceased until arrangements can be made. To my knowledge, family and/or special religious people pray over, wash, and wrap the body right away, and male relatives and friends carry it to the cemetery for burial the next day.]

Sela's youngest brother, Orhan the doctor, had been staying with their father; he'd first suspected appendicitis, but it turned out to be stomach cancer. It was so sad. He was such a good man, such a good father. And poor Sela. He loved his father very deeply and hadn't seen him since he took Hikmet there a year ago. As they say in Turkish, it's "kismet." Fate....

The happier news is that I've made a resolution: as soon as Melike is able to trot around, I'm taking the children for a vacation in Spokane! The catch is, of course, that I have to earn the fare, but I've already started with five private pupils. Plus, Sela said he would round up a group of men who desperately need English for their work. I was even approached recently by someone sent by the Headmaster of the school here, who wanted to enlist me as a regular teacher, but I said no. As it is, I manage to get the house in order, do the laundry, then leave the children at play with the houseboy and the maid to do the private tutoring sessions in the mornings. Afternoons, I cook and sew and take the children for walks or visiting. We have a nice daytime routine all worked out, but it certainly doesn't allow for extra activities!

Although, last night I did "step out," in a manner of speaking. After the little ones were in bed, Hikmet was busy writing her lessons and Naime was struggling with the first-grade primer, I took my mending bag along to visit a neighbor whose geologist husband was also away (out in the summer camp). We had a glass of tea and chatted for a pleasant hour.

When I came back, there was a small slip of paper from Hikmet on my pillow:

ANNE BENI ERKEN UYADIR ÇÜNKÜ DERSIM VAR

[Mother, wake me up early because I have a lesson.]

With only one spelling mistake, and very carefully printed. I was so thrilled. Her teacher said she had the neatest printing in the class today. Another big thrill. All last year, she'd copy and memorize pages of lessons, without really *comprehending*. I wasn't really sure if she would ever catch on to reading. Last year, her pals Ferhan and Selma were already reading. None of this "Look, Mehmet! See the ball!" stuff either. They were reading *newspapers*! On reflection, though, the other children weren't working out two language systems in their head, like Hikmet. She never confuses Turkish with English, or vice versa.

Wish you could have seen the second grade marching past our apartment building yesterday: about fifty little boys and girls in black smocks and white collars, two by two. Naime, Kâmuran, Melike and I were watching and waving from the kitchen window as the teacher nodded in our direction. We were so excited. We could see Hikmet pointing out her new rabbit's house on the balcony as she and her schoolmates filed by. She was "ready to bust a button."

Tell Camilla we're awaiting word. What a conversational ice-breaker. Never fails when I'm stuck for polite conversation at an afternoon tea. All I have to do is bring the neighbors up to date on the latest number of your grandchildren. It's "phenomenal!"

To wind up this news report, we're all doing fine here; in the words of Walter Winchell, "That's thirty for tonight!"

Your loving daughter, Anna Maria

PS: All the birthday cards came. T. and K. wore theirs out almost the first day, showing them off. H. took hers to school in her school bag, so it lasted longer. When Sela finally caught on to the punch line, he got a big bang out of Wally's card.... Special regards to all the Neighbor Ladies of the Rimrock.

Letter to Tulsa Friends

TPAO Sitesi, Batman
November 8, 1959

Dear Brownfields and All: Hello, hello, hello!

This letter will be good for only one cup of coffee, since there's no news of great note to report. Just a few comings and goings. There was the national election, of course, but everyone knew what the outcome would be: no changes in the President Celal Bayar/Prime Minister Adnan Menderes regime, alack and alas, and so that's *that* on that subject....

150

The Asiatic flu hit here but we didn't get it; it was only a matter of three or four days of fever and achy bones, according to the neighbors who did get it. Evidently there are various strains of the virus, varying in potency, and this was not the drastic type. I had a touch of tonsillitis and so did Sela, Timmy, and Kâmuran, but the Company now has an experienced baby doctor, and we've laid in a winter's supply of vitamin drops, so all is now well in that department.

Interruptions.... Hikmet is the last one ready for bed tonight. We're on the third chapter of *The House at Pooh Corner* and she can hardly wait. She would like to "stamp her name on this letter" first, please. HIKMET

Her Turkish is improving by leaps and jerks, — but improving may not be the word. The latest addition to her vocabulary is socially unacceptable, I think, or perhaps even taboo. She's now sound asleep on the top bunk in the children's bedroom, with her Mary-doll in her arms.

Can't remember if this is news or not: Sela is now the Chief Production Engineer at the TPAO refinery. Since there was no other production engineer left at the refinery after the previous one returned to Ankara, the promotion seemed inevitable. However, if he'd been NG [No Good] he wouldn't be CPE now, I guess. Anyway, I think he's invaluable. On the job or off. Well, enough of these cryptic comments!

The "Moonlight Ball" at the Swimming Pool

We've had a run of social engagements lately, lots of Guest House dinners for visitors from the Central Office in Ankara, and so forth. My fuchsia poplin party dress and Lucite high heels (from Spokane) were the topic of conversation amongst the ladies the first night I wore them, at the "Moonlight Ball."

This party was the last poolside event of the season. Quite fittingly, a harvest moon shone down, sparkling and glittering on the black waters of the swimming pool. Strings of colored lights festooned the bath houses and created a magical atmosphere. Everyone was in a highly festive mood when the after-dinner dance music (phonograph records) started playing and couples crowded onto the dancing area.

Before I knew it, Sela and I were caught up in a dance competition with two other couples vying for "best dancers." The whole thing was pretty contrived, if you ask me; I think they were all waiting to see whether I'd taught Sela the rock-and-roll. (Now, where would I have learned that on my last trip home, in my "condition"?) At any rate, after several lively waltzes and a snappy fox trot, the music switched to a samba. Sela says he "draws the line" at sambas, so the other two couples split the prizes. What a relief! I can take only so much limelight!

This the end of the page and my ration of paper, so bye for now, and love to all. A

.... Next day, Page 2: I just scared up more paper. How's the coffee pot holding out? Between one thing and another, this may turn out to be a long letter.

Dinner for Sela's Boss

The main interruption was an American-style dinner for Director Suat Çalıslar, and his charming wife Ruhsan hanım. (Actually, they're *both* charming.)

Early in the morning, I started the food preparation from scratch and cooked all day long: cheese sticks for appetizers, roast turkey and dressing, fresh spinach, peas and diced carrots, mashed potatoes and gravy, baking powder biscuits, and cherry pie and applesauce cake for desert.

Also, Emine helped prepare shell a bowl of hazelnuts and squeeze a jugful of orange juice. The before-dinner orange juice and vodka whet the appetite, and if the biscuits are tough, who cares? It was, if I may say so, a first-rate turkey dinner.

Note: There are some members of my family who don't think I can cook, namely brother Pete. My only comment is, "I get driven to it." As when bachelor engineers drop in from one of the camps, with a freshly plucked turkey....

Our latest visitor was a German pump-equipment representative. [TPAO, as you know, is a Turkish government enterprise, but the government has recently issued numerous exploration concessions to foreign companies.] The visiting pump agent spoke only German, but Sela and a couple of his old school mates here are trilingual, having studied in Germany, and then in the U.S. so they were all quite at ease with the visitor. Modestly, Sela says: "Nah, I'm not really much of a *languist* myself!"

Today is full of sunshine, the tenth of November. It's the anniversary of Atatürk's death (which is observed rather than his birthday) so the big red flag in front of the Guest House is flying at half-staff.

Timmy is out talking to the garbage man's horse, and Hikmet is making mud pies on the front steps with her girl friend Selda. It's "Indian summer" weather or, as they say here: "pastrami summer," good weather for drying pastrami. Any day now, the rainy season will begin, and then the cold.

Things have reached a lull, so I'll stop and make a stab at getting these six carbon copies off in the next post. A
PS: Just have to include this "hot one" from Sela:

It's nightfall in the city, and a man from the village stops a passerby.

"Begging your pardon, brother, can you please tell me the name of that star up there?"

The passerby answers the villager: "Unfortunately, no, brother. I'm a stranger here, too!"
PPS: Several days later, alas. I'm beginning to grow fainthearted about finishing this. Meant to get at it bright and early.
Scorpion and Flea Control

You wonder why these letters are few and far between? Early yesterday morning, Emine cut her finger in the kitchen, I found another flea in Kâmuran's bed, and then much to my great consternation, found the offspring of the adult scorpion we had dispatched a few days ago in the basement. This little creature was crawling up the dining room wall in back of the oil heater, and probably has siblings somewhere downstairs. I tried to alert the other tenants in this four-family building, then decided not to wait. With the help of Emine, Mehmet the houseboy, and a janitor-at-large, we cleaned out all the basement storeroom spaces. (It took all of my morning energy.) We didn't find any more scorpions, but now they'll be easier to spot if any show up.

Fleas come in from the villages, where they thrive on the earthen floors. Hiring a new maid is always a mixed blessing because it means sewing up a new outfit for her and disposing of her old clothing; each visit home to the village

152

means an immediate bath on her return, and fresh clothing. Fleas brought in by the workers from the villages abound on the wooden floors of the movie house as well. Before and after each film showing, maintenance men spray the floors with refinery creosote to kill the pests.

I've developed my own method of flea control. After Sela and I walk home from a movie, I carefully gather my full skirts at the door, and hop into the bathtub, where I vigorously shake out all clothing into the tub. Any lurking fleas slide down the white porcelain sides and I simply flush them down the drain. But Sela's approach is even simpler. He relaxes in the easy chair, picks them off his white cotton work socks where they seem to gravitate instinctively, and drops them into a bowl of water. Thus we both manage to hold our own with these invaders. They definitely do not deter us from going to the movies, our rare link with the fantasy world of Hollywood.

Movies in the Site and Other Celebrations

Attending a movie, I should explain, is a real treat for everyone. TPAO's central office sends fresh films down from Istanbul by train every week, and their posters announce the showings on the movie house door. Each film is shown twice, earlier in the evening for the TPAO workers from the villages, and after dinner for the employees in the TPAO Site here. (This allows time for the aforementioned spraying between showings.) Unlike attending wedding celebrations, children are not taken along to the evening movies. There are special film showings on the weekends for children only.

Finally, attending a movie is a special occasion for me because there's no custom of baby-sitting. If we have no mother's helper such as Emine, I stay at home with the children. It's part of being a parent here.

Speaking of weddings, there was one in Batman today. An open truck bearing the bride and groom and joyful celebrants made the rounds of the marketplace and our neighborhood, with musicians seated in the back energetically beating the big drum, tootling flutes, and shaking tambourines. I think this symbolizes a wedding tour from the bride's house to her husband's. In this case, I suspect the families may not live far from each other, so to dramatize the event, they just kept going until the truck ran out of gas....

And now back to Hikmet, who's just emerged from her evening bath. She's clattering about in her wooden bath clogs, a necessity on these cold terrazo floors, and wants to stamp HIKMET. She doesn't believe this is the same letter! PPPS: I hope Mary, Mrs. Bieber, and all get a chance to read these letters? I wake at night with guilt complexes, thinking I should write more personal letters. Too many interruptions. A

Journal: Promotion to Chief Production Engineer, and Other Moves Up The Director and his wife held a farewell dinner last month for the UN petroleum consultant from Great Britain, John and Sylvia Macleod. I miss them, especially when I see their house on "Executive Row" sitting empty. There has been much speculation about who will be eligible to occupy it.

Now for the good news and the bad news since the MacLeods left:

The good news is that Sela has been promoted to Chief Production Engineer. I think he really deserves it, working so hard. As I understand it, this is an Assistant Director's position and I'm very proud of him. He came home at lunch today to give me the news, also the surprising news that we'll be moving into the empty house!

For Sela, this is a doubly prestigious promotion. More importantly for the family, it's a roomier living space and the house is surrounded by a large garden for the children to play in.

Bad news followed on the heels of the good, however.

My very pleasant and attractive new neighbor across the hall, Leila hanım (*not her real name*), knocked on the door this morning to tell me she'd heard the news about our imminent move. Instead of offering congratulations on Sela's promotion, she made a startling announcement: They had been expecting to move into the empty house themselves!

Now, she continued coolly, she cannot accept the fact that *we* are moving into the house her husband, the refinery's chief accountant, "rightfully deserves." Therefore, we are no longer friends and she will no longer be speaking to me. In her eyes, apparently, we are usurpers.

I was shocked. I mumbled that it was not our decision, it was the decision of the General Director in Ankara, and I was sorry she felt that way.

In such a close community, where we all live in similar circumstances, share the swimming pool and Guest House, and pay social calls on the same neighbors, I can't imagine not speaking to someone you know.

I haven't related any of this to Hikmet, who shares a desk with Leila hanım's daughter in elementary school. ❧

In the New House on Executive Row

TPAO Sitesi, Batman
January 15, 1960

Dear Camilla,

After all those wonderful Christmas cards, pictures and notes, I owe the whole family letters! I trust they understand that whenever I write, it's for everybody — I'm thinking of them all when I write.

We had a waffle breakfast this Sunday morning (using the old trusty-dusty waffle iron, which has burned out its coils and been repaired so many times that there's hardly any of the original wiring left). Dr. Necdet bey and his bride Sündüs were our guests. The new Company doctor is a psychiatrist, trained in Bellevue Hospital, NY. He says he's looking for work in his field, but people apparently don't believe in going to psychiatrists in Turkey.

For the special breakfast occasion, Hikmet and Kâmuran put on their party dresses, Timmy wore his beige orlon sweater like his daddy's and his white shirt from Andy Paul. They got little Melike all dressed up like an old-time Pasha's daughter with beads and fringed scarves, and she came out all preening and posing. Timur and Kâmuran don't "take" to many people, but they're both very fond of Necdet bey and Sündüs hanım. They've now gone off to the doctor's house to sail paper boats in their bathtub.

Sela is napping off a cold. Melike has a cough, and has to content herself watching the pigeons and sparrows feeding on the balcony. We inherited these pigeons from the former director, Suat bey, who lived next door. The birds roost in fancy dove cotes under the eaves of the children's window, and except for Hikmet's rabbit, who disappeared, they're our first successful pets. Tahir the houseboy has tamed several to follow him. His secret? He brings them wheat from his village.

Travel Conditions

My dear "name friend" Ançi Köksal [Ançi is an Austrian diminutive for Anna Maria], tried for the second time to go to see her family in Linz. She had all the papers: sponsorship, doctor's statement affirming her father was ill with cancer, tickets from Vienna. This time, thinking all was in order, she got on the train and rode as far as the border. There, they stopped her because of some minor error on her passport. It's so discouraging.

I've been daydreaming about taking just Hikmet on a trip to Spokane. Since Sela may go to Sürmene this summer to see his mother, the three small ones could spend part of the summer there and get the best of care. Hikmet and I could hop on a bus from New York easy as pie and cut expenses, instead of flying across the US. Such a trip would really broaden her life. And Sela says, "It's been a long time since you saw your mother." Well, I continue to daydream....

Batman School Conditions

The school situation here is really poor this year. The new Batman primary school is still under construction, so the children go to class at 6:30 in the morning and come home at 10:15 — three hours of school a day for 85 pupils. Sometimes the teacher is so overworked he doesn't even give homework; the parents are expected to do the drilling and practice at home. Even if the school were up to the usual standard, which is excellent in a city like Ankara, there is no outside intellectual stimulation for the children at all.

My latest (temporary) responsibility is lining up four other mothers in the Site to take turns one afternoon a week supervising our children. Hikmet and four of her classmates do arithmetic one afternoon, nature study lessons, and general reading the other afternoons. I pick out stories for them to read that are not in their lesson books: fairy tales, lives of famous men, and so on. I hope this project doesn't fall by the wayside, because if school keeps on at this rate, the children's elementary education will wither on the vine.

At least Hikmet gets all kinds of additional reading in English — we're on *Black Beauty* now. She just found a picture of Atatürk for her collection, and informed us, for example, that Atatürk's horse has check reins and a double bit. She has an active curiosity and a developing vocabulary.

Substitute Teaching in the Middle School

The days just run on, one into another. This week I have to tote up grades for the fall semester. Some days I get so discouraged, and regret having promised to fill in as English teacher at the middle school. I'm not at all trained for this kind of teaching situation. My main approach is what the teachers in Ankara Koleji practiced: mainly question-and-answer drills, traditional rote learning and grammar translation. I wish I were better trained for teaching huge classes.

English has become a required subject in the curriculum, and in order to complete school, the pupils have to pass minimal English. How sad, I think to myself, that most of these Kurdish children don't speak Turkish fluently and now they're expected to learn a *really* foreign language. While some of the pupils come from the Site, many come from villages. They have no paper to write any homework on, so I can't give them exercises to write out. Some boys are taller than the school principal, and already sprouting moustaches. I guess many have to work in the fields and can't attend regularly. That seems to be the stark reality.

I admire Headmaster Atilla bey for taking on this difficult job. He not only has to oversee the teachers and curriculum, but attends to health check-ups in this region where tuberculosis is endemic, fleas roam, and trachoma lingers. He checks the children for head lice and smacks the boys if their hair is too long. (It's easier to check for problems if the scalp is visible). He also oversees the administration of public health inoculations.

When I heard that the public health nurse uses the same hypodermic needle for the whole classroom, I was aghast. Sela visited the school learned the health workers were given very few needles; the best they could do was give Hikmet the first injection from a fresh needle. I have such conflicting emotions here: deep compassion for all children, versus fiercely protective instincts for my own children.

Meanwhile, Home Entertainment in Batman

Timur and Kâmuran had a "delicious" lunch at Necdet bey's, and when Tahir went after them, K. refused to come home because she likes it there so much!

Hikmet was invited for lunch down the street at the Pierces (one of the Parsons Company families from California). "I ate so much I nearly bust a

156

button," she said. (One of her favorite new expressions.) At my frown, she reminded me: "It's rude to refuse food, Mother."

Melike and Sela have waked up, and are eating onion soup; it seems to help their sniffling and wheezing. The weather has been bitterly cold, with a wind that blew all night long. Today it looks heavily gray outside, like impending snow. We're fortunate to have an endless source of fuel for our oil stove so we can keep toasty warm despite the cold temperatures.

With no television, what does one do at home with children on dreary days, you ask? We read a lot of stories. We look at picture books and photograph albums. We play cards, play phonograph records, play the little electric organ Mr. Crawford brought us. We play house and dress-up and make up games. We take turns visiting and having afternoon tea parties with our neighbors. In short, we create our own entertainment.

The thought of those nine little pen pals in Spokane has been hanging over my head for weeks, Camilla. I've decided finally, since Hikmet can't write English yet, that she could write one letter to the school class as a group, and I will translate. Maybe next year she'll be able to write well enough herself. Right now, she's copying her drawings of life in Batman to send to Grandmother.

And now, I'll have to call a halt to this writing. There's too much pressure from the traffic around here. So, here's a Hello to everybody there, from body here!

Your loving sister, Anna Maria

Residents of TPAO Sitesi 1959

12

SELA IN HEYEBELI SANATORIUM

Letter to Family and Friends

TPAO Sitesi, Batman
April 9, 1960

Dear Brownfields and All: Greetings of the Springtide!

April showers and lots of news. I've put off writing for so long, it's difficult to begin. Things go along smoothly, and then we get pulled up with a jerk!

We've Moved "Up"

Since Sela's promotion some time ago, we live across the street in a single house on "Executive Row." It has a cool, concrete verandah in front, bordered by a wide green lawn. This is mowed periodically by a line of five or six gardeners wielding long scythes in unison; I admire their rhythmic expertise from a respectful distance.

At the side of the house is a wooden garden swing and a newly planted rose arbor. The garden is always full of our children and the neighbor children from across the street. They have a happy time together and thrive in the spring sunshine.

I've stopped all my lessons except the refinery class three times a week. My project for this month is spring sewing. Did I mention that I finally got a Singer treadle machine last fall? It hardly ever collects dust and is the joy of my domestic life. I make easy children's garments: shirts, shorts, simple dresses, aprons, Hikmet's school smock and collars, also curtains. And whenever we get a new maid, I buy material from Diyarbakır and sew her salvar (bloomer-type pants), scarf, apron, etc.

Sela Has TB?

The startling news is that Sela is leaving next week for Heyebeli Ada, an island near Istanbul. He became quite ill with a high fever during this last holiday, at the end of Ramazan. The Company doctor found a "small shadow" on his lung. It was quite a shock, as you can imagine, but "nothing really to worry about," Dr. Tarık bey says. So, Sela will spend a month or two at Heyebeli Island Sanatorium on the beautiful Bosphorus (the strait connecting the Sea of Marmara with the Black Sea). He should come back here fully recovered and rejuvenated. Insallah!

This past year he's been terribly overworked. The only time he had off was when Melike was born, and when he went to Sürmene for his father's funeral. This enforced sanatorium stay is a blessing in disguise. He simply needs rest.

This automatically cancels my trip next Christmas. At first, I considered taking the children to Spokane while he recuperates, but the expense ruled that out. Who knows, maybe next year, Sela can come for his one-month yearly vacation…. Just daydreaming again!

But the Children Are Thriving

Otherwise, all is well with us in Batman. Melike is trotting about and climbing now: onto Hikmet's desk, the kitchen step-stool, the divans, and up and down the front steps. Her head is tenderly covered with golden curls, and she very much resembles Hikmet. Never still a minute, happy all the time.

Darker haired Kâmuran is more winsome than ever at this stage. She still shies off from strangers, but when she warms up she chatters like a magpie, in an enchanting kind of Turkish baby talk all her own.

Timmy is irresistible when he smiles. He can now ride Hikmet's new child-size bicycle, with learner's wheels attached.

Hikmet, naturally, rides "like the wind" and can even manage a standard-size bike. At school, she's started handwriting and two-digit division problems. She can recognize all the fruit trees the Company gardeners have planted in our backyard this spring: apple, cherry, pear, apricot, and peach. She's planted her own lettuce patch. At the moment, she's busy hunting up all the sunflower seeds she hid away last fall. Sad to say, I think she and her pals served up most of them at their tea parties.

More visitors have arrived to wish Sela well before his departure. Bless their generous hearts, they send all kinds of delicacies to "fatten Sela up" and the rest of us are getting plump on the leftovers!

When he gets settled, I'll send on the address and perhaps everyone can send him things to read. He's responded to the treatment the doctors here have started, and already he looks and feels "like a new man." He'll completely recover in a very short time, they say.

Much love as always. A

Letter from Sela

Heyebeli Island/Istanbul
Thursday afternoon
April 28, 1960

My Dearest Wife Anna Maria,

A couple of days ago, I had written to you. Since then, I have received two or three letters from you. They were very nice letters, darling. I am very glad that you all are fine and everybody is helping you.

Don't work hard and make yourself tired painting and whitewashing or other things around the house. See what happened to me! I am glad you got the divan and chairs covered and got new light fixtures and faucet.

Dr. Tarık bey came to the hospital yesterday. He is going to take the express tomorrow and will be in Batman on Sunday afternoon. He said he will come and talk to you.

Today the Sanatorium doctor came back from vacation, and examined me. He said that what I have got is probably a slight cold infiltration in my lung,

159

which is almost gone. The cold, not the lung! He said it is probably not tuberculosis. I said, "Insallah!"

This doctor is Güntekin Köksal's relative, Dr. Haydar Aksugur. I talked to almost all of the doctors today and they all say the same thing. Almost all of them had a phone call or letter from our friends in Ankara and Istanbul asking them to take good of me, etc. etc. So I have become a famous patient in this hospital. Dr. Faruk bey [Dr. Turhan hanım's husband] has been very nice, asking me all the time whether I need anything. I haven't seen Edith and Güler Oyhon yet.

We just heard over the radio that the Government has ordered "special conditions" in Istanbul and Ankara. Nobody will be allowed on the streets after 9:00 p.m. and all the night-life places will be closed. This is curfew under martial law. The university students are rioting over the actions of the Prime Minister, the President, and their friends. Traditionally, if things get out of control in the government, the Army takes over to calm things down. So you better stay where you are for a while and take care of yourself. I don't think there is anything serious, but you never know.

Say hello to Güntekin and Ançi, to Yilmaz M. and everybody else. My best to Ruhsar hanım and please thank her for everything. Say hello to Hessie and Pete Williams.

Is Timur a good boy? And is Kâmuran a good girl? How is Melike? I am glad that Hikmet had a good Children's Day on April 23. Thank you for the letter, Hikmet. I will write to you next time.

My best love, Your Sela

Heybeli Sanatoryumu
Bina 2 Oda No. 30
Heybeli Ada/Istanbul

Letter from Sela

Heyebeli Island/Istanbul
May 1, 1960

My very dear wife!

Today is Sunday and the weather here is windy but not cold. I am staying in the room since I caught a cold a couple of days ago, and have a sniffling and runny nose.

Yesterday, I went to Istanbul to get my laundry and tried to call Ankara, but no luck because of the special conditions here. I was very sorry that I left here! I almost got tangled up with one of the mob gatherings protesting against Prime Minister Menderes. I ran into Tafi (Rafit Taviloglu) from U of W, remember?) and we had a nice little chat.

I also bought a bouquet of carnations and went to see Edith and Güler; Edith was in the hospital with some kind of kidney trouble, I think. We had a long talk and kidded each other about who's going to see who, and who is supposed to be in the hospital. Their house is fairly close walking distance from TPAO's Istanbul guesthouse and from the hospital she is staying in.

Tomorrow, the doctors are supposed to let me know what's up with me. They might not let me stay here if I don't have tuberculosis; they're afraid for me (as much as I am) in catching TB microbes from the other patients. I probably will stay in the TPAO guesthouse, or here, 'til things cool off politically in Istanbul.

Tafi, Edith, Güler, all send their regards. Say hello to everyone for me.

Yours alone, Sela

Card from Mother in Spokane

Route 4, Box 188, Spokane
May 1, 1960

Dear Sela,

Anna Maria wrote that you were in the sanatorium in Istanbul, for a month's rest and treatment. Hope that you will make use of the rest and enjoy it.

I'm looking around for some books you might like. If you'd drop a line, I'll know what to send. Otherwise, you'll probably get some Who-Done-Its.

Mom (*that's Mother, and Grandmother Jones*)

Heyebeli Ada Sanatorium 1960

161

Postcard from Sela

Heybeli Island/Istanbul
May 10, 1960

Dear Mom!

This picture shows the sanatorium I am staying in. Thank you so much for the nice card and the well wishings. Anna Maria must have written to all of our friends about my condition, which brings me lots of mail.

I have stayed almost 25 days in this hospital, but they could not decide whether I have TB or not. The doctors are saying that what I have most probably is an infiltration of a slight cold into my lung. The only thing I need is a little more rest. After resting a month I feel grand.

I am leaving the hospital on the 13th. Anna Maria is coming to Istanbul on the 14th. We will stay here a week or so, then go to Ankara and from there to Batman in a month.

Best wishes and regards to everyone. Sela

Letter from Mother in Spokane

Route 4, Box 188, Spokane
August 25, 1960

Dear Anna Maria,

Your picture arrived, now reposing on the mantelpiece. Much discussion on which one is really the most, but everyone agrees that all four children are "very good-looking and appealing." I intend to frame the picture.

Terry and Marty (Hikmet's girl cousins) are much impressed. "Imagine, she speaks two languages! Besides reading *Treasure Island!*"

I sent H. an insect book parcel post, found out the parcel post takes around two months to get there. Anyhow, I'll send a couple at a time, so two months from now, start looking. And those German textbooks Aaron got from a Gonzaga prof, I'll mail those also, but one at a time, air mail. That way, it won't be so much.

Have news on the grapevine that Joyce and Nona are expecting in Sept. and Nov. but don't let on I said a word. Hush, hush!!!
Ma

Journal: A Little Detective Work Is Necessary, Now and Then From time to time, I meet up with a different endemic nuisance, and usually deal with it by consulting with my much more experienced neighbors, or, in this case, by having Sela consult with one of the doctors at the hospital here.

The first inkling of trouble was during the children's "potty check" in the bathroom yesterday. Timmy is still too small to use the grown-up toilet, so both he and Kâmuran share the little wooden chair with its removable, enameled chamber pot. This is where I start my daily cleaning. For once, I couldn't believe what I was seeing. I bent over to take a closer look. Yes, there *were* tiny pinworms crawling around in the little potty. "Ohmigawd!" was my immediate reaction. "Who *did* this!"

From the children's room, Timmy responded, " *I* didn't do it, Mama, I *swear* I didn't do it!" He, of course, couldn't see what I was looking at; this was just an automatic reaction on his part. He was also trying out a newly-learned adult expression in Turkish.

Kâmuran immediately echoed him: "*I* didn't do it either, Mama!" Immediately, I realized that was the wrong approach, and tried again.

"Ooh!" I cried out, in a pleased tone. "Who did *this*?"

"*I* did it, Mama, *I* did it!" Timmy shouted out.

"No, *I* did it, Mama, *I* did it!" Kâmuran echoed.

On general principles, Sela and I administered Dr. Tarık's dosages to all four children. Later, our neighbors told me more than I wished to know about other endemic parasites, and some truly horrific stories about tape worms.

My newest mottos now are: "Cleanliness and Vigilance for Good Health" and "Cook All Meat Thoroughly." 🍂

Journal: A Day for Forgiveness Our former neighbor Leila hanım *(not her real name),* who'd taken umbrage when we moved into the empty house on "Executive Row," had been silently snubbing me. At official dinners and afternoon teas, she exchanged polite greetings but otherwise she never spoke a single word to me. On the street, she turned her head. I tried not to let it bother me and I never mentioned it to anyone. I doubt anyone else was aware.

Winter passed into spring. One afternoon, it was my monthly "at home." I baked an applesauce-walnut spice cake, lined up coffee cups and tea glasses on a tray, arranged a bowl of fresh-cut garden flowers on the table. It's always a pleasure to entertain and chat with my neighbors because they're always so kind and helpful to me — and I learn so much from them.

A few women had already arrived and were chatting together in the living room when I went to answer another knock at the screen door. I could scarcely repress a gasp. Standing there as cool as a cucumber was my formerly friendly neighbor, Leila hanım.

Somehow recovering equilibrium, I greeted her as if it had been only yesterday, not last year, when she had last spoken to me. And she, equally coolly, walked on into my tea party and back into my social life!

Later, my curiosity was too much to bear and I went to talk to my close friend Meral hanım. She found it unbelievable that I'd been snubbed for so long by a mutual neighbor, and that no one ever noticed. I explained the reason for Leila hanım's coolness, but why the sudden change of behavior, I asked, as if nothing had ever happened? This was what I couldn't understand.

But Meral understood. In her soft, gentle voice, she explained that on this particular day of the religious calendar, there are special Moslem prayers for forgiveness. If someone who has harmed you comes to ask you for forgiveness, you are expected to forgive them.

My erstwhile neighbor and friend had knocked on my door, and I had opened it to let her in. How poetically symbolic. 🍂

Birthday Card from Mother in Spokane

Route 4, Box 188, Spokane
September 5, 1960

Dear A. M.,

We have not gotten around to answering the BOX [a carpet from Sela] because it came just when the house was flooded with company in July and August. The company was: Aunt Birdie *[from Alaska]*, Cousin Joy & family *[from Alaska]*, Cousin Donald & family *[from Duke U]*, Aunt Edna *[from Portland]*, Mike *[from Hawaii]*, Uncle Harris/Aunt Edith & family, Cousins Paul/Virginia & boys, Cousins Betty Jean and Dale.

We are now back to normal. Ma

Letter to Family and Friends

TPAO Sitesi, Batman
September 18, 1960

Dear Brownfields and All: Greeting and Salutations!

We've had the busiest spring and summer imaginable. Here's a brief flash-back for those of you whom I've neglected for so long.

The children and I flew to Istanbul in May to join Sela when he was released from the sanatorium after a month's stay. There isn't a trace of anything on his lungs; perhaps, they say now, he didn't even have TB after all.

At any rate, he's fatter than ever and twice as sassy! After a week's stay with relatives in Istanbul, we took a ship to Zonguldak, the coal-mining region on the Black Sea, where we visited Sela's married sister Sülhiye and husband Süleyman Atalı for four days.

"Special Conditions" in Ankara

From Zonguldak, we went by train to Ankara, arriving in the capital the night before the Turkish Army took control of the government. While it was termed a "benevolent takeover," it was, in fact, a real *coup d'etat*, and a very exciting time for us, as you might imagine. We had been invited to stay overnight enroute in Alice hanım's apartment house (our friend from the Raman camp); we had planned to rest up there and then take the Kurtalan Express back to Batman.

Very early the next morning, however, we were awakened by strident voices on the national radio station, broadcasting repeated messages rapidly and frequently: "Prime Minister Adnan Menderes has been apprehended and deposed by the Army, along with President Celal Bayar and their top officials. General Gürsel is now acting head of the Turkish Government."

Sela and the excitable tenant downstairs were discussing the news reports as they came over the air. When we heard that the repressive and corrupt prime minister was finally removed from power, the immediate reaction was relief, and everyone rejoiced: "Long life to General Gürsel! Then we all ran outside to the balcony to listen to the directives being broadcast from a loudspeaker atop a military truck moving slowly up and down the street: "All residents to remain

164

within their homes until further notification." This was an instantaneous curfew, trapping us in Alice hanım's apartment!

My reaction was to wash, dress, and feed the children, pack up, and be ready for any exigencies. Sela was already on the phone to family members, including his elder brother Sabri, who now lives in Ankara. Shortly thereafter, Sabri, who has a remarkably commanding presence, commandeered a taxi and arrived at the door. While Sela was communicating with his main office on the phone, Sabri agabeyi, Hikmet, and I took the waiting taxi to the train station to try to buy return tickets to Batman. Along the way, we were stopped at several checkpoints and questioned by militia, but were allowed to enter the nearly deserted station to buy tickets....

Later — again with Sabri agabeyi's help — Sela and I managed to get all of us and our baggage onto the train without undue complications. The other train passengers were excited and abuzz with the breaking news and predictions of the outcome: What would happen now to the Prime Minister Adnan Menderes and his cronies? From what I understand of the situation, he finally went too far constitutionally with his many restrictions, including repression of the press. While Sela had been in the Heyebeli Island Sanatorium nearby, there were riots in Istanbul: university students were protesting Menderes' abuses of power; even the elite War College cadets were marching against his repressive regime. Sela explained that traditionally the Turkish military serves as a safeguard when "things get bad" in the government. They take over until the political parties sort things out, then after a free and open election to choose a new political party, they step down.

The only direct effect all this has on us, personally, is that I would have great difficulty in leaving the country now, were I to try. Too many people need to be cleared of political suspicion and accusations of criminal wrongdoing before the present restrictions against travel abroad can be lifted. This stringency is justifiable, I think, in view of the fact that the country was being bled dry of gold. I imagine the banks in Switzerland are full of Turkish gold taken out of the country illegally. But by next year, it should be possible to get visas for travel again.

At any rate, we returned safe and sound to Batman, where life goes on as usual.

Sela's Appointment as Assistant District Director

Right in the midst of the whirl of visitors from the new refinery in Izmit, and a round of inspection tours from the new General Director of TPAO, Sela received his Good News of the Year: He has been appointed Assistant to the District Director here in Batman. There are two Assistant Directors here, one for the refinery and one for field operation — drilling, production, etc. Sela is now in charge of field operation. The raise in salary is not substantial, but the position is an important one and he will get a lot of valuable experience.

My English course at the refinery finished up after seven months. Some of the engineers will be sent to the new refinery in Izmit to work with the Caltex people. Caltex is now joint-owner along with the Turkish Petroleum Company, I understand. I don't know how much of what I tried to teach the trainees will stick, but they're guaranteed to know when to say OK.

Hikmet the Philosopher

The children are blooming. Hikmet, now eight, has finally taken a real interest in reading, which makes me very happy. I'd intended to start her reading in English this summer, but since she's still a bit shaky reading in Turkish, she's been reading aloud to me in Turkish every morning. Yesterday, she found a recipe for little cakes in a Turkish children's magazine, baked them, and served them to her friends at a tea party in the garden. That's real "reading comprehension!"

On her own, she's also learned to embroider, swim, and ride a bicycle. One of her recent bed-time conversations — the best time to pin her mind down –– had to do with the life span of human beings and why people die. I told her they're like flowers, and after they've lived a long, long time, they get tired and die. "But flowers grow again," she said.

"That's because they drop their seeds into the ground," I answered.

"Oh, I see," she said. "Like people have children. But what about the people who have no children?"

"Everybody leaves memories in other peoples' hearts so they don't really die, either," I explained.

"Of course," she responded thoughtfully. "Just like Atatürk!

In school, she has memorized reams of poetry about the First President of the Republic and his visionary and heroic efforts to bring Turkey into the twentieth century.

Children's Talents Galore

As for Timmy, he's passed one great milestone, going to buy the daily loaf of bread all by himself. He trots off down the street and around the corner with his coin purse in one hand, a clean string bag in the other. He always comes home with the right change, but with some of the bread missing. As Hikmet says, "He just sits down on the curb and chomps off a very large *hunch*." Now over four, he's decided to speak English, and manages whole phrases like: "Mama, Kâmuran poked the cake!" and "Mama, Melike is biting Sinan!"

Kâmuran, now over three, sings songs that we can recognize easily. Her two favorites are "Spring Is Come, The Roses Are Blooming" and "Jandan Is a Beautiful Girl," a song about Sleeping Beauty. Most of the verbs in Turkish have an "r" in the ending and try as she will, she can't pronounce the sound. It's quite delightful to listen to her sweet voice, but it takes practice to recognize her words. Each child has a personal repertoire, and sometimes there are minor altercations over who's singing whose songs: "No, *you* can't sing 'Twinkle, Twinkle' unless *I* can sing 'Little Ayse, little Ayse.'"

As Mama would say, there are no flies on Melike, either. She wriggles through the balcony railing, dangles her feet over, hanging on backwards, and drops the remaining foot to the ground. Then she's off! For a year-and-a-halfer, she's pretty fast on her feet and keeps the houseboy Tahir on his toes chasing her. She collects keys to open things, and likes to pick flowers — in the garden, and in the vase on the dining-room table. So far, she has a limited vocabulary of about seven or eight words, but this is compensated for by the fact that she understands both Turkish and English, also some Kurdish.

166

Best Wishes, Congratulations, and Circumcision Festivities
    Well, it's nearing dinner time and I must rise to the task. After dinner, Sela and I plan to pay a short call on the neighbors because their children departed for boarding school in Istanbul today. In this case, it's customary to offer best wishes with the expression: "May God bring you together again." We'll stay just long enough to be polite.

    Then, we have to express best wishes at another neighbor's for a speedy recovery, congratulations, and hopes that God will keep the family together. This is for the parents of Hikmet's school-mate who was circumcised yesterday.

    In a Moslem boy's life, the occasion is a religious rite of passage, comparable in importance, I believe, to a First Communion or a Bar Mitzvah. The boy's proud father invited about 150 people to a dinner party at the Guest House. Little Talat lay abed in a far corner of the dining hall, under a lavender satin coverlet, surrounded by piles of gifts and crowds of well-wishers. Not to mention the hungry guests who were busily stoking it away at the nearby buffet table.

    The long table was resplendent with an array of the chef's most popular dishes, which waiters continuously replenished from the kitchen. At the stroke of midnight, the chef himself emerged wearing his tall, white, French-style chef's hat and bearing a huge platter of "wedding rice." [The unique feature of this special dish is a sweet syrup containing saffron, the most costly spice in the world and literally worth its weight in gold, I just learned from a visiting Canadian engineer. This dark yellow powder comes from the powdery strands of the crocus blossom, and each tiny flower bears only three strands. To gather one pound of this exotic spice requires the painstaking harvesting of 75,00 blossoms.]

    The appreciative guests proclaimed the chef's wedding rice "fit for a sultan," and consumed it in the twinkling of an eye.

    All evening long, the three-piece jazz band played French, German, Italian, and American popular songs. Then they hit the roof with a wild Black Sea dance, especially to entice Sela onto the dance floor. He and his handsome cousin Yılmaz Malkoç immediately joined hands to stomp to the beat.

    This folk dance reminds me of an American Indian war dance, if it were played by Scottish bagpipes. The music is actually produced by a wooden flute, a kind of stringed lute, and a large drum, with the cheering audience clapping along in a one-two-three-FOUR-hunh rhythm. At the end of each round, the dancers wave their silk handkerchiefs and yell "Hosaka!" with great fervor. I don't know what that means, but it has an exciting sound. And it rounded out the celebration.

    Now I must take leave, with our greetings to everyone.

Love as ever, Anna Maria

Letter from Mother in Spokane

Route 4, Box 188, Spokane
September 26, 1960

Dear Anna Maria,

Just a mere line. Do you have the *Golden Book Encyclopedia*, illustrated in color? Seems in your before-the-last-letter, you spoke of Hikmet studying ants in an ency. but darn it, I can't lay hands on the letter. If you haven't the set, let me know pronto; I'll mail the first volume at once. Have A, B, C, D books, but will mail them air mail, one at a time. They are sold at all the Super markets, service stations, etc. at 99 cents per copy.

Have been canning like mad and have the cellar stocked up again. You know since Aunt Mill, Pete, and Mike are gone, no one eats all that food, and I myself don't make a dent in it. But I hear that there may be some extra lil' kids here, come spring, so that's why the fruit, pickles, jelly, jam, conserves — all from the garden — are ready on the shelf.

Will write a formal note of invitation to you all next time I write. The thought of company is very stirring. Quick, wash the windows! My god, we must fix that leak in the roof!

More about this.... Ma

Round Robin Letter from Tulsa Friends

Tulsa
November 13, 1960

Dear Anna Maria, Sela & Family in Batman, Turkey:

Our love to you and the children. We are pleased by Sela's recent promotion. Bill Brownfield

-Your ears should be burning. We've been thinking of you and wishing you could join us. Hope everything is good with you. Come see us. Thelma Brownfield [Bill's mother]

-Greetings from Tulsa, USA. We are yearly making new friends — young friends, from your part of the world. They soon will be very influential in their countries and can do much to further good will and good living throughout the world. We are proud of all of them and hope they have as much affection for us as we have for them, and as we have for you, Sela and Maria! Tom Brownfield [Bill's father]

-We are all thinking of you tonight. I hope to visit you next year. If you see Rolf V., who works with Esso, tell him hello for me. Eric Nelson [Kathryn's brother]

-Dear Anna Maria, This evening, we've been invited to Kathryn Brownfield's house for dinner. We're having a really good time. Very nice people, and I really like all of them. Thank you for arranging to introduce us. I kiss your eyes. Meral Özkan [*translated from Turkish*]

168

-Having a perfect evening. Its memory will remain for me forever, and I would be glad if you were here too. Knowing Erik was so pleasure for me. He just arrived from my hometown in Iran. Mohammed K.

-I had the privilege of meeting Anna Maria during her last visit here, and having heard Bill and Kathryn speak so often of Sela, I feel that I know him also. Best wishes and good fortune to you and your family. Fred Nelson [Kathryn's brother]

-Dear Ana Maria, I hope you are quite alright. Tonight was a nice party in Kathryn's home, and she was talking of you. So everybody decided to write to you. Anyway, as a friend, good luck and happiness to you and your family. Manon I., Iran

-Howdy! I'm still late the late-hour pest that I was while you all were living below the Days on 10th in the garage apartment. Be nice if we could see you both soon. Best of everything. Bruce Phillips

-Hi! I'm still going to write — a book! I'm glad to hear Sela is doing fine. Meral and Selahattin O. are certainly nice folks. We're glad to have them here, any time. I have no excuse for not writing now because I'm not working anymore. Deanie Day *[Deanie, like her mother before her, has the onset of Alzheimer's.]*

-Howdy! By golly, next to seeing you two, I guess the best thing happened; we met two very marvelous people who know you well, Meral and Selahattin O. Very fine folks. We feel like we've known them for a long time. We're very glad to hear of Sela's rapid and complete recovery. The Turks are notoriously tough anyway, and Sela is the epitome. And a mean card player. Keep writing to us. Keep us posted on your whole family. Maybe one day—even before we make that "million dollars" — we can be together again. Alan Day

-Hi, Anna Maria, Sela & family, I am Ann, Kathryn's sister-in-law. I have heard of you both so often, I feel as if I know you. We wish you had been here to share this evening with us. I hope you and you family are well. Looking forward to knowing you. Ann Nelson

-We had a good night, and I enjoyed very much. I wish you were here, and I would be glad to know you too. Abbas K.Y. from Iran

- I must end by telling you that "Terra Explorations" became "Day & Brownfield" when some investors helped finance their prospects. At the beginning of this year, they moved to new offices: "Oakes, Day & Brownfield." It's really quite remarkable, what they've done, with no capital, during the worst oil slump in years. Wish us luck!

We are all in good health. Lisa & Valerie started kindergarten this year. Kay is in high school, Betsy is in junior high, and life is never dull. Except it has been mostly all work and no play, so perhaps the next year will bring a vacation or a few more evenings like this.

Your friends, the Özkans, were wonderful. I want to call Meral "Merry," she has such a merry expression. Oh, what a good time we had. I so wish that you all could have been here to enjoy it with us.

Our love to all of you. Kathryn

13

BATMAN NEIGHBORS COME AND GO

Christmas/New Year's Card 1960

Card to Mother in Spokane

TPAO Sitesi, Batman
December 18, 1960

Dear Mama,

Hikmet and I made a few of these screened silhouette cards, but then everything went wrong. At a Guest House dinner for visiting generals from Ankara, dear Mr. Williams, the UN consultant from the Caltex company in Texas, had a heart attack after dancing with all the ladies at our table. He just sat down and fell over. It was a terrible shock, naturally, and so sad. The Company made all the arrangements to send him home. Sela took his wife Hessie up to Ankara and saw to it that she was escorted home. Some neighbors and I packed up her household things; they were all crated and sent to Port Arthur.

Sela is still in Ankara, working on the yearly budget. The children all have the flu. We don't feel much like Christmas, but I'm going to get some kind of a tiny tree or bush, mainly for Hikmet and Jim Crawford, the only other American here now. (He's the kind UN geologist who brought us the little electric organ). We've invited an engineer's mother who is German, Hilda hanım; also Ançi Köksal. I hope Sela will be back in time for our 10th anniversary this week.

Hikmet says to tell you her hair is cut; the page-boy bob is neat and makes her look less like a long-legged stork.

I got the copy of my *Spokesman-Review* article, thank you. Did I get a by-line or check? Did anything ever come of my travelogue?

When the last director and his wife, Ruhsar hanım, left this summer, I lost my German language study-mate, so I'm now studying with Sündüs, the wife of the new psychiatrist, Dr. Necdet (who sent the letter from NY). He says they're biding time here in Batman until he finds a place in his own field, psychiatry.

Say hello to everyone! Your loving daughter, Anna Maria

Letter from Mother in Spokane

Route 4, Box 188. Spokane
January 25, 1961

Dear Anna Maria and All,

Got your Christmas card; it must have been a trying time for you. My sympathy to Hester Williams. Hope you are back on the beam.

The grade school is waiting with bated breath for a letter from Hikmet, according to Mrs. Adler's friend, Sylvia Purcell. We work together at the Blood Bank.

So far, the only piece of yours in the *Spokesman-Review* has been the "Cooking Turkey in Turkey for Thanksgiving" article. I have two extra copies saved up for you.

We are having air transportation strikes now: everything goes to the coast by West Coast, and then down south, and then east. Well, it'll all be settled in due time.

I mailed you three books (encyclopedia) last week, and three this week, by printed matter parcel post. Takes anywhere from three weeks to a month. So watch about the end of Feb. We'll mail them as we get them, and will let you know the dates.

I'm waiting diligently for Aunt Birdie to show up. She's through with her job in Alaska, and is retiring to spend her time in Wash. and Ore.

I see Uncle Harris and the kids often. Gosh, his kids are growing. They're really not kids in size and looks anyway.

Would I know Hikmet, Timur, Kâmuran, and Melike? The older I get, the faster they grow! Tell Hikmet to hang onto some hair to braid. I like it that way.

Mom
PS: And a special hello to Sela. How I wish I could visit with you. I enjoy hearing him talk about things!

---

*Journal: **Snakes in the Grass, etc.*** We are enjoying the luxury of having a green lawn around our house, and a vegetable garden in the back. In this hot, dry region, it's like an oasis in the desert. But, like the Garden of Eden, no garden is without its snake in the grass, I've discovered!

One evening last week, I'd called to all the children playing in the garden to gather up the toys, it was almost supper time. One condition for sharing toys with the neighbors is that they all have to help gather them up later, so the older children obediently carried the wagon and tricycle to the verandah, the younger ones put all the balls and other toys into a large wicker basket by the door. When I glanced out the French doors to check up, I saw several toddlers standing near the basket.

"Don't move, children!" I called out in Turkish. A long, green serpent was twining itself about the handle of the basket. "Don't move! There's a snake!" Instantly, every child stood stock still. Only Behiye the maid reacted, instinctively reaching down for a wooden stick the children had been playing with. She dispatched the intruder with several sharp blows so quickly no one had time to be frightened.

Children in the area are taught at an early age to recognize poisonous varieties of spiders, scorpions, earwigs, and other large insects. I'm learning to be extremely cautious myself, as in dealing with fleas from the movie house. And now I'm learning to be wary when entering the house after we've been out all day. As, for instance, when we returned late last evening from a day's outing with the neighbors. Sela waited at the door with the children while I turned on all the lights and went through every one of the six rooms in the house. I shouted to him to attend to a very large earwig in the children's bedroom. Then, for the first time ever — call it a premonition — I walked over and lifted up one of the children's sleeping cots and looked underneath.

A foot-long, inch-thick, pink earthworm was looping up and down like a roller coaster on the bare, clean terrazo floor. "They've been plowing out there in the open field next to our house," Sela muttered as he reached for a towel. "That's where all these things are coming from. They come out when the earth is turned over!" He caught the snake-like intruder, took it outside beyond the house, and flung it far out into the open field.

I was aware that, unlike the earwig, the earthworm was not poisonous, but it still made my skin crawl to look at it. Before preparing the children for bed that night, we checked out the corners of every room again. From now on, we're making it a general routine. ❦

*Journal: **It's Ramazan, And My Heart Is Wildly Pounding*** *In Arabic, whence the word originated, the word is Ramadan. "Borrowed" into Turkish, it's pronounced and spelled Ramazan. It is the ninth month of the Moslem calendar, the period of religious fasting. It may also be the given name of a child born during this period.*

Last night, I woke from a deep sleep to feel my heart pounding wildly in my ears. The pounding slowly grew louder and louder, then gradually receded until everything was quiet again. Was it something I'd eaten before going to bed, I wondered, that was causing palpitations? Or a nightmare? At breakfast, I idly mentioned this "heart disturbance" that had awakened me so violently in the middle of the night.

"That's not your heart! It's the night watchman's big drum," said Sela. "He goes around the neighborhood waking people for prayers before the first light of dawn. It's Ramazan fasting period, you know, so that's the last chance they can eat or drink until sunset."

"Don't people use alarm clocks if they have to wake up to pray? Does he have to wake up the whole neighborhood?" I asked petulantly. And ignorantly.

"The watchman always does that; people expect him to. Ignore it," he advised. So I did. I was relieved to know, at least, that my heartbeat was normal. Being a pretty sound sleeper, I'd never been aware of this night-watchman duty before.

The month of Ramazan fasting finally ended, and the first day of Seker Bayram — literally translated as "Sugar" Holiday, or "Sweets" Holiday — dawned bright and sunny. "Happy Seker Bayram!" Sela called out to everyone in the household. Already dressed, he was filling the silver candy bowl with foil-wrapped chocolates. "Here he comes!" he announced, and pointed out the window.

The now-familiar drumming grew louder, and shortly we saw the watchman coming down the street, beating rhythmically on an enormous bass drum strapped to his shoulders. Like the Pied Piper of Hamlin Town, he had attracted a crowd of children, laughing and shouting in his wake.

Sela waved and stepped out on the verandah with the bowl of candy for the crowd. For the drummer, he had holiday greetings and a fistful of heavy coins.

This was a special day for children to wear new outfits and be indulged with gifts and sweets. Though not a Moslem, I, too, had respectfully dressed up for this festive occasion. As a family, altogether, we paid first holiday respects to the director's wife. Then Sela walked down to join the other men at the refinery, where they would pay respects to the director and other officials ensconced there for the occasion, exchange holiday greetings, and generally socialize all day.

The four children and I set off down the street to visit the various elderly mothers, mothers-in-law, grandmothers, widowed aunts, and other relatives staying with their families. At each brief visit, we exchanged greetings, were seated and served bayram treats. For the children, this meant endless amounts of ready-made chocolates from Istanbul candy factories, home-made cookies and cake, and a kind of soda pop called gazoz.

In each home, I was served the same sweets as the children, plus a tiny cup of Turkish coffee, followed by a tiny glass of Turkish liqueur, flavored banana, cherry, tangerine, or peppermint. After several visits, I had to politely turn down the liqueur....

By noontime, we'd paid respects to all the elders on our street, and made our way back home. Not surprisingly, no one was hungry for lunch. The children napped all afternoon and I, too, fell into a deep slumber until dinner time.

Later, we all agreed that we'd had "a lovely bayram time!" ❦

TPAO Sitesi, Batman
May 4, 1961

Dear Mama,

We got Camilla's letter last week and I've been depressed ever since, not so much about the ticket details, but because there seems to be a recession, and it's affecting you all. Well, I guess by next year, things may ease up here on travel. I hope to start another English course here where I can earn more; I received 40 kurush per lesson hour at the high school last year. (Pity the poor teachers!)

Not much news. We're all well. The children have the bloom of health, so don't take the enclosed picture seriously. (It has such a pre-Victorian quality!)

I couldn't resist having it taken. The marketplace photographer was in front of the shoemaker's shop; he and his ancient camera were hidden under a draped black cloth, with another black cloth hung on the adobe wall as a backdrop. The children were soon surrounded by curious passersby, which partly accounts for their grim expressions. Kâmuran never likes to have her picture taken anyway, so she looks as if she's about to cry.

More soon. Your loving daughter, Anna Maria
PS: Hikmet is sending you some stamps. "Watch for the Arabic stamp," she says.

Photography in the Marketplace 1961

Journal: Behiye, A Polyglot Some of my neighbors had seen Behiye begging in the market place, and wanted to find a place for her to work as a live-in mother's helper. They came to ask if we needed a helper, explaining that this young girl's mother had died, her father was a night watchman who drinks up his meager wages, and she tries to take care of herself and her younger sister by running errands or simply begging in the marketplace.

Our last helper, Naime, had gone back to her village to be married off, so we did need a new helper. But before making a decision, I consulted with my neighbors Sühendan hanım and Zehrah hanım. "Make sure she gets a good soapy tub bath, and washes her long hair thoroughly," they reminded me.

[These same experienced women had taught me how to cope when one maid had carried in head lice after a visit home to her village. To my horror, the nits showed up in little Kâmuran's braids; even Baby Melike's scalp was infected with the eggs. That was my very first glimpse of these creatures.]

Sela agreed to take in Behiye, and asked the houseboy to bring her over the next day. That gave me time to sew up a salvar, blouse, and overskirt. These were ready for her, with clean underwear, apron, house slippers, and a head scarf, when she arrived — and emerged from the prescribed bath. (All her previous clothing was carefully disposed of.)

Behiye has now been with us for some months, sleeping on an extra bed in the children's large bedroom. She's proved to be very bright, and speaks to me in quite clear Turkish, though I still can't make out if her first language is Kurdish or "Suriyandji." She seems to have picked up a smattering of several languages and has a good ear for mimicry, evidenced by what happened yesterday evening.

I'd asked her to call the children in from the garden, where they'd been playing after supper. She went outside, stood on the steps, and called out their names: "Hikmet! Timur! Kâmuran! Melike! Commeer! Commeer! Washerfaysnhanz! Putcherpijammazon! Brashurteef!"

It took me a moment to decipher her commands, but I finally recognized my stress and intonation: "Come here, come here! Wash your face and hands! Put your pajamas on! Brush your teeth!" ❧

Letter to Mother in Spokane

TPAO Sitesi, Batman
August 15, 1961

Dear Mama,

Hadn't realized it's been so long since the last letter — until I looked at the calendar. Hikmet has been in Sürmene for a month now. Has she written you? She's probably afraid she can't manage by herself in English, although she can read simple words.

She went with Sela's brother Muammer [moo-a-mehr] and his wife Nezihe [nay-zee-heh] when they went left on vacation. First, they visited Sela's older brother Sabri [sah-bree], his wife Seyyare, and sons Sinan, Ilhan, and Ayhan in Ankara. They took her to see Atatürk's mausoleum (her dearest wish), also to the big Luna Park amusement center.

Then, upon arriving in Sürmene, she asked her Grandmother Malkoç to take her and cousin Sirin [She–rin] to see their Grandfather Malkoç's grave. That evidently took care of all her formalities there.

She goes swimming everyday in the Black Sea, just across the road, with her third and youngest uncle, Orhan. He's now the local government doctor in Sürmene.

Well, what other good news? Oh, yes! Sela got a special letter of commendation for his work in the Company this year. I'm very proud of him. (To say nothing of a previous raise.) In my opinion, he really deserves it. He's on the go all day long with the new wells and drilling locations and bigwigs coming in on business.

The children are blooming. Timmy seems to be taking after his Grandfather Jones: he loves to tinker with a screwdriver in one hand and a wrench in the other. He spends half of the day breezing up and down the street on his tricycle, the other half pumping its tires, tightening bolts and "fixing things." He has made friends with the visiting Halliburton and Schlumberger engineers here. They can't understand Turkish of course, so he is frequently forced into speaking English.

Kâmuran has blossomed since Hikmet left for Sürmene. She is my "helper" around the house and dotes on going visiting with me. Now that Timur is in the "machine stage," she and Melike trot about together quite amiably. They play house on the balcony, chase butterflies, watch the storks on the telephone pole across the street, and visit all the children in the neighborhood.

Melike had a mishap recently climbing up on the tricycle, which rolled away with her because she can't reach the pedals. She fell off and broke one side tooth; a second front tooth had to be pulled later. At the Company hospital down the street, the doctor gave her one stitch inside her upper lip (no scar), one tetanus and one penicillin shot. Once back home, she was ready to get right back on that trike, too. Can you imagine!

Sewing Projects

Most of my time is taken up with sewing now. Everything seemed to wear out all at once. I send such worn-out clothing and scraps of material to Sela's relatives in Zonguldak on the Black Sea. They cleverly cut the material into strips and weave them into rag rugs. Sela says one family with four small fatherless children is quite destitute there. The father was killed by a runaway car coming down the steep hill; he saw it coming and heroically pushed his customers out of the way before it smashed into his coffee house. So I send boxes of whatever I can to them every year for their rag-rug weaving.

This summer, I've made T. five cotton shirts, K. and M. each four cotton dresses and a charming button-on sunbonnet, plus two nightgowns apiece, and outfitted H. for the trip to Sürmene. Also sheets, pillowcases, tea towels, and things for myself. None of these things, I should mention, are ready-made here. But I do have to hire a seamstress to sew my dresses for me, since I'm not that advanced!

My next project is a closet-door shoe-bag, if I can find the right material in Diyarbakır. While I'm there, I plan to visit a new Royal Dutch Shell Company family. It makes a pleasant diversion to take the morning post train into Diyarbakır, go shopping, have lunch, do more shopping, visit over tea, and then take the evening post back.

Public Transportation in Batman: A One-Horse Phaeton

"Going to the train" keeps the children in trim. Very often we all walk down to the train station just to see someone off. It's about a mile and a half, and even little Melike steps right along. And then usually we catch the phaeton to go back home. It's the only carriage in Batman, a life-saver when we have a lot of fresh produce and groceries to carry back up to the Site. (We're not allowed to ride in Company vehicles on personal errands.)

Instead of riding inside the carriage with us, Timmy is often invited to sit up with the driver behind the horse, hold the reins and squeak the bulbous horn. What moments of glory for a five-year-old boy!

Well, time to do the ironing, then fry the eggplant fresh from the garden. This summer, we have tomatoes, cucumbers, green squash, okra, string beans, corn, parsley, onions, artichokes, cress, dill, and mint for soup. Also seven peaches off the peach tree, and one watermelon.

And no, Mama, I hasten to add, I did *not* plant the vegetables. The Company gardener got miffed when I suggested I'd like to plant something myself. That was *his* job, and he would lose face!

Please say hello to EVERYBODY.

Your loving daughter, Anna Maria

Route 4, Box 188, Spokane
August 17, 1961

Dear A. M.

   Just came back from the Blood Bank and have an hour before catching a ride home.

   There has been plenty of company: Lucile and her three just left for Portland; Cuz Donald and Sue are coming. Linda and Cherry were up from the ranch; Linda backed into a post at 11 p.m. in the dark and lost one tooth, so she comes up to the Spokane dentist regularly. You wouldn't know those girls, young ladies now.

   Bess Smith spent a week with me; she says hello.

   We are all busy as bees. Outside of taxes and the high cost of living, things are on an even keel here.

   Have the tail end of the Ency. Will send you some more book packages, and will drop a card the day I do.

Love to all. Ma
PS: Look out for Camilla!

Journal: More Festivities: The Poolside Wedding   The Olympic-sized Company swimming pool is conveniently located in back of our house. There the Guest House kitchen staff sets up a bar of sorts and serves tea and coffee, also lemonade and gazoz, a kind of soda pop, for the children. In the late afternoon, after doing house chores and preparing the evening meal, I like to freshen up and join other mothers and their children at the pool. We order a beverage and a bowl of sunflower seeds to snack on, and socialize until twilight falls. Sometimes the husbands join us; occasionally they enjoy a round of poker in the Guest House before dinner.

   Each year, the poolside activities become more evolved and offer the TPAO employees other entertainment in addition to swimming. The "Moonlight Ball," for instance. This colorful event has been surpassed by a recent wedding, when one of the young electrical engineers married the daughter of a refinery technician. The families arranged a poolside reception for 300 friends and relatives of the popular pair.

   The groom, "as handsome as a movie star," appeared wearing a smart tuxedo suit; the exotically beautiful bride was wearing a hand-stitched, white silk wedding gown and veil. (The bride's mother had called on neighbor women to help the dressmaker complete the gown; I was thrilled to be invited to watch this communal effort, and hand-stitch part of one sleeve!)

   As the bridal couple walked the length of the pool and paused for photographs, the guests broke into appreciative applause — they looked like models for a wedding cake decoration. At a signal, the electricity was turned on, instantly transforming the scene.

178

Colored lights glowed in the weeping willows, and strands of colored lights strung across the pool glittered as they swung gently in the evening breeze. Their swaying, sparkling reflections created a magical effect, like colorful molten streaks in glassy black water. The full moon rose up, silently and dramatically, and cast its pale light over the seated guests, the scurrying waiters, the electric light wires, the weeping willows. It hung in the black sky, adding a silvery reflection to the floating colors in the pool. The total effect was beautiful, breathtaking, a "Midsummer Night's Dream."

The groom's buddies — and Mother Nature — had outdone themselves with the lighting effects. And the best was yet to come. The young electrical engineers' creative genius was amazing. [Partly inspired, I was told later, by an article in *"Popular Mechanics Magazine."*] By lashing together a number of empty oil drums painted bright silver, they created an enormous barge, added a wooden platform strong enough to hold the old Guest House piano, and a charismatic master of ceremonies with a microphone.

From beneath the weeping willows, a three-piece jazz band from the Officers' Club in Diyarbakır sounded a musical fanfare. This alerted the guests to the barge as it was maneuvered to the pool's edge and launched into the water at the deep end. Phonographic strains of Lohengrin's "Wedding March" signaled the bridal couple's arrival.

Amidst wildly cheering applause from the crowd, the newlyweds gingerly stepped aboard the barge, picked up the microphone, and broadcast a general greeting and thank-you to all their admiring friends and neighbors They disembarged carefully, slowly making their way from table to table to greet the guests personally, then sat in state at their flower-bedecked table of honor. [Earlier in the day, the pair had signed the marriage contract in the presence of the Batman marriage clerk and had repeated the marriage prayers read by the local imam in the privacy of the Guest House bridal suite.]

Waiters emerged from the Guest House with bounteous plates of wedding fare for every table. Children cheered and frolicked about. The three-piece band struck up a lively tune; the emcee sang all the latest popular Italian songs, followed by an endless repertoire of old-time crowd-pleasers. It was really and truly a wedding to remember. ❧

Journal: Visitors of All Persuasions The Guest House staff sometimes direct foreign guests to our house when in need of a translator, in hopes that Sela might be coming or going. Or, as a last resort, I might be able to help.

One sizzling hot day, a well-dressed man about Sela's age dressed in crisply ironed shirt and slacks knocked at the screen door. He introduced himself as a visiting engineer from someplace I didn't catch, speaking English with a French accent. He apologized, saying that the Guest House had run out of cold beer, and the attendant had suggested perhaps he might find a cold beer at our house. I invited him in, said I'd be happy to make a pot of tea, or a Turkish coffee. I couldn't offer lemonade, I explained; there was a shortage of lemons in the market place.

But no, he was really looking for a cold beer, thank you. Then I explained we'd had no beer for months, and, in any case, we had no ice. I apologized that all I had to offer was a glass of very cold, clear water. I did not apologize profusely, however. I'd already surmised he was the "Count X" from Paris whom Sela and his friends had mentioned would be arriving for a tour of the drilling sites. Where did he think he was, looking to find a cold beer way out here in the boondocks? This house was not a well-stocked Schlumberger or Royal Dutch Shell Oil camp, I thought to myself....

Besides, aristocratic royalty really goes against my democratic American grain. ❦

Birthday card from Mother in Spokane

Route 4, Box 188, Spokane
September 10, 1961

"Those born in September have the qualities of steadiness and reliability,
are highly esteemed by those who know them best,
and make successful designers and editors.
If they permit the bright side of their character to prevail,
it will lead them to happiness."
Flowers: Aster and morning glory
Birthstone: Sapphire

This is advance notice that the family is getting around to wishing you a happy birthday, but are still card shopping.

Love, Mom

Letter from Mother in Spokane

Route 4, Box 188, Spokane
September 21, 1961

Dear Anna Maria and all,

Just a line to let you know that dear Aunt Matilda arrived here on a visit. You know how we adore her....

And now, Clint [Uncle Harris' older son] is here with me, going to college in Cheney. Don't know what he really is going to study, but he'll get settled. Seems to fit into the hodge-podge here at Rocky Acres. Plus, he's handy too, with hammer & nails, which is a blessing for me. Things have a way of disintegrating.

Uncle Harris is as busy as ever, coming into town now and then for tractor parts or what not. Always leaves a passle of fresh fruit on the back porch [from his garden on the Columbia River]. No cream, because we have a cow now.

Well, must stop, the bus is coming. Tell Hikmet she will receive a Letter.

Love to all, Mom

TPAO Sitesi, Batman
September 22, 1961

Dear Brownfields and All: Greetings!

It's been a hot and hectic summer. Hikmet was the lucky one, having spent a month and a half with her Malkoç grandmother on the Black Sea. Most of our old friends, including Hasan Göker and family, have departed for the new refinery in Izmit, leaving a big gap. Then a lot of neighbors left on vacation. I did an enormous amount of sewing for the children, tutored Hikmet's mandolin teacher in English, baked cakes for the Halliburton and Schlumberger bachelors, and where did the time go?

The vacationers have returned, the government trials in Ankara have ended, and Menderes, *et al* — the former, late Prime Minister and his top officials — have gone to their just rewards. There will now be a brief respite until the elections....

The Prakla Seismic Crew

Things have brightened immensely for me since Ançi, one of my dearest neighbors, has come back to stay. She's the Austrian wife of one of the drilling engineers and they've been out on location this past year, where she learned more Turkish in one year than I did in five! On returning, the first thing her husband, Güntekin Köksal, did was to invite "a few of his friends" from the German Prakla camp where they do seismic work. They "dropped in," sixteen strong. It took Ançi and me, with the help of the doctor's wife next door, all morning to cook up enough food for the outfit.

It was wonderful to see them devour our home cooking — that was our reward! After a swim in the pool, they came back for Ançi's fresh cake, my ice cream, and our coffee. Then they piled into their Jeeps for the long road back to their campsite in the hills.

My Sister-in-Law Güher

Sela's younger sister, Güher, is visiting with us now. She came with Hikmet and Sela's brother Muammer's family, when they all returned from Sürmene.

Güher, with heavy, dark blond hair, bright blue eyes, and a rose-petal complexion, is almost as tall as Sela, and well-proportioned. I think she's been teased about her size, which has made her shy. Especially when it comes to the prospect of finding a husband — or, rather, of accepting a prospective one that's been found for her. At 27, she's very particular, and still unmarried. But she's a hardy soul and an energetic housekeeper, sews like a house a-fire, and loves to cook. For her trousseau, she is making the most unbelievably delicate lace and fine embroidery, which she learned in the girls' fine arts class in Sürmene.

Yesterday, we had the living room and dining room painted. All of us worked like troopers to finish cleaning up by evening, and I was ready to collapse but Güher was still going strong. She insisted on ironing all the curtains so she could hang them back up for the night. When she finally sits down to rest, she either knits or crochets something!

I have just sneaked out of the house to come across the street to Ançi's, where there is peace and quiet, to finish this letter. Timur and Kâmuran are riding their tricycles. Hikmet's friends Ferhan and Selma are showing her how to string okra and peppers from our garden "for the winter."

School started this week but some of the teachers haven't arrived as yet; things are in such a turmoil with the school construction that the children have been sent home until next week. Güher and Melike just went down the street to visit my married sister-in-law, Nezihe, Muammer's wife.

I'm very fond of my sisters-in-law and consider myself lucky to have two here right now in Batman. Nezihe, Güher's age, has dark blond hair, light blue eyes, a peaches-and-cream complexion, and a pleasant disposition. She is always helpful in a crisis. She and Muammer now have two children: daughter Sirin [Shirin] and son Serdar, roughly the ages of Timur and Melike. Nezihe manages her housework most efficiently and, like Güher, also sews, crochets, and knits industriously, producing handsome sweaters, caps, scarves, and leggings of wool or cotton for her children, as the season dictates.

It is only because of my baking abilities, if I may say so, that I can hold my head up at all in the presence of such housewifely marvels as my sisters-in-law and my neighbors.

Last week, to celebrate my birthday, I took a train trip to Diyarbakır with Timur and Hikmet, who were due for eye check-ups. Then I did a lot of shopping: shoes for Sela, things for the kitchen, material for the living-room chairs and divan. I found a blue-green upholstery material that is very fetching with our rust brown curtains, dark brown carpets, and the pieces of copper Sela brought from Gaziantep last year.

Before we took the train back to Batman, we three had tea with the wife of a Royal Dutch Shell engineer. She speaks very good English and her young daughter speaks a little, enough to tell me her name was Anne Marie. (With Ançi, that's three of us "name friends" now.)

This afternoon, I'm going with neighbors Sühendan hanım and Meral hanım to welcome the newest bride in our neighborhood. Sometimes I get so involved in this custom of making social calls on new arrivals that I feel like a Welcome Wagon Lady. But it has its compensations. When Nezihe and I gave a tea for Güher at the Guest House, all the women in the neighborhood came to welcome her, which warmed my heart.

Now I see it's time to round up the little ones, so I must take my leave.

With love, Anna Maria

Letter to Mother in Spokane

TPAO Sitesi, Batman
September 23, 1961

Dear Mama,

Thanks for the pretty card and note. The children were so pleased with their cards. Even Melike trots around clutching hers, only showing it to special people.

All is well here. School has started, but without me. And not without a lot of pleading on the new principal's part. I just can't spend so much time on schoolwork. I've got to concentrate on Hikmet this year. She has eight subjects plus English.

Timur so far hasn't shown any interest in drawing, or reading books, although he and Kâmuran will look at picture books for hours on end, and carry on split dialogues — one starts a sentence, the other finishes it. T. does like "tinkering," as I mentioned before, and he now has a fancy combination saw-hammer-screwdriver that's a marvel. It was a gift from a Schlumberger guy just back from home leave.

Well, they've found my hideout, so I have to quit! Love to all.

Your loving daughter, Anna Maria

Journal: Sela Takes a Short Business Trip   Without much ado, TPAO has decided to send Sela on a short trip to Europe. Although he's been too busy to go into details, I assume he's being sent to confer with petroleum companies who send their representatives and personnel to the Batman region. ❦

Postcard from Sela

Paris, December 9, 1961

Love from the Eiffel Tower. We just had lunch on the second floor. Sela

---

Postcard from Sela

Milano Airport *[typed]*
December 12, 1961

Dearest,

They have Olivetti typewriters to type letters to your sweetheart from Milan Airport!

After arriving here last night, Melih Genca and I walked around the city and saw the famous churches, etc.

In the morning we went to ENI office and talked about our trip to Sicily, where we will see an oilfield producing heavy oil like our Batman/Raman oil. We are taking a plane at 1:30 pm to Catania, Sicily, stopping about one hour in Rome.

Forest Love lives in Rome; I will give him a call. We will arrive Catania tonight, from there will take a two-hour ride to Gela. Tomorrow will visit the oilfields and then fly to Frankfurt day after.

With all my love, yours only, Sela
PS: Hello from Melih.

Postcard from Sela

Rome Airport
December 14, 1961

Dear Mom,

I am having a 15-day business trip through Europe. Have been 4 days in Paris, 2 days in Geneva, 2 days in Rome and Milano. Today I am flying to Frankfurt and Hannover, Germany. Will stay in Germany about a week, and will be back home for Xmas eve. I hope!

Yours Truly, Sela

14

A TRIP WITH HIKMET TO AMERICA

Letter to Mother in Spokane

TPAO Sitesi, Batman
February 28, 1962

Dear Mama,

In the last letter, I was not going to ask you for an affidavit; Sela said it would be a lot of trouble and I probably wouldn't need it. But after having talked with friends here, I think it may help me avoid exchanging more money than I really need.

Travel Plans for Spokane

It used to require an affidavit of support just to leave the country. Now getting a tourist visa is easier. However, I also have to exchange lira into dollars ($200) at the cambio office. Most travelers need the money anyway, and it helps cut down on black market exchange. At 13.50 lira to $1, it's about 2700 lira, quite a bit for me, especially after buying the tickets. With a letter of support from you, I may be allowed to take along the minimum $50. It should be easy for you to get a new one within a couple of weeks, sending the enclosed old affidavit special delivery to Chicago and including special delivery stamps for return mail to Spokane. (There's no special delivery here, only air mail.) You can take the money out of the kitty. And thank you for doing all this, Mama.

We still haven't gotten any word from the travel agency in Ankara. Imagine trying to make plans when you don't know the schedules!

I'm trying to "indoctrinate" the children about my trip gradually. Our dear neighbor Ançi, with no children of her own, unfortunately, is very fond of ours and has promised to take all three. She knows quite well how to manage them by now. Plus, our houseboy Hasan is extremely efficient and responsible, and will help out at Ançi's house, so I won't be worried about them.

What's most important, Sela encourages me: "It's time you take Hikmet to visit your mother," he says. If there's anything anyone would like from here, please let me know. I've already collected lace work from Diyarbakır and the village women here. I do hope all is well. Sela sends his best. We'll keep you posted.

Your loving daughter, Anna Maria
PS: I missed Camilla's birthday letter, but have her birthday present tucked away.

Letter from Mother in Spokane

Route 4, Box 188, Spokane
March 30, 1962

Dear Anna Maria,

About Hikmet's Turkish dancing outfit you mentioned in your postcard: Yes, the Cheney Cowles Museum in Spokane is glad to get any native dress as a gift to the Museum. The curator said to please get all the info you can, for their records. Anything from another country is greatly appreciated.

Haven't heard from Chicago, but should get the papers any day. Shall I send them to you?

Well, Pete's in San Jose, now, and so is Mike. They'll be real glad to see you two down there.

And we're all yipping in the meantime!

Ma

Card from Mother in Spokane

Route 4, Box 188, Spokane
April 3, 1962

Dear A. M. and all,

Well, got the affidavit so I'm sending it to you. Sent the $20.00 to Gloria Gaston, but what about Hikmet? Have you her tkt? Let me know if and when or whatever. That would clear out the kitty, but that would be OK, huh? You can always wire me collect.

Mom

Postcard to Mother in Spokane

Rome
April 4, 1962

Dear Family,

This is our first stop and Rome is wonderful. Hikmet and I are staying with friends, Mr. and Mrs. Love, who've taken us to the Vatican City and to the famous Trevi fountain, where we made a wish and threw in a coin. My head is in a whirl with all the marble statues and antiquities. Just *beautiful*.

Hikmet is watching television now. Oooh, how wonderful! I can't believe it! We're leaving tomorrow for Geneva. Will keep you posted.

Hello to everybody!

Your loving daughter, Anna Maria

186

Geneva
April 7, 1962

Dear Mama,

Everything is delicious and delightful here but, unfortunately, it's only a short stop. We're visiting one of Sela's old friends, Abdi bey, and his family here. We're on our way to the airport. Next stop Paris, where we will visit Schlumberger friends Rolande and Gilbert Domps. Bon Nuit! YLD

Postcard to Mother in Spokane

Washington, DC
April 16, 1962

Dear Mama,

We made New York OK. Got the M.O. from Gloria. NY is too rich for me! Spent 24 hrs with Gloria; she sent 2 suitcases off from 34th Street Greyhound Bus station. They said it would take 3 days. Give them a week; if they don't arrive in Spokane, then check, OK? Hikmet and I are waiting for connections through Tenn. & from there to El Dorado, Ark. where we will sojourn for a day. Hikmet is holding up great. I keep feeding her ice cream. xxx Anna Maria

---

Postcard to Mother in Spokane

Austin, Texas
April 19, 1962

Howdy, y'all!

We're on our way to Austin to see Hessie Williams from Batman. Had a nice stop-over in El Dorado, Ark. to see Alta and Chuck Sternberg, a UN consultant we also knew in Batman. Land, but this is purty country!
Luv from YLD

Letter from Sela

Ankara
May 6, 1962

My Dearest Anna Maria,

I am writing these lines in Suat bey's apartment, after a comfortable ride around Ankara with Ruhsar hanım and Suat bey in his new Opel sedan. I came to Ankara Friday with Gültekin and Sait on business and will stay until Wednesday.

I received your card from Oakland and was glad you are coming to the end of your travel. By now you should be in Spokane. All that traveling from New York by Greyhound bus must have tired you out. I hope you enjoyed all of it.

187

I received a nice letter from Mr. Love in Rome with a picture of Mrs. Love, and Hikmet. I also got a card from the Sternbergs from the Fiji Islands. They said that you looked very tired when they saw you in Eldorado.

Ançi is taking care of Melike and Kâmuran very nicely, and Timur is staying with Muammer. He is doing his eye and foot exercises with Güher every night, sometimes with me. After we sent you off, I took Timur to another eye doctor, who examined him very thoroughly [for his "wandering eye"]. He said that the exercises must be kept up, and glasses must not be used until the eye corrects itself, which is a 70% chance. So he is not using glasses, and I think the exercises are helping him. This doctor said it's too early to think about an operation.

Kâmuran is getting taller, and is not looking for you as much as Melike. Saturdays and Sundays I take them out and we pick wild flowers. Sometimes Melike says, "When is my mother going to come?" and "I thought she went to Ankara." But she is forgetting as the time goes on.

I already got your table made, the kitchen whitewashed and all the cupboards painted blue. I am getting our bed repaired at the moment.

I am thinking to take a month vacation starting next Friday, to take Güher back home to Sürmene with Timur for Kurban Bayram.

If I can manage it, I will take a ship from Zonguldak to Istanbul with Timur and show him to another famous eye doctor. Of course, if my money lasts that long. From Istanbul, I will go back to Batman via Ankara.

I have been invited to many Wednesday and Saturday dinner parties in Batman. So last week, I had to give one at the Guest House to the people who invited me. We had a good time. But without you, everything is getting to be lonely and poor. I am longing for you, darling, so much that you could not imagine.

Don't worry about the kids at all. They are being taken care of very nicely.

Kisses for Hikmet. I hope she is being a nice girl.

Give my best to Mom and everybody else.

I love you. Sela

PS: Ruhsar hanım helped me buy some dress material for Ançi yesterday. I thought about such a gift since she doesn't take money for taking care of the children.

PPS: from Ruhsar:

Dearest Maria, I hope you are enjoying your liberty, beginning with Geneva, Rome and Paris. O-la-la! We were awfully glad to see Malkoç in Ankara and to spend a few hours with him. Our deepest love and respect to you and your family. As always, Ruhsar

---

188

Letter from Sela

TPAO Sitesi, Batman
May 24, 1962

My dearest Anna Maria,

Your last letter came couple days ago. I already wrote you a Turkish letter; I hope you understood all of the things I wrote in that letter.

We all are fine and dandy, don't worry about us kids. Ançi is doing fine and she says that you should not be in a hurry if you are thinking about the kids. I sent another $500 to your account so buy some beautiful things for yourself with the money, to be beautiful for this poor Sela (though you are already beautiful and lovely).

I will be taking a month vacation and going to Sürmene with Timur, also taking Güher on the 28th and coming back via Zonguldak and Ankara. So take your time and enjoy yourself. Ançi and Güntekin do not want anything; they only say hello. Everybody says hello from Batman. Hello to everybody and kiss Hikmet for me.

I love you, SM

Journal: Hikmet's Dancing Costume Visits the Schools and Goes to a Museum
In preparation for this trip, many hands helped to assemble a dancing costume for Hikmet to wear when she visited her grandmother, cousins, aunts, uncles, and pen pals in Spokane. Rather than a costume specific to one regional, it was an amalgamation of pieces from many parts of Turkey.

For Hikmet's headgear, our neighbor Emirhan hanım donated an heirloom silk scarf fringed with tiny crocheted carnations, to wear over a satin striped toque (or "pillbox" cap). When I protested that the 150-year-old scarf was too precious to accept, Emirhan hanım said she would be proud to have it go to America, "so people could see the beautiful Turkish handwork."

Hikmet's Aunt Nezihe sewed a black velvet salvar sprinkled with colored flowers. Her Aunt Güher embroidered tiny tulips on a white silk blouse with long puffed sleeves, her Aunt Sülhiye embroidered a vest to wear over the blouse. In Diyarbakır, I found a gold fringed scarf for her cummerbund, and Sela brought home a pair of red and gold brocade slippers with turned-up toes. Even more spectacularly, he had discovered a pair of "antique bell bracelets" in a hole-in-the-wall silversmith's shop. These were small silver bands with tiny silver bells attached, to be worn on the wrists or ankles. "She'll jingle while she dances," he said, proud of his find.

This, then, was how she was dressed when we entered the Whittier Elementary School in Spokane, intending to visit her cousin Andy Paul's and Matt's classrooms. Instead, we were ushered into the school gymnasium, packed with curious children! I introduced ourselves, explained the folk dance Hikmet had learned for them, "Harmandalı," [Harvesting Sheaves] and slipped to the back row to watch her answer the children's questions before she began her performance.

189

She started singing and dancing slowly, making her way from the front of the crowded auditorium down the long aisle to the back, whirling and dipping and swirling from side to side. When she reached the back of the room, she whispered in Turkish, "That's the end of my song and dance, Mother. What shall I do now?"

"Make up something, sing a song about spring and birds, dance back again," I whispered in Turkish. And like a trooper, she broke into a lilting children's song, improvising little dance steps as she went along. The black velvet salvar and the white silk scarf with its dangling carnations billowed gently as she moved; her silver bracelet bells tinkled as she swooped her wrists airily and gracefully. Her audience loved it.

She also visited her nine pen pals in Adams Elementary School. To her surprise, they all burst out singing the "Friends" song. In return, she sang two Turkish songs: "Bahar Geldi" [Spring Has Come] and "Küçük Ayse" [Little Ayshe], then answered questions from the audience to the best of her ability. The last one was, "What is the temperature of Turkey?"

To which she responded, "About 70 degrees." This satisfied the young questioner and everyone else.

She wore her precious dancing costume at a special family gathering for her grandmother, and many other times during our visits in Spokane and Seattle. Before we left, she presented the outfit, with a written explanation of its origin, to the Cheney Cowles Museum for Spokane schoolchildren to admire.

How proud Emirhan hanım's great, great grandmother would be to know that her exquisite bridal scarf had danced in America! ❦

15

BACK TO BATMAN, UP TO ANKARA

Kamuran and Auntie Güher

Waiting for Mother

Letter to Sister in Spokane

TPAO Sitesi, Batman
July 25, 1962

Dear Camilla:

Hope Mama got my card from Ankara. We arrived back in Turkey on the 14th. Our kind Schlumberger friend brought Sela to meet us at the Diyarbakır airport, where we had to wait three hours in heat over 100 degrees Fahrenheit. However, that longest part of the journey came to an end, and we finally got back to Batman.

Ançi was waiting with the children in front of the Guest House. Timur did his best not to smile, Melike looked bewildered but clung to my hand, and Kâmuran burst into tears whenever I opened my mouth. Here was her long-awaited mother, talking like a regular foreigner!

Readjusting to a Strange Mother

What a shambles that night was. Sela had had the walls whitewashed, the furniture polished, even a bowl of cut flowers on the table. In five minutes, all the suitcases were adrift, all the gifts from Grandmother and everyone had been opened, admired, and strewn about. And Kâmuran was still crying! By the time I got her calmed down, Melike decided *she* was losing out. She couldn't understand a word of English either! She made faces and complained loudly in Turkish, "Stop *talking* like that! Talk *plain!*"

Well, after ten days now, they've all calmed down and gotten used to English again, more or less.

And Catching up on the News

Oh, the things that happened while Hikmet and I were a-roaming: two weddings, a broken engagement, and three babies hardly count. Ançi got pregnant, at long last. Unfortunately, it was a tube pregnancy, and she had to go to a doctor in Ankara. Sela had taken Timur to see his parents in Sürmene, so one neighbor took care of Kâmuran, and sister-in-law Nezihe took Melike in. Everyone was wonderfully good about watching the children. Seems they were all quite "charming" in my absence. Now that I'm back, they're once again at their little squabbles over this and that.

Ançi has now returned to Batman, still a bit weak but hopeful for the next time. We've started her English lessons.

Then a few days later at noontime, it seemed that all hell broke loose when the refinery's dynamite shelter exploded. Sela had just finished his lunch at home. In a split second, he was off running down the road toward the explosion area. Amazingly, only one man got a scratch from falling glass. There were no other casualties, although here in the Site (half a mile away) almost everyone's windows shattered. They say the shelter was "overloaded." Fortunately, the earthworks about the building were built extra high, otherwise the refinery and all souls there would have mushroomed right up.

Price Fixing Affects Our Marketing

Our main problem now is buying food. The county commissioner has set price ceilings, so now there's no bargaining. As a result, the villagers don't want to sell their produce in the marketplace. They've started coming up to the Company housing development here to hawk their fresh produce in the Site streets. Personally, we're lucky to have squash, tomatoes, peppers, cucumbers and parsley right in our back garden. And resourceful Sela bought a cow in the village up near Raman, and pays to have it tended to. When the service truck comes down from Raman camp each morning, we get a bottle of fresh milk. Now that I've finally learned how to make yogurt, it's perfect food for this heat.

More Catching Up

Hikmet has started her "catch-up" lessons. Thought I'd be able to manage to help her myself, but instead arranged with the teacher I gave English lessons to last year to come five mornings a week for an hour or so.

I still haven't caught up with the task of changing winter to summer clothing; this means opening each trunk in the storeroom and airing out the contents on the back clotheslines in the bright sunshine. Also shifting winter to summer clothing, summer curtains, etc.

The first day back from the Spokane trip, I burned my hand frying chicken and Hikmet had to pinch-hit washing dishes. It's my right hand, too, darn it. Now, after doing three day's worth of hand laundry, it somehow got infected. By the time I catch up on the ironing, it should be healed enough to use the washboard in the bathtub again. I just sighed thinking of my sister-in-law Nona with her seven little ones in Spokane. I'm so happy for her that she has a washing machine!

The sad news in our house is that the brother-in-law of Hasan, our helpful houseboy, got stoned to death, so Hasan had to hurry off to the village to see to family responsibilities. Can you imagine that!

Hasan's replacement hasn't really caught on to our house routine yet. The houseboys [janitors] are hired by the Company to tend to the single houses and apartment buildings. They check on basic maintenance in the building they're responsible for, run general daily errands like bringing fresh bread from the bakery to every household, deliver the newspaper when it comes in on the train, carry invitation/responses between neighbors in the community. In general, they try to cope with emergencies as they arise.

Keeping Cool in Batman

The heat's enough to choke a horse this summer. Most of the men here are out in the intense sun — working on construction at the refinery, or at the drill sites, or on the rigs, where they sometimes drop from heat exhaustion....

Thankfully, in our house we now have a window air-cooler. I close the curtains, drapes, and windows early in the morning, and except for errands to the neighbors, the children and I usually don't emerge until sundown. That way, the house stays cool during the day. As soon as the sun starts going down, and the outside air begins to cool, we escape from the house, where the concrete walls now give off the heat absorbed during the day. We often take tea at the poolside; it's a wonderfully relaxing and pleasant area.

The children love to listen to their new records from Spokane. You should see Hikmet do the "Twist." She's got it down pat, and even little Kâmuran is picking it up. In fact, they're all struggling to "twist."

Sela was so pleased with his records, please tell Rosemary. We've invited several UN men here, and Sela loves to play something "different" when they come for after-dinner coffee and cake. Next Sunday, we're having a waffle breakfast. That's a big treat for everyone, and for many visiting engineers it's a first experience with waffles.

The first night back from the Spokane trip, I was taking out my new contact lenses when Sela came in. He remembered my explanation of what it was like getting used to them. "Hi, Kiddo. Taking off your wooden leg?" he asked.

Remember how the extra weight I gained on the visit bothered me? No longer! Everyone thought the trip improved my appearance. Shows you how people differ. Anyone considered "slim" in the States is "skinny" here. In any case, I'm slowly losing it and feel fine.

You should see Timur in his cowboy regalia! He keeps everything carefully packed away in his suitcase in the closet and uses Sela's clothes brush for his cowboy hat. Someone at the refinery made him a tin sheriff's star to pin on his vest. Then he puts on the chaps and the rest of it and roves about in this heat — — sweat trickling down under his hat brim — flipping his Gene Autry gun like crazy. Eventually, he tires and forgets he's a cowboy. Then he re-assembles the train set and is lost in another world of his own, watching the little engine go around and around and around....

The girls are playing graceful "Indian princesses" now. H. and K. have the feather headdresses, and Melike has colored pencils stuck in a headband. They're parading and dancing about in wild abandon....

Hikmet has just volunteered to make the afternoon snack: cocoa and cookies. Yesterday, she and neighbor pal sweet Ruhan made cookies with the new cookie cutters. They spent hours in the kitchen and the net results are so precious they get doled out only on special occasions.

She has a real "schedule" now: after breakfast she helps in the house, then goes down the street to the hospital to see Dr. Çetin bey, the dentist who's studying orthodontics and plans to put caps on her crooked teeth. Next, she's home for her lessons, then off to the big swimming pool with one of the young engineers who supervises her swimming. This is another trade-off for English lessons here.

[While we were gone a-visiting in the States, a young child drowned in the smaller pool — right in the midst of a crowd! After that tragedy, there's always a lifeguard posted at each pool. But I don't worry about Hikmet, especially since she goes with Turgut.]

Melike has just asked for permission to play in the garden. "I'm not going to play with anybody, because I have a cough," she says, dragging out the dolls in her doll buggy. Whooping cough is going around, though this may not be it. They've all had shots, but the doctor says they could still get it lightly.

It's time to clear the decks for Sela to come home. Poor guy, the new district manager is away and he has too much to handle. There's lot of dissension in the office with the new regime, and I think Sela wants to move to Ankara. It's up to him, of course. Right now, all I want to do is take good care of the children. Well, we'll see....

Another thing, Camilla, about your young neighbor Kenny's request for a Turkish souvenir. We were in a rush in Ankara and I couldn't mail anything. I saw a delightful Turkish fairy tale book (about $4.50) that should more than make up for the $2.00 bill Kenny gave me. (I spent my last *dime* before getting on the plane in New York, and I needed $2.00 for the new airport tax in London. Big shock!) As soon as someone goes up to Ankara, I'll ask them to send you two copies. If you think he'll be disappointed with a book, I'll try to find something else.

Hope Wally got settled in that job, and you and the children are OK.

I miss you all. I'll try to send pictures when we get them developed. Please give everyone our best!

Your loving sister, Anna Maria
PS: Camilla, I thank you for that final donation. Someday I'll try to make it all up to you.

Letter from Mother in Spokane

Route 4, Box 188, Spokane
August 17, 1962

Dear Anna Maria and all,

Hope you are all back safe and snug in your own domicile. Didja get the parcel with Hikmet's glasses yet? Found 'em by the tarragon bush, by pure chance. If I hadn't been chopping out wild rose bushes in the back garden, they would have been there for a long while.

Well, anyways, we do miss you two after your visit, but maybe not so much your own there in Batman. At the moment, young Sue Roy and Jon Smith are sleeping upstairs. Cuz Joy comes Monday for Jon, then Cuz Donald and Virginia to pick up Sue. Also, Lucile is here with her young ones to visit before going out to Aunt Ann's in the Valley.

The clothing you left to be sent has to be certified by the dry cleaners first. Had some packages all ready, but the PO refused them without certification. I think because of the polio scare.

So, keep looking. Mom

Journal: The Kurdish Women's Delegation As I was clearing the breakfast table one morning recently, I noticed a group of seven or eight village women clustered at the end of the sidewalk steps outside the house. They were milling about uncertainly, so I walked out to see if I could help them.

The woman who appeared to be the head of the group introduced herself by name. "I'm happy to meet you," I responded, shook hands, and waited with a smile.

"We're of the . . . family ," she continued. Clearly, she was waiting for me to be impressed by the name, which I didn't catch. "You know our name?" She repeated it. When I indicated I didn't know it, she seemed surprised at my ignorance.

[Truth to tell, the only famous local name I know is that of "Hasso," the regional Kurdish "Robin Hood" who, they say, robs from the rich and helps out the poor. He's on the run from the gendarmes for having robbed a Royal Dutch Shell Oil camp in the nearby hills. Cleverly eluding the Turkish police, he found refuge among sympathetic villagers in the region. It's said that no Kurdish village would ever betray him; he could hide indefinitely, if not in a village around here, somewhere in the caves along the Tigris. With the help of my big dictionary, I've read accounts of his escapades in the little weekly Batman newspaper. Otherwise, I know only the names of the women and girls who come to work in the site, and the men who work in the maintenance jobs. I don't know the family or tribal name of anyone in this area. I'm still struggling to learn about the various members of the Malkoç family and their complicated histories!]

"What is it you wish?" I asked politely, trying to make amends for my ignorance. The gist of what the speaker for the group was saying in Turkish seemed to be a grievance against Sela for firing one of the men in the family. I could see that the women were agitated and could only guess they wanted him reinstated.

I tried to tell them they had to talk to my husband at the refinery, but I didn't know the Turkish words for influence, or intermediary, or intercede, so I simply repeated: "I'm sorry. I don't work at the refinery. Please talk to my husband." My words were in vain, I knew. These women would no more approach the directors at the refinery than the man in the moon, but I didn't know how to help them, and didn't know what else to say to them.

To myself, I was thinking their husband/son/brother must have broken important work rules if, indeed, Sela had fired him. Being the ethical person he is, I believe he would never dismiss any valuable worker without just cause. My guess was the worker had broken rules. And I know how dangerous it can be working around refineries and oil rigs, where infractions of the rules cannot be tolerated. But these were all just guesses on my part.

Except in unusual circumstances, Sela never brings home any "ills of the office" that would distress me. He discusses work problems with the other engineers at the head office or after dinner, elsewhere. So, of course, I knew nothing about the women's complaints. When I told him about the women's visit to the house, he became angry, and promised me it wouldn't happen again. ❦

Journal: Turkish Wrestling (from an article for the Spokesman-Review) The ancient art of wrestling dates back, according to some authorities, to Theseus, the Athenian king of Greek legend. Not so legendary are the actual remains of Egyptian monuments depicting the sport in hundreds of different poses.

Perhaps one of the most colorful of wrestling figures in the modern world is the "Pehlivan" wrestler of Turkey. This gladiator-type athlete belongs to the classic rather than the modern school of Turkish wrestlers. Usually of imposing stature and proportions, clad in skin-tight, knee-length leather breeches and anointed from shaved head to bare feet with olive oil, his very appearance is enough to dismay the weak in heart.

Pehlivan Wrestler Is World Champion Wrestler

Compared to the more or less standardized forms of western wrestling, the Pehlivan is a primitive wrestler. His style was set by "Big Joseph," a strong man of great renown, born over 100 years ago in the village of Kırk Pınar in Thrace, the arm of Greece reaching down across Turkey.

"Big Joseph" wrestled his way to glory across Europe and during his appearance in the United States, he won the world championship in heavyweight wrestling — a crown he never relinquished. Tragically, when the ship on which he was returning to his homeland capsized, he went down with it. However, he brought such long lasting fame to his village that "Greased" wrestling is also termed "Kırk Pınar" wrestling.

Like the old Greeks, these Pehlivans engaged in Kırk Pınar bouts are set no time limits and one match may last several interminable hours. The victor is acclaimed when one man is felled, not necessarily with both shoulders touching the grass, but face up, with his chest partially or fully exposed to the sky.

As opposed to the oil-besmeared Pehlivan of the classic school, there is also the modern or "mat" wrestler in Turkey. These men wear regulation gym suits and shoes and compete under rigid restrictions on regulation-sized mats, 6x6 or 8x8 meters. The mat wrestlers are judged in either of two fields, the Graeco-Roman (where all holds are taken above the waist) or the Free Style.

Wrestling Matches in Batman

Turkish wrestlers are world famous and generally walk away with firsts or seconds in the Olympic Games. I've always had a hankering to see an authentic Turkish wrestling match, and this year I had an opportunity to see TPAO's Sport Club compete against the National Railways Central Repair Shops Sport club from Sivas [the railroad headquarters located in Central Anatolia]. The series of bouts held here in Batman were part of the Seker Bayram [Sweets Holiday] following the month-long Ramazan fasting.

The local TPAO team didn't look too feeble to me: a couple of hefty gendarmes, the chief toolpusher from the oil rigs, and the Company butcher — who, rumor had it, was filling up on fresh lamb chops and raw ground beef. The men had next to no training, true, but they packed a lot of muscle. All of which was to little avail, sad to say. The men from Sivas were formidable.

And small wonder. Some 25 years ago, according to one source, the government railway central repair shops in Sivas set up a school where likely young village boys are sent to study. Later, they're set up as apprentices in the workshops and, if promising, trained in the Sport Club. They learn to swim, play soccer, climb the rugged mountains nearby, become excellent riflemen, and learn to wrestle. Now here were a dozen of these young Sivas stalwarts flexing their muscles for the fray. The first match, western-style, was held at the TPAO tennis court on a mat 26 feet square.

All in all, it was a fair scene to behold. The spring weather was balmy. The newly arrived storks were building nests on the telephone poles. Narcissus were blooming in the open fields. The children were dressed in holiday attire: girls in ruffled dresses and hair ribbons, boys in new jackets, shirts and ties. Grown-ups crowded along together and the wrestling began. Great cheers went up: "Bravo, Mustafa!" "Hurrah, Ali the Lion!" and an occasional "Yuuuuh!" which rhymes with "Boooo!" and means the same.

One after another, the TPAO men went down, shoulders pinned to the mat, but struggling manfully. The manliest was the meat-eating butcher, emerging with a bruised shoulder, mat burns and enough scratches to satisfy the most bloodthirsty in the audience. The second engagement was noticeably tamer, held in the Company cinema, several days later. This gave the wrestlers time to recuperate while a wooden apron large enough to accommodate the mat was built to extend out from the theater's stage. Again, the audience was teeming; everybody goes to these free wrestling matches.

Wrestling Rules and Regulations

This time the trainer from Sivas explained some rules and regulations: Each bout of 12 minutes is divided into 4 intervals, the first of which lasts 6 minutes. The side referees reckon the points during this first interval and refer them to the mat referee; the man with the greater number of points during this first 6 minutes chooses positions to start off the next interval, of 2 minutes. In case of a tie, a coin is flipped, to decide who's up and who's down, so to speak. Then this same position starts off the third interval, only the men reverse. The fourth

197

interval, again only 2 minutes, is simply a continuance of the third, making 12 minutes in all.

It was all deadly serious. And very confusing to me. The most exciting moment occurred when the two brawniest wrestlers nearly fell off into the orchestra pit and into the lap of somebody's grandmother. ❦

Journal: I Will Always be a Yabancı, a Stranger Although Sela and I have been here in the oilfields for the better part of a decade, and I have learned to adjust to my life in the TPAO Site, I was reminded for the first time in a long time that I am still an "outsider" here.

In a sense, though, so are the other people in the Site as well. Sela himself, as a Turk, is an outsider to this part of the country populated by Kurdish villages. So I, being neither Turk nor Moslem, am doubly a "yabancı." This struck me acutely on my walk to the market this morning.

With my crocheted shopping bag in hand, I was taking a short cut across an open field, heading for the little shops near the train station. Some fifty yards distant, on a parallel path criss-crossing the field, a young village girl of about 13 or 14 was walking in the opposite direction. The moment she spotted me going down my path, she quickened her steps and pulled a fold of her headscarf across her face, keeping her head turned as she hurried toward her own destination.

Some extremely devout Moslem women, I've heard, will avert their eyes and shield their faces from infidels — non-believers — to protect themselves from breathing in "evil emanations." That young girl's gesture struck me with great force, reminding me that in the eyes of some (many? most? all?) people around here, I am a "yabancı." In her eyes, this seems to be synonymous with "gâvur," a person beyond the pale, like a leper, or an "untouchable."

I had an urge to run after her, to tell her I wasn't evil at all, just another female human being.

But I didn't, of course. I simply continued on down the path to the vegetable stalls to buy potatoes and leeks for my family's supper. ❦

Postcard of Ancient Greek ruins in Side, Turkey

---

mailed from Ankara Airport
August 20, 1962

Dear Mama,

Very shortly, our house will be in this state of disassemblement (see picture other side).

Sela sent me to Ankara to find a house to rent, which I have just done. Now I'm returning to Batman. (I'm writing this at the terminal for the plane back to Diyarbakır.) Then, I'll pack up and take the children to Ankara next week. H. and T. will start school in Ankara next month.

Sela expects to be transferred to Ankara later. All is very well. Sorry I haven't written, but things are hectic. Love to all. More anon.

YLD, Anna Maria

Journal: "Mama, Is There Chewing Gum in Ankara?" In the fall of 1962, Sela put in for transfer to the main TPAO office in Ankara. He himself couldn't leave until he'd arranged all his business in the field, but it was essential that I first go to find an apartment in Ankara, return for the children, get settled in the new place, and enroll Hikmet and Timur in school for the fall semester.

So, after finding a suitable apartment in Ankara, I went back to Batman. The children and I packed up our things and we said goodbye to our friends in the neighborhood. Sela took us to the train station, where so many times we'd stood waiting to welcome bewildered newcomers, and where we'd stood waiting to bid sad farewells to departing friends.

To me, these arrivals and departures were a symbolic metaphor of the passages of our life. Now, after tearful hugs and promises to write, it was our turn to board the train, to say our farewells in Batman.

Perhaps I may see some of these friends in Ankara or elsewhere, I thought as we waved from the compartment window, but in all probability, we will never return to this remote area where we have lived eight eventful years of our lives, where Baby Cemile died in Raman Camp, and where Melike was born at home in the TPAO Sitesi in Batman. We waved and waved, until our friends were tiny pinpoints on the receding tracks, and we were well on our way to the nation's capital.

For Hikmet, of course, this was not the great adventure into the mysterious unknown that it was for her younger siblings. Timur and Kâmuran had been too young to remember the few times they'd visited Ankara. Melike had been only an infant.

In their immediate world, the ancient walled city of Diyarbakır was the "Big City." For days now, they'd been discussing our forthcoming move to Ankara. They asked many questions of "Miss-Know-It-All" Behiye about traveling on trains, since she had actually been on a train herself! Was the train nice inside? Where did it go? Where did it stop? Did you buy anything there?

Behiye told them she'd actually gone as far as Bismil (a small village station about 50 kilometers down the track). In her young eyes, Bismil was a big place compared to her own village, or compared to Batman. They sold chewing gum in Bismil, she told them in an awed tone. Like nylon, the new "miracle material," chewing gum was something marvelous and rarely seen in Batman.

In my own way, I've been trying to paint for them a picture of Ankara, this strange place that will be our new home. I've told them it's full of big houses and very tall buildings. There are no horse-drawn phaetons; people ride in buses and taxis. There are many stores that sell lots and lots of things.

"And chewing gum?" Kâmuran asked timidly. "Is there chewing gum in Ankara?" I assured her there was lots of chewing gum, and in different flavors! This was almost too wonderful to imagine.

Now, in fascinated silence, they all watched the train conductor skillfully turn our compartment seats into sleeping berths. They readied themselves for bed, drifted off to sleep as the steam engine chugged on through the night, transporting us to Ankara. To the Big City. ❦

Journal: A First Elevator Experience in Ankara Sela had planned ahead and made arrangements for our arrival in Ankara. Kind friends were waiting at the train station to take us to our hotel accommodations.

During the swelteringly hot, two-day train trip to Ankara, we had opened the train windows to cool off. As a result, we were grimy from the sooty coal smoke blown back into our compartment. We were also tired and hungry, but hot, soapy baths took first priority. The bath water immediately turned inky black from the soot on our skin and hair. In no time at all, I'd bagged all the sooty laundry, laid out fresh clothing, scrubbed and shampooed us all, dressed, and ordered room service. We devoured the simple supper and slept like logs.

After a restful night's sleep, room service brought us a large tray of breakfast. "Such luxury," Hikmet remarked, enjoying it thoroughly. The younger children were in a state of mild shock, overawed by everything. In polite whispers, they made observations to each other, or lapsed into total, watchful silence.

Now that we were clean, well-groomed, and refreshed, we were ready for our morning venture out into the city. "Follow me," I said to my brood, and led the way down the hall to the elevator. They had been so tired and sleepy the night before, they'd paid no attention to the elevator, or to how they'd gotten up to our room on the fourth floor.

"Walk in," I motioned, and pressed the down button. An elderly businessman, already inside, watched the children's reactions as the elevator started its slow descent and our "room" began dropping down. I winked conspiratorially at Hikmet; she winked back. But the younger ones exchanged startled glances with each other in silence. I smiled at them. The other passenger calmly continued to read his morning paper, easing their alarm — but not their mystification — as we descended and emerged into the hotel lobby. "That was an elevator, children," I announced, walking straight out to hail a taxi. "And now, here we are in The Big City!" ❦

Journal: Neighbors Old and New Part of Sela's advanced planning included a list of likely apartments for me to choose from, gleaned from information his Ankara friends had sent him. I decided on the first apartment on the list, across the street from old Batman friends Meral and Selahattin Özkan, and their sons Semih and Bülent.

What cinched the choice for me was meeting the American family upstairs: Pete (Sergeant Willis Jones, U.S. Air Force) and Lois Jones and their children Beverly, Victor, and Joy, about the ages of Timur, Kâmuran, and Melike. What a golden opportunity to meet American children and really speak English!

Özkan immediately telegraphed Sela that I'd chosen a place to rent, so he could have our belongings sent up by train. And it seemed no time at all before Sela arrived, we were registered with the muhtar [the local municipal official], Hikmet and Timur were enrolled in their schools, our crates were delivered, and were all happily settled into the Gazi Osman Pasha neighborhood, a hillside area not far below the crest of the hill where the presidential palace overlooks the capital.

One morning after the older children had gone off to school, our new neighbor Lois brought her youngest daughter down to pay us a welcoming call.

Five-year-old Kâmuran was helping me arrange our tea things on a tray. Melike came in, wearing her "best dress" for the visit, arranged herself on the sofa beside little Joy, the same age and also in her "best dress." There they sat, side by side, watching us in unmoving silence: fair-skinned Melike with wispy blond tendrils and bright blue eyes; brown-skinned Joy with glossy, jet-black curls and sparkling brown eyes. The pair of three-year-olds looked like exquisite, life-sized dolls.

I was busy with the refreshments, but happened to glance over at Melike, whose eyes were fixed on Joy in a sideways, searching stare. Slowly, she reached out her hand, lightly touched Joy's arm, inched it back into her lap and into a fold of her skirt. Ever so slightly, she turned her head to see if we were watching, but Lois was asking Kâmuran about the tiny tea spoons on the tray, and Joy was totally absorbed in their conversation.

Without seeming to move at all, Melike turned her hand over, looked down, took another look at Joy's arm and then at her face. Still absorbed in Kâmuran's comments, Joy seemed quite unaware of this delicate scrutiny. After another thoughtful moment, Melike finally spoke.

"Want to see my dolly?"

"OK!" said Joy, and the two ran off to play in the children's room. ❦

Journal: Gazi Teacher Training Friends have told me about part-time teaching jobs for native speakers of English at the Georgetown Program [GELP], funded by the U.S. to develop new English teaching materials and field-test them at the Gazi Teacher Training Institute (a three-year normal school to train high-school graduates to become middle-school and high-school teachers.) I've already had an appointment with Patricia Matthews at the GELP office, and signed up to teach morning classes at Gazi.

It's a long bus ride across town to Gazi, but we've all learned the public transportation system and can go wherever we need by bus. When in a hurry, we take a dolmus [shared taxi]; it's more expensive than a bus, but cheaper than a private taxi. For shorter distances, of course, we walk. We all walk a lot.

I've already met the admirable members of the English Department at Gazi and have mentally categorized them:

The "Old Guard," the most experienced, trained after World War II, have translated British and American literature, and teach traditional English grammar and translation;

The "Fresh Blood," the Fulbright scholarship students returning from Georgetown University with MA degrees in linguistics;

The "Peace Corps contingent," the several energetic volunteers who've had some teacher-training sessions and a brief cultural orientation to Turkey; and lastly;

The "Others," the few, including myself, who don't fit into the above categories.

The mix of teachers makes for a stimulating atmosphere. I expect to learn much by teaching here — from the other teachers, from the Georgetown pronunciation materials I've been given to teach, and from the students. ❦

Hikmet's Fifth Grade Class and Teacher at Çankaya School 1962

Timur's First Grade Class and Teacher at Çankaya School 1962

202

Xmas Card to Mother in Spokane

Gazi Osman Pasha/Ankara
December 1962

Dear Mama,

    We ran behind schedule this year. Thought we'd all never get these cards signed; Kâmuran, with her beautiful handwriting, was the proudest signer.

    We're all full of happy energy. Just baked and frosted five dozen green cupcakes for Hikmet's National Home Products week at school; she plans to wear her new green dress from Auntie Camilla and "will be a pear."

    Yesterday, President Gürsel passed by H. and T.'s grade school on his morning walk and actually spoke to them as he passed: " Good morning, children! How is your school?" This was their thrill of the week!

    Our neighbors, Lois and Pete Jones, offered to let us use their new tape recorder, so we'll start filling the tape before the children become totally bilingual. Already, when I'm baking a cake, Kâmuran says: "Mama, kin I lick the beater?"

    Happy, Happy New Year to all! Your loving daughter, Anna Maria

Sunday Tea Party for Gazi Students December 1962

Gazi Osman Pasha/Ankara
January 23, 1963

Dear Mama,

This is to wish you Happy Birthday from all of us. We wanted to get the tape filled up to send, but it's hard to get everybody lined up and borrow the neighbors' recorder at the same time. We did about five minutes on New Year's Eve. Hope we tape more of the children before they're completely bilingual.

Yesterday Kâmuran, Melike, and I were walking home from the neighborhood dressmaker's and the girls were fussing for chewing gum. I said, "Oh, Kâmuran, why should we buy chewing gum? It's just throwing away money!"

Kâmuran rolled her blue eyes at me and said, "I wouldn't throw it in the garbage can. I'd just chew it and chew it and chew it." In perfect English. I simply had to reward her linguistic efforts with some gum!

Hikmet, a sixth grader, is now a "Wolf Cub" (a younger Girl Scout). In Batman, she wore a simple uniform, stood at attention, learned some folk dances, · and marched down the street by the train station while playing the snare drum.

In Ankara, she's learning a number of handcrafts, different folk dances, and marching for the national holidays in the enormous municipal Hippodrome. I think she's trying for the honor roll; this pleases Sela, especially since she was behind in her new class, coming from such a provincial region as Batman.

Timur, a second grader, came home with a 2 (2 out of 5) in his first test. H. tried to impress on him that he'd *flunked*. This didn't disturb him a bit.

"Oh, yes, lots of children got 4. But on the other hand, Ergün and Recep got 1 and Mustafa got 0!" He just grinned. However, some of H.'s lecture must have sunk in, because today he came home with a 4.

Ten of the boxes you sent have arrived. Thank you, Mama! It was terrible trouble to get them out of customs. Plus all the trouble and expense it cost you. Never again. Next trip, I'll return with everything right along with me.

It was 5 degrees centigrade [41° Fahrenheit] last week in the Gazi classroom barracks, so they closed the school for ten days before semester vacation. Since I'm really hired by the Georgetown University English Language Program, I'll do some substitute teaching at GELP's intensive program and some tape recording, etc. Just a few hours a week, but I'm on their payroll, which is good.

Sela says hello. Our best to all.

Your loving daughter,
Anna Maria
PS: How do you like this linen note paper? They just started making it in Turkey.

Gazi Osman Pasha/Ankara
March 2, 1963

Dear Camilla,

Hikmet and I had meant to write you a proper birthday message. I had also meant to write about the Middle East Airlines crash that you may have read about in the newspaper (the MEA plane and a Turkish Army training plane collided over downtown Ankara). That day, I happened to be on a bus going downtown to a doctor's appointment with Kâmuran and Melike. The crash just missed the doctor's office where we were heading. People on the street outside the building died of burns from the jet fuel.

Sela saw one of the two planes right outside his office window, flying south; Özkan saw the other one outside *his* office window on the corner, flying *north*, and each thought it was only one plane crashing. The whole office nearly went crazy arguing about the directions. Sela, especially, was distraught, thinking we were in our doctor's office on that street. As fate would have it, the girls and I had missed the first bus and were a half-hour late for our appointment. Unfortunately, one of the Schlumberger Oil men we had known in Batman was on the MEA plane. He was such a nice family man, and we were all so very saddened. I really do believe in fate. Or destiny.

Life in the Capital

I've just finished a series of shots for slight anemia (again), and feel really energetic. Too high a cholesterol rate, though. So, I had to tell Sela no more fresh butter. Last month, when Orhan came back from leave, he brought a half-gallon wooden tubful from Sürmene just for me, since he knows how I like butter. But enough is enough!

I'm busier than ever since I had to let the maid go. She didn't always show up on lesson mornings and I could never leave for the bus to go to my English classes at Gazi until she arrived to do the housework and take care of Kâmuran and Melike. This left me a nervous wreck. Now I do the housework, and have arranged for the girls to go to kindergarten every day by special bus and come back at 5:30. They have lunch, a nap, and an afternoon snack at the "Toy School."

Hikmet is a "Wolf Cub," a kind of local Girl Scout, junior level. She goes to ballet twice a week and to the orthodontist once. Alone on the bus, too!

Kâmuran has Saturday morning ballet lessons with Melike. (I'm writing this in the ballet school waiting room now.)

Finally, I've been relieved of the extra grammar hours now that school has resumed after semester vacation and Ramazan holiday. So I only have three mornings and one afternoon at Gazi.

Still, I just can't seem to keep to an even schedule. We had visitors from Rome for a week, Mr. and Mrs. Forest Love: they had invited Hikmet and me to visit them on our trip to Spokane last year. Here in Ankara, they stayed in a hotel, but we entertained them. About the only time Sela and I ever go nightclubbing is at such times, so we really enjoyed the diversion.

205

The Ramazan fasting ended recently with a three-day holiday, rather like Easter. I got all four children attired in new outfits (Timur is so proud of his red jacket from Spokane) and took them to pay respects to their elders. We went first to visit Sela's mother, then the parents of Sela's friends from Batman.

Güher Is Married

On the third day of Ramazan, Sela came back from Sürmene, where he'd gone with Orhan and his older brother, Sabri, to see their younger sister, Güher, married off. I'm so happy for her. They say she didn't like any of the potential suitors her brothers had lined up for her, but I think they did well by her. Everyone agrees her husband, Recep Eroglu, [Re djep Air olu], is a really nice fellow. (He's a young agricultural engineer in the sugar refinery where Sabri agabeyi has been in the directorate.) Personally, I think Güher is very lucky, and will make a *wonderful* housewife. She's so capable, and a marvelous cook with an artistic flair.

Orhan is finally doing his specialization as radiologist at the Medical University here in Ankara. Until he finds a house, he's staying with us and will start studying English at night school. He's so amiable, charming, and likable. We're going to work hard on his English, knowing it makes all the difference in a profession.

Sela says Orhan wants to get married, but is "holding out for a girl with money." In the meantime, when he finds a house, he'll bring his mother here to live in Ankara. Also his grandmother, whom they call Nine [nee-neh]. She tells people she's 104 years old, but Orhan says she's only 93.

It's just one event after another…. Remember Hasan Göker from U of W? His sweet wife, Esin, is staying with us for a few days. We were neighbors in Batman for a while and we're all very fond of her. Hasan is working in the new refinery in Izmit.

Many of the former "Batman wives" have been visiting, in little waves. There's a group of about ten, most of whom went to Batman as brides. Now that their husbands have been transferred to Ankara, they're here, like me, with their children, trying to adapt to life in the Big City….

Ballet School

My! My! The pupils in the class inside are getting a workout this morning! This dance school is run by an Englishwoman, Beatrice Applegate Fenmen. I've heard that in her time, she danced in The Sadler's Wells Ballet, then came to Ankara to teach and eventually open up her own ballet school. She's married to Mithat Fenmen, a well-known pianist and head of the State Conservatory.

Mrs. Fenmen is a terrific teacher, especially for Kâmuran, who is apt to be tense and jerky sometimes. Now she's gradually learning to "unflex" her muscles. In these beginning lessons, she has to first listen to the rhythm, recognize the notes, then write down what she hears on the blackboard. I was very impressed by the last lesson she wrote on the blackboard. Mrs. F. was impressed, too.

Hikmet, who looks quite "artistic," goes twice a week with Kâmuran. For the two of them, it's been worth all the effort this year.

Now, you should hear Kâmuran and Melike when they bound out of the school bus after a day in kindergarten, just bubbling over in English! They love to tell Timur and Hikmet all about their teachers and their school. It's really been good for Kâmuran; she's gaining so much in self-confidence and poise.

Well, lessons are coming to a close inside. The little darlings are about to take their little bows and come out of class, and I'm becoming surrounded by the incoming mothers of the next class and *their* little darlings.

Haven't heard from anyone for so long. Hikmet was thrilled with Marty's letter. She read it easily, but can't write an answer too well yet.

Kisses to Andy Paul, Matt, Marie, Sarah, and Wally xxxxx

Your loving sister, Anna Maria

Letter to Mother in Spokane

Gazi Osman Pasha/Ankara
March 25, 1963

Dear Mama,

One package of *Pocket Book*s came. Thanks very! They're much appreciated by many friends here; we exchange back and forth.

Went looking at vacuum cleaners last week: the shops now have imports from Germany, Denmark and Russia [in trade for Turkish lamb and mutton exports]. Will probably settle for a modest Danish "Nilfisk" at 1500 TL — approx. $150. I just can't manage without either a cleaning woman or a vacuum cleaner, so I'm going to teach extra classes this summer to earn this "modern housewife's helper."

Now I'm back to only 12 hours a week at the school, but it still keeps me hopping to do the grocery shopping, cooking, etc. It costs more to put Kâmuran and Melike in kindergarten than it does to hire a maid, but it's much better for them, of course. The two perform together at home every evening, demonstrating their latest games and folk dances. Even Timur, aspiring to be a Wolf Cub, looks envious.

A New Contract at Gazi Teacher Training Institute

It looks like I'm being raised, in a manner of speaking. Now that one teacher has resigned from Gazi Teacher Training Institute, the English Department has an open slot for one "foreign expert" on their teaching staff, and though I don't have a master's degree in linguistics, the head of the department wants to give me the position. Same hours and classes, but 500 TL more per month, plus summer salary. Also a professional teacher's rating. I think the department head figured that my teaching experiences, plus my Turkish, override the educational requirements. (I should mention that on several occasions, foreigners have taken me for a Turk — but only during short conversations.)

Note: As I understand it, Gazi Teacher Training, a Turkish government institute, funds the salaries for a "foreign expert" and three native-speaking English teachers. Georgetown English Language Training Program, through US/AID money, funds the salaries of six to eight Turkish teachers of English, whom they have sent to be trained in linguistics at Georgetown University in Washington D.C. These American and Turkish teachers of English all end up teaching together on the Gazi staff, but may receive their salaries from several different sources.

The annual issue of *Spokesman-Review* finally arrived. Thank you! Everyone is enjoying it, especially Sela.

Our greetings to everyone. Your loving daughter, Anna Maria
PS: Kâmuran's and Timur's birthday cards just came from Camilla. They'll be thrilled. Now that he can read, Timur loves to get letters. He wrote his first letter to a friend in Batman and when the answer came, he looked at the envelope and blinked, his eyes got bigger and he started to grin — like a slow-motion close-up. "Bay Timur Malkoç" the envelope said. [Mr. Timur Malkoç] He read it and just laughed out loud, he was so tickled.
PPS: Hikmet wants you to know she is going to join the extra-hour English class so she can "improve her writing." A

Card from Mother in Spokane

Route 4, Box 188, Spokane
May 10, 1963

Dear Anna Maria,

This congratulation card is for the school promotion. (Believe me, I spread the word!)

David overhauled the tape recorder and we heard the Malkoç family in person. It was very exciting. Hikmet, of course, mature from travel, and Timmy just like his dad. But we can't spot the difference between Kâmuran and Melike, in tone, that is. We will have us a ball playing the tape this summer when the in-laws congregate. The tape came intact, in that little box. Should have thought it would be squashed or lost.

By the way, the kitty is OK.

We are going through a real lively spot now. Today is the day that *[expletive]* in Alabama will stand in the doorway of the University and try to buck President Kennedy and the Constitution of the United States. You know *my* sentiments! More anon.

Mom
[Note: This kind of language from Mama is unheard of. In self-defense, she says strong sentiments about racist bigot George Wallace and his segregationist policies "drive her to profanity."]

Letter to Mother in Spokane

Gazi Osman Pasha/Ankara
May 28, 1963

Dear Mama,

This is a quick note to catch that kind family before they leave for Turkey. Could you manage to send some shoes for me, I wonder? Neat, smart looking black shoes for next fall and winter which I can wear for walking and at school. (I teach all my lessons standing, by the way.) I just have no luck with shoes here; either they're too fancy or too uncomfortable. I don't have a Turkish foot size, it seems.

Sela is working hard, as usual, and getting ready for his business trip to the States. He hopes to save enough extra from his allowance to buy a car in Europe on his way back, sell it in Turkey and use the money to help buy an apartment. He should show up sometime in July, and will keep you posted.

I'm writing this during my lab hour; the English language students have to listen to tapes so many hours a week. They're all sitting in booths in front of me with headphones on, very earnestly repeating recorded conversations. All this equipment was given by USA/AID. (Or ICA? They keep changing the name for Foreign Aid.)

Well, I've got to get along now. We're all doing well. Hope you and Camilla can manage about the shoes. If not, it's nothing to fret over. More soon.

Your loving daughter, Anna Maria

Journal: Summer Goals: Saving, Moving, and Timur's Eye Operation My main reason for working extra classes this summer is to earn enough extra to buy — oh, rapturous joy! — a vacuum cleaner. This spurs me on whenever my spirits flag.

During the three months Sela is on his trip, I hope to accomplish several other more important goals, the first being to move from our apartment in Gazi Osman Pasha to a place much nearer to Gazi Teacher Training Institute where I teach. Friends have helped me find a suitable apartment in the Bahçelievler area, close to a good middle school for Hikmet and directly across the street from an elementary school for Timur. City buses there run more frequently, and there are more shared taxis operating in the neighborhood so Sela will be able to get to his office in less time. Again, with friends helping me make the move, we will be all settled in by the time Sela returns.

I'm also taking time off to have Timur's "lazy" eye operated on. For some years we've had it checked on by different doctors. The ophthalmologist here told me that now would be a good time to have it done, before Timur begins the school semester and starts to read books and do homework. Ruhsar hanım's family doctor is making all the arrangements at the new Children's Hospital connected to Hacettepe University. And as luck would have it, the head nurse on the floor is the sister of Sabahat Tura, a dear Gazi colleague. It will be a short stay in the hospital. For a seven-year-old, Timur is a real trooper about following doctor's orders, and I think it will go well. Insallah! ❦

209

16

SELA'S TRIP TO THE U.S.

Letter from Sela

Aboard Alitalia
June 9, 1963

Dear Anna Maria,

The flight to London over Athens, Munich, Frankfurt was enjoyable and comfortable. We [he and Tüncer Alpay, the junior petroleum engineer traveling with him] stayed in Mount Royal Hotel, at the corner of Hyde Park in London, and had a very good time. We were hosted by Mr. Dawson and Mr. Leith from Continental Emsco Company [who had visited Ankara]. I gave them your regards.

One evening, Mr. and Mrs. Dawson and Mr. and Mrs. Leith took us to have dinner in the famous Ivy restaurant right across from the Ambassador Theater. On Saturday morning, we went to see trooping the colors and change of guards in the presence of Queen Elizabeth at Buckingham Palace. This happens once a year, were we not lucky!

The same night Mr. Eyman from Oilwell took us to a play called "Lock Up Your Daughters," a comedy at Her Majesty's Theater, then to a famous night club called "Talk of the Town." We watched the show, and the people dancing. I wished you were there and danced with me, darling!

Today, before going to the airport, Mr. Eyman took us to Windsor Castle, where we saw Queen Elizabeth again and the change of guards.

I hope that everything is fine and the children are well. How is Hikmet's school? Hope she will do all right, not that I doubt it.

With all my love, kissing all the children, Your husband, Sela

---

Letter from Sela

Hotel Roosevelt, New York City
June 12, 1963

My Dearest Anna Maria,

We had a nice flight to New York and were met at Idlewilde airport by Mr. Balaban, the president of Inter-Drill Supply Company, who drove us to this hotel in his 1962 Cadillac. After a couple of drinks, he took us by cab through China Town and Greenwich Village. This week is Art Week in New York, so we walked around Greenwich Village and watched artists painting. Then Mr. Balaban took us to the "International" night club on Broadway, right next to the famous

"Birdland." We had dinner and watched the show and went to our deluxe hotel. (Very expensive — $18.00 a day!).

On Monday, we made contacts with the oil companies and had lunch with some salesmen in Rockefeller Center where they ice skate in winter. We watched some sport events during the lunch hour. In the afternoon, Tüncer and I roamed around a little. New York has changed quite a bit: more skyscrapers, some downtown slums have been torn down, and newly rebuilt. With the exception of electrical equipment, prices are terrifically high. I am flabbergasted at the many, many new products you can see on the market. I get sick when I look at them and think what we have been missing and probably will miss for a long time to come in Turkey.

Monday night, Mr. Balaban's assistant and her husband took us to dinner at Chez Vito, and from there to a private club called "Gas Light." (He is a member and has a private key.) Maybe you heard about this club; the waitresses are beautiful blonds, brunettes, etc. etc. Tüncer almost lost his mind.

We went to the Majestic Theater last night and saw "Tovarich," a romantic musical comedy with Vivien Leigh and Jean Pierre Aumont. We enjoyed the show and I wished you were with me.

In New York, I dropped a pin for you and for Özden [Sela's assistant petroleum engineer at TPAO]. She had given me one to drop in Europe and one in USA. If you see Özden, tell her that I dropped her pins.

We have finished talking business with the people here, and have arranged visits in Tulsa and California. We will be in Tulsa tomorrow evening.

I hope everything is fine, and you all are healthy and the kids are not making you nervous. Please write to me to Tulsa or Dallas, and you know I will bring you whatever you want.

I will close now with kisses for Hikmet, Timur, Kâmuran, and Melike.

I love you, and miss you very, very much. Sela

Journal: Travel Highlights from Sela As was his habit, Sela continued to write postcards and letters home regularly. After leaving New York City, he and Tüncer flew on to Tulsa, and arranged to rent Bill Brownfield's empty garage apartment.

They talked to people at Tulsa University, and went to an evening get-together with the Days, Brownfields, Mary Fitzgerald, Ann Lancaster, and other old friends from Tulsa University days. Sela found time to call his elderly landlady, Mrs. Bieber, to pay his respects.

He and Tüncer visited the Sinclair Research, Pan American, Jersey Production (ESSO) Research companies. Because they faced a lot of driving outside Tulsa, they rented a car to visit the Failing Companies factory and rigs in operation in Enid. They talked to U.S. Bureau of Mines officials in Bartlesville, and visited Mr. Johansen and his family [Özkan and Meral's friends] to collect technical literature for their project, and delivered Özkan's gift from Ankara.

When they arrived at their next stop, Core Labs in Dallas, they were provided with "a wonderful, fully automatic, 1963 model Chevy Impala with air conditioning; black outside and red patent leather inside." According to Sela, driving it was a *thrill*.

They met with Turgut Ulug of IDECO, visited his home, and saw the Fourth of July fireworks in the Dallas Cotton Bowl. They went on to Longview, where people from the Lufkin Company took them to see installations and their plant in Lufkin, Texas.

In Houston, they visited more oil companies and drilling equipment manufacturers, stayed at the Shamrock Hilton. Evenings, Sela wrote his letters home sitting by the courtyard pool. (He and Tüncer never passed up a chance to swim.) One evening, Sela visited old Tulsa neighbors, the Mc Guinns. Paul was doing the same job as 11 years ago, and Sela couldn't recognize their children!

On a side trip to Port Arthur, they had a brief visit with Hessie Williams, in her lovely home with the copper and Turkish rugs she'd acquired during her time in Batman. (Hayri Adanali, also from our days in Batman, was staying in Hessie's home while working at the Texaco refinery there.)

From Houston, the two travelers flew on to visit fire-flood projects in Oklahoma and Wyoming. Before more appointments in California, they arranged to fly to Washington State. ❦

Letter from Sela

Route 4, Box 188, Spokane
July 22, 1963

My Dearest Anna Maria,

Here I am, sitting at the round dining table and thinking about you right in your mother's house, and writing to you! Aunt Mill is washing the dishes and Mother Jones is working around here. Joyce and her children were down here 10 minutes ago, and just went back up the hill.

I had written you last from Houston. Since then we flew to Ponca City and visited Continental Oil Company's labs one day, and then drove down to oilfields near Oklahoma City. In Casper, we tried Jim Crawford, but he was vacationing at his cabin 200 miles away. He had left a note for us to go up there and visit him, but we decided against it. We saw the fire-flood projects in Casper and flew to Spokane on July 21.

Mother Jones and your sister Camilla were at the airport waiting for us, bless them! They took us to stay at Mother's house: Tüncer is in Mike's room, and I'm in the other bedroom.

Aunt Mill is visiting from Nebraska, and Cousin Donald's son Marcus is here from Duke U.

On Sunday, we went to Uncle Harris' farm on the Columbia River and had a very good time with Wally and Camilla and their children, Mother Jones, Aunt Mill, and Marcus. After lunch, your godmother Linden and her family came out and we all picked cherries, apricots, and cucumbers. We swam in Lake Roosevelt on the Columbia River and came home around 10:00 p.m.

We will be staying here till the 30th of July, then will fly to Seattle and spend a few days there before flying to LA.

212

Our upstairs neighbors from Ankara, Sgt. Pete and Lois Jones, haven't been transferred to Spokane yet. I hope they will arrive before we leave here.

Everybody says hello. Give my regards to everyone there. Love to the kids.

I love you missingly. Your Sela

Letter from Sela

The Space Needle, Seattle
August 2, 1963

My Dearest Anna Maria,

I wrote you right after arriving in Spokane 10 days ago. I had a very good time; so did Tüncer, I think. People were very, very nice to us, God bless them.

Your brother Aaron and I went shopping for children's things. One night Aaron and Nona and I had a wonderful dinner with Kemal Satır and wife Gülten at the Matador Restaurant in the Davenport Hotel; then we visited Alex Schön and his family. We had dinner with Joyce and John in their house with another couple who know you; he's an accountant. [Gertrude and Bernie Habbestad]

Last Friday, Mother Jones and I went to see our old neighbors Sgt. Pete and Lois Jones, who finally were transferred from Ankara, and invited them to a family lunch. Camilla and Nona arranged a potluck dinner in the garden; Tüncer and I made delicious shish kebab. Mother Jones, Aunt Mill, Wally's brothers John and Orval Phillipson and their wives, the Schöns, your brothers Aaron and John and families, your godmother Linden and her husband Norman, your Harms cousins, etc. were all there, and Camilla's neighbors and a few other couples whom I don't know. Anyway, it was lots of fun and everybody enjoyed themselves.

One evening, we went to with Mother Jones and Aunt Mill for dinner at David and Rosemary's. They have a very nice place.

When Tüncer and I left Spokane for Seattle on the 30th of July, everybody came to Geiger Airfield to say goodbye and see us take off. God bless them all! They were wonderful to us.

Liz [old friend from Spokane] met us at the Seattle-Tacoma airport; she's going to put us up for a couple of days in her house. Liz and Tüncer went to see her sailboat on Lake Union while I went to see Douglas [his UW roommate] and wife Margery. We had a nice visit, talked about old days at UW, drove around the town, then had dinner at Four Winds Restaurant on Lake Washington.

Next day, Tüncer and I went to the Expo 62 Fair Grounds, saw Zeki Beyaz in his office, and had lunch with him at Crawford's Sea Food Restaurant at the dock. We borrowed Zeki's car and went to see Nihat Balci (you met him on your last trip, he said) and visited the UW campus. In the evening, we went to see Joyce and Zeki's children and had dinner on Aurora Way.

We are flying to LA this afternoon. Everybody says hello and send regards from here. Will write you from Dallas again. We should be there around the 10th of August.

How are you and the children doing? I hope you are not working too hard, darling. I sure miss you all very much. Kiss Hikmet, Timur, Kâmuran, and Melike for me.

Yours only, Sela

Letter to Tulsa Friends

6th Avenue 76/1, Bahçelievler/Ankara
August 5, 1963

Dear Kathryn & Bill, Deanie & Alan:

Sela sent a postcard about the good visit he had with you all! According to the latest schedule, he'll be in Dallas around August 10, address: Core Laboratories, Inc.

I've been having an eventful summer myself, frequently escorting the children to visit their Grandmother Malkoç. (She moved from Sürmene to Ankara after Sela's father passed away.) We also visit the Fun Fair at Luna Park, Zoo Land, and Playground and I'm getting tired of crowds and city buses!

Georgetown U English Language Program

Mornings are so peaceful by comparison. I put in four or five hours a day at the Georgetown Program (GELP), partly in their Materials Branch as a junior editor, partly in the Gazi Teacher Training Branch, copy-reading composition materials, guided exercises, etc. In the first department, teachers/writers are working on new textbooks to be used in the public high schools' required English classes. I have a feeling someday this will all prove valuable experience, though I find the linguistics a bit thick at times. That is, having adult students learn English written only in phonemic symbols, to aid in their pronunciation. It certainly doesn't help their spelling! I think some linguists have to be different just for ego's sake, and rewrite the teaching materials based on their own particular linguistic schema. (As if every student learns in the same way, and in the way these linguists *think* they will!)

The children and I have a Gazi Institute student staying with us this summer. Everyday, Münire [myew nee reh] dictates sentences in English for Hikmet to write, and they're both improving in the process. At the moment, Münire's taken the little ones off to the Children's Park.

I'll be so glad when Sela gets back. There's absolutely no motivation for cooking. We live on fresh fruit and vegetables, mainly. This evening's meal was fava beans cooked with olive oil, onion and tomatoes; fresh wheat bread; and yogurt. Plus the daily watermelon. Hikmet roasts all the seeds, and snacks on them later…. Yes, we're all keeping busy!

With much love per usual, A

Journal: More Travel Updates from Sela Sela and Tüncer had appointments in Long Beach, and visited Parsons Company friends who'd worked on the TPAO refinery in Batman: the Pierces, Kays, Van Wingens, Vic Fawcetts. They returned to Tulsa via Dallas, according to a rather complicated itinerary of meetings scheduled with oil company officials.

Before they left Tulsa, Sela dropped by the Biebers' boarding house for another nostalgic visit. Their son Harry Jr., a stamp collector, requested Turkish "Freedom from Hunger" stamps issued April 14, 1963 (45 kurush for one, 65 kurush for the other).

If he has time, Sela plans to "get a car and drive it to Turkey, bringing a Mickey Mouse watch for Timur, and surprises for everyone." The two left Idlewilde Airport on August 22 and flew non-stop to Amsterdam.

Sela mailed his next postcard from The Hague. He's already looked at cars with an eye to resale value in Turkey. Because of the large demand for cars by Turkish "guest workers," he hasn't found what he's looking for. Now he's decided *not* to buy a car, but will be home as planned. ❧

Letter from Sela

Den Haag, Holland
August 30, 1963

My Dearest Anna Maria,

After receiving your last Sunday's letter, I felt much better and was glad that you found a place for us to live especially to your liking in Bahçelievler.

I wish I was there right now, and present at Timur's eye operation. I feel awfully bad that I can't be there to help you with the children, and the moving.

Well, I changed my mind again, and finally decided to buy a car. I've started the necessary papers today for the purchase, export licenses, etc. It will be a dark blue Simca 1300, just out of the factory. (It's a French car assembled in Holland.) I don't know when I will leave Holland. Here, they do things like in Turkey, and you never know when the papers will be ready. It's exactly like Turkish government departments; nobody knows what to do, it seems.

Since the car is new, I won't be able to drive it over 70 kilometers per hour. Money-wise, I am just about managing, if not a bit short. I might be wrong, but this is a chance of a lifetime to buy a car and sell it for a down payment on an apartment. I don't want to pass up the chance. Who knows when I get to go abroad again? If ever?

I bought Hikmet a nice watch. I think she will love it, and I have something for every little darling!

Will see you soon. I love you. Sela

Postcard from Sela

Amsterdam
August 31, 1963

Dear Mother Jones,

It has been 10 days since we arrived here in Holland, very close to your ancestors' hometown, if I remember right. We will be driving a car to Turkey on the 5th of September and I will be home on the 9th, I hope!

I do thank you, and all the others in your family who made my stay enjoyable in Spokane. Please give my personal regards to Uncle Harris.

Respectfully yours, Sela

17

SELA'S TRIP ENDS

Letter to Mother in Spokane

6th Avenue 76/1, Bahçelievler/Ankara
September 9, 1963

Dear Mama,

We've had grievous news from Zagreb, so please sit down to read this.

We waited and waited for Selahattin to come back but he isn't going to. Ever. He bought a car in Holland like he wanted to, and had an accident in Yugoslavia. I guess he died on the spot. Tüncer did, too.

We have lots of friends and Malkoç family here, and have moved into a house close to all our schools, so I guess I'll eke out this coming school year here.

People are very kind. The general director of TPAO offered me a job. I won't need it, as they're eager for English teachers in Ankara. Financially, we'll manage. The children and I are going to be all right.

I had been thinking all summer about the children's future, and how we were ever going to manage to send them all to the States. I guess this is the answer. But oh, what a price.

Your loving daughter, Anna Maria

Letter to Friends

6th Avenue 76/1, Bahçelievler/Ankara
September 10, 1963

Dear Friends,

This is a grievous task to have to write you such sad news.

We have lost Selahattin. He died in a car accident in Yugoslavia with his junior engineer Tüncer Alpay. Sela's brother Muammer is leaving tonight for Zagrep to settle things.

As far as I'm concerned, I'm settled for this coming school year. The children are all registered in their new schools close by. Our new apartment is all arranged and convenient, so we'll make do until school is out. I dare say we'll be coming to the U.S. then. Right now we're all being taken care of; we have family and fine friends here. I'm so glad Sela got to see you all. He loved you all so much. As do I.

Always, Anna Maria

217

Çankaya/Ankara
September 13, 1963

Dear Camilla,

Your sister Anna Maria has asked me to write to you. I have known Anna Maria for about ten years and, like her, I am an American married to a Turk. Her husband and mine did part of their military service together and have also been friends the same length of time.

You probably know by now of the terrible tragedy that befell Anna Maria and her family. She was able to get a letter off to her mother the day the news came in, but she feels incapable of writing any more and I am taking care of her correspondence.

Anna Maria wants me to reassure you that she is not in any financial difficulties. And I would like to reassure you too. She has a teaching job at the Teachers' College here. Her salary is more than the average salary and she puts in 30 hours a week. If she cares to, she can augment this salary by teaching also at Georgetown University program, but even without this, she can manage all her expenses. She also has a bank account to take care of any extras. She will also, no doubt, receive a small monthly pension from her husband's firm. We both want you to know that no difficulties exist financially.

Anna Maria's in-laws have been very good to her, and Sela's office have been extremely helpful, taking care of all the expenses and arrangements needed in Yugoslavia and here. They have also installed a telephone in her new apartment, which is a great help. Telephones are not exactly easy to get; people wait on the waiting list for years.

She has a student staying with her as a mother's helper and she is a great help. Her Austrian friend from Batman is also here, and one of her sisters-in-law. Both she and Sela have lots of friends, so please rest assured that all her physical needs and also the children's are being taken care of. The children are all fine. With the possible exception of Hikmet, I doubt that they fully understand the significance of what has happened. Anna Maria has my admiration. She is handling herself superbly. Although all her friends, Sela's friends, relatives, and office are all behind her, there is nothing any of us can do to relieve the hurt and grief that is hers alone to carry. This is the sad part that makes every one feel so helpless.

Anna Maria also says that she hopes to come to the States next year. On what basis, I'm sure she doesn't know yet, but for the present, it is best that she remain here where she knows she can manage quite well. I feel, and I think she feels also, that she and the children will be better off in the States for the future. But for the present, they are better off here.

There is nothing more I can really say. Please be assured that we are all taking care of her, and assure the rest of your family. She is rich in friends. I am sure as soon as the clouds clear up a bit for her, she will write you herself.

Sincerely, Marion Türker

Letter from Sister in Spokane

Spokane, Washington
September 15, 1963

Dear Mr. Brownfield,

The enclosed clipping explains my reason for writing this note. We were stunned over the tragic news, and now we are hoping to help Anna Maria when she comes home in June (?). There seems so little we can do at the present time. She has recently moved and her new address is:

6nci Avenue 76/1, Bahçelievler

Ankara, Turkey

I'm sure you will hear from her if you haven't already. We know very little about the accident other than what the papers said. Sela bought a new Simca in Holland, Sept. 5th and hoped to reach Turkey around the 9th.

If you know anyone that knew Sela, would you pass the news on? Thank you so much.

Sincerely, Camilla Phillipson (*Anna Maria's sister*)

Spokesman-Review **article:**

Woman Hears of Kin's Death

Mrs. Ethelbert Jones, Route 4 learned today of the death of her son-in-law in an auto crash on a mountain road in Yugoslavia. Dead is Selahattin Malkoç, 42, Ankara, Turkey, a petroleum engineer for the Turkish Petroleum Co. Killed with him in the crash according to the letter received by Mrs. Jones, was his assistant Tüncer Alpay.

Met as Students

Mrs. Malkoç is the former Anna Maria Jones of Spokane. The two met when both were students at the University of Washington in 1947. Malkoç, a scholarship student from Turkey, later received degrees in petroleum engineering at Tulsa University in Tulsa, Okla. Mrs. Jones said that Malkoç and Alpay, in this country on a three-month tour of oil fields and petroleum plants, visited her here in August.

Long Trip Taken

"When they left to return to Turkey, they purchased a car in Holland, drove across western Europe and were in southern Yugoslavia when the accident occurred," Mrs. Jones said. Her daughter and her four children are remaining in Turkey indefinitely. An instructor in English, Mrs. Malkoç formerly taught at Ankara Koleji, and now is a teacher at the Gazi Teaching Training Institute, Ankara. *end of article*

Letter from Bill Brownfield

Tulsa, Oklahoma
September 16, 1963

Dear Anna,

We got your letter this evening. I am trying to think of words that might lessen your grief, but there are none, of course. We are so far away. As you know, we will do anything for you and the children, now or later, if we can only see the way. You have a home here, as needed. Just as I think Sela was at home here. You have no idea how happy it was, how good a visit.

I guess we are all only visitors here. That is what makes it sweet, and bitter.

Sela and I were closer than ever before, and for me, it was rich. Everything was rich for Sela because he was so real, the most real and vivid person I knew. He was a fierce man with a fierce mien, who demanded himself and others stand up to their stature; and everyone loved him for this because he respected them when they did, and they respected themselves. But as I saw, his gentleness and generosity were so large behind that fierceness that they weren't even concealed. He was as hard as a man should be and as soft as a friend needed.

I got some idea of the scope of Sela's work, and however much or little they realize, the Turks have been much hurt. His contribution to you and his family, to his friends, and to his country were large and tangible. At this point, it may be no consolation, yet all us, and you, are so much richer because of his touch and influence.

Oh, Anna! What hurts the most is that he never even got home. He was so anxious about you and anxious to be home. It is some consolation to us, and I hope to you, that because you and Sela are the kind of people you are, there must be a thousand homes over this globe that feel, as ours does, that they are your home, too. We would offer anything we can, Anna. It is important to us that we be allowed to help you with any need we can fulfill. Please ask us when there is any need. Whatever it is; it will be with great love.

Bill & Kathryn

Letter from Bill Brownfield to Sister, Camilla

Tulsa, Oklahoma
September 20, 1963

Dear Mrs. Phillipson,

Thank you so much for your letter. Anna wrote me on the ninth, but she gave no details, such as what happened to Tüncer Alpay. This is understandable, of course.

Sela was a close friend of mine at school before Anna came down here to Tulsa so that they could be married. They lived by us, and we were very close friends. Later, after I moved to Wyoming, they came up there to live shortly after Hikmet's birth and Sela got his master's.

220

I am not able to talk about how I feel about this. It is enough to say that I have grown to love them over the years.

I don't know why it should make that much difference, but the fact that he didn't even get home again makes everything worse. We spent that last few days shopping for presents for Anna and the children, especially for the watch for Timmy. And Sela was so anxious to get home. I notified all their friends in this part of the country immediately. I wrote Anna the same day, and I am sure several others have already written. As you say, there is very little we can do from here. If you know of anything — anything at all — I can do, now or later, I would certainly be appreciative if you would inform me....

I think you should find consolation in the fact that Sela was, and Anna Maria is, such a fine and really noble person that her — their — friendship is dear to many people in many places, who will not let her down. Thank you, again, for your letter.

Sincerely, Bill Brownfield

Letter to Mother in Spokane

6th Avenue 76/1, Bahçelievler/Ankara
October 12, 1963

Dear Mama,

Things have quieted down a bit. I've gone back to work. The children are all settled in their schools, and doing well. This is the first time since the funeral that I've felt like writing.

It all seemed to take so long, almost two weeks before Muammer could get to Yugoslavia and arrange things and arrive back.

Fortunately it is not the custom, I am told, for women to attend the funeral procession. All the men walk though the streets from the mosque to the cemetery. After almost two weeks of callers every day and each evening, it would have been too much for me. Sela's mother came to our house each day for three days and sat in state. She held forth, weeping and wailing, rocking back and forth. It is her way of mourning. Relatives came and sat with her. So I sent the children across town to their old neighbors. They didn't quite understand all this anyway, having waited so long for their father to come back from his summer-long trip.

Well, it seems that a great truck swerved directly across their path. The driver is sitting in jail in Yugoslavia. The TPAO company is trying to collect damages. This sounds so cold-blooded, but then, not when there are four fatherless children at home. There was nothing left of the car, but Muammer very faithfully brought back all the suitcases which were undamaged in the trunk. Kâmuran and Melike each had gifts lovingly marked; Timur got his Mickey Mouse watch, and Hikmet got hers....

I am so sorry for Tüncer's family, too — his elderly father and mother, and his sister.

221

Sela was insured by TPAO for a goodly sum, I'm told. This means I can buy an apartment next spring. And/or invest some money for the children. I have several very shrewd friends to ask advice of in these matters.

I'm hoping that after all this financial business is cleared up, Sela's private insurance will cover a trip to the States next summer. This would not cut into the capital, so to speak.

I can't think about a complete move now to the States, because I don't think I could find such a job as I have now, where I could support four children so well. I also have help here while I'm working, so that when I come home at night I can spend my free time with the children. I'm hoping that what I learn on this new job, half-days, will maybe help me later on. There are several language centers that teach Turkish. Right now, my spoken Turkish is much more fluent than other Americans around here, but I need to study grammar and translation.

I'll be teaching 12 hours a week at Gazi and working 15 hrs a week at the Georgetown U Program. They want me to take on the editing of a new textbook for a tape recorder course, and later on to do some writing for it since I've written some bits for another book. I keep learning, and this all keeps leading into better things.

It's a pleasant office here with a quietly stimulating atmosphere. A quiet change from the Gazi Institute, which I am also fond of. So, you see, I'm really very lucky about all this work. I could find teaching positions here in a dozen places, but I prefer these two places, and fortunately they work together: Georgetown sends part of their staff to teach at Gazi.

Financially, we are all right. I have a houseful of furniture and no debts to anyone. Except what Sela borrowed from you and Camilla to buy a car this summer. I'll be able to take care of that as soon as I can settle things.

I'll be getting another girl student to come live with us and help with the housework. This is a very good arrangement for us and for her; plus, her English will improve!

Would you ask Aaron to please thank Elaine H. and Elizabeth K. in the Welsh Society for the lovely card. And Mrs. Harke, too? I appreciated Joyce's letter and Rosemary's. Please thank them all for me. Also, thank Kemal Satır for his kind letter.

Let me know what you think about a trip next summer. I'd like to think about it. It takes my mind off things.

Your loving daughter, Anna Maria

Journal: Four Austere Officials Pay a Condolence Call Sela's brothers Sabri and Muammer came to break the news early in the morning. Then every day for three days, his mother came with relatives and sat in a corner, praying and rocking and keening. To me, it is such a very different way of showing grief.

When news of the death of Sela and his assistant Tüncer Alpay appeared in the newspaper, I received dozens of telegrams, handwritten notes, and cards expressing sympathy. Close friends and business associates made personal calls at the house; sometimes couples, families, or small groups came together. Thankfully, there was always someone around — relatives and friends — to answer the door, occupy the children elsewhere, and generally ease the flow of visitors.

Not long after the funeral, a somber group of dignified TPAO directors came to express their condolences, as is customary. They seated themselves in a half-circle in the living room and spoke in hushed tones about the memorable qualities of the deceased and the great loss for the Company. They used many religious expressions intended to provide solace and comfort; the listener's heart may not embrace them all, at the time, but they are soothing to the ear.

Their voices drifted down the hall to the children's room, where four-year-old Melike was brushing her pony tail with the new hair brush from her father's fateful trip. One familiar voice drew her into the living room, where she recognized her father's director from Batman. Silently, she stood by his elbow, obviously longing to sit on his lap. When I leaned forward to tell her to sit next to me, Suat bey said "Let her sit." He nodded and she hopped up onto his lap, adjusting her skirts daintily, hairbrush still in hand.

"What is that, dear?" he asked.

"My new hair brush, Uncle Suat bey." It was very soft and made of camel's hair, she explained, demonstrating with a light stroke across the director's forehead. I was embarrassed and about to admonish her, but held my tongue when I saw the quiet smile on Suat bey's face.

Tenderly and painstakingly, she smoothed and brushed back his thinning locks. Finally, satisfied with her work, she smiled and slid gracefully off his lap. He looked as if he'd been touched by an angel's wing.

The two dignified gentlemen sitting next to Suat bey now looked at Melike expectantly. One by one, she climbed upon their laps to administer her delicate brush strokes, adjusting here and there, gliding over their balding spots with the gentlest of care. No one spoke a word. We all sat watching her, mesmerized.

She turned to look at the fourth visitor, sitting in the far corner. He was a stranger to her, and she hesitated. His sad, lonely look did not escape her notice, however. She approached him shyly. "Uncle, shall I brush?"

Shefik bey nodded, and with a happy little sigh, she brushed him with the angel's wing. ❦

18

LIFE GOES ON IN THE CAPITAL

Letter to Tulsa Friends

6th Avenue 76/1, Bahçelievler/Ankara
November 3, 1963

Dear Brownfields and Days,

Your latest letter arrived, thank you, Bill! And shortly thereafter, the marriage certificates, for which I'm most thankful as they're necessary for documentation here.

It's a strange sort of adjustment I find myself making. I tend to drift toward the acquaintanceship of people who never knew Sela, and away from those who did, like the families of his old school friends here. It just seems to be too much to take, now that the numbness is wearing off. Also, with some people there is no longer a common bond. I had always made a point of keeping in touch with certain circles here because their husbands or relatives were old classmates and they all held Sela in such esteem. And I always felt accepted because of him. Now, somehow, I prefer different faces, people who accepted me because of myself, not accepted of necessity, being Sela's wife. A form of escape now maybe, but it's better to avoid, rather than trying to endure too much, I think.

Yesterday, I had 30 Gazi students here for a jolly evening. Entertaining Gazi students will probably form most of my extracurricular activities now. They're so sweet with the children and so grateful for a little homey atmosphere since many come from small towns/villages far from Ankara. The apartment I moved into so hopefully this summer is considerably larger and more comfortable. It is also much more convenient to all our schools, the children's and mine.

I now have another Gazi student staying with us: gentle Nevin, who failed English for the year and can't return until she passes her makeup exams. She helps me about the house and helps the children with their lessons. Three times a week a housekeeper comes to cook, iron, and clean. As long as this arrangement continues, I think I'll manage very well. And I expect Nevin's English to improve significantly, since I speak only English with her and the children.

My next project is French lessons because Hikmet is getting bogged down in her French class at school. (She's required to study one foreign language this year.) I plan to hire a tutor — a third year student from the Gazi French department — who spent last summer in Paris. He promises to come and give us both lessons twice a week.

I have another request for you: several copies of Hikmet's Tulsa birth certificate. I have a feeling that both her birth certificate and the marriage license were left at the American Embassy here, but no one could find any trace. I need a whole set of papers to file another type of claim.

The children have just trotted off to bed, having spent the last hour practicing "some folk dances for Grandmother." Nevin plinked out the tinkly tunes on the mandolin and they all lined up behind Hikmet, snapping their fingers in time and solemnly following the leader. If our trip ever materializes for next summer, I'd dearly love to assemble some costumes and put them through their paces for my mother and the rest of the family in Spokane. They're really quite a charming sight. But it would probably mean my taking mandolin lessons, too.

And I'll never catch up on my letter writing! Please pass along my best to one and all.

With much love, as always, Anna Maria
PS: Thank you again for all your letters. I reread them occasionally and when I think of you all in Tulsa, it buoys my spirits.

Letter to Tulsa Friends

6th Avenue 76/1, Bahçelievler/Ankara
November 19, 1963

Dear Brownfields and Days,
Sorry I neglected to include Hikmet's birth date: Feb. 6, 1952. St. John's Hospital, Tulsa. And, yes, Timur *did* get his Mickey Mouse watch. Bright red! Thank you very much. He's so proud of it.

I've been rushed this past couple of weeks — but pleasantly, I should add, and things are slowly getting back on a more or less even keel. A former UN consultant from Batman flew in from Arkansas recently and kindly took us all out to dinner at a very fancy restaurant. That was a big treat!

Occasionally, old friends from Batman and from the new refinery in Izmit drift in and out. Last Saturday night, we had the second group of Gazi students for an evening's dinner and entertainment: 35 students plus three Peace Corps volunteer teachers.

I've decided this social life, in moderation, is just what I need. Tomorrow night, I will have my first experience going to the theater with friends. It's so hard to get tickets, and that makes it all the more special. And by now, I should be able to understand some of the fast dialogue.

This evening, since it's so early, we're all "stepping out" for a bus ride to the park and a treat at the pastry shop. Will keep you posted.

Much love, Anna Maria

6th Avenue 76/1, Bahçelievler/Ankara
January 5, 1964

Dear Camilla,

You've probably wondered at the long silence. I've been too depressed. I try not to write at such times.

I've never answered Kemal Satır's generous offer either, mainly because of the indefinite state of my financial affairs. I'm going to try to buy a small apartment, invest a little, and still have enough for a trip this summer. Financially, we're well off, but on the other hand, I have no health or life insurance, and the children need more tutoring help with their lessons than I can manage. It's six of one and half dozen of the other. Well, I'm trying to provide for all contingencies.

I've thought about your offer to telephone on a regular basis, but I just haven't felt I could manage. We'd only get around to asking each other how everyone is, and I'd just start crying. But thank you for the kind offer.

Please tell Aaron his tape arrived. Next weekend, I'll take the children to listen to it on their Uncle Sabri's tape recorder. They're listening to their little phonograph now and dancing to the records from their Aunt Rosemary. Hikmet's doing "the Madison" with Timur, Melike and Kâmuran are "cat-walking."

Just can't get up steam to write thank-you notes yet. To say nothing of answering a whole drawer full Christmas cards. I didn't send any, it's so difficult. I don't even like to sit down to read. I work a crossword puzzle or two every night and read the morning papers. Just too restless.

We visit Malkoç's here often: Grandmother Malkoç, Sela's brother Sabri and wife Seyyare, and Orhan; they always send their best regards. Sometimes I send the children over to visit their Büyük Anne [Grandmother]. Hikmet prefers to go alone. She says, "Büyük Anne likes Timur best, of course, because he's a boy! You'd think girls would be more valuable. They're the ones that have the babies!"

If you've time, could you ask about the cost of tickets at that travel agency, for the last of May or first of June: one adult, four children, round trip tourist? Also life insurance that would be valid in Turkey. Thanks in advance!

Love to all, Anna Maria

Letter to Sister in Spokane

6th Avenue 76/1, Bahçelievler/Ankara
February 25, 1964

Dear Camilla,

A late Happy Birthday! Hope you're having a nice one.

We're just getting over a long, three-week semester vacation at Gazi. I put in two full weeks at the Georgetown English Language Program. We're editing and rewriting a teacher's handbook to be used with an English textbook, written by people in the office here. It's very interesting for me as a novice, but it's hardly a vacation.

Nevin (the sweet Gazi student who's been helping with the children) took off to visit her family in Adana; she really deserved a holiday. Hikmet helped at home on the days the maid didn't come, so we made out all right, though it called for close scheduling.

We now have Altan, a 15-month-old little boy staying with us while his mother, Ellen Yazar is in the hospital with their new baby daughter, Deniz. (Ellen's father was a dean at Stanford, where her future husband, Nüsret, was a student in his class. Another romantic marriage!)

Haven't had a chance to relax much. Some friends invited me to the opening of the new State Ballet, a wonderful treat! The invitation called for "evening dress" and I'd hoped to wear the dress and mandarin jacket you sent me. The dressmaker was making it over into a sheath with a moderately slit skirt, but it wasn't ready in time, so I wore my old black velvet dress and still had a lovely time.

Haven't gotten the Dr. Seuss book yet. Please thank the family for all the lovely valentines. Everyone here was charmed. While I was at work, Hikmet made the cookies from her valentine's recipe and sprinkled on the red sugar. We served them to guests, who thought she was the ultimate in capability.

I just get things settled into a schedule, and then something pops up. Now I have to go apartment-hunting. Also have to get sharp on this summer itinerary. Even if Hikmet is only half-fare, 30,000 lira is so much money. I haven't had time to stop by for a real chat at an agency.

But here are a couple of things you could be seeing to, when you have time: Life insurance for me. And what is usually sold at an August fur sale and about how much? Also tell Eleanor Meenach that I'll try to bring the meerschaum pipes she wrote about. Sometimes I feel absolutely sunk when I think of all the unanswered letters. But I just can't manage to do everything.

The children are all fine. We're all in good health. I get out once in a while now, so the time is passing more quickly. We're all waiting for June.

Your loving sister, Anna Maria
PS: The *Spokesman-Review* came with my article about traveling in the U.S. with Hikmet last year. Please thank John and Aaron for me. I'm taking one copy out to Gazi; the students always enjoy reading about America!

Letter from Mother in Spokane

Route 4, Box 188, Spokane
May 19, 1964

Dear Anna Maria,

Got your M's Day card day before yesterday. We were all so thrilled to hear from you. We're all happy that you have that good job. (Things are pretty tight all over.)

Just came from Boberg's Travel agency, I think they're the best, and here's the dope: For 3 children, approx. ages 10, 8,6, the round trip fare is $1,998.20. The 10 and 8 are 50% off, the smallest is 100% off. Now, there is

$1,333.80 in the kitty. So that leaves $600 to scrape up. There is no way I can whittle it down, as everyone here is pretty much on edge financially. So would have to float a loan, if you think it's necessary. Mike is still in Japan, and Pete is in Calif, unemployed at present. Many are out of work there. Just want to let you know how things are.

We'd be tickled pink to see the kids. There is lots of food and room, and everyone is healthy and able to help look after them, so that part is OK. It's just that the fare has to be figured out. You cogitate on it, and answer pronto, so we can go ahead. So far, we're all OK. No weddings, and no new progeny to date. I'm planting a good garden, so there will be plenty to eat. And we have lots of milk and eggs.

Saw Kemal Satır yesterday. He sends regards, and says not to worry if some of those packages didn't get to his folks in Ankara, whatever that means. I think Sela was going to bring back some things for his parents (?).

I'm writing this in the Crescent department store lounge. That's why it's so scraggly. And now, lots of love to you all, and tell the kids to look forward.

Buck up, Banny! Mom

Letter to Mother in Spokane

6th Avenue 76/1, Bahçelievler/Ankara
June 8, 1964

Dear Mama,

Well, here we are, on another verge. This time, of moving again.

Yes, I finally *bought an apartment!* All the proceedings have been quite long and drawn out, with inheritance papers, deeds, etc. Also, closets and cupboards have to be built, walls painted, etc. My teaching friend Molly Emre's husband Sinasi Emre and his brother Orhan Emre (who have a construction business) kindly checked out the building first, then sent people to do the work and oversee it. I was very lucky there.

It's a new apartment, large and pleasant. One of the persuasive points was that our dear friend Perihan hanım lives across the hall. She was a lawyer with Sela's company, and she's been very helpful with the legalities. Since I already know most of the inhabitants in this eight-unit apartment house, it will be a comfortable move.

When you wrote that the tickets would be $2,000 for the three children, it settled me here for another year. Sounds like I'm really better off here and I'd better not look a gift horse in the mouth! One important disadvantage in my employment, however, is a complete lack of any kind of insurance, as I'm employed by the Turkish Ministry of Education on a special foreigner's contact arranged for me by the head of my department. (It pays much more for the same teaching hours but does not provide for the usual benefits granted to regular teachers.) I wrote Camilla, asking for info on insurance and whether it's possible to establish anything from here.

228

Kâmuran has a light case of measles. Her Uncle Orhan (yes, he *did* finish medical school, some time ago) just stopped by to prescribe some medicine for her.

Hikmet failed in Turkish, as did some of her friends, and her other lessons weren't up to par either, all of which means she needs tutoring this summer. Also, the other children have to be transferred to our new neighborhood's schools, so I suppose it's just as well we give up traveling now. I have my work cut out for the whole summer.

Elsewise, we are all well and pursuing further goals. I may take up French. It often comes in handy in certain circles here in Ankara.

Hello to all. Your loving daughter, Anna Maria
PS: Sorry we spilled nail polish on your letter, trying to fix Kâmuran's Barbie doll's lipstick.

---

*Journal: **Making Friends in the New Neighborhood*** Unfortunately, the children were uprooted again when we moved into our new apartment in the Kavaklidere area of Ankara. The girls seemed to be making the best of it, but eight-year-old Timur despaired of making new friends. "How can I play here?" he grumbled. "I don't have any friends!" I tried to comfort him by reminding him that when school opens he'll meet lots of boys in his new class.

Uncomforted, he meandered off after breakfast with his little marble bag, looking for marble players in the neighborhood. When he came back, it was nearly lunchtime. He was whistling.

"That's a good sign," I thought to myself. Then I spotted his marble bag, chock full of new glassies. "Timur!" I exclaimed. "Where'd you get all those marbles?"

He was grinning broadly. "Won 'em from my friends!"

"Is that the way to make new friends, winning all their marbles from them?" I asked.

"Mother, sometimes you lose, sometimes you *win*," he explained. "That's the way it goes!" His father's poker-playing philosophy, exactly, I thought to myself. 🐦

*Journal: **Some Names Are International*** I took a different approach meeting our new neighbors. Since Perihan hanım had mentioned that the children upstairs seemed very quiet, I thought perhaps they are shy, and we should take the first step. So, after lunch, Kâmuran and Melike went with me to introduce ourselves.

I knocked on the heavy door. It was opened by an extremely tall, handsome Chinese man, who stood smiling down at us. I greeted him in Turkish, explaining we were downstairs neighbors, and we were welcoming his family to the building. I gave him my name, then introduced Kâmuran and Melike. "And my name is Hikmet Ma," he responded in Turkish, bowing elegantly and smiling at the girls. Ever poised, seven-year-old Kâmuran bowed right back.

But five-year-old Melike just gaped up at him. It was the tallness, and the unexpected strangeness of this man, who was *using her elder sister's name!* — a kind of triple shock — that took her time to adjust to.

We quickly made friends with his sweetly smiling wife and their two sons, Djevdet and Shevket, who looked to be about Timur's age. They were also marble shooters, we learned.

We also learned that Hikmet bey had been appointed to the War College in Ankara, had studied Turkish diligently, was from a Moslem sect in China (hence the Moslem name), and loved to cook delicious dumplings for his family and friends as a special treat. The Ma family doted on Timur, and taught him many Chinese words each time he went to visit them. Which was often. ❦

Letter to Sister in Spokane

Güniz Street 6/7, Kavaklidere/Ankara
July 19, 1964

Dear Camilla,

I'm relaxing from a terrific cleanup after my first housewarming party. We invited Ruhsar hanım and Suat bey (Sela's director from Batman), their family doctor, neighbor Perihan hanım across the hall, and husband Samim bey, their daughter Perin's former nursemaid, Mat, from Brussels, and Samim bey's relatives from Izmir. It turned out that many guests knew each other, or had some "connection." It was a somewhat disorganized but very interesting dinner.

Mat, short for Mademoiselle, has promised to help me with my lessons at the French Cultural Center. That's my vacation this summer, instead of a trip. There's a Turkish saying: "A change is as good as a vacation!"

A Private School for Hikmet

Hikmet and I took the train up to Istanbul to see about a French school for her next year, but no luck. The Sister at Dame de Sion explained that Hikmet would lose a year, probably two, learning enough French to get started, so I was dissuaded. (French is her "foreign language" class this year.)

Now some friends in the Ministry of Education have written me about Esenis, a new private school in Istanbul, that teaches most lessons in English and will take a few boarders. Hikmet's friend Aysegül (her mother, Naciye hanım teaches at Gazi) will be enrolling there. So, I may take another weekend off, stay with Ançi in Istanbul, and get Hikmet registered there.

The younger ones are doing well. This house-moving has taken their mind off the prospect of a trip. They were disappointed, but they do well in hiding it. They're pretty good little sports. Our new apartment home gives them a feeling of security, I think, because it *belongs* to us.

Hikmet has to take a make-up exam in Turkish in the fall, so she and Münire have set up a study schedule. (Münire's back now, to help with the children, thank God.) Hikmet doesn't have much time to write now, but she sends her "respects." In fact, we all send our "respects."

Your loving sister, Anna Maria

Route 4, Box 188, Spokane
September 20, 1964

Happy Birthday, Daughter!

Hope this year is whatever you wish. No matter what, we sail through. The Recession is still on, but I believe things will clear up.

So many of the neighbors send their respects: the Browns, the Frankes, Mrs. Angeloff, Mrs. Sandstrom, all want to put in a special word.

And Aunt Ann and Lucile were here, with the two small sprigs. If Lucile doesn't write, she means to. You two must have had a big time at Aunt Edna's in Portland. She talks about you all the time!

"A loving wish for a very happy birthday and a wonderful year." Mom

[Note: When Cousin Lucile and I graduated from high school, we went to live with our Aunt Edna in Portland. All three of us worked as welders in the Swan Island shipyards during WW II.]

19

HANDWRITING ON THE WALL

Letter to Sister in Spokane

Güniz Sok. 6/7, Kavaklıdere/Ankara
September 26, 1964

Dear Camilla,

Thank you for that magnificent barrage of birthday cards! They inspired the children to great achievement, under Münire's leadership. I was told not to come home until eight o'clock — it was the last night of my French course, anyway — and when I arrived at the door, I was met by the whole family, all dressed up! Hikmet and Kâmuran were wearing their taffeta dresses you gave them, and Timur was sporting his bow tie from Vivian.

All the birthday cards were on the table with candlelight and a bouquet of flowers. Münire outdid herself arranging an elaborate salad. Hikmet had made a chocolate cake and colored some sugar to sprinkle on it. Imagine how it sparkled with all the candles!

The best, though, was my birthday present: two little pottery ashtrays, which they had bought with their own allowance! I should explain that we — rather the children — have rented out our share of the carport in the back to the American Army major next door. Every month they collect 50 liras from him, about five dollars, which they split four ways.

After this splendid birthday feast, disturbed only slightly by the hardware store fellows arriving to put up our new curtains, they all practiced the Limbo on the curtain rods. It was altogether a delightful evening, and I thank Andy Paul, Matt, Marie, and little Sarah very, very much! I especially thank the sender of the card with the "57-piece trained flea band," which stuck to everybody's nose, hilariously.

A few days ago, Hikmet set off for boarding school in Istanbul with Münire. She called to say they'd arrived there all right; she had deposited H. all in good order, with her bedding, Barbie doll, stamp album, precious box, three pairs of my shoes, and a letter from her old orthodontist to her new one. Now that Hikmet and Münire have gone, the little ones and I rattle around in our four-bedroom apartment. But Münire will be back soon to start her last year at Gazi. We think she'll be able to get week-end permission to spend Saturday afternoons to Sunday nights with us.

I have a new housekeeper who is a life-saver but can't stay nights, which makes it difficult at times. Looks like I will be doing the entertaining this winter, rather than waiting to be entertained. Next Saturday night, the Georgetown Materials Branch (30-40 lively souls) will have a potluck dinner here, partly to wish me good luck on our new apartment, and partly to initiate the new school year.

As soon as the head of the GMB gets back from vacation, I'm going to talk with him about working towards a master's degree in linguistics or education in the U.S. where I can study Turkish. There are a few places where I might be able to teach English to foreign students. (At the same time, the tuition charges would be waived, I think.)

I've got our ticket money salted away for next summer, drawing interest. It seems like such a tearing up of roots and all, and so much to be arranged for.

I trust all is well with you all. Give my best to everyone. More later, because this is just typewriter practice.

Your loving sister, Anna Maria
PS: You can write to Hikmet at:
Hikmet Malkoç
Esenis Özel Okulu, Set Üstü
Arnavutköy/Istanbul

Letter to Mother in Spokane

Güniz Sok. 6/7, Kavaklıdere/Ankara
November 20, 1964

Dear Mama,

Just a note to let you know that we're all fine.

You should receive a draft for around $400, sometime in December. This is my accumulative Gazi salary "cambio." When the Ministry of Finance finally granted permission for me to send a part of my Gazi salary (I've been moved to a "foreign expert" slot on a special contract) they allowed me to make it retroactive. After this, it will be around $40 a month.

I wonder if Camilla ever found any insurance policy that I could get without a check-up? It bothers me that I don't have any kind of life insurance.

I've just been asked to be on a 10-member Board of Language Study (along with two of my bosses and the head of the Turkish-American Language Center.) They meet once a month to ponder the problems of language teaching. I did tell them that I wouldn't be here after next June, but they still wanted my "experience." They're all linguists, which is beyond me, except for what I've absorbed at Georgetown training workshops these past two years. If I can get into a school where linguistics is taught, I could really improve myself, so I'm writing to places about this now.

The children are all well. Hikmet sends word that she's fine: "Sometimes my friend Aysegül and I get homesick. We get sad and sit down and cry together. But then we try to be happy and satisfied." At least she's writing in English!

Despite their homesickness, the two girls really seem to love their school, Esenis Özel Okulu, a huge old mansion that sits overlooking the Bosphorus Strait from atop a high, wooded hill. The place is fabulously beautiful.

233

Melike sends regards, and wants to know if you have any used comic books.

Your loving daughter, Anna Maria

Letter from Mother in Spokane

Route 4, Box 188, Spokane
February 5, 1965

Dear Anna Maria,

Just a mere line, with "Hafta tell" news notes:

The last box went off, but the charges came to a little over $60.00, which is stupendous, but as it was a gift, that was all right.

Everyone here has a nose to the grindstone. We don't know when a depression will come. By the time your vacation starts, I expect to have the garage finished, which will be much nicer when kids are around. They zoom in and out, but I know the Malkoç clan will fit in very well. That is, if they like a sort of rural atmosphere. Everyone is looking forward to their coming. Will answer your letter pretty quick.

Love to you all. Ma

Journal: Sinan Brings Sad News Late one afternoon, on March 12, 1964 to be exact, when the children had arrived home from their various schools and I was preparing to go to an evening teachers' meeting/dinner, there was a knock on the door. I opened it to find my nephew Sinan (son of Elder Brother Sabri) standing there.

Startled, I mumbled a welcome greeting and something like, "What brings *you* here, Sinan?"

I should note here that Sinan and his brothers Ilhan and Ayhan had never been playmates with my children, who were some years younger. When they visited us once at far-off Raman Camp, Hikmet was only a toddler and they were already schoolboys. When we were living down in Batman, they were in distant government sugar refinery sites in Malatya and Kutahya. Later, all of us ended up in Ankara, but they were always seriously occupied with lessons, so my children and I rarely saw these tall, handsome boys except on special visits.

I was therefore quite surprised to see Sinan standing there so unexpectedly in my doorway. "Do come in, Sinan," I said. "Please sit down."

"No, Yenge, I have to tell you Baba Anne has died. Heart attack."

The unexpected news was such a shock that I couldn't react immediately. My mother-in-law had doted on all her grandchildren, I knew, but Sinan, her first grandchild, must have been the apple of her eye, and I sensed he was striving to hide his emotions. He quietly delivered the sad message and left.

So I cancelled plans to attend the teachers' dinner, of course, and went instead to sit with my in-laws. Orhan, who had been living there with her, Sabri and his devoted wife Seyyare, and various other grieving relatives were already in the apartment where my mother-in-law had moved after leaving Sürmene. Her 94-year-old mother Nine, who had accompanied her from Sürmene, had passed away the year before.

As is the custom, beloved Grandmother Ayse Malkoç was laid to rest on the following day. She lies in peace, next to second son Selahattin, in the Ankara Cemetery. 🐾

Journal: Timur's Birthday Party and the Deaf Cat For his 10th birthday, Timur invited friends to a game of soccer in the back courtyard. Two boys in our building are Turkish, the other two are learning Turkish, but their first language is Chinese. Several other friends are Turkish, studying English in school, and several are American boys, learning Turkish in the neighborhood.

The boys' common bond was a mutual love of soccer. As backup activity in case of a rain-out during the soccer game, I borrowed the neighbor's 8mm film projector with a couple of "Mickey Mouse" reels. The mothers who would be picking up their sons were joining us for tea, so I baked an extra cake.

Timur greeted his birthday guests at the door and introduced them to each other. They all shook hands politely, then tore downstairs to start their game. Kâmuran and Melike helped Münire fill snack bowls with peanuts, raisins and salted leblebi [roasted chick peas]. I'd just put the finishing touches on the cake and added candles when the threatening storm clouds erupted and rained out the game.

"OK, everybody, we have "Mickey Mouse!" I consoled the boys as they came back upstairs. "Let's get it set up!" The children all sat cross-legged on the floor in a semi-circle, munching from the snack bowls, waiting excitedly. Münire loaded the reel in the machine, adjusted the focus, aimed the projector at the bare, white wall, and turned on the switch. Nothing happened. Kâmuran rushed across the hall to ask the neighbor for help with his machine. Apparently it lacked a vital part. The boys began to grow restless.

"OK, everybody, we have popcorn!" I cheerfully announced, and frantically heated up the largest cooking pot in the kitchen with a matching lid, opened up the precious can of imported popcorn saved for "a rainy day." It didn't take long to pop, and soon Melike and Kâmuran were trotting out snack bowls of the popped corn to the eager crowd. Münire started up a game of "Pin the Tail on the Donkey."

The doorbell rang. This was Billy, the last invited guest, arriving with his mother and a large, snow-white, blue-eyed Angora cat! They were moving back to America, Billy explained; he wanted to give Koko to Timur as a birthday present. Before Timur could even say "Thank-you," Koko leaped out of Billy's arms and into the nearest escape hatch — the china cabinet, with its doors yawning wide open. I had been about to take out the tea glasses when the bell rang.

Unbelievably, in that one phenomenal jump, Koko had leapt *inside* the cabinet. Amazingly, it was now hunched atop the rows of crystal tea glasses, without moving a single one! Mute and still, it remained there despite all our cajoling and coaxing. I even opened up a can of tuna fish to no avail. No matter how we pleaded, she did not budge.

235

"Oh, I'm so sorry," said Billy's mother, coming to the rescue. "Koko's deaf! All blue-eyed Angoras are deaf," she explained, reaching in with both arms and skillfully extracting the cat — again, without dislodging the tea glasses.

Immediately, Koko leaped out of *her* arms, tore down the hall, and hid under the nearest bed for the remainder of the party.

In the meantime, during the excitement of pinning the tail on the donkey and awarding prizes to the winners, the bowls of popcorn had all been overturned, and white snow puffs of popcorn lay sprinkled on carpets and coffee tables in riotous abandon. The boys began tossing the kernels about in some kind of impromptu competition.

But there was no need to despair. Münire quickly brushed up the debris in the living room; the three younger girls quickly washed and dried the tea glasses. The scene was comparatively calm by the time the other mothers arrived for tea. They seated themselves comfortably on the sofas, Timur and his guests lined up around the dinner table, and I lit the candles for the birthday cake. ❦

Timur's Tenth Birthday Party

Letter to Mother in Spokane

Güniz Sok. 6/7, Kavaklıdere/Ankara
March 30, 1965

Dear Mama,

Camilla's Valentine card and pictures of the boys just arrived. How handsome they look on my bureau!

Things are just settling down after several hectic birthday parties, and a farewell potluck dinner for Mrs. Rae Hall, with all the Gazi English teachers celebrating in our apartment.

Several weeks ago, I had Kâmuran checked up after her tonsillectomy. At the advice of a number of doctors, Timur and Kâmuran had had their tonsils removed because of chronic problems. Timur suffered no after effects, but K. complained of pain in her abdomen, so our kind medical friends arranged for her to have tests.

One report came back: "Hospitalize immediately, highly suspect typhoid." In spite of our yearly typhoid shots! So she had to go through more tests, which turned out to be normal. There had been a mix-up in the lab tests. The whole business, naturally, was nerve-wracking, especially for nine-year-old K.

Our doctor said, "Don't take her for any more lab check-ups!" She seems to be recovering her good health, now, I'm happy to report.

In appreciation to all these people who were so kind to Kâmuran, I invited them to a special dinner. Guests always expect something "American" in our house, so I try not to disappoint them. I've gotten to be a whiz at stuffed meatloaf, potato salad with mayonnaise, also Sunday morning waffles.

Our living room is large enough for folk dancing, and the children can usually be persuaded to put on their costumes and dance for the guests before retiring for the night. They've learned a number of regional dances from Münire and my other Gazi students, in readiness for the summer.... Yes, we're really getting ready for the trip this year!

I've received several interesting job offers for next year, one from an old school friend of Sela's, in the directorate of the new iron and steel mill near Zonguldak. They're bringing in 100 American experts with their families; the children will carry on their education via Calvert correspondence courses. (The American families in Batman had done this; when I visited them in California on the trip with Hikmet, I saw how effective that course was. Not one child failed or missed a grade when they returned to U.S. schools. They did "exceptionally well.")

Anyway, they want me to supervise these Calvert courses in Zonguldak. It's an interesting offer I may consider if I don't have any luck with a university.

Someone asked me about teaching at the U Maryland extension courses here. This didn't interest me much, although it's nice to know I would never be without job opportunities here.

Today I was called into the Georgetown Program director's office. (I attend a small class with him every morning to read Turkish newspapers; although I'm not a Stateside US-AID employee, he got special permission for me, to have someone to study with.) Now that the Georgetown Program will be phasing out this summer, he's recommended me for a job with the Peace Corps. There are PC teachers at Gazi now, and in quite a few towns.

So, I had an interview with the Peace Corps representative looking for a supervisor for the 30 PC English-teaching volunteers in Turkey. This would mean traveling to the schools around the country where the volunteers are located, advise them on their teaching materials, problems, etc. (I got a good insight into such situations when I did substitute teaching one semester in the Batman Middle School. This experience is now considered "impressive.")

I felt really honored. This would be very much down my alley, with a handsome salary, and a cambio permit to bank a portion in Lincoln Savings & Loan. Anyway, I don't have to even turn around for a job. Gives me a secure feeling. I told him I was waiting to hear from a university in the U.S.

Finally, I finished my extra job of proofreading the English translation in the government report, and now spend several hours every evening at the printer's, checking the galley proofs and trying to learn the processes.

Last week, I took Timur with me so he could see the presses. The next night, there was a box of visiting cards engraved "Timur Malkoç" on the desk. He was so thrilled. He's quite a personable child, I think, and impresses people as being business-like and dignified. At the same time, he likes to play soccer, and participates in the Cub Scouts' national folk dances in the national Hippodrome.

We frequently telephone Hikmet in Istanbul. She may come home with her roommate Ayşegül for next holiday. She reaches up to my ear now, and has walked off with all my flat-heeled shoes. She isn't doing too well in math, but she's a terrific dancer. Aren't all 13-year olds now?

Melike says, "Tell Grandmother I *özlemek* her." [I miss her.] M.'s really the live wire. She expects to perform on TV this summer!

Kâmuran is just as quietly industrious and elegant as ever.

Hello to all. Your loving daughter, Anna Maria

Journal: Summons to the Fourth Precinct Police Station Last week, Naciye hanım, the Gazi English Department's director for this year, handed me a mystifying letter requesting me to report to the Fourth Precinct Police station. It's the office where they check foreign passports, she explained. She offered to accompany me.

"No, thanks anyway. I'll be all right," I said. "I'll just stop by there on my way to school tomorrow morning. Hope I won't be late for classes."

"Don't worry, Anna Maria, we'll take your classes," she assured me. There had been something in her tone of voice when she said "Fourth Precinct" that should have given me pause. But I was not unduly anxious the next morning as I entered the building and walked into the room indicated in the letter.

I introduced myself to the clerk at the nearest desk, and showed him the letter, along with my Turkish registration certificate. "Please, sit down" he said, and gestured to a chair along the wall. Shortly, he asked to see my American passport.

Usually, I never carry this precious document around with me, because I never use it in Turkey, but today I felt I might need extra identification. As I handed it over, I regretted turning down Naciye hanım's offer to accompany me. The atmosphere was beginning to feel like a village coffee house, where females never enter. Or like some place women would enter only if they had business to conduct, and only if escorted by a male who would speak for them. My next thought was: I should have asked one of my brothers-in-law to come with me. They are always so willing to help.

As I waited, the first clerk passed my passport around to the other clerks. They all wanted to take a peek, it seemed. Instinctively, I felt an urge to snatch it back, but I resisted it.

Eventually, someone escorted me to a chair in the director's office. Then the director himself, tall and imposing, swept in with a sheaf of papers in hand and sat down at his desk. We exchanged greetings. He riffled through the sheaf, held up one document and began to confirm the information in it:

"Were you born in America?" he asked.

"Yes," I nodded in agreement.

"Do you have an American passport?" "Did you marry a Turk?" "Do you have a Turkish registration card?" "Are you presently teaching at Gazi Teacher Training Institute?" I responded affirmatively to all his questions. He then informed me that I was not eligible to hold a position as a "foreign expert" on the Gazi teaching staff.

This was a shock, but not totally surprising. Indeed, I was under the impression that last year's department head at Gazi had tried to help me out by moving me to this more lucrative slot in the teaching staff. (People here are especially kind to widows and children; I think it's a tenet of the religion.)

I remember pointing to my Turkish registration and asking if I would still be eligible as a foreign expert? "It's all arranged, Anna Maria," he had reassured me. "The slot is vacant, you're an American teacher, so don't worry!" But when someone tells me that everything is all arranged, and not to worry, I've come to believe there may actually be something to worry about....

Now the Fourth Precinct director is telling me, in essence, that my misgivings about the foreign expert contract had been well-founded. I struggled to control my rush of anger at the well-intentioned department head, embarrassment at having to go through this official reprimand, disappointment at losing the additional salary, bewilderment over what my next step should be.

For a long moment, I couldn't speak. The director assumed I hadn't understood what he was saying about the importance of possessing a Turkish registration card, that it was a privilege conferred upon me by the Turkish government. He sent for a translator.

By the time the translator came in, I'd gathered my thoughts and was on my feet. Ignoring him, I addressed the director as calmly as I could in Turkish. I expressed appreciation for my Turkish registration card and informed him I had never used my American passport while in Turkey, I obeyed all the laws of the country to the best of my ability, and I was following orders from the head of the Gazi English Department.

As a parting shot, I told him that before my deceased husband had done his military service, the Turkish government classified me as a foreigner, and therefore my husband was ineligible to become a commissioned officer. So we had gotten a divorce. Now, I added, the government is saying because I have a Turkish registration card I was not eligible to teach English as a foreigner. My remarks were becoming increasingly more impassioned.

The director stood up, apologizing profusely for my distress. He bowed and apologized again as I collected my papers and struggled to remain cool and lady-like. It was quite a dramatic exit, under the circumstances.

As I informed Naciye hanım back at Gazi, it was "the handwriting on the wall" for me. It was a "sign." I had taught my last class at Gazi. It was time for me to leave Turkey, and return to the States. 🍂

Güniz Sok. 6/7, Kavaklidere/Ankara
June 3, 1965

Dear Mama,

I must say, these past few months have nearly undone me. So much going on!

Job Offers

I have finished teaching at Gazi. And that flattering Peace Corps offer that kept me waiting for a month while the director went off to Washington for conferences? The official decision, finally, was to hire a male supervisor to travel about to the different schools where PC volunteers are teaching English. Too "risky for a female." (I guess they were right, generally speaking.)

There were several other offers, but nothing spectacular, except for the nicest one from Beirut, from the American University group, which is setting up language centers for training teachers of English as a foreign language. Dr. Nasr came to interview me at home so he could meet my family. Good salary, free American school for the children, medical services, transportation from Spokane, etc. etc. When he reported back to Beirut, the Board told him the position required a master's degree, even though I have "highly qualifying experience."

So, now I've written to my old school friend Liz (from Latin class at Lewis & Clark High School), who now lives in Seattle, asking her about applying for graduate school. I hear they have a linguistics department and also a Turkish department at the U of W. I might have a chance to earn an MA in teaching English as a foreign language.

Camilla could inquire about colleges in Spokane, but I doubt there's any equivalent offered there. I'm going to make a desperate attempt to get that degree. You see what a difference it makes in job qualifications.

Travel Plans to Return

Last week, I booked six bus tickets from Ankara to Münich on July 6. From there to Paris or London, we'll fly across the Atlantic, and take a bus from then on.

Tentatively, we should be in Spokane the last of July. I'm hoping to take Münire with me, at least for the trip. I rather doubt that the Ministry of Education would let her stay, but just in case, and if it's not too much trouble, could you get an affidavit for her? You have her info, just write the same old paragraph showing proof of support, etc.

When I get this trip all figured out, I'll ask you to send a Railway Express or Traveler's Check to Münich or Paris, where we have friends. This will take everything I have to get there, but I'm told I'll be able to have our pension transferred. Or I may sell the apartment, in which case I'll be able to pay for my tuition.

My sisters-in-law are busily sewing and embroidering costumes for the children. Now the four are really quite professional in dancing, especially when Münire plays the mandolin. I wish they could capitalize on it!

They send respects, and say they would like "peanut butter, comic books, and a new pair of shoes." Melike is embroidering "something for Grandmother."

Until this last week, everything was so hectic, I didn't know which side was up!

I'm sorry I never wrote to Aunt Tret, and I'm sorry we missed a ride with her from Philadelphia. But I have to settle the deed for the apartment on July 1, so we couldn't have left before, in any case. Please give her my apologies.

Your loving daughter, Anna Maria

Letter to Mother in Spokane

Güniz Sok. 6/7, Kavaklıdere/Ankara
June 20, 1965

Dear Mama,

Just realized I hadn't answered your question about the children. Here's the info:

1. Hikmet Malkoç, born Tulsa, Okla, Feb. 6, 1952
2. Timur Malkoç, born Ankara, Turkey, March 25, 1956
3. Kâmuran Malkoç, born Spokane, Wash., March 24, 1957
4. Melike Malkoç, born Batman, Turkey, Feb. 9, 1959.

Where they're going to stay depends on whether I can get into U of W and/or work in Seattle.

Of course, it would be nice if Münire could stay in your house. She's a wonderful help, quiet and steady, and willing. But maybe the three little ones would be too trying for you? If you want to consider it, OK.

More later.

Your loving daughter, Anna Maria

PS: The enclosed affidavit for Münire just came. I guess this is all the info you need. We're waiting to see if Camilla can get some letter from a college or university in Spokane so Münire can enroll as a student. Even as a special or probationary student. Otherwise, she can't stay. She'll have to go back in the fall. But I still want to bring her for the experience of the trip. She deserves a reward and I'll take care of all her expenses.

We're selling off our odds and ends. The rugs and copper pots are washed and ready to be packed. I'm trying to tidy things up here and leave as few loose ends as possible. It's time-consuming.

If anyone wants anything special, write quick. xxx

Güniz Sok. 6/7, Kavaklidere/Ankara
July 3, 1965

Dear Mama,

Things are shaping up! I'm off to arrange the sale of the apartment with my friend and neighbor, Perihan hanım. She's a lawyer and is helping me with all the legalities.

Have reservations on Icelandic Airlines, from Luxembourg to New York July 21. We should make it to Spokane somewhere toward the end of August if we take a Greyhound and stop along the way. Could you please send $5.00 to the U of Wash. per enclosed application instructions? This has to be in before July 15.

xxx Anna Maria

PS: Back from a long day with Perihan hanım.

The sale of the apartment, 100,000 TL [Sela's life insurance from the Company, the equivalent of $10,000] was cash on the barrel head.

I have just invested half of it in the new State Eregli Iron and Steel Company, which Sela's friends also have shares in.

Then we went to the bank and deposited the other half in my account. This should see us through next year, while we all adjust to life in the States. A

20

TOUR BUS OUT OF TÜRKIYE

Journal: Preparations and Packing Up The die has been cast. I have officially finished my employment at GELP [Georgetown English Language Program] and at Gazi, sold the apartment for cash, bought Turkish tour-bus tickets to Münich, and Icelandic Air tickets from Luxembourg to New York. The consular clerk at the American Embassy instructed me to have our American visas stamped properly for transit through Bulgaria, which means a visit to the Bulgarian Embassy. We should also have typhoid and/or other inoculations for our World Health cards, in case these should be required on our way through Europe.

We have many to-do lists: the children's registration papers/school records, my registration/work records and letters of recommendation. Also, what to keep/sell/give away; what to pack/crate up to send to Grandmother; what to pack for the trip itself. Each of us will have one suitcase to check in on the plane, one tote bag to carry on, and one string bag for snacks and a beverage. This means agonizing decisions for the children, who have many "little treasures and precious keepsakes." Most will be boxed up and sent by ship/surface. The days pass in an accelerating flurry of activities. 🐦

Timur Packs His Footlocker, Ankara 1965

A Last Visit to Ankara Cemetery 1965

Journal: Farewells to Family and Friends Our goodbyes have been long and drawn out. The children and I first of all paid a visit to Sela's grave. I think I can bear to leave the place behind, because his spirit is deep in my heart; I will take that with me. But it is still difficult for me to say his name aloud.

Taking leave of his family has been perhaps the hardest — thanking his faithful brothers Sabri, Muammer, and Orhan for all their unstinting care and attention to me and the children. And my dear sisters-in-law: Seyyare, Sülhiye, Nezihe, and Güher. All the relatives in Istanbul. I don't have enough words. How I shall miss them in America!

I think of all my earliest friends whom I met at Sela's old institute, MTA [Mining and Metallurgy Research]: Perihan Turgay, lawyer and neighbor; Fikret Bayri and Ferda Oyhan, the lady biochemists….

My dear and close friends at Gazi Teacher Training Institute: Pat Matthews, Mollie Emre, Sabahat Tura, Naciye Öncül, Ferhunde Aker, Ülkü Bilgen….

The GELP friends: Dorothy Pedtke, Betty Segland, Betty Siglin, Selma hanım; Shafiga and all the "Tatar contingent." The list is so long….

My friends and dear neighbors from TPAO Batman: Ruhsar Çalıslar, Ançi Köksal, Meral Özkan, Sühendan Baytan, Senol Sahankaya, Perihan Tolgay, and another long list….

My TAA friends (Turkish-American Association): Edith Oyhon, Eloise Enata, and Marion Türker who saw me through a burst appendix and other serious crises. How can I ever thank them — and all the other friends — for their kindness, thoughtfulness, and generosity. I can never repay them. Given the chance, I can only hope to help someone else in turn.

244

Saying goodbye to all these dear souls is one heart-wrench after another. I don't really say "goodbye." To myself, I think: *Au revoir, 'til we meet again.* For who knows if, when, or where our paths may not cross again?

The invitations to farewell lunches, teas, and dinners carry us along through these hectic days, keeping our spirits exhilarated to the very eve of departure. When morning dawns, relatives and friends are already waiting to help us make our final exit from the apartment. Willing hands transfer our take-alongs into cars that carry us to the Ankara train station. Kind hands help us board the train, press us with small mementos, load us with boxes of fresh confections and savory pastries. Our string bags are full. Our hearts are overflowing.

The train whistles, wheezes and shudders into motion, belching clouds of steam. As we begin to move down the tracks, we wave goodbye to the dear ones standing on the platform. They slowly diminish into memory and my mind flashes back to the Batman train station….

This train will take us from Ankara to Haydarpasha, the terminal on the Anatolian side of Istanbul. As planned, I spend the night with friends, and the children overnight at Münire's mother's. Next morning, bright and early, we all converge at the small tour bus station near Taxim Square on the European side of Istanbul. Once again, there are kindly helpers — Münire's family members — to make sure we're all intact and nothing has gone astray. They wish us a good journey, and a happy return some day. There are more hugs and kisses, more baklava, lokum, and chocolates for the string bags. Somehow, we disentangle ourselves, get on the bus with Münire, and wave goodbye to her family.

The tour bus is modern, spacious, and already more than half-full. We drive through the city, making scheduled stops along the way to pick up more passengers on the outskirts of Istanbul. At the Küçükçekmece stop, I see my sister-in-law Sülhiye, husband Süleyman, and daughter Refiye through the bus window, standing patiently by the side of the road to say goodbye to us enroute. Quickly we all climb off for hugs and kisses, a few snapshots, more hugs. For Sülhiye and Süleyman, I know that saying farewell to us, in essence, is taking leave of Sela all over again. The children are a part of him, and our departure from Turkey is fresh grief for everyone.

Several minutes later we're back on board and settled into our seats. We wave our farewells from the window as the bus pulls away for the long journey to Münich. It seems impossible to contain our feelings; we are brimming over at one and the same time with inconsolable sadness and travel excitement. 🐦

Münire, Timur, Sülhiye, 1965

A, K, T, & M with Sülhiye, Süleyman, Refiye Atalı at Küçükçekmece, 1965

Journal: A Close Call at the Border Our sleek, new tour bus has high-ceilings and spacious overhead racks. The efficient-looking bus driver has a young assistant and — oh, glory be! — a uniformed bus hostess who is dispensing tiny snack packets and cups of fruit beverage. On her second round, she sprinkles drops of lemon cologne into our outstretched palms. It is fragrant and refreshing.

Every seat on the bus is now taken. I think some passengers had boarded earlier in Syria, some perhaps in Lebanon. They're speaking Arabic. Their suitcases, frequently open to view as they tend to their small children's needs, seem to be crammed with embroidered slippers and brightly colored scarves, perhaps for sale in Germany.

The morning passes. Münire helps comfort the children and tries to interest them in the passing scenery. We reach the dusty town of Edirne [Adrianopolis] and travel on to a tiny, deserted-looking outpost to its other side, on the border between Turkey and Bulgaria.

Our bus pulls over and stops, the driver gets out, goes into the small building in a grove of dusty trees, comes back with a gendarme-looking official who strides to the rear of the bus. The Lebanese and Syrian passengers pull down their baggage from the overhead racks to reveal the contents under his official scrutiny. No one has anything to declare. The bus driver busily collects our passports. The two men go back to the little office, where other officials look over the documents. The two men come back out and return the passports to us. The border official returns for more consultations with other officials inside.

Outside, the noonday sun is beating down on the silvery bus roof. The other passengers are stirring restlessly in the back seats. Something is out of order, apparently. We wait patiently and Münire starts a "20 Questions" game with the children.

The official enters the bus again, confers with the driver. He comes back to our row, to my seat, and apologetically requests to see my passport again. Assured that everything is in order because I'd carefully followed instructions from the American Embassy clerk, I calmly hand over my passport. The man leaves, and we continue Münire's game. But not for long. From the window, I see the brown uniform returning to the bus for yet another passport check. I've lost count; is this his third or fourth trip, I wonder?

This time, the bus driver comes back to tell me, apologetically, that the officials would like to see me inside the office, and please to bring my passport. Now, I feel a faint foreshadowing of something like apprehension. I tell the children I'll be right back, the officer just wants to ask something. I get off the bus and walk into the office where the official is looking at me. "Madame," he says, pointing to my Turkish passport, "No visa!"

"There is, sir," I tell him politely, and take out my American passport to show him the page with the Bulgarian transit visa clearly stamped on it. [This was according to instructions I'd received from the American Embassy official: show my Turkish passport at the border, then use my American passport to enter Bulgaria and onward.]

Now there is a general confabulation amongst the several border guards. The senior official shakes his head, and points to the picture in both passports.

"Impossible, Madame!" He is telling me, in so many words, that because of document irregularities, we cannot cross the border. We have to return to Istanbul.

I stand there dumbstruck. I don't know what to say, so I say nothing. He continues to shake his head and seems personally indignant that I am not only taking four children — *four Turkish citizens* — from their homeland, but taking them with *no permission from their father! Where is their permission paper from their father*, he wants to know.

My stomach begins to churn as I try to grasp the total situation. The man waits impatiently for my response.

Sometimes in times of crisis, by forcing myself to remain calm and collected, I find that some kind of divine inspiration comes to me.... And sure enough, the Turkish words I need slowly come into my head.

"Long life to you, sir," I say to him. "The deceased father of my children is sleeping in celestial light. May he rest in peace." I pause a moment, then conclude, "I am taking my children to my mother."

These few words seem to work like magic. *Click! Click!* goes the rubber date-stamper on the ink pad. *Scratch! Scratch!* goes the official's pen across the passport page. In a twinkling, he hands back my Turkish passport and my American passport, and is wishing me a safe and happy journey, with a multitude of God's blessings on my fatherless children.

I walk back out to the bus on trembly knees, rejoin my children and Münire. *Never again,* I vow to myself. *Never again will I set foot in Turkey. Life is complicated enough.*

Or, I amend myself after a moment's thought, *if ever I do come back, it will be under the aegis of a higher power!*

These words just pop into my head. Whatever they mean, only God knows. ❧

APPENDIX

TIME LINE

Dec 1952 Departure from New York
Jan 1953 Arrival in Istanbul
Feb 1953 Arrival in Sürmene
April 1953 Return to Istanbul
April 1953 Train to Batman
April 1953 Arrival in Raman Camp
Sept 1953 Military Duty/Divorce in Ankara
May 1955 Sad Return to Raman Camp
Nov 1955 Move to Batman Site
Dec 1956 Trip to Grandmother's with H and T
Aug 1957 Return to Batman with H T and K
April 1960 Sela's Stay on Heyebeli Island
June 1962 Trip to Grandmother's with Hikmet
Aug 1962 Return to Batman
Aug 1962 A & Children Move to Ankara
Aug 1962 Sela's Transfer to Ankara
Sept 1963 A's Teaching in Ankara
June 1963 Sela's Trip to USA
Sept 1963 Heartbreak in Zagrep
Aug 1964 Buying Apartment
May 1965 Leaving Gazi
July 1965 Departure

See also **A Brief Post-Turkey Biography: 1965-2005**
following **Photographs**

APPENDED PHOTOGRAPHS

Tulsa U Engineers' Ball 1951   *[Bill Brownfield standing behind Sela]*

Visiting Parsons Families' Barracks, Batman 1956

250

Sela Fishing on the Tigris River   *S & H Meet the Kurtalan Express*

Visiting the Kutahya Sugar Refinery 1957

Muammer, Süleyman Kıralı [Aunt Saadet's brother], Ayse Malkoç [in doorway], Güher, Mehmet Ali Malkoç, Seyyare [on rail], Nezihe, Orhan [seated], Sela [holding Sirin]

251

New Year's at the Guest House 1957

A&H, Dr. Turhan, Jane MacLeod at Selçuk Cemetery, Ahlat 1958

252

Folk Dancing at the Guest House 1958

Batman Refinery 1958 (?)

A & S at the Guest House with Esin Göker. Sylvia & John MacLeod 1959

Neighbor Senol Sahankaya and Baby Melike 1959

Ancient Houses at Hasan Keyf on the Tigris River 1959

Family in Batman Apartment 1959

255

New Year's at the Guest House with Muammer & Nezihe 1959

Hessie William's Dinner Table 1960

Sad Farewell to Hessie 1960

front row: Hessie Williams, Ruhsar Çalislar
back row: Suat Çalislar, Sermet Idil, Hasan Göker, Selahattin Malkoç

Noel Baba and His Helpers' Surprise Visit 1960

Guest House Party 1961

UN Consultant Jim Crawford (center) and friends

258

Timur and Kamuran on House Steps 1961

New Year's Frivolities at the Guest House 1961

1962

Last Dance, Guest House

Last View of Batman Site Street Traffic

Last Glimpse of Batman Skyline

260

Sela & Timur in Ankara 1962

Welcoming Gazi Students 1962

Welcoming Munire and Friends 1963

Recep & Güher Eroglu, Sürmene 1963

Timur Recites a Poem

Children's Day, April 23, 1963

Sela & Tüncer at Spokane Airport 1963

Strolling through Luna Park, Ankara 1963

264

Kamuran Smiles for the Camera 1964

Fresh from the Hair Salon, Ankara 1964

265

EPILOGUE

A Brief Post-Turkey Biography 1965-2005

1965-1966 Enrollment in Schools My four children attended Rich Whitman School, a small private day school in Seattle fall semester, and Whittier Elementary in Spokane spring semester. Within three months, they were reading and writing English, had stopped speaking Turkish, spoke only English to each other. I was studying Turkic language courses at the UW in Seattle, with the intent of becoming a translator or interpreter.

1966-1970 Move to Northwest Washington DC Enrolled children in Janney Elementary/Alice Deal Middle/Woodrow Wilson High schools. To maintain my Turkish language skills, I decided to speak only Turkish at home with the children. Now, they understood me but answered only in English, the reverse of our earlier communication in Turkey!

Joined the American-Turkish Association, hoping it would ease the cultural transition for the children and give them a real sense of pride in their Turkish heritage. They performed as folk dancers for the Embassy's festivals and numerous other places. I worked as bibliographer/information specialist at the Center for Applied Linguistics and, taking evening classes, earned an MA in applied linguistics at American U.

1971-1974 Teaching/Jobs/Schools Hikmet started working at the TPAO office in Ankara. Timur, Kâmuran, and Melike attended Box Hill boarding school in England. During long holidays and summers they visited relatives in Turkey, or stayed with me in Poland where I had a two-year Fulbright grant to teach English at Adam Mickiewicz U in Poznan, and taught in summer seminars. The third year, I planned and ran a State Department-funded pilot refresher course for English teachers in Lodz.

1974-1975 Foreign Service Application Applied to the USIA (FS) as an English teaching specialist. While waiting for application results, the children and I lived at Grandmother's in Spokane. They attended nearby schools in Cheney; I took a course at Eastern Washington College.

1975 New Position Entered the Foreign Service, USIA as English Teaching Officer *(specialist)*.

1975-1979 Assignment in WashDC The older children were living in Turkey/Washington State, Melike was a boarding student at nearby Sandy Springs School as I sometimes traveled on assignments. My main domestic assignment was in the Materials Development Department, preparing an ordering catalog of English teaching materials for Agency posts overseas.

1979-1983 Assignment in Turkey The older children were working/studying in various places. I was assigned as English Teaching Officer (ETO) to the American Embassy in Ankara. *Note: This was my prophetic return to Turkey "under the aegis of a higher power."*

Since Melike was a dependent at the time of my assignment, she traveled to Ankara with me, then returned in the fall to study at Spokane Falls Community College.

266

My new responsibilities in Turkey included planning/implementing teacher-training workshops with the Ministry of Education and the British Council. Because of terrorist activities and violent unrest between Leftists and Rightists, the new Gazi English Department director was loath to let me visit my old classroom: "There's still blood on the walls from the last shooting, Malkoç hanım." And at Middle East Technical University, armed militia had to unchain the gates to allow official cars access to the campus; guards with bayonets patrolled the halls to protect the student factions from one another.

Various regions in the southeast were not open to travel without official permission. Arrangements were made to visit Diyarbakır [where in a previous incarnation I had often taken my children on the train for check-ups and shopping]. I was to pay a follow-up/thank-you call on the University's English department director who had sent his entire staff to the six-week Istanbul course the previous summer. After formalities, the senior teacher invited us to tea. The Secret Security man detailed to follow me was confused by this new task, so I offered to share my cab with him. Happily, it turned out, our hostess was his child's English teacher at the Anadolu High School. He was charmed, everyone relaxed, and we all thoroughly enjoyed the hospitality. Other visits, to seminar participants in Malatya, Konya, and Bursa, were less problematic but no less enjoyable. I felt a deep kinship with all these dedicated teachers.

Returned to Washington DC at the end of this four-year assignment in Turkey, and to my astonishment, received a Superior Honor Award.

1983-1987 Assignment in Poland My ETO duties in the American Embassy in Warsaw were similar to my previous assignment, but because of the Cold War behind the Iron Curtain, travel activities for US embassy personnel were limited and closely monitored. Although I enjoyed the seminars and workshop assignments and became fond of all the hard-working participants, I could never become close friends with anyone for fear of jeopardizing their jobs, travel permits, etc. So I spent my free time completing *Easy Plays in English*, started in Turkey. It was later published by Metro Books in Istanbul.

While on home leave from Warsaw, daughter Melike (drama student at UW) helped me have the book recorded professionally in Seattle. Amazingly, the State Textbook Publishing House of Warsaw published it in 1986. (English language teachers were hungry for fresh materials, as none were being imported from the West.) Many high school English teachers had their students perform the plays and wanted to invite me to their performances, but were forbidden because I was an official in the American Embassy. Instead, their students sent me letters and crayon drawings of their enactments. This was a highlight of my tour in Poland.

Also memorable were the USIA/British Council summer refresher courses for high-school English teachers and university philology students from institutions throughout Poland. From 1971 on, I spent 11 summers teaching in these courses in Czestochowa, Krakow, Poznan, Suleyuwek. Adjusting to dormitory life with teachers and students was an education in itself. It was this experience that gave me the model for the 6-week summer course in Turkey in 1981, and inspired me to develop many teacher-training materials.

1987-1990 Reassignment to WashDC Last USIA assignment was as Materials Development Chief, preparing the USIS ordering catalogue, teacher-training pamphlets, and other low-budget "Americana" materials. Earlier, as a "home hobby," I'd compiled selected poems for language teaching, *On Wings of Verse*, wrote an accompanying teacher's manual, and donated it to the Agency to print and distribute to USIS posts worldwide. My next special project was compiling a songbook, *Old Favorites for All Ages;* volunteer colleagues recorded the songs at the Voice of America. The book and cassettes were also available to posts worldwide. This final assignment gave me my greatest joy.

1990 Mandatory Retirement from the Foreign Service Moved back to my hometown of Spokane WA and set about remodeling the old family home, which my mother had whimsically dubbed "Rocky Acres." I spent much time enjoying the garden and visiting with my extended family in Spokane.

1991 Revision of "Easy Plays" First retirement project was to reformat the book and find a local artist, David Clemons, to illustrate it.

Joined a group of volunteer teachers from Baltimore to do teacher-training in Xiamen, their Sister City in China. This was another enriching experience. Returning via Japan, I visited my brother Mike, sister-in-law Miyako, children Karen and Ryuto, and their Tada grandparents in Niihama. Also met a Tokyo publisher interested in *Easy Plays*. [It was published later by Regents Prentice Hall.]

1992-00 Gathering Notes for "Conversational Dialogues" In 1990, Mukogawa Fort Wright Institute [MFWI, a branch of the Mukogawa Women's University in Nishinomiya, Japan, Spokane's Sister City] opened near my home in Spokane. I visited the MFWI Library to learn about Japan, ended up teaching classes full-time. Working with hundreds of bright, eager students and with the creative, stimulating faculty were golden years for me.

Worked on *Conversational Dialogues and Cultural Notes* (the Tokyo publisher's suggestion). And worked vigorously on my house and garden.

2000 Second Retirement Taking leave of my MFWI colleagues was a great wrench. Director Takaoka said he felt he was "saying Goodbye to Mr. Chips" (one of his favorite American films). Celebrated with a grand garden party for extended family, neighbors and friends, sold the family house (an even more heartbreaking wrench) and moved to live in an apartment in my son's home in Mukilteo WA.

Settled into a happy life with son Timur, beautiful daughter-in-law Paige, and endearing grandsons Dylan and Miles. My first project was to put finishing touches on *Conversations in American English*, recorded by colleagues before leaving Spokane. But by this time, the Tokyo publisher had gone out of business. [It was published several years later in Osaka.]

Found new formatters in Mukilteo for *Tales from Rocky Acres: The Wildlife in My Garden*, a book I'd prepared during retirement years in Spokane. [Some stories had appeared earlier in students' publications in Poland, Germany, and Turkey.] After several kindly rejections from U.S. publishers, I opted to have it formatted as an electronic "print-on-demand" book available on the Internet. It's a memento of my mother's garden and cherished family home in Spokane.

268

2005 Closer Family Ties My children and I all live in the Puget Sound area, within half-hour driving distances from each other. When Timur sold his house in Mukilteo, I moved to Edmonds with daughter Hikmet. After working many years at the Smithsonian Museum, she's now helping me with the computer complications of my book projects. I visit Timur, Paige, seven-year-old Dylan and four-year-old Miles for Sunday dinners, cookouts on the Mukilteo beach, and many family occasions. Less frequently I go to Shoreline to see daughter Kâmuran, deep in studies at Bastyr University. Most frequently, I see daughter Melike, son-in-law Kim Jack Loop, and fourteen-year-old first grandson, Gordon, in Seattle.

I often visited Gordon's school in Seattle for volunteer activities: introducing the Japanese Doll Festival, doing Turkish plays, teaching thank-you letters and easy poems. Gordon, an all-round sportsman, now writes acrostic poems for his family and new classmates in Bellevue, Washington.

Because my three grandsons have other grandmothers, I've taught them Turkish names for myself: Timur's sons call me Baba Anne [father's mother]; Gordon calls me Anne Anne [mother's mother]. He loves visiting his doting relatives in Turkey, eating Turkish food, swimming in the Aegean Sea. Little Dylan and Miles are looking forward to "going to Turkey some year." ❦

And Whatever Happened to Münire?

My dear student from Gazi Teacher Training, Münire Baylantahtacı, never did visit me in the States, or go to college in my hometown, although nearly 30 years later, after retiring from the Foreign Service, I ended up teaching in the very institute she had applied to in 1965! [The school had changed hands in the meantime; it is now Mukogawa Fort Wright Institute, a branch of Mukogawa Women's University in Nishinomiya.]

It was only by a strange quirk of fate that I ever discovered the outcome of Münire's application letter to which she'd never received a reply, and for that reason could not accompany us to the States. At the time of this strange revelation, some 15 years after the children and I had left Turkey, I was once again in Ankara. I was an English Teaching Officer in the Foreign Service/USIA, on tour of duty at the American Embassy. (My prophetic return to Turkey!)

My ETO assignment for the summer of 1981 had been to plan/direct a six-week summer refresher course for 100 teachers of English from high schools all over Turkey. USIA and the Fulbright Office were funding 12 instructors to teach the classes, as well as an assistant of my own choosing. I immediately thought of Gül hanim from Gazi *(not her real name,* a brilliant linguist, one of the best teacher trainers I knew, and a true friend of many years. She was free for the summer and would be willing to take on the job. I was thrilled. Even more so to learn that the program was to be held at Münire's school in Moda [a suburb of Istanbul], and she'd already signed up for the course!

Moda Anadolu Lisesi [Anatolian High School in Moda] was a huge, gray stone building with dormitory accommodations and enormous subterranean kitchens, ideal for housing the summer-course residents. After a long day of workshops and language-related activities, it was always a pleasure to sit out on the second-story balcony and enjoy the spectacular sunset over the Bosphorus.

Gül hanim and I were on the balcony one evening, reminiscing. "Who would have ever thought," I mused, "that you and I would be here running this summer course.... And what a coincidence it should be in our Gazi student's school!"

"Yes," she nodded. "The Director says Münire is now a senior English teacher, very popular with the students. And their parents."

Still musing aloud, I wondered how different Münire's life would have been — and mine and my children's — if the college in Spokane had accepted her application 15 years ago. When a reply never came, I was bitterly disappointed. I'd been looking forward to helping Munire get a BA degree, and counting on her to help me with the children. Münire, of course, had been crushed.

My friend took a deep breath. "Anna Maria, I've something to tell you."

"About Münire?"

"Yes. Actually, that school *did* accept her." Before I could even gasp, she went on. "But I destroyed the letter." A double whammy.

"Why?" I managed to ask. "Why ever did you do that?"

"Because you already had four children to take care of. And I felt you shouldn't be burdened by another responsibility," she confessed.

At first, I was too shocked to feel anger. Then I decided to just let it go. What was the use of anger so long after the fact, after so many convolutions of destiny?

During and after my four-year assignment in Turkey, I've had numerous occasions to visit dear, diligent Münire, who continues to teach English in school and at home. From time to time, my children and I communicate with her by e-mail or phone. Her son Oguzhan is an established medical doctor, her daughter Aslıhan is working on her Ph.D. in linguistics on a full scholarship at Brown University.

We all seem to be following the same inspiring motto: "Strive ever upward and onward." ❦

Author's Articles on Turkey
"Four Turkish Weddings" in *Spokesman-Review: Inland Empire Magazine: Sunday Family Section Part II: October 25, 1959.*
"The 'Hindi' Bird in Turkey Land" in *Spokesman-Review: Inland Empire Magazine, Nov. 20, 1960.*
"Giant Turkish Pehlivan Wrestlers in Action" in *Spokesman-Review: Inland Empire Magazine, July 29, 1962.*
"Bus Trip to Samsun" in *The Ankara Scene: vol viii, no. 21, July 31, 1981* [U.S. Embassy Ankara in-house publication]; also in *USIA World, vol 4, no. 1, January 1985.*

Work in Progress:
"Stories from Here and There" *(working title)* will include stories from Turkey.

INDEX of People/Places/Topics

GLOSSARY *[in use at the time of writing]*

PEOPLE / KINSHIP TERMS
abla > older sister
agabeyi > older brother
amca > uncle (*father's brother*)
anne > mother
baba > father
bey / bey efendi > mister / sir
efendi > gentleman / sir (*old form*)
gelin > bride / daughter-in-law
hala > aunt (*father's sister*)
hanım / hanım efendi > Miss / Mrs.
kardes > brother / sibling
kayın anne > mother-in-law
kayın baba > father-in-law
kayın birader > brother-in-law
kız > girl
kız kardes > sister
teyze > aunt (*mother's sister*)
yenge > sister-in-law

FOOD / BEVERAGES
baklava > a sweet, flakey pastry
bal > honey
börek > flaky or steamed pastry
çay > tea
cezve > a long-handled coffee pot
demitasse > small, after-dinner coffee cup
dolma > stuffed vegetable dish
kabak > squash, pumpkin
kahve > coffee
köfte > meatball, minced meat roll
manda yagı > water-buffalo butter
pide > flat bread
pismaniye > a kind of shredded taffy confection
rakı > a strong, anise liquor
sarma > grape leaves stuffed with rice

GREETINGS / EXPRESSIONS
Afedersiniz. > I apologize. Pardon.
Allaha ısmarladık. > Goodbye.
Güle güle. > (*polite response to Allaha ismarladik.*)
Evet. > Yes.

Güzel! > Nice! / Beautiful! / Fine!
Hayır. > No.
Hos geldiniz > Welcome *[hosh]*
Hos bulduk. > (*polite response to Hos geldiniz.*)
Insallah. > God willing.
Lütfen. > Please.
Masallah. > Wonderful!/May God protect! (*to keep a child from harm*)
Merhaba! > Hello! Hi!
Tesekkür ederim. > Thank you.

GENERAL VOCABULARY
ada > island [Heybeli Ada]
ayıp > shame, disgrace
bayram > religious festival/ national holiday
cami > mosque **Yeni Cami** > New Mosque
dag > mountain; **Raman dagı** > Raman Mountain
hamal > porter, basket carrier
harem > the women of a household
hoca > religious teacher
imam > Moslem priest
kolej > a foreign-language high school
kurus > 100th of a lira, small coin no longer in use *[kurush]*
lira > 100 kurus
lojman > housing, apartment units
minare > minaret, mosque tower
misafir > visitor, guest
muezzin > a Moslem caller to prayers
muhtar > an official village elder
pazar > an open market / bazaar
salvar > baggy pants *[shalvar]*
site > *[sit-eh]* housing development [TPAO Sitesi]
sokak > street
TPAO > Turkiye Petrol Anonim Ortaklıgı [Turkish Petroleum Co.]
yabancı > stranger, foreigner
yorgan > a hand-quilted coverlet